Perth to Pilbara

Atlas and Guide

Including the Goldfields & Coral Coast

Michael & Jane Pelusey

Your ultimate guide to the ultimate experience!

Perth to Pilbara – Atlas & Guide

This is another title in a series of outdoor guides, published by Hema Maps Pty Ltd and originated by Rob van Driesum. The guides complement the maps that Hema produces, with a focus on outdoor activities.

The Authors of this Book

Western Australia-based travel writers and photographers, Michael and Jane Pelusey contribute to many magazines and newspapers, including *Australian Geographic*, and have authored numerous guidebooks, children's educational books and audiovisual presentations. For Hema Maps they have *authored WA 4WD Top 50 Atlas & Guide* and *WA Caravan & Camper Trailer 50 Best Road Trips.*

Change is Certain

The information presented in this book is always subject to change. Roads change, rules and policies are amended, and new facilities and services spring up while existing ones go out of business. Quoted schedules, prices and contact details were correct at the time of research, but you should always check with operators to avoid disappointment.

This book can only be a guide and should not be taken as gospel. The best advice is to keep an open mind and talk to others as you explore this beautiful land - it's all part of the adventure.

Please Tell Us

We welcome and appreciate all your comments and any information that helps us improve and update future editions of this book. Please write to Hema Maps Pty Ltd, PO Box 4365, Eight Mile Plains, Qld 4113, Australia. Email: manager@hemamaps.com.au

PELUSEY PHOTOGRAPHY

Fishing at Eighty Mile Beach on the Pilbara coast.

Published by

Hema Maps Ltd
PO Box 4365
Eight Mile Plains Qld 4113
Australia
Ph (07) 3340 0000
Fax (07) 3340 0099
manager@hemamaps.com.au
www.hemamaps.com.au
1st edition – 2010
ISBN – 978-1-86500-557-7

Photographs
Front cover:
Fishing along the Coral Coast
Photo: David Kirkland
Chichester Ranges at sunset
Photo: Pelusey Photography
Flap: Grevillea, red sand and spinifex grass tussocks in the Pilbara region.
Photo: Jeff Drewitz Photography

Publisher: Rob Boegheim
Cartographic Publishing Manager: Gavin James
Editor & Project Leader: Natalie Wilson
Authors: Michael & Jane Pelusey
Cartographers: Will Martin
Designer: Debbie Winfield
Printing: Toppan Leefung Printing Ltd, China

National Library of Australia
Cataloguing-in-Publication entry
Author: Pelusey, Michael.
Title: Perth to Pilbara atlas & guide : including the goldfields & coral coast / Michael Pelusey; Jane Pelusey.
Edition: 1st ed.
ISBN: 9781865005577 (pbk.)
Notes: Includes index.
Subjects: Roads—Western Australia—Perth—Maps.
Roads—Western Australia—Pilbara Region—Maps.
Perth (W.A.)—Description and travel.
Perth (W.A.)—Guidebooks.
Other Authors/Contributors: Pelusey, Jane.
Dewey Number: 919.41

Contents

Chapter 4

Coral Coast 41

Chapter 5

Pilbara 73

Chapter 6

Gascoyne and Mid West 95

Chapter 7

Goldfields 109

Perth to Pilbara Atlas 123

Index 158

Introduction

This book covers the area north of Perth to just south of the Kimberley and east of Perth to the South Australian border: incorporating Western Australia's Pilbara, Mid West and Goldfields. To present this large area easily it has been broken up into regions based on the designated Western Australian Tourism categories.

Australia's Coral Coast covers the beautiful coastal strip of Western Australia from Perth to Exmouth. The name came about because the southward flowing Leeuwin Current in the Indian Ocean bathes offshore reefs in warm water conducive to coral growth. Rottnest Island, the holiday playground just off Perth, even has pockets of coral growth. Even so, most of the coral that you can see pictured vividly in scuba-diving magazines occurs further north in places such as the Abrolhos Islands, Shark Bay, Coral Bay, Ningaloo Reef and Exmouth. Ningaloo Reef is largely the epicentre for coral diving and snorkelling in Western Australia. In some sections, coral outcrops are within a short snorkelling distance of beautiful white beaches such as Turquoise Bay. Scuba divers can dive on coral reefs that rate among the best in Australia after a short boat trip to the outer reef. Snorkelling boat tours from March to June take excited divers to see rare and imposing whale sharks and more common manta rays.

By far the biggest population base on Australia's Coral Coast is the farming, fishing and tourist service city of Geraldton. It has all the amenities visitors need as well as plenty to see and do. Other centres such as Dongara, Jurien, Carnarvon and Exmouth feature a multitude of attractions and activities to keep visitors busy.

When the Pilbara is mentioned in business circles, more often than not, iron ore and natural gas are the major topics. Towns such as Tom Price and Newman offer tours of mining sites that give a spectacular insight into how big mining is in this part of the world. Standing on the waterfront in Port Hedland at certain times you can marvel at the size of iron ore carriers coming and leaving the port. But the main reason for travelling in the Pilbara is to experience nature, adventure, wilderness and unique landscapes.

No other place in the Pilbara has those three features in greater abundance than Karijini National Park. This ancient landscape of ranges and plateaus etched by deep crisscrossing gorges is for many visitors one of Australia's best scenic highlights. For the adventurous, you can tackle walks of various degrees of difficulty from easy right up to abseiling, canyoning and rock climbing for the experienced only. For the more sedate, superb views into deep gorges are awesome. For the real adventurous four-wheel driver, the Pilbara features some iconic locations such as the remote wilderness of Rudall River National Park and the Canning Stock Route. On the coast, Port Hedland, Dampier and Karratha are obviously mining-orientated towns. But away from these bustling industrial centres is a remote and spectacular coastline bristling with angling, diving and boating opportunities.

The Gascoyne and Mid West is a region often off the tourist radar and perfect for the traveller who likes to get away from it all. The two big attractions are Mount Augustus, said to be the world's biggest rock, and the remarkable landforms of the Kennedy Ranges. These areas are also the hub for wildflower journeys in spring.

The Goldfields is the area responsible for Western Australia's first mining boom: the gold rushes of the 1890s. Ghost towns, booming Kalgoorlie, stark desert landscapes and salt lakes, fascinating rock formations and intriguing history await the visitor to the Goldfields.

Travelling through these regions of Western Australia evokes strong emotions in people as they experience nature and uncompromising landscapes combined with an exciting pioneering spirit often missing or tamed in other parts of the country. This book is largely for self-drive travellers who are planning a trip to this part of Western Australia. After your trip you will have come away with some of that pioneering spirit.

Sunset at Cape Peron JEFF DREWITZ

Cape Peron is a feature of the Shark Bay area.
COLIN KERR

Red Bluff is a spectacular coastal cliff in Kalbarri National Park
COLIN KERR

Blankets of wildflowers cover the landscape in good seasons.
PELUSEY PHOTOGRAPHY

Crystal-clear pools at Millstream-Chichester National Park
STEVEN DAVID MILLER, NATURAL WANDERS

There are numerous gorges in Karijini National Park
PELUSEY PHOTOGRAPHY

Mount Augustus is considered the world's largest rock.
COLIN KERR

The sculptures are striking against the immense Lake Ballard
PELUSEY PHOTOGRAPHY

The woodlands are integral part of the Goldfields landscape.
PELUSEY PHOTOGRAPHY

chapter one

Backgrounds

Highlights

We are indulging ourselves a bit here by selecting what we think are some of the 'not to miss' highlights from Perth to the Pilbara.

Australia's Coral Coast

- **Lancelin (p45)** – The wind surfing capital of Western Australia, Lancelin attracts windsurfers from all over the world, and the huge white dunes are legendary too.
- **Kalbarri (p55)** – Kalbarri has the lot. You can hike and marvel at the views of spectacular coastal cliffs and Murchison River gorges. For anglers, Kalbarri is fishing paradise.
- **Ningaloo Reef (p68)** – Ningaloo Reef is one of the few places where you can get out of your car, step off a white beach into aqua waters and dive luxuriant coral reefs teeming with life. You can also snorkel with giant whale sharks.
- **Exmouth (p68)** – Supremely well located on a cape between the North West Gulf and the Indian Ocean, this well-serviced town is the base for exploring Ningaloo Marine Park and Cape Range National Park.
- **Coral Bay (p67)** – On a wide sweeping bay at the southern end of Ningaloo Reef is a Western Australian holiday favourite. It's a place offering great swimming, fishing and superb coral reef diving.
- **Abrolhos Islands (p52)** – They are low, rocky, largely barren and devoid of coconut palms, but these islands provide a smorgasbord of seafood to catch. And the diving, on one of the world's southernmost coral reefs, is up there with the best.
- **Carnarvon (p63)** – The great climate makes Carnarvon ideal for growing bananas, avocados, pink grapefruit and mangoes as well as attracting tourists. Dangling a line off its one-mile long jetty is a popular pastime too.
- **Shark Bay (p58)** – Featuring a huge variety of marine and terrestrial habitats teeming with fauna and flora, Shark Bay was declared a World Heritage site in 1991 with good reason. The fishing possibilities are endless.

Gascoyne and Mid West

- **Kennedy Ranges (p96)** – The Kennedy Ranges rise dramatically out of parched plains east of Carnarvon. Several gorges are accessible by short walk trails and watching the sun set over the battlement-like cliffs is nothing short of amazing.
- **Mount Augustus (p95)** – Considered the world's largest rock, Mount Augustus is worth visiting for that fact alone. There are several walks of varying degrees of difficulty, with the 12km return hike to the summit the toughest and most rewarding.
- **Wildflowers (p100)** – This region's stark barren landscapes turn into a blaze of colour during spring with carpets of pink, yellow and white paper daisies. There are also colourful grevilleas, kangaroo paws, banksias, wattles and the rare wreath leschenaultias to see.

Pilbara

- **Karijini National Park (p73)** – It doesn't get much better than Karijini where numerous gorges cut deeply into an ancient and weathered plateau producing spellbinding vistas. The vivid red rock, white snappy gums and bright blue skies overwhelm the senses and walk trails range from easy to demanding.
- **Warlu Way (p74)** – The newly instituted Warlu Way is likely to become a classic drive trail as the scenic route includes such iconic locations such as Karijini National Park, Chichester Ranges and Millstream.
- **Chichester Ranges (p76)** – A drive near sunset through the mesas of the Chichester Ranges is absolutely magical for photographers. Python Pool surrounded by sheer rock faces is the spectacular starting point for a couple of walk trails that offer wonderful views of mesas and vast desert landscapes of red dirt, snappy gums and spinifex.
- **Millstream (p76)** – Crystal-clear pools teeming with fish and waterlilies await the surprised visitor numbed by travelling through barren landscapes.
- **Rudall River National Park (p93)** – This remote national park is a bit like Karijini without the people. It is WA's largest national park in area and incorporates unspoilt desert landscapes, rugged ranges and gorges, and pristine waterholes.
- **Canning Stock Route (p110)** – The old cattle route between Halls Creek and Laverton is one of the world's greatest 4WD treks. To undertake this one requires planning, teamwork and self sufficiency.
- **Pilbara Coast** – The coast between Onslow and Port Hedland is full of contrasts from busy iron ore ports trading with the world to isolated pristine islands and mangrove inlets teeming with marine life.
- **Tom Price (p81)** – A drive up Mount Nameless, WA's highest 4WD track, near sunset is worth the giddying climb. A stay at the caravan park gets you up close and personal with cockatoos, galahs and several friendly euro kangaroos.

Goldfields

- **Kalgoorlie (p115)**–Step into gold-mining history while enjoying the modern day wealth gained from the Super Pit. Absorb the architecture that characterises Kalgoorlie's golden ages.
- **Coolgardie (p116)** – Explore historic Coolgardie and stand in awe at the workmanship of the grandiose buildings in the wide main street. The historic cemetery has Ernest Giles' grave as well as those of other hardened pioneers.
- **Gwalia (p111)** – When walking amongst the mining humpies of Gwalia, you are experiencing life on the Goldfields at a real personal level. See the legacy of Herbert Hoover, a tenacious mining engineer who later became the President of the United States of America.
- **Golden Quest Discovery Trail (p115)** – Soak up all the history and scenic wonders along one well-marked drive trail. Don't rush it as this trail's charms are revealed to those with patience.

- **Kookynie (p113)** – Stay at the Grand Hotel and wander into the tiny but atmospheric bar where prospectors and the occasional German backpacker chew the fat. It can get quite lively, especially considering there's less than a handful of permanent residents.
- **Lake Ballard (p114)** – Picture an immense salt lake shimmering into the distance. Then imagine skinny naked people spaced widely apart under a vivid blue sky. Well they are not real people I might add, but the work of a gifted world famous artist.

History

First Inhabitants

Australia's first inhabitants arrived from South East Asia at least 40 000 years ago. At that time sea levels were much lower so the northern Indonesian islands and New Guinea acted as a land bridge for the movement of people. The first human inhabitants quite likely entered Australia somewhere in the North West.

The Aborigines adapted to the harsh conditions by living a nomadic hunter-gatherer existence. When hunting, they often used fire to flush out animals. Fire helped shape the landscape by promoting native grasses, the main food for kangaroos. Indigenous Australians travelled in family groups within their specific tribal areas, and strictly adhered to complex social structures and laws that united their group.

Spiritual beliefs centred on the concept of the **Dreaming** or **Dreamtime**. Dreamtime is a belief that all the features that make up earth were formed when time began. Spirits that took the form of major animals created natural features, all other animals, humans and even the moon, sun and stars. Each major physical feature has its own story of creation. These places are sacred sites or places of worship to the local Aboriginal people. This reinforces the Aboriginal people's strong bond between the tribal group, nature and the land itself. There are thousands of sacred places scattered throughout the Pilbara, Gascoyne, Murchison and Goldfields. Some of the most notable are Millstream and Karijini in the Pilbara and Mount Augustus in the Gascoyne.

The arrival of European settlers and the development of the pastoral industry had a huge impact on Aboriginal people. Sheep and cattle took over traditional hunting grounds which inevitably led to conflict. Introduced diseases from European settlers caused huge numbers of deaths as the Aboriginal people had no natural immunity. Some Aboriginal communities came under the influence of missionaries spreading Christianity.

Over time many cattle and sheep stations employed Aborigines as drovers and station workers in exchange for food and lodging for them and their family. In 1968, Aboriginal people were granted full citizen's rites that resulted in equal pay. The result was many Aboriginal people already displaced from their homelands lost their station jobs. With nowhere to go they moved to the outskirts of towns in makeshift housing. Despite these incredible setbacks and the resulting health and social problems many Aboriginal people still follow their traditions. Land rites legislation has led to some Aboriginal communities reclaiming their land.

Rock art on Burrup Peninsula

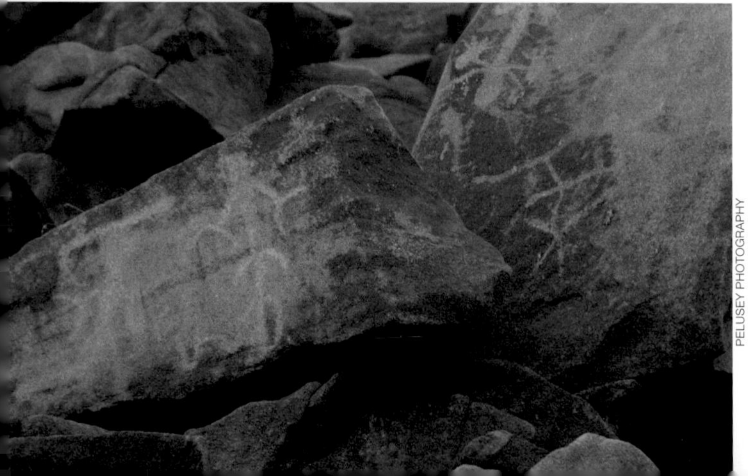

PELUSEY PHOTOGRAPHY

Early Mariners

When explorer **Captain James Cook** made landfall in Australia in 1776 he was not the first to do so. About 150 years before Cook, a Dutch captain by the name **Dirk Hartog** in his ship the *Eendracht* landed on an island just off the west coast of Australia. The date was 1616 and to commemorate the momentous occasion he left an inscribed pewter plate nailed to a post. The exact location of what is the first recorded European landing in Western Australia, and possibly Australia, is Cape Inscription on Dirk Hartog Island in Shark Bay.

The English had a bad start to their eventual claim over Australia when a trading vessel called the *Tryall* ran aground on the Montebello Islands in 1622. Only a few survivors made it back to England.

About 80 years after Hartog's landing, another Dutch explorer, **Willem de Vlamingh**, dropped by and replaced Hartog's plate with his own. The original Hartog plate made its way back to the Netherlands, but there is a replica at the Shark Bay Discovery Centre in Denham. Although the Dutch had early claims on the western side of Australia, other maritime nations soon followed.

An English pirate, **William Dampier**, explored a group of islands off the north west coast of Australia in 1699. What he saw of the barren coastline near Dampier did not impress him one little bit.

The French also did a fair bit of exploration and mapping of the Western Australian coast. The French named many landmarks on their visits such as Henri Freycinet Harbour, Thevenard Island and Peron Peninsula. Not only did the French name everything in sight, they actually claimed the western side of Australia. This led to renewed interest by the British who began settling the western part of the country.

Batavia Mutiny

Further south, roughly 60km west of Geraldton, are the **Houtman Abrolhos Islands**. This group of low lying and barren islands have a very dark history. In the winter of 1629, a Dutch ship called the *Batavia* was wrecked on Morning Reef in the Wallabi Group in the Abrolhos Islands. The survivors out of 316 men, woman and children hung on surviving while Captain Pelsaert and some crew set off in an open boat on an epic rescue mission to Batavia (later to be Jakarta) in Indonesia. In the following months a group of sadistic mutineers, with the aim of taking over Pelsaert's ship when he returned, murdered 125 survivors including women and children. About three months later, Pelsaert and his heavily armed forces arrived and overpowered the mutineers who were subsequently executed by hanging.

Land Exploration

From the very beginnings of European settlement in Western Australia, brave explorers set out on foot and horseback looking for greener pastures. **George Grey** led two expeditions into the unknown. The first was an ill-fated attempt to find suitable places for settlement in the Kimberley. His second journey in 1839 took him and his men by two whaling boats to Shark Bay. While exploring the region on foot he found a wide dry river bed which he named the Gascoyne. The land must have had recent rain for Grey noted the area would be most suitable for habitation and agriculture. Running out of supplies, the party had to return to Perth. They rowed for 10 days and then walked 700km back to Perth after the boats sank. Luckily some Aborigines took pity and rescued them from certain starvation.

Grey and some of his party were finally rescued by John Septimus Roe. This near fatal journey resulted in new land being opened up.

In 1858, **Francis Thomas Gregory** explored Grey's old battleground, the Gascoyne region. Like his compatriot, Gregory's expedition helped opened up future pastoral areas. But, it was Gregory's second expedition in 1861 that really achieved results. Interestingly, his second expedition was sponsored by the British cotton industry. With that in mind Gregory and his team landed off a boat near what is now Dampier and planted some cotton to see what would happen. Obviously it never came to much. They then ventured inland discovering and naming a number of well known physical features of the Pilbara, including the Hamersley Ranges, Fortescue River, Hardy River, Ashburton River and De Grey River.

John Forrest in 1874 and **Ernest Giles** in 1875 and 1876 explored inland regions east of Geraldton as part of much bigger expeditions. Giles was a gifted writer with *Australia Twice Traversed* a classic. His grave is in Coolgardie cemetery.

Early Development

Due to its harsh arid climate, crops such as **wheat** never took hold north of Kalbarri on the coast and beyond Southern Cross in the east. Reports of potentially good pastoral country from explorers such as Grey and Gregory quickly sparked the pioneering spirit. From the 1870s to late 1880s stoic pastoralists transported **sheep** to the Gascoyne and Murchison regions. Despite extreme heat, lack of water and constant harassment from Aborigines these pastoralists produced **wool** for Britain. To ship wool out, ports such as Carnarvon, Onslow, Point Samson, Cossack and Port Hedland became thriving centres. Further north, into the Kimberley, **beef cattle** replaced sheep. However, beef cattle in subsequent years began competing with sheep in the Pilbara and Gascoyne.

People living in the North West and inland areas were dogged by isolation, but this problem was lessened in coastal areas serviced by the State shipping lines. The real turning point for North West residents happened in 1921 when Western Australian Airways started Australia's first regular airline service, between Geraldton and Derby. One of their pilots became a famous aviator: **Sir Charles Kingsford Smith**.

Canning Stock Route

The famous outback adventure, the Canning Stock Route, had an unlikely starting point. In the early 1900s, there was a ban enforced to prevent the spread of red water fever from ticks. The ban meant cattle were prevented from moving from the disease-ridden East Kimberley region into the disease-free West Kimberley. This meant cattle had to be shipped south, which was a very expensive exercise. To overcome the problem, a 1750km-long route from Halls Creek in the Kimberley to Wiluna in the south was devised – the offending ticks could not survive the desert climate. In 1906, **Alfred Canning** and seven men set out to survey the track, an incredibly demanding and dangerous undertaking. Two years later Canning returned and sunk 54 wells. The track was last used for cattle driving in 1959. Today the Canning Stock Route is regarded as one of Australia's greatest 4WD trails (see p110).

WWII & After

In the early years of WWII, Western Australians felt fairly isolated from the battles occurring in the northern hemisphere. That dramatically changed in 1941, when a German raider, the *Kormoran*, had an encounter with the Australian warship, *HMAS Sydney II*. More than 600 seamen died only 50km off the coast, between Carnarvon and Geraldton. It wasn't until 2008 that the wrecks of *HMAS Sydney II* and the *Kormoran* were found. A moving **memorial** is located in Geraldton.

PELUSEY PHOTOGRAPHY

Conditions for the Batavia survivors on Abrolhos Islands were very tough.

David Carnegie (July to Dec 1896)

By Mick Hutton

David Carnegie's ambition was to explore the desert country of the Gibson and Great Sandy, and with the sale of his gold mine he could finance his own expeditions. Carnegie searched for minerals, grazing land and a possible stock route to link the northern and southwest goldfields. Although nothing of value was found, he successfully crossed one of the harshest areas on earth and the expeditions filled in many blanks on the maps.

Departing Coolgardie in July 1896, Carnegie pushed into the desert country deliberately choosing to travel in areas that were unexplored. Being a dry year, water was difficult to locate. So many of the rockholes and soaks that the expedition found were dry. Months dragged by as the party continued north, adding to the lack of water the heat of the oncoming summer began to tell. Several of the camels died of poison plants as they broke out of the desert and entered better country.

Carnegie and his party soon found creeks and waterholes aplenty as they neared the Margaret River, south of the Kimberley. Charles Stansmore was accidentally shot and killed while hunting alone along the Margaret River as the party slowly recovered from the desert crossing. This left Carnegie and the party numb with shock after what they had all just endured together.

Leaving the river they followed the Telegraph Line east and reached (Old) Halls Creek early in December 1896. The young Scotsman had successfully crossed one of the harshest areas on earth. After a few months rest in 1897, Carnegie and his party started from Halls Creek and successfully returned across the desert to the southwest goldfields: an incredible feat of endurance.

Members of Carnegie's expedition – A Breaden, Hon David Carnegie, Warri and Godfrey Massie.

When the Japanese entered the war, Australia came under immediate threat. Attacks were unleashed on Darwin, Broome and even Wyndham in the Kimberley. A lesser known is the fact that the **Exmouth Gulf Base** was attacked in 1943. Obviously the pastoral industry was affected during the war and mining was minimal throughout that time.

Soon after the end of the war, relations between Russia and the allies cooled dramatically and the threat of nuclear annihilation was a real fear. Britain decided to test its atomic bombs in 1952 and 1956 on the **Montebello Islands** off the Pilbara coast. Successful as the tests were, the islands were out of bounds for decades.

John Forrest (Apr to Sep 1874)

By Mick Hutton

In 1874, 26 year-old WA Surveyor John Forrest successfully crossed the arid interior west to east. John Forrest and his brother Alexander were both Western Australian born. They grew up on a farm, so were capable horseman and bushman from an early age. Both men became surveyors, John showed considerable aptitude and, under the guiding hand of Surveyor General Roe, was given greater responsibilities. In 1869 and 1870 John led expeditions into unexplored country, adding considerably to the colony's knowledge.

The arid interior was the next challenge, and John was given leadership of a major expedition to cross the central deserts west to east. The small party left Geraldton in April 1874. Tracing the Murchison River, the expedition entered the desert and pushed to the east going from one waterhole to the next. Numerous times they were held up while searching for water. Eventually they broke through to Giles' Warburton Ranges. From that point they had known waters ahead thanks to Gosse' 1873 chart John carried. However, the year was dry and water was still hard to find. Several of the horses had to be left behind as the terrible conditions continued. In September, John led his men onto the Overland Telegraph Line and comparative safety.

In later years, he entered politics and was Premier of WA for many years. During that period he was instrumental in the expansion of WA. Forrest went on to become a member of the Federation Parliament as member for Swan, a position he held until his death. He held continuous offices through seven Federal Ministries for the next 18 years, which included Treasurer for five years. The climax of his career was as Acting Prime Minister for four months in 1907. John Forrest was the first native born Australian to be knighted for his efforts.

John Forrest and his exploration party leaving Perth in 1874.

In 1964, NASA built a **space tracking station** at Carnarvon. It played a vital part in the Apollo space program that eventually resulted in landing on the moon. The station closed in 1975. During the height of the cold war in 1966, America built a series of very low frequency radio towers at **North West Cape** near Exmouth. There were nearly 1000 people working and living in Exmouth at the time – mostly American.

Agriculture

Almost half of WA's total agricultural production comes from the Wheatbelt region, with the Mid West and Goldfields/Esperance areas adding a further 12% and 8% respectively. Being primarily a mining area, the Pilbara contributes only about 1%.

Although **meat and wool production** remain the main pastoral activities, many stations are now diversifying into goats, turkeys, marron, yabbies, emus and ostriches, snails, worms, deer and alpacas as well as outback tourism. **Sheep** were introduced to the Gascoyne region in 1876, and they remain an important part of the area's pastoral industry. There is also an increasing interest in the export **goat** market. **Beef cattle** contribute most to the Pilbara's agricultural output with sheep and lambs for meat as well as nursery produce, such as cut flowers, being other major commodities. Meanwhile the Wheatbelt region is the largest producer of sheep and lamb meat in WA. In the Mid West, sheep are mainly farmed for their wool. **Wool production** is also a major product of the Goldfields/Esperance region, as well as eggs, honey and milk.

In the Wheatbelt region cereal crops, primarily **wheat** and **barley**, contribute about 67% of the region's agricultural value. Lupins and hay are also grown, as well as oranges, wine grapes, olives, carrots, cauliflowers, lettuces and potatoes. This region is also WA's main producer of **cut flowers**. Major cereal crops, including wheat, barley and oats are also grown in the Mid West region, along with lupins, canola, hay and cut flowers. Wheat, barley and canola are also important crops in the Goldfields/Esperance region. Today the banks of the Gascoyne River near Carnarvon are the centre of the Gascoyne region's **horticulture industry**, thanks to the use of a micro-drip irrigation system. Bananas, tomatoes, table grapes, capsicums and mangoes have traditionally been significant crops but peaches, nectarines, plums and red grapefruit are also being grown.

Another important contributor to the Gascoyne region's economy is the **fishing industry** with prawns and scallops from Shark Bay and the Exmouth Gulf providing the bulk of the state's catch. Crabs, snapper, whiting and mullet are also commercially harvested, with processing factories in Exmouth, Carnarvon and Denham. In the Wheatbelt region rock lobster is the predominant part of the industry, with freshwater marron and yabbies also produced commercially. Dhufish, snapper, mullet and shark are common catches. The Pilbara region has emperors, snapper, cod, Spanish mackerel, barramundi, threadfin salmon and sharks as well as prawn, crab and mollusc fisheries.

Although it is the Kimberley region that is known for its **pearls**, the hatcheries at Carnarvon and Exmouth supply farms in the Exmouth Gulf and Montebello Islands. In addition, the Pilbara region produces about 15% of the value of WA's pearl production with sites in the waters of the Dampier Archipelago and Montebellos area. The Mid West has an emerging black pearl industry at the Abrolhos Islands.

Although the Goldfields/Esperance region only contributes a small percentage of WA's total production value from **forestry**, it does produce all of the State's **sandalwood**. The region's acacia and eucalpyt woodlands are also known for producing good timber that is valued for its density and attractive grain. Forestry is also a minor industry in the Wheatbelt region.

Mining

Without doubt the Pilbara and Goldfields of Western Australia are the nation's major iron ore and gold producing regions. (In 2006/2007 the Pilbara region contributed about 60% of the total value of WA's mining industry with the Goldfields/Esperance region adding a further 19% and the Mid West 8%.) Iron ore and petroleum are Western Australia's major commodities, with alumina, gold and nickel also being important. About half of Australia's mineral and energy exports are contributed by Western Australia. In 2008 Western Australia produced 110 million barrels of crude oil and condensate, and 27 296 million cubic metres of natural gas: equating to 66% and 71% of the Australian production respectively.

Mining really hit its straps in the 1960s with the opening up of iron ore mines in the Pilbara and nickel mining in the Goldfields. When mining for **asbestos** began in the Hamersley Ranges near Wittenoom the industry attracted many migrants. Although mining for asbestos ended in 1966, the horrific legacy of fatal lung diseases continues.

WA is the only place in Australia to produce **nickel**. About a third of the State's nickel production comes from the Mid West region, and the Goldfields-Esperance area is rapidly becoming one of the world's prime supply zones. Nickel is also mined in the Pilbara.

About 60% of the State's **copper** is produced in the Pilbara, and it is the only base metal mined in significant quantity in the region. **Manganese** is also mined in the Pilbara. Deposits of zircon, ilmenite and rutile are mined at Eneabba, and the Tiwest mine at Cooljarloo is Australia's largest titanium dioxide pigment producer.

In November 2008 the State Government revoked the ban on mining **uranium** in Western Australia. As the State has known resources of uranium, the Government is now focussing on developing this sector. Five companies already have projects are that expected to start mining in or after 2012.

Gold

Gold was first found in the region back in 1882 between **Cossack** and **Roebourne**. But it was 10 years later that the gold rush really started when prospectors **Arthur Bayley** and **William Ford** discovered the precious metal near **Coolgardie**. In 1893 **Patrick Hannan**, **Dan Shea** and **Tom Flannigan** found gold in what is now **Kalgoorlie**. The region became known as the Western Australian Goldfields. As these gold discoveries became known, many people rushed to the goldfields to find their fortune. Many died of thirst, while others died of diseases such as dysentery due to unsanitary conditions. Most prospectors panned for alluvial gold in riverbeds.

Gold was also found as nuggets just under or on top of the ground. As these two sources of gold gradually diminished, miners dug deeper underground to find more sources. To support these mining ventures, towns such as Kalgoorlie and Coolgardie grew into big thriving communities. This wealth spread to Perth, resulting in many new buildings there. The Gascoyne and Murchison also had their fair share of gold, with **Cue**, **Mount Magnet** and **Meekatharra** becoming important centres. But as the elusive metal ran out many other communities, such as **Malcolm**, **Niagara**, **Kanowna** and **Bulong**, became ghost towns.

The value of gold production has steadily declined since its peak in the mid-1990s but the Goldfields/Esperance region still produces about three quarters of WA's total gold production by value. The **Super Pit**, at Kalgoorlie, is today one of Australia's largest gold mines. The Mid West also has an active mining industry in the **Wiluna**, **Meekatharra** and **Mt Magnet** local government areas. While the Mid West contributes about 20% of WA's gold production, the Wheatbelt contributes only about 4%.

Mount Whaleback Iron Ore Mine near Newman

PELUSEY PHOTOGRAPHY

Iron Ore

During World War II, an embargo on exporting iron ore was in place because it was needed to make machinery and weapons for the war effort. So, in the 1950s, mining companies looked for more iron ore deposits. Huge deposits of iron ore were discovered in the Pilbara region by miners **Lang Hancock** and **Peter Wright**. In 1961, the embargo was lifted when it became clear Australia had large deposits of iron ore. Soon after, mining for iron ore began. In 1966, the first mines in the Pilbara began excavating iron ore from **Mount Tom Price** and **Mount Goldsworthy**. The first shipments left the port of Dampier in the Pilbara.

Today the Pilbara is responsible for producing about 96% of WA's total production of iron ore with the majority exported. Major producers in the region are Rio Tinto's subsidiary **Hamersley Iron** and **BHP Biliton**. The Wheatbelt region only contributes about 2% of WA's total mineral production but almost 40% of this value is from iron ore.

Oil and Gas

In 1953, oil was discovered at **Rough Range** near Exmouth. The yields were small and soon petered out, but 11 years later a much bigger oil field was discovered at **Barrow Island** off the Pilbara coast. Currently the Pilbara produces about 96% of WA's crude oil and 99% of the petroleum condensate. There are also major crude oil operations in the Mid West region.

In 1971, oil and gas were discovered on the **North West Shelf** off the Pilbara coast. The **North Rankin gas reservoir**, discovered in 1971, is the largest deposit in Australia. Liquefied natural gas, liquefied petroleum gas and natural gas are all produced. Significant gas fields in the Mid West region include Dongara, Woodada, Xyris, Beharra Springs and Beharra Springs North.

Today many of the world's largest oil and gas production companies have interests in the Pilbara, including **Woodside Energy**, **Chevron** and **BHP Biliton**. The demand from China for gas and iron ore has seen these industries continue to expand.

A major gas explosion at the **Varanus Island** gas processing facility in June 2008 cut Western Australia's domestic gas supply by 30%. The facility, operated by Apache Energy is located about 115km west of Dampier.

Salt

The Pilbara boasts Australia's largest solar salt fields with sites at **Dampier**, **Port Hedland** and **Onslow** producing about three quarters of the state's annual value for salt production. **Dampier Salt** is WA's principal salt producer. The main mining activity in the Gascoyne region is also salt, with operations at **Lake MacLeod**, north of Carnarvon, and **Useless Loop** in Shark Bay. The Gascoyne region contributes about 21% of WA's salt production value. Salt is also mined in the Wheatbelt region at **Lake Deborah**, north of Southern Cross. Salt is used extensively in the South East Asian chemicals industry.

Geology and Landforms

By world standards, the rocks in Western Australia are very old, which partly explains the relative flatness of the terrain. Put simply, what were once big mountains are now little more than hills worn away over many millions of years. The **Pilbara Craton**, which was formed more than three billion years ago, runs from Karratha and Port Hedland to Marble Bar and Nullagine. Further south the **Yilgarn Craton**, which reaches from Meekatharra to Mt Barker and east to Kalgoorlie, is about 2.6 billion years old. In some areas of the Pilbara, rocks have been found dating back 3600 million years. The oldest rock in the Pilbara is a mix of granite and greenstone formed under great heat and pressure. Major geological components of the Pilbara include the Hamersley and Chichester ranges, and the Fortescue and Roebourne plains. The Gascoyne region is characterised by low granite ranges and broad valleys, such as the catchments of the Ashburton and Gascoyne rivers.

Not much later in geological terms, simple life forms such as bacteria and **stromatolites** came into existence. Evidence of this life is found in parts of the Pilbara, making these fossils some of the oldest found on Earth. Living forms of stromatolites are found at Hamelin Pool, in Shark Bay. With so much of this ancient rock exposed, geologists and scientists from around the world come to the Pilbara to study the Earth's early history.

The spectacular landforms that visitors marvel at today, particularly in the Pilbara, date back to about 250 million years. During that time, glaciers carved out the landscape and subsequent erosion over millions of years has formed the Pilbara landscape we know today.

Cape Range

PELUSEY PHOTOGRAPHY

Mount Augustus

PELUSEY PHOTOGRAPHY

Mount Augustus

Rising abruptly 715m above the scrubby plain, and 1105m above sea level, the solitary Mount Augustus is one of outback Western Australia's great sights. It is claimed to be the biggest rock in the world. Mount Augustus is 430km east of Carnarvon and 850km north of Perth.

About 1600 million years ago ancient river systems and later sea encroachments laid down sand and conglomerate deposits. About 800 million years ago this layer of rock and even older underlying granite was uplifted. Subsequent erosion over countless millennia shaped this rock into its present form. To the geologically knowledgeable, Mount Augustus is one of the best examples of an asymmetrical anticline.

Karijini Gorges

The 100m deep gorges that crisscross Karijini National Park are possibly Western Australia's most spectacular scenic wonder. These gorges have an incredibly ancient look and feel about them, and for good reason. Most of the rocks that occur in the region originated some 2500 million years ago as iron and silica rich sediment layered down under the sea. Over millions of years further layering occurred, which exerted incredible pressures on underlying sediments. The result was hardened layers of rock. Subsequent earth movements buckled and lifted the rock to form a plateau that makes up much of Karijini National Park. Over time erosion caused by water movement has worn away softer rock to form the gorges seen today by enthralled visitors. What's more, iron that was once sediment on an ancient sea floor is now a major contributor to Australia's monetary wealth.

Cape Range

Cape Range is 100km long and nearly 400m high in places. The range forms a dramatic sight for visitors and has a quite different geological history to other parts of WA. It is mainly made up of limestone, a sedimentary rock that formed up to 30 million years ago. As you walk amongst the ranges, well away from the sea, shell and coral fossils can be found. Over millions of years, uplifting of marine sediments has slowly taken place, forming the rugged ranges we see today. Over time many caves formed as rainfall penetration eroded softer limestone. Similar erosive forces carved out the steep arid canyons. The western side of the range was eroded by waves as uplifting took place.

Wave Rock

One of Western Australia's best-known attractions, Wave Rock was formed more than 2700 million years ago. It is 345km east of Perth and 4km from the little town of Hyden. This granite formation resembles an enormous dumper about to come crashing down on your head. The 'wave', actually the northern side of Hyden Rock, is about 15m high and 100m long, and the colourful, vertical stripes are a result of algal growth. The rock also acts as a water catchment for the area, hence the rather ugly concrete barrier along the 'crest'.

Kennedy Range

The Kennedy Range National Park protects an ancient eroded plateau with cliffs rising up to 100m above the surrounding plain. These spectacular sandstone battlements are a remnant of an ancient land surface isolated by the process of erosion. The top of the range is a waterless red dunefield dominated and stabilised by spinifex and small shrubs. On the eastern side of the range a maze of steep-sided canyons lead back into the mesa where ancient marine fossils can be found embedded into the sandstone cliffs. Some ancient rock art engravings (petroglyphs) can be seen in the southernmost gorge.

PELUSEY PHOTOGRAPHY

Spinifex, Chichester Ranges

JEFF DREWITZ

Grevillea, red sand and spinifex grass tussocks in the Pilbara.

Habitats

Desert

Many people think deserts are boring places, devoid of life and blisteringly hot. Though they are indeed very hot in summer, the desert regions in Western Australia are also diverse and full of life. Although they are mainly arid, just add some rain and the deserts come to life. Within days, green shoots sprout turning the desert sands green with life and shrubs blossoming with flowers. Paper daisies also paint the land in colourful pinks, yellows and whites.

The largest desert in the State is the **Great Victoria Desert** at nearly 500 000 square kilometres. Red sand dunes are a major landform in this desert, which stretches from near Laverton across the border into the Northern Territory. Here tree steppes of eucalyptus species and mulga exist over hummock grassland.

Further north, the **Gibson Desert** is characterised by flat-lying sandstone with mulga on the plains and shrubs such as acacia, hakea and grevillea on the red sand plains and dune fields. There are occasional stands of coolabah along the creeks.

Stretching from the coast, above Port Hedland, east into the Northern Territory is the **Great Sandy Desert**. This desert's gently undulating uplands support acacia shrublands over hummock grass, but some dunes reach over 20m in height. The extensive salt lake chains feature samphire and low melaleuca shrublands.

For further information on WA's deserts see Hema's *Australia's Great Desert Tracks Atlas & Guide*.

Spinifex Country

At least 20% of Australia is dominated by one form of vegetation: spinifex. This spiky clumping grass is found in arid parts of Australia and it grows in profusion in the Gascoyne, Pilbara and inland regions of Western Australia. Spinifex species are often found near mallee and acacia species. Although it forms a seemingly impenetrable barrier of spikes, this plant provides a safe haven for small reptiles such as dragons and geckoes, insects and small marsupials. Spectacular red **Sturt desert peas** (*Clianthus formosus*) and **purple mulla mullas** (*Ptilotus exaltatus*) are often seen growing amongst spinifex.

Gimlet and Salmon Gum Forests

Dominating uncleared areas of the northern and eastern wheatbelt and vast areas of the goldfields are forests of **gimlets** (*Eucalyptus salubris*) and **salmon gums** (*Eucalyptus salmonophloia*). The smooth colourful trunks of these trees glisten after rain and provide an awesome sight. For about 100 years up to the 1960s, most of one of the world's largest temperate forests was cleared for timber to fuel the booming gold industry around Kalgoorlie and Coolgardie. Although almost destroyed, the forests have grown back with vengeance and are now protected in various national parks including Goldfields Woodland.

COLIN KERR

Typical Pilbara landscape

Mangroves

Mangroves are found in sheltered coastal waters from Carnarvon into the Kimberley region. There a significant stands found on the Burrup Peninsula, near Dampier. Other sites include at the mouths of the De Grey, Harding, Cane, Fortescue and Robe rivers. These trees thrive in hostile saltwater estuarine environments. Mangroves provide shelter and nursery grounds for many species of fish including threadfin salmon, barramundi and mangrove jacks. They also provide the main habitat for the tasty mud crab and many water birds nest in the dense leafy canopies.

Grassland Savannah

Savannah is the term used to describe the vegetation type that dominates the tropical zone in areas where there are distinct wet and dry seasons, such as the Pilbara. Here the dominant trees are eucalypts with an understorey of spinifex and tall grasses such as **spear grass** (*Sorghum intrans*). The **Themeda grasslands** of the Pilbara are dominated by perennial **kangaroo grass** (*Themeda triandra*) along with various other annual herbs and grasses.

Riparian Strips

Most lowland streams originate in the higher rocky country, where heavy rain during the Wet brings floods that frequently invade the adjoining savannah. By July the seasonal creeks have mostly stopped flowing and become strings of pools overhung by tall **paperbarks** (*Melaleuca sp*). Zones of riparian vegetation can be found along the Fortescue, Maitland, Turner, De Grey, George, Nichol and Sherlock rivers.

Coral at Turquoise Bay

PELUSEY PHOTOGRAPHY

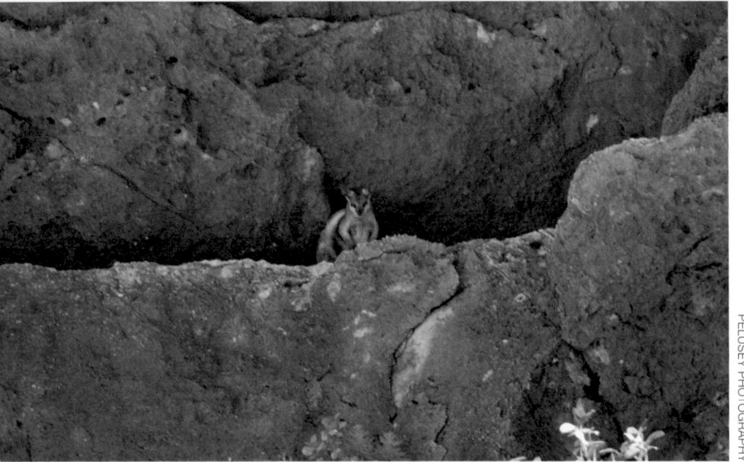

Black-footed rock wallaby

PELUSEY PHOTOGRAPHY

Millstream

In a predominantly arid Pilbara landscape, the lushness of vegetation and abundance of fresh water at Millstream results in a habitat of tropical exuberance. Fresh water rises from an immense underground aquifer forming deep permanent pools and creeks. The Jirndawurrunba Pool is located near the old Millstream homestead, which is now the visitors centre. This series of deep crystal clear pools are full of fish and water lilies with dense reed beds and exceptionally tall cajuput trees. This unique habitat protects a number of rare plants and animals. With the exception of a couple other locations in the North West, the native Millstream Palm (*Livistona alfredii*) is found nowhere else in the World. There are also dense stands of date palms introduced by the station owners well before it became a national park. The area also supports over 30 species of dragonflies and damselflies, with one particular damselfly only found at Millstream.

Millstream

PELUSEY PHOTOGRAPHY

Wetlands

In the mainly arid Pilbara region, the few permanent waterholes and swamps become significant refuges for many species of wildlife. Wetlands of national significance in the region include Millstream (see boxed text), the Fortescue Marsh and the pools in the gorges of the Hamersley Range, particularly in Karijini National Park. Other important wetlands include Weeli Wolli Spring (north of Newman), Palm Spring (northwest of Tom Price) and pools on the Robe River.

Coral Reefs

Coral reefs are one of the richest ecosystems on Earth and Western Australia has many scattered along the coastline in subtropical and tropical waters. The **Ningaloo Reef** – the largest fringing coral reef in Australia – is located down the western side of the North West Cape and extends for 300km. The reef has over 500 species of fish and 200 types of corals. One of the World's southernmost coral reefs is located around the **Houtman Abrolhos Islands**, 60km from Geraldton.

Fauna

Mammals

With the exception of kangaroos, and to a lesser extent possums, most native mammals are shy retiring types not easily seen by humans. Having said that, northern and inland Western Australia have areas where viewing other mammals is more likely. In fact 19 small ground-dwelling mammals have been recorded in the region. **Shark Bay** on the Peron Peninsula, **Karijini National Park** and **Cape Range National Park** are just three locations where a little stroll at night with a torch may reveal some nocturnal happenings. The same stroll early next day will reveal all sorts of footprints in the sand. Some of the world's rarest mammals are found in Shark Bay including five threatened species. Four species can now be found in the wild nowhere else in the world. Other species have been introduced to the area after being almost wiped out elsewhere in Australia. (See the boxed text next page.)

Both the **red kangaroo** (*Macropus rufus*) and the **euro** (*Macropus robustus*) are common throughout the northern half of Western Australia. Stay at the caravan park in Tom Price and you should be visited by tourist-friendly euros who like lazing about under the shady awnings. Although it is regarded as a threatened species in Western Australia, the beautiful **black-footed rock wallaby** (*Petrogale lateralis*) can be spotted along the ledges at Yardie Creek and Mandu Mandu Creek in Cape Range National Park if you have sharp eyes. Doing the boat tour up Yardie Creek offers the best vantage point. When they move, sit back and admire their agility on precarious rock ledges and steep cliff faces. Restricted to the Hamersley Range, Chichester Range, Burrup Peninsula and some islands of the Dampier Archipelago, the **Rothschild's rock wallaby** (*Petrogale rothschildi*) looks similar to the black-footed rock wallaby but doesn't have its dorsal stripe. This wallaby lives along cliffs and scree slopes. The endangered **rufous hare wallaby**

Euro at Tom Price

(*Lagorchestes hirsutus*) and **banded hare wallaby** (*Lagostrophus fasciatus*) are both only found on the Bernier and Dorre islands in Shark Bay. The rufous hare wallaby has been introduced on Trimouille Island in the Montebello Islands and a small population of the banded hare wallaby has been established on Faure Island, near Monkey Mia. Once one of Australia's most widespread small mammals, the **Shark Bay boodie** (*Bettongia lesueur lesueur*) is now only found wild on the Bernier and Dorre islands in Shark Bay. Also known as a burrowing bettong or rat kangaroo, the boodie is the only member of the kangaroo family that regularly inhabits a burrow.

One of only two mammals that lay eggs, the **echidna** (*Tachyglossus aculeatus acanthion*) is fairly common throughout Western Australia. Echidnas use their long sticky tongue to eat ants and when approached curl up in a ball with spines pointing outwards.

Other common mammals include the **dingo** (*Canis lupus dingo*) and the introduced **red fox** (*Vulpes vulpes*). The latter is often seen around Hyden and Carnarvon and considered a pest throughout the state. Intensive fox control programs have seen the populations of some native mammals improve, including the black-footed rock wallaby.

The rare **western pebble-mound mouse** (*Pseudomys chapmani*) is very elusive and not easily sighted. But evidence of their habitats is there to be seen amongst the rocks and spinifex – big piles of pebbles are the giveaway. If you are lucky you may see one in the spinifex country of Karijini National Park. Now only found wild on Bernier Island in Shark Bay, the **Shark Bay mouse** (*Pseudomys fieldi*) has been extinct on the mainland since European settlement. Also known as **djoongari**, this mouse has been introduced on Doole Island in the Exmouth Gulf, Trimouille Island in the Montebello Islands and Faure Island near Monkey Mia. Classified as vulnerable to extinction, the **greater stick-nest rat** (*Leporillus conditor*) has been introduced to Salutation and Faure islands in Shark Bay.

Extinct on the mainland since the 1940s, the **western barred bandicoot** (*Parameles bougainville bougainville*) is now only found wild on Bernier Island in Shark Bay. Populations have been introduced to Heirisson Prong and Faure Island in Shark Bay.

Birds

The northern and inland regions of Western Australia are home to hundreds of bird species. In what is predominantly arid land, birds are often found in big numbers around areas of permanent water. One area of particular consequence is the **Fortescue Marsh** – which is one of Australia's most important wetlands. When inundated, the Marsh supports up to 270 000 **waterbirds**, including waterfowl, cormorants, grebe, heron, ibis, stilt and tern. The uncommon **grey falcon** (*Falco hypoleucos*), vulnerable **slender-billed thornbill** (*Acanthiza iredalei iredalei*) and critically endangered **night parrot** (*Pezoporus occidentalis*), have all been reported in this marsh area too.

Important Bird Areas (IBA)

Fortescue Marsh is just one of various sites of international significance in central and northern Western Australia – known as Important Bird Areas (IBA).

In the Goldfields district IBAs are located at **lakes Barlee, Ballard and Marmion**. All three lakes have recorded large breeding events of the **banded stilt** (*Cladorhynchus leucocephalus*).

A cluster of three IBAs in the Wheatbelt district – **Karroun Hill**, **Karara** and **Lochada**, and **Mt Gibson** and **Charles Darwin Reserve** – all have populations of the vulnerable **malleefowl** (*Leipoa ocellata*). The latter two areas also have **western corella** (*Cacatua pastinator*).

Project Eden, Shark Bay

Many of Australia's unique marsupials are either extinct or endangered due to feral cats, foxes and habitat destruction. To save these marsupials from extinction, the Department of Environment and Conservation started Project Eden. The aim of the project is to rid Peron Peninsula of feral cats and foxes, and introduce rare species in a relatively safe habitat. To keep feral animals from entering Peron Peninsula, fencing was built across a narrow isthmus near Shell Beach. A widespread and ongoing cat and fox extermination followed; with reasonable success. As a result, rare malleefowls and bilbies are now breeding in numbers. Introduced woylies, banded hare wallabies and other endangered marsupials are hanging on despite cats remaining in the area – albeit in smaller numbers. In the future, more rare mammals will be introduced with the aim of increasing their numbers.

PELUSEY PHOTOGRAPHY

Feral proof fence near Shell Beach

Pelican at Monkey Mia

STEVEN DAVID MILLER, NATURAL WANDERS

Off the coast of Geraldton, the **Houtman Abrolhos** group of islands is recognised as the most important seabird breeding site in the eastern Indian Ocean. It has populations of the wedge-tailed and little shearwater; white-faced storm petrel; pied cormorant; roseate, fairy, bridled and sooty tern; and common and lesser noddy. It is the only place in Australia where the **lesser noddy** (*Anous tenuirostris*) breeds.

In Shark Bay there are IBAs on the **Faure, Pelican and Freycinet islands** that support populations of the **pied cormorant** (*Phalacrocorax varius*). In addition, the Faure and Pelican islands have breeding colonies of the vulnerable **fairy tern** (*Sterna nereis*) as well as the **pied oystercatcher** (*Haematopus longirostris*) and **red-necked stint** (*Calidris ruficollis*).

North of Carnarvon the **Lake MacLeod** IBA is home to the vulnerable **fairy tern** (*Sterna nereis*) as well as the **red-necked stint** (*Calidris ruficollis*), **curlew sandpiper** (*Calidris ferruginea*), **banded stilt** (*Cladorhynchus leucocephalus*), **red-necked avocet** (*Recurvirostra novaehollandiae*), **red-capped plover** (*Charadrius ruficapillus*), **dusky gerygone** (*Gerygone tenebrosa*) and **yellow white-eye** (*Zosterops luteus*).

The mangroves of the **Exmouth Gulf** also support populations of the **dusky gerygone** (*Gerygone tenebrosa*) and **yellow white-eye** (*Zosterops luteus*), as well as the **grey-tailed tattler** (*Heteroscelus brevipes*) and **pied oystercatcher** (*Haematopus longirostris*). North of the Exmouth Gulf, **Sunday Island** has a substantial population of **roseate terns** (*Sterna dougallii*).

Off the coast between Onslow and Karratha, **Barrow Island** and the **Montebello Islands** are also recognised as IBAs. Barrow Island is the only known location for a vulnerable subspecies of the **white-winged fairy-wren** (*Malurus leuconotus*) and the vulnerable **fairy tern** (*Sterna nereis*). It also has populations of the **pied oystercatcher** (*Haematopus longirostris*), **red-necked stint** (*Calidris ruficollis*), **grey-tailed tattler** (*Heteroscelus brevipes*) and **spinifexbird** (*Eremiornis carteri*). The vulnerable **fairy tern** (*Sterna nereis*) is also found on the Montebello Islands, as well as the **roseate tern** (*Sterna dougallii*), **sooty oystercatcher** (*Haematopus fuliginosus*) and the near-threatened **beach stone-curlew** (*Esacus neglectus*).

Small numbers of the **dusky gerygone** (*Gerygone tenebrosa*) can be seen around the **Dampier saltworks**, as well as populations of the **red-necked stint** (*Calidris ruficollis*) and **red-capped plover** (*Charadrius ruficapillus*).

The **Port Hedland saltworks** IBA also has populations of the **dusky gerygone** (*Gerygone tenebrosa*) and **red-necked stint** (*Calidris ruficollis*), as well as the **sharp-tailed sandpiper** (*Calidris acuminata*) and **yellow white-eye** (*Zosterops luteus*). North of Port Hedland, **Bedout Island** IBA has the **brown booby** (*Sula leucogaster*) and an important breeding population of the **lesser frigatebird** (*Fregata ariel*).

At the northern end of the Pilbara region, **Eighty Mile Beach** sees more than 400 000 migratory shorebirds. Those commonly sighted include the **bar-tailed godwit** (*Limosa lapponica*), **eastern curlew** (*Numenius madagascariensis*), **great knot** (*Calidris tenuirostris*), **greater sand plover** (*Charadrius leschenaultii*), **grey-tailed tattler** (*Heteroscelus brevipes*), **oriental plover** (*Charadrius veredus*), **oriental pratincole** (*Glareola maldivarum*), **red knot** (*Calidris canutus*), **red-necked stint** (*Calidris ruficollis*), **terek sandpiper** (*Xenus cinereus*), **pied oystercatcher** (*Haematopus longirostris*) and **red-capped plover** (*Charadrius ruficapillus*). When flooded, the nearby **Mandora Marsh** is home to the **plumed whistling duck** (*Dendrocygna eytoni*), **hardhead** (*Aytha australis*), **white-necked heron** (*Ardea pacifica*), **glossy ibis** (*Plegadis falcinellus*), **straw-necked ibis** (*Threskiornis spinicollis*), **brolga** (*Grus rubicunda*), **little curlew** (*Numenius minutus*), **banded stilt** (*Cladorhynchus leucocephalus*), **black-winged stilt** (*Himantopus himantopus*), **red-necked avocet** (*Recurvirostra novaehollandiae*), **oriental plover** (*Charadrius veredus*), **oriental pratincole** (*Glareola maldivarum*), **gull-billed tern** (*Gelochelidon nilotica*) and **whiskered tern** (*Childonias hybrida*).

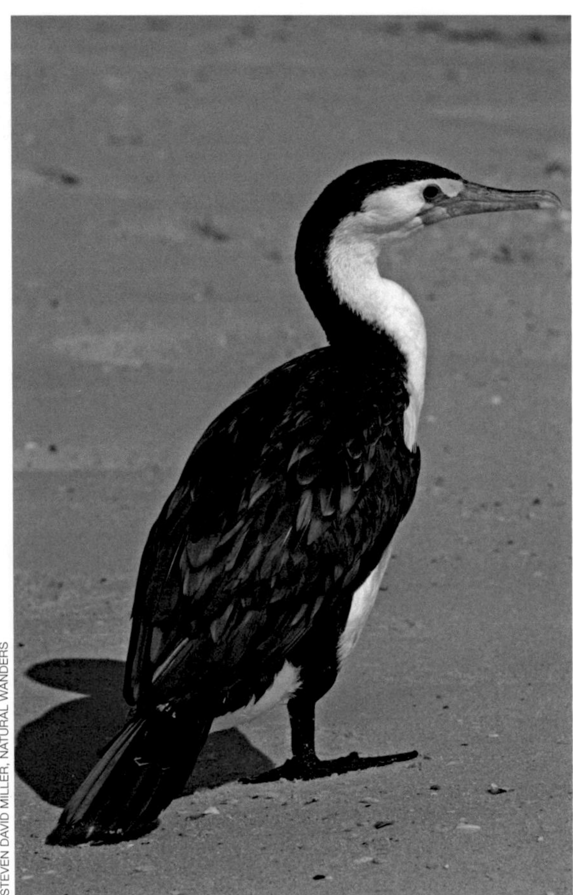

STEVEN DAVID MILLER, NATURAL WANDERS

Pied cormorant

Commonly Seen Birds

Probably the most conspicuous birds in northern and inland areas of Western Australia are colourful **parrots**. Seen in huge flocks are the noisy **galahs** (*Cacatua roseicapilla*) and **corellas** (*Licmetis*). Driving along outback roads it is not uncommon to see flocks of the wild form of that favourite pet: the **budgerigar** (*Melopsittacus undulatus*). Other parrots such as the **mulga parrot** (*Psephotus varius*), **Bourke's parrot** (*Neopsephotus bourkii*) and **Major Mitchell cockatoo** (*Cacatua leadbeateri*) are less commonly seen but well worth looking out for.

The **Australian bustard** (*Areotis australis*) is a large ground-loving bird second only in size to an emu. Historically it was a favourite meal for Aboriginal people. In the North West the Australian bustard is also known as the **bush turkey**, and it can sometimes be seen from travelling vehicles.

Often found gorging on road kill, the **wedge-tailed eagle** (*Aquila audax*) dominates the clear blue skies of northern and inland parts of Western Australia. These magnificent birds of prey can reach a length of a metre with a massive wing span of up to two metres. They are quite capable of preying on wallabies, rabbits and other mammals as well as road kill. Be aware that they can be slow to fly off the road kill, so be prepared to slow down.

Almost as big as a wedge-tailed eagle, the **white-breasted sea eagle** (*Haliaeetus leucogaster*) is a predominantly coastal bird,. Australia's second largest bird of prey, it is an impressive sight.

Kingfishers live near permanent water and mangrove areas with the imposing looking **blue-winged kookaburra** (*Dacelo *leachii*) sometimes seen around permanent waterholes in the Pilbara. Flittering amongst the mangroves is the **collard** or **mangrove kingfisher** (*Halcyon senegaloides*).

The squat-looking **spinifex pigeon** (*Geophaps plumifera*) is a colourful little bird with a banded face, red eye and conspicuous crest. As the name implies, this pigeon is a common resident in areas where spinifex dominates. The **crested pigeon** (*Ocyphaps lophotes*) is larger and more common than the spinifex variety. A common bird call in the north west is the chime of the quite small **diamond dove** (*Geopelia cuneata*).

A variety of tiny **finches** inhabit the dry regions of the Gascoyne, Goldfields and Pilbara. As they are seed eaters, finches require easy access to water. Seeing a flock of finches usually indicates water isn't too far away, an often heart-warming sight for the early explorers. The **zebra finch** (*Taeniopygia guttata*) is the most often seen species.

Mangroves and tidal mud flats attract **wading birds** in huge numbers, including many **migratory birds** that have made the incredibly long journey to escape winter in the northern hemisphere. These birds include dotterels, plovers, sandpipers, stints and curlews. Common wading birds seen at most times of the year are oystercatchers, banded stilts, several egret species, spoonbills and reef herons. There are several migratory hotspots in the North West, including **Eighty Mile Beach** between Port Hedland and Broome. (See Important Bird Areas pp15-16.)

Reptiles and amphibians

To the casual observer, besides flies, the visitor could be excused for believing the northern and inland regions of Western Australia are the land of reptiles. Reptiles dominate the fauna of the region, coming in all shapes and sizes. Occasionally the dangerous **estuarine crocodile** ventures southwards into Pilbara waters, but is much more of a threat in the Kimberley.

Of the 97 reptile and amphibian species found in **Millstream-Chichester National Park**, 15 are endemic to the Pilbara and five are endemic to Western Australia. Species endemic to the Pilbara include two **geckoes**, two **legless lizards**, six **skinks**, two **elapid snakes** and one **monitor lizard**.

Lizards

By far the most spectacular lizards in size and appearance are members of the **goanna** family. The most commonly seen goanna in the region is the **bungarra**, or **sand monitor**, (*Varanus gouldii*). It can often be seen near roads and is considered tasty bushtucker by the Aboriginal people. Other monitors found in the region include the **ridge-tailed monitor** (*Varanus acanthurus*), **stripe-tailed pygmy monitor** (*Varanus caudolineatus*) and **short-tailed pygmy monitor** (*Varanus brevicauda*). The biggest lizard in Australia is the **perentie** (*Varanus giganteus*), which can grow to over 2m in length. It is capable of killing and eating a small kangaroo, but more often consumes smaller prey. Although it is not a common lizard, if sighted it is never forgotten. Its range is from the North West coast, inland through to Central Australia. Another imposing goanna is the **desert-spotted monitor** (*Varanus panoptes rubidus*), which exists only in central Western Australia. They grow to more than 1.5m long and are fond of consuming road kill. Confined to small areas of the Pilbara, the **Pilbara rock monitor** (*Varanus pilbarensis*) prefers rocky hills, cliff faces and gorges. This monitor has been seen sheltering in the rocks in **Karijini National Park**.

The **Burton's legless lizard** (*Lialis burtonis*) is very common in the Pilbara.

Geckoes are found throughout Western Australia and are well represented in the State's northern and inland parts. They are soft

STEVEN DAVID MILLER, NATURAL WANDERS

Plumed Whistling-Ducks

STEVEN DAVID MILLER, NATURAL WANDERS

STEVEN DAVID MILLER, NATURAL WANDERS

L to R: Blue-winged kookaburra, Spinifex Pigeon

JEFF DREWITZ

STEVEN DAVID MILLER, NATURAL WANDERS

L to R: The wedge-tailed eagle (Aquila audax) can have a massive wing span of up to two metres., Galahs are often seen in huge flocks

The perentie is Australia's biggest lizard

STEVEN DAVID MILLER, NATURAL WANDERS

PELUSEY PHOTOGRAPHY

Yellow spotted monitor

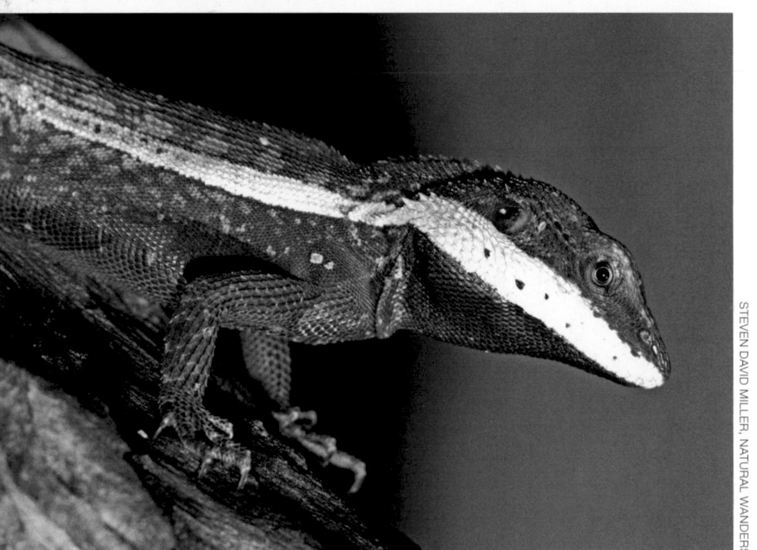

STEVEN DAVID MILLER, NATURAL WANDERS

Ta-ta dragons are commonly seen in the Pilbara

Snake Bite First Aid

If you are unlucky enough to be bitten by a snake, it is important to follow the appropriate first aid. It can save lives.

- Do not wash the area of the bite. Hospitals can swab the area to identify the snake.
- Immediately wrap a wide bandage firmly around the bitten area and most of the inflicted limb. Bandage down the limb to the extremity and then back up again. It should be firm but not so tight it cuts off circulation.
- Keep the victim still and reassured they are going to be okay.
- Splint the limb to immobilise it. You must not remove the bandage or splint. Medical staff will do this when they are ready.
- It is better to bring transport to the victim rather than attempt the reverse as any movement can aid poison distribution.
- The victim should be transported to the nearest hospital or if in an isolated place, contact the Flying Doctor Service via satellite phone.
- Once in hospital, tell staff if the victim suffers from any allergies that could effect antivenom treatment.
- Identifying the snake makes treatment simpler, but it's not essential as universal antivenom is available. Although presenting a dead offending snake to the doctor is helpful for identification, having two bite victims certainly is not.

bodied animals that generally shelter during the day and hunt for insects at night. The **smooth knob-tailed gecko** (*Nephrurus levis*) is one of the most beautiful looking lizards you are ever likely to see. Along the northern Pilbara coast, the **northern spiny-tailed gecko** (*Strophurus ciliaris*) can often by seen at night near roads during the summer months. The **thick-tailed gecko** (*Underwoodisaurus milii*) is also found along the coast, but south of Shark Bay. In the inland parts of the Pilbara, as well as the Goldfields, the **marbled-velvet gecko** (*Oedura marmorata*) can be found. Other geckoes commonly found throughout the region include the **tree dtella** (*Gehyra variegata*) and **Bynoe's gecko** (*Heteronotia binoei*). **Millstream-Chichester National Park** has many geckoes, including several endemic species.

Go for a walk around rocky areas in the Pilbara and you will invariably see small large-headed lizards basking in the morning sun or dashing about at great speed. There are many species of these **dragons**, including the **Gilbert's dragon** (*Lophognathus gilberti*), a slender elegant-looking lizard often found in trees and shrubs along permanent waterways. It is quite common along the coastal Pilbara region. Other common species include the **western bearded dragon** (*Pogona minima*), **western netted dragon** (*Ctenophorus reticulatus*) and **long-nose ta-ta dragon** (*Lophognathus longirostris*).

The **thorny devil** (*Moloch horridus*) is one of the more unusual lizards in both habits and appearance. It is a slow moving, dumpy looking lizard covered in sharp looking spikes. It feeds entirely on ants eating as many as 5000 a day. Able to cope with a lack of water, this lizard is supremely adapted to life in the Pilbara and inland regions. It is commonly found throughout Western Australia's arid regions, and can often be seen on the sands of the **Peron Peninsula**.

Snakes

No doubt the one reptile that strikes fear into most people is a snake. Northern and inland parts of Western Australia are the home of many species of both venomous and nonvenomous snakes. Most snakes are harmless to humans unless they are suddenly disturbed or feel threatened, but unless you are an expert they should all be left alone.

The most fearsome snake is the **king brown** (*Pseudechis australis*), which can grow to two metres and is found throughout most of Australia. Also known as the **mulga snake**, it should be avoided at all costs, because its bite can be fatal. The **spotted mulga snake** (*Pseudechis butleri*) is found in a small part of the Gascoyne and Goldfields regions – inland from Geraldton up to Meekatharra and southeast to Leonora. Occasionally the king brown is mistaken for the **western brown snake** (*Pseudonaja nuchalis*), another resident of WA's drier regions. Also commonly known as the **gwarder**, the western brown is also poisonous. The **desert death adder** (*Acanthophis pyrrhus*) is found throughout Western Australia's arid and semi-arid areas. This venomous snake can be found in spinifex, sand dunes and rocky outcrops as well as gibber deserts and coastal dunes. Another dangerously venomous snake is the **Pilbara death adder** (*Acanthophis wellsi*), which is only found in the Pilbara. They live around Dampier and Port Hedland, inland to Newman, as well as in Cape Range.

Nonvenomous snakes such as the huge **olive python** (*Liasis olivaceus*) and the smaller **Stimson's python** (*Antaresia stimsoni*) are also found in parts of the North West. The tiny **pygmy python** (*Antaresia perthensis*) is only found in the Pilbara. Also harmless are the **Australian bockadam** (*Cereberus australia*), **white-bellied mangrove snake** (*Fordonia leucobalia*) and **Richardson's mangrove snake** (*Myron richardsonii*). All three are found along the coast south to Port Hedland. The **black-headed python** (*Aspidites melanocephalus*) is also found along the coastal and northern areas of the Pilbara. The **woma python** (*Aspidites ramsayi*) is found along the coast north of Port Hedland, as well as in areas of the Mid West, Wheatbelt and Goldfields from Shark Bay down to Geraldton and across to Kalgoorlie.

Frogs

In a region more known for its aridity, it may be surprising to find frogs but they are common residents near permanent water. In more arid parts, certain **burrowing frogs** lay dormant or aestivate under dry riverbeds and lakes. After a rare spell of heavy rain these watercourses fill up, triggering these frogs into a breeding frenzy. The most likely place you will see frogs is in the warmer areas in the toilets.

Eleven different frogs are found in the **Pilbara** area including the **Main's frog** (*Cyclorana maini*), **desert tree frog** (*Litoria rubella*), **desert trilling frog** (*Neobatrachus centralis*), **shoemaker frog** (*Neobatrachus sutor*), **desert spadefoot toad** (*Notaden nichollsi*) and **Spencer's burrowing frog** (*Opisthodon spenceri*). Three **toadlets** – **Douglas's** (*Pseudophryne douglasi*), **glandular** (*Uperoleia glandulosa*) and **Russell's** (*Uperoleia russelli*) – are found only in very small areas of the Pilbara.

In the **Mid West** region, 21 different frogs are found. In addition to the Main's frog, desert tree frog, shoemaker frog, Spencer's burrowing frog and desert trilling frog that are also found in the Pilbara, there are also the **water-holding frog** (*Cyclorana platycephala*), **sandhill frog** (*Arenophryne rotunda*), **tawny trilling frog** (*Neobatrachus fulvus*), **Kunapalari frog** (*Neobatrachus kunapalari*) and **goldfields bullfrog** (*Neobatrachus wilsmorei*). The **Gunther's toadlet** (*Pseudophryne guentheri*) and **orange-crowned toadlet** (*Pseudophryne occidentalis*) are also found in the area, along with the Russell's toadlet.

There are no frogs found only in the **Goldfields** region, but 12 live here including the Main's frog, water-holding frog, desert trilling frog, Kunapalari frog, shoemaker frog, Spencer's burrowing frog and orange-crowned toadlet.

Groundwater fauna

Animals that live permanently underground in water are called groundwater fauna, or **stygofauna**. The majority of stygofauna are crustaceans, but they can also be fish, worms, snails, mites and insects. These subterranean animals have been found in calcrete and alluvial aquifers in the Pilbara and Yilgarn plateaus, Cape Range Peninsula and Carnarvon Basin. Two threatened species of **stygofaunal fish** are found in the Cape Range area, near Exmouth. These are the **blind cave eel** (*Ophisternon candidum*) and **blind gudgeon** (*Milyeringa veritas*). The entire suborder **Tainisopidea** is restricted to karstic groundwater of the Pilbara and Kimberley.

Nonvenomous python

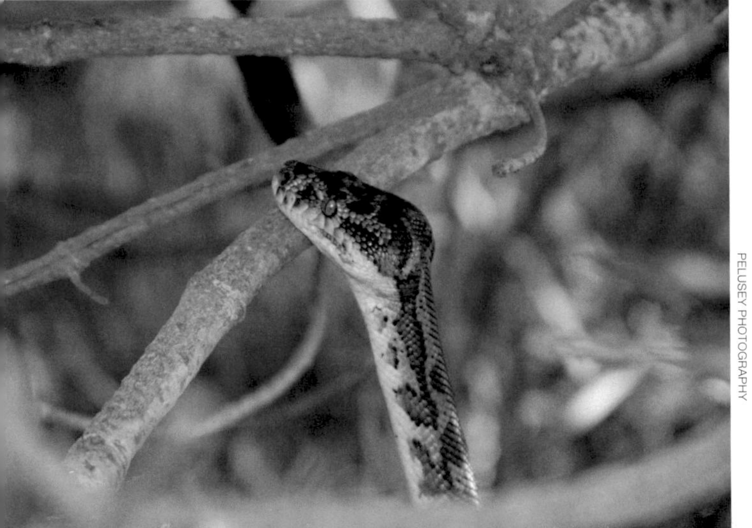

PELUSEY PHOTOGRAPHY

PELUSEY PHOTOGRAPHY

Green tree frog

Weeli Wolli Spring: A priority ecological community

By Stephen van Leeuwen, Department of Environment and Conservation Science Division

Weeli Wolli Creek in the central Hamersley Range supports a permanent series of pools which are fed by Weeli Wolli Spring. This arid zone wetland supports a unique community of plants and animals some of which are endemic to the Spring.

The Spring, which has considerable spiritual and cultural significance to traditional owners of the Hamersley Range, is located at the base of a large banded ironstone ridge that intersects the Creek, providing an impermeable barrier to the subsurface downstream flow of water. The subsequent surface expression of water at the Spring varies from a trickle to a significant flow which is expressed as pools and billabongs on the surface for up to 10km.

The vegetation of the Spring and surrounding creek channel is typical of most Pilbara drainage features that support permanent water. It is dominated by a fringing forest or tall woodland of silver paperbark (*Melaleuca argentea*) and river red gum (*Eucalyptus camaldulensis*) over trees of coolibah (*E. victrix*) and a dense shrub layer dominated by an assortment of wattles, in particular Pilbara jam (*Acacia citrinoviridis*). The presence of permanent water and very moist sediment also provides suitable habitat for many sedges and herbs. The area is a haven for birds and other fauna including many bats and also supports a rich community of surface and subsurface aquatic invertebrates.

The Spring is recognised as a focal point for birds in the Pilbara with over 60 species recorded along the creek. Similarly, the diversity of habitat types and rough landscapes provide many opportunities for bats, with the Spring being the only known Pilbara and most northern locality for the chocolate bat (*Chalinolobus morio*). The ghost bat (*Macroderma gigas*), a threatened species, has also been recorded foraging above pools downstream of the Spring.

The most significant biological values of the Spring and its creek system are associated with the aquatic invertebrates that inhabit the Spring, pools and the underground water body. Three species of water mite and three crustaceans are only known from Weeli Wolli Creek and one other locality in the Pilbara. Similarly, two underground aquatic invertebrates, a water mite and an oligochaete, are only known from Weeli Wolli.

The DEC is currently working with industry and traditional owners to manage impacts on Weeli Wolli Creek and the Spring with the primary objectives to protect cultural values and maintain the biological assets of the area. To this end the State Government will establish a reserve at Weeli Wolli in 2015.

chapter two

Planning the Trip

Information Sources

There are many places to find out information on the Perth to Pilbara region.

Visitor Information Centres

The area covered by this book encompasses the Pilbara part of the Australia's North West WA tourism region, as well as the Australia's Coral Coast and Australia's Golden Outback regions. Within each region there are visitor centres that are able to answer most questions relating to their particular areas.

Australia's Coral Coast

www.australiascoralcoast.com

- **Carnarvon Visitor Centre** – 11 Robinson St, Carnarvon; Ph 08 9941 1146; www.carnarvon.org.au
- **Dongara Tourist Information** – 9 Waldeck St, Dongara; Ph 08 9927 1404; www.irwin.wa.gov.au
- **Exmouth Visitor Centre** – Murat Rd, Exmouth; Ph 1800 287 328; www.exmouthwa.com.au
- **Geraldton Visitor Centre** – 90 Chapman Rd, Geraldton; Ph 1800 818 881; www.geraldtontourist.com.au
- **Greenough Visitor and Interpretation Centre** – Brand Hwy, Greenough; Ph 08 9926 1084
- **Kalbarri Visitor Centre** – 70 Grey St, Kalbarri; Ph 1800 639 468; www.kalbarriwa.info
- **Milyering Visitor Centre** – Cape Range National Park, near Exmouth; Ph 08 9949 2808
- **Mullewa Telecentre & Tourist Information Centre** – Jose St, Mullewa; Ph 08 9961 1555, www.mullewatourism.com.au
- **Northampton Tourist Centre** – Old Hampton Rd, Northampton; Ph 08 9934 1488
- **Shark Bay World Heritage Discovery & Visitor Centre** – 53 Knight Tce, Denham; Ph 08 9948 1590; www.sharkbayinterpretivecentre.com.au

Australia's Golden Outback

www.australiasgoldenoutback.com

- **Central Wheatbelt Visitor Centre** – Barrack St, Merredin; Ph 08 9041 1668, 1300 736 283; www.wheatbelttourism.com
- **Coolgardie Tourist Bureau** – 62 Bayley St, Coolgardie; Ph 08 9026 6090
- **Cue Visitor Centre** – Lot 2 Austin St, Cue; Ph 08 9963 1041
- **Great Beyond Explorer's Hall of Fame & Visitor Centre** – Augusta St, Laverton; Ph 08 9031 1361
- **Hyden Visitor Centre** – 20 Marshall St, Hyden; Ph 08 9880 5200
- **Kalgoorlie Goldfields Visitor Centre** – Cnr Hannan & Wilson Sts, Kalgoorlie; Ph 08 9021 1966; www.kalgoorlietourism.com
- **Leonora Tourist Information Centre** – Cnr Tower & Trump Sts, Leonora; Ph 08 9037 6888
- **Mount Magnet Tourist Information Centre** – Lot 366 Hepburn St, Mt Magnet; Ph 08 9963 4001

Australia's North West

www.australiasnorthwest.com

- **Karratha Visitor Centre** – Karratha Rd, Karratha; Ph 08 9144 4600; www.pilbaracoast.com
- **Newman Visitor Centre** – Fortescue Ave, Newman; Ph 08 9175 2888; www.newman-wa.org
- **Onslow Tourist Centre** – Onslow; Ph 08 9184 6644; www.ashburton.wa.gov.au
- **Port Hedland Visitor Centre** – 13 Wedge St, Port Hedland; Ph 08 9173 1711; www.porthedlandtouristbureau.com
- **Roebourne Visitor Centre** – Old Gaol, Queen St, Roebourne; Ph 08 9182 1060
- **Tom Price Visitor Centre** – Central Ave, Tom Price; Ph 08 9188 1112; www.tompricewa.com.au

Government Offices

Department of Environment and Conservation

The Department of Environment and Conservation (DEC) manages Western Australia's national parks, conservation parks, nature reserves, marine parks and state forests. The useful website (www.dec.wa.gov.au) has plenty of information on facilities and attractions in the State's parks and reserves. For enquiries regarding parks in a particular region, contact the offices listed below:

- **Goldfields region** – 32 Brookman St, Kalgoorlie; Ph 08 9080 5555
- **Mid West region** - 1st floor, The Foreshore Centre, 201 Foreshore Dr, Geraldton; Ph 08 9921 5955
- **Carnarvon** – 211 Robinson St, Carnarvon; Ph 08 9941 3754
- **Shark Bay** – 89 Knight Tce, Denham; Ph 08 9948 1209
- **Pilbara region** – Lot 3 Anderson Rd, Karratha; Ph 08 9143 1488
- **Exmouth** – 20 Nimitz St, Exmouth; Ph 08 9947 8000
- **Wheatbelt region** – 7 Wald St, Narrogin; Ph 08 9881 9222
- **Merredin** – 33 Bates St, Merredin; Ph 08 9041 2488

Department of Fisheries

In Western Australia fishing is recognised as the most widely enjoyed of all recreational activities. It is also considered to be one of the most dangerous as deaths and injuries occur regularly, particularly in rock fishing. Please take extreme care and ensure you are safe from any unusually high waves or other dangers. Always keep alert and never turn your back on the sea.

Along the coast you can fish for abalone and crayfish which both have restricted seasons. Many fish and other catches also have minimum legal sizes and restricted bag limits. Although there are no season restrictions or licences required for crabs or prawns, size and bag limits do apply.

Driving is really the only way to get around this vast area.
ROB BOEGHEIM

Remember that annual fishing licences are required in Western Australia for abalone ($44), rock lobster ($38), marron ($26) and net fishing ($31). The Freshwater Angling ($26) licence applies in south-west Western Australia for fishing in any waterway that is not affected by the tide, below 29° (Geraldton). A combined licence is also available for $87.

Licence applications are available online or can be obtained at post offices and Department of Fisheries offices. A licence will take about 30 days so allow plenty of time. For further information see the very helpful website, www.fish.wa.gov.au.

Offices:

- **Carnarvon District Office** – 59 Olivia Tce, Carnarvon; Ph 08 9941 1185
- **Denham District Office** – Knight Tce, Denham; Ph 08 9941 1210
- **Dongara District Office** – Fishing Boat Harbour, McIntyre Cove, Dongara; Ph 08 9927 1187
- **Exmouth District Office** – Cnr Payne & Riggs St, Exmouth; Ph 08 9949 2755
- **Geraldton Regional Office** – 69-75 Connell Rd, Geraldton; Ph 08 9921 6800
- **Karratha District Office** – Unit 1, 17-19 Crane Circle, Karratha; Ph 08 9144 4337
- **Perth Regional Office** – 3rd floor SGIO Atrium, 168-170 St George's Tce, Perth; Ph 08 9482 7333

Books and Magazines

There are various useful publications that are worthwhile reading when you are planning a trip. Local libraries in towns can often have interesting publications about their area. The main branches of the DEC offer a multitude of fascinating reading material about the northern part of Western Australia. *North-West Bound and Shark Bay: Twin Bays on the Edge* are recent additions to the DEC book list, with plenty of information and stunning photographs. Other DEC publications include *The Golden Pipeline: Heritage Trail Guide, Gascoyne Murchison Outback Pathways* and *The Marine Life of Ningaloo Marine Park & Coral Bay.*

For around $6.50 you can pick up handy palm-sized books by DEC covering such diverse subjects as *Geology & Landforms of the Pilbara, Common Plants of the Pilbara, Common Trees of the Goldfields, Wattles of the Pilbara, Hazardous Animals of North-Western Australia* and *Mammals of North-Western Australia. Discovering Shark Bay Marine Park and Monkey Mia* is a 64 page DEC publication that covers walk and dive trails in the region.

For current information about DEC activities and in-depth articles on Western Australia's flora and fauna, check out *Landscope* Magazine. It's available from some DEC offices and most newsagents.

Len Zell's Wild Discovery Guide to *Shark Bay – Ningaloo Coast & Outback Pathways* includes plenty of useful information, including great guides to the plants and animals of the regions.

GPS navigating, near Steep Point

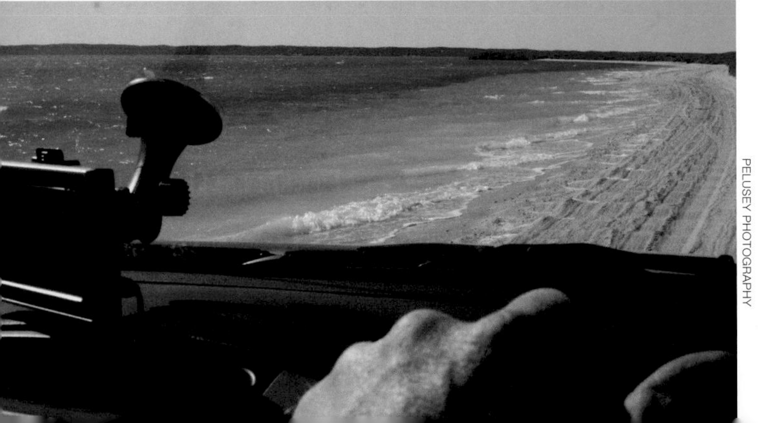

PELUSEY PHOTOGRAPHY

Bird-watching

Birds Australia's WA office (Ph 08 9383 7749, www.birdsaustralia.com.au) is at Peregrine House, 167 Perry Lakes Dr in Floreat, a Perth suburb. It has a number of regional bird guides and lists that you can download off the website.

Canoeing & Kayaking

The *Canoe & Kayak Guide to Western Australia*, by Martin Chambers (Hesperian Press, 2000), is a handy reference available from DEC information centres, tourist offices and canoe shops. Also useful (if you can get hold of them) are the canoe notes put out by the Department of Sport & Recreation. They're out of date, but still make good references.

For river levels, refer to www.water.wa.gov.au (WA Department of Water site) and follow the Maps, data & atlases link to River level information.

Diving & Snorkelling

DEC publishes two guidebooks, *Dive & Snorkel Sites in Western Australia* and *More Dive & Snorkel Sites in Western Australia.*

Fishing

The following state-wide references are worth getting hold of:

- *Fishing the Wild West*, by Ross Cusack and Mike Roennfeldt (West Australian Newspapers, 2002), is a handy glove-box sized reference that describes a number of sought-after species and how and where to catch them.
- Kurt Blanksby & Frank Porker's *Fishing Guide to Western Australia* (Australian Fishing Network, 2003) is too big for the glove box, but makes a good reference during the planning phase. Its maps are excellent and there are plenty of interesting fish facts.
- *Western Fisheries* is a publication similar to *Landscope*, published by the Department of Fisheries. It focuses on the marine world, particularly around research regarding amateur and professional fishing.

Also check Friday's edition of *The West Australian* newspaper, which has several pages devoted to fishing.

Channel Nine's website www.fishingwa.com has plenty of useful information including fact sheets, species, fishing tips and wheelchair-accessible fishing spots.

Finally, speciality tackle shops are invariably founts of knowledge on all aspects of the local scene.

Wildflowers

The DEC book *Wildflower Country* covers the Gascoyne and Murchison regions from Jurien Bay to Shark Bay and inland to Meekatharra. DEC also publishes several pocket references to regional wildflowers, including *Common Wildflowers of the Mid-West, Wildflowers of Shark Bay* and *Threatened Wildflowers of the Mid-West.* These cost $6.50 each and are available at DEC information centres and tourist offices. Tourism WA's free publication *Western Australian Wildflower Holiday Guide* details several self-drive tours you can do.

Maps

The maps in this book come from Hema's *Western Australia Road & 4WD Atlas.* Hema also publishes maps of *Pilbara and Coral Coast* (1:1 250 000), *Mid West Western Australia Including Gascoyne & Batavia Coast* (1:1 250 000) and *Goldfields, Esperance & the Southern Coast of WA* (1:750 000). Hema's *Camping Atlas of Western Australia* covers the more popular campgrounds in the area.

These days, many travellers are using GPS devices that show your location on downloaded maps including the **Hema Navigator**. They work well and are easy to use, but don't rely 100% on them in isolated areas. Have a good selection of maps and a compass as well and make sure you know how to use them.

PELUSEY PHOTOGRAPHY

Packing them in at Coral Bay

When to Go

Climate

You must take into consideration climate when timing your visit in the area covered in this book. As the regions covered by this book vary we'll consider the climate region by region.

Coral Coast

Generally speaking the area covered here extends from Yanchep in the south to the North West Cape in the north.

The southern part of this region, from just north of Perth to Kalbarri, experiences a typical Mediterranean climate with summers that are generally hot and dry. Afternoon sea breezes are often strong from December to February, making these months the peak time for kite surfers and windsurfers on the west coast. From late February and March the winds are generally lighter.

Inland, temperatures are usually much hotter. Every summer, both Geraldton and Kalbarri get temperatures reaching into the mid-40s. Spring is the best time for wildflowers: from July to September. Carnarvon has a beautiful year round climate with mild sunny winters and windy hot summers tempered by regular sea breezes. The Exmouth North West Cape area is constantly windy and very hot in summer. In late autumn and winter this area is usually less windy and perfect for boating activities.

Gascoyne & Mid West

The region around Gascoyne Junction often tops the maximum temperature in the state on weather reports with temperatures near 50°C not uncommon. So if you can you should avoid travelling in summer. Winter and early spring on the other hand are delightful, with warm sunny days but sometimes cold nights. Wheatbelt locations are hot in summer with cold nights in winter. Spring is peak wildflower season: August to October.

Pilbara

Winter and early spring are also the best times for visiting the Pilbara as summer is exceptionally hot. In places like Marble Bar and Roebourne 40°C is a cool day in summer, and heatwaves are measured in months not days. The Pilbara coast is also very vulnerable to cyclones. Torrential rains accompanied by destructive winds also occasionally make road touring in summer very problematic. However the winter months are wonderful when gloriously sunny days nudging 30°C are the norm. Nights are still cold inland, even in the summer months. In particular, do not underestimate how cold it gets at night in Karijini National Park during winter.

Goldfields

In a nutshell expect hot to very hot summers and cool sunny winters with regularly freezing desert nights. Infrequent thunderstorms can cause disruptions in summer, but winter is normally dry. Spring and autumn are great times to explore this area.

Cyclone Alert

Cyclones are intense tropical storms that are also known as hurricanes in the Americas and typhoons in Asia. The Pilbara and Gascoyne coastlines are particularly vulnerable to these destructive storms that regularly bring winds of up to 300kph. The Pilbara coast experiences more cyclones than any other part of Australia with the cyclone season for northern WA **between November and April**. Intense cyclones not only produce destructive winds, they can also bring severe flooding from torrential rain and storm surges. Cyclones are rated in **categories** from the weakest at 1 to the strongest at 5, depending on the maximum wind gusts experienced.

Historically, **Onslow** has the dubious honour of being the town with the most hits. But towns such as **Carnarvon**, **Denham** and **Exmouth** have also seen their fair share of destruction. Although cyclones primarily affect coastal areas, strong winds can persist as a cyclone moves inland. However, even when the strong winds weaken as the cyclone heads inland the flooding that occurs after heavy rainfall can still cause significant damage.

If you are in an area where a cyclone is threatening, you must follow **emergency procedures** to the letter because cyclones are life-threatening events. Listen to a radio for regular updates from the local ABC station. Make sure the radio has fresh batteries as power is the first thing to go in a cyclone.

For weather forecasts, warnings and further information check the **Bureau of Meteorology** website (www.bom.gov.au/weather/wa/) or Ph 1900 955 366 or 1300 659 210 (WA Tropical Cyclone Information).

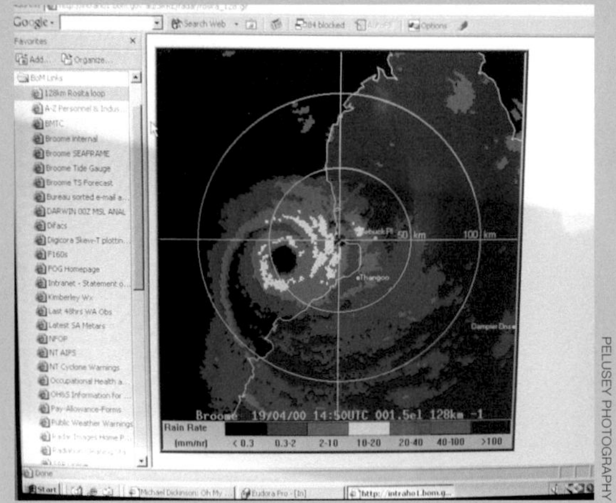

PELUSEY PHOTOGRAPHY

Cyclone heading down NW coast from Bureau of Meteorology website

Crowds

Generally speaking, if you don't like crowds then you should avoid travelling in Western Australia's **school holidays**. This timing is particularly important during the winter months in the Coral Coast and Pilbara. But, places like Exmouth, Kalbarri, Carnarvon and Coral Bay are always busy in the **winter months**. This is largely due to the migrating caravanning fraternity seeking out the winter sun. Booking for accommodation well in advance is always advisable during this time. Away from the coast, with the exception of Karijini National Park, bookings are not so essential. *Here's a tip*: crowds are generally smaller in the Pilbara and northern

Coral Coast between March and June, just before the annual migration north. Of course, any earlier and the crowds will be even smaller but then you are talking about summer and that's best avoided for the reasons mentioned above.

School holidays vary in timing from year to year so check before you go. Term dates for WA's public schools are available on the Department of Education and Training website (www.det.wa.edu.au).

Permits

National Park Passes

Many great attractions are located in national parks where visitor fees apply. It therefore makes sense to purchase national park passes from DEC branches in major towns or some manned national park entry points. Fees listed were correct as at September 2009 – check the DEC website for the latest prices. (Where they apply, camping fees are in addition to these entry fees.)

Parks With Entry Fees

- Cape Range National Park
- Francois Peron National Park
- Kalbarri National Park
- Karijini National Park
- Millstream-Chichester National Park
- Nambung National Park

Day Pass

The day pass allows entry into national parks on any one day.

- $11 per car, with up to eight legally seated passengers
- $5 per motorbike
- $5 per passenger if on a commercial tour

Holiday Park Pass

This pass covers any four-week period and is a cost effective alternative for multiple entries into national parks.

- $40 per car, including up to eight passengers

Annual All Park Pass

As we regularly visit national parks, this pass is very cost effective. Again it applies to one vehicle with up to eight passengers. It covers unlimited national park access over a 12-month period.

- $80
- $50 for seniors, aged pensioners and veterans
- $110 - gold star pass, which includes a subscription to Landscope magazine

Monkey Mia Reserve

The National Park Passes listed above do not cover access to Monkey Mia Reserve.

Special entry fees apply:

- $8/day or $12/month for adults
- $6/day or $10/month for concession holders
- $3/day or $5/month for children under 16
- $15/day or $30/month for a family (2 adults, 2 children)

Entering Aboriginal Land

A **transit permit** is required to travel through Aboriginal-owned land, and local visitor information centres can generally advise on the requirements. If you have any doubts, contact the Department of Indigenous Affairs (DIA) in Perth (Ph 08 9235 8000), South Hedland (Ph 08 9140 2577), Geraldton (Ph 08 9964 5470), Kalgoorlie (Ph 08 9021 5666) or Midland (Ph 08 9274 4288). The DIA website, www.dia.wa.gov.au, has information on entry permits and an online permit application.

It is now necessary to get permits for the **Canning Stock Route**. For wells 15 to 40 a permit is required from the Ngaanyatjarra Council (Ph 08 9425 2000). The sections from wells 40 to 50 and from well 50 north to the southern boundary of Carranya station both require permits from the Kimberley Land Council (Ph 08 9194 0100). Although the public have access rights along the Canning Stock Route itself, any deviation from this route into adjacent areas is unlawful without prior permission from the traditional owners. The Australian National Four Wheel Drive Council website has more information, see: www.anfwdc.asn.au/canning_stock_route.

Travelling east of Laverton to **Uluru** requires transit permits from the Central Land Council in the Northern Territory, www.clc.org.au/Permits/permits, as well as the DIA.

Environmental Concerns

Despite its tough looking exterior, northern and inland regions of Western Australia are environmentally quite fragile and susceptible to human impact. The usual minimal-impact guidelines apply to outdoor activities, such as bushwalking and camping.

Marine Parks

Western Australia's vast coastline and offshore waters include a huge range of unique and sensitive marine habitats. Certain areas of special significance are protected within marine parks. The most significant marine parks within the scope of this book are **Ningaloo Reef** off North West Cape, **Shark Bay**, **Jurien Bay** and **Montebello Islands**. Within these parks are sanctuary zones where any marine creatures, including fish, are totally protected. Certain parts of Shark Bay and Ningaloo Reef come under such sanctuary zone protection. Please obey signage or risk serious penalties. Information about marine parks in these areas is readily available from DEC offices and visitor centres. Other areas within marine parks offer some limited exploitation, but strict bag limits and size limits will apply for anglers. The Shark Bay pink snapper, which is an isolated breeding population, is a case in point. Any angler wishing to catch a snapper needs to know these restrictions. (See the earlier section on the Department of Fisheries, pp21-22, for contact details.)

Henri Freycinet Harbour

In Shark Bay's Henri Freycinet Harbour, you must buy special tags in advance that are obtainable from the Department of Fisheries. Do not try to catch a snapper in this area without having purchased tags. Fishery officers police the area. You can only buy two tags per year per person, which means catching and keeping two snapper. Special size restrictions also apply here. (See the Department of Fisheries website for details – www.fish.wa.gov.au.)

National Parks

Not surprisingly, some of the best natural places to visit in the regions covered in this book are protected within national parks. Special rules apply within national parks. It is a good idea to visit www.dec.wa.gov.au for information about Western Australia's national parks. Specific national park details are obtainable from district DEC offices in major towns (see p21).

Some general rules for visiting national parks:

- Obey all signage.
- No campfires unless otherwise stated.
- Camp only in designated campsites.
- Leave your pets at home.
- Stick to designated trails that are open to the public.
- Leave wildlife and plants undisturbed.
- Pay all relevant fees.

Special Precautions

First Aid

First but foremost, do a designated first aid course before starting your travels. Then pack a comprehensive first aid kit to take with you. St John Ambulance suggest you take the Off Road (4WD) first aid kit on camping and caravanning holidays. (For more information on first aid kits contact St John on Ph 1300 360 455 or visit www.stjohn.org.au.)

Basic Survival Skills & Emergencies

Emergencies can happen, so be prepared, especially if you will be travelling on isolated tracks. The Gascoyne, Goldfields and Pilbara are unforgiving places, particularly in summer.

- Always **notify somebody of your journey** and the estimated time of arrival when taking on isolated country. Most importantly, remember to contact them again on arriving at your destination.
- **Take plenty of water**: say three litres per day per person. You can last a couple weeks without food, but potentially less than a day without water in extreme heat.
- If you break down, **never leave the vehicle**. A vehicle is much easier to spot in an air search than a person wandering around aimlessly in the scrub.
- Take an **emergency beacon** or EPIRB.
- Install a **HF radio** in the vehicle or take a **satellite phone**.

Snakes

For international visitors and people from snake-less New Zealand, snakes often cause feelings of fear and loathing. Most snakes are not dangerous to people, but there are some exceptions (see pp18-19). But here's the thing: snakes are generally shy, retiring creatures that would prefer to avoid human contact at all costs. Problems can arise if you come across a snake that has no real escape route. They strike out in defence, but to say this is a rare possibility is probably overstating it. To markedly reduce the risk from accidental contact, and peace of mind when bushwalking, wear long pants and or gaiters, plus stout boots.

It is a very good idea to have a first aid kit with you that includes a snake-bite pressure bandage. Of course, it is a good idea to know how to use it by doing a first aid course. (See p18 for information on first aid in case of snake bite.) A good way to avoid being bitten is to not try to kill the snake yourself. We have all heard of the inebriated bloke trying to do the 'superhero' thing in front of his mates or family.

Camping in a designated site at Karijini Eco Retreat

PELUSEY PHOTOGRAPHY

PELUSEY PHOTOGRAPHY

Stick to designated trails when walking in national parks, Chichester National Park

Responsible Camping Etiquette

One area where travellers can personally exhibit their environmental credibility is to follow responsible camping techniques

- **Firewood** should be collected from designated areas only. Do not take wood from standing trees dead or alive. For environmental reasons, many places in WA do not allow collection of wood, so bring your own in those cases.
- If provided always use **fire rings** or if none, where there is an existing fireplace. If there is no existing fireplace, site your fire in a cleared area at least 3m from the nearest flammable material including overhanging trees. In windy conditions, make the cleared margin bigger or do without a fire altogether. Keep the fire small as possible. Make sure the fire is well and truly out before breaking camp.
- Where **toilets** aren't provided, bury toilet waste at least 50m, and preferably more, away from any watercourses, campsites or walking trails. Bury toilet waste properly or if not possible due to terrain, take it out. There's nothing worse than seeing toilet paper draped around the place like Christmas decorations.
- Camp in **designated areas.**
- While camping, **secure bags of rubbish** in strong plastic bags and place in vehicle. Birds and animals such as dingoes are skilled at getting into food scraps. Take rubbish out with you unless there are bins provided for the purpose.
- **Use generators with discretion**. In some places they are banned.
- **Feeding wildlife is prohibited** – not only is the practice harmful to animals, it encourages aggressive behaviour towards campers.
- **Polluting streams**, waterholes, stock-watering points, etc with soap, shampoo or detergents is prohibited.

Blood-sucking Insects

Mosquitoes

Mosquitoes are incredibly annoying when you are enjoying drinks or a barbecue around dusk. But, there's more to these little blighters than itchy bites. Mosquitoes can carry several diseases, the most serious being **Australian encephalitis**. This disease, although rare, can be fatal. Most cases occur after heavy rain in northern regions. More widespread, and far more common, is **Ross River Virus**. Again, it's more prevalent after rain. Although considered not fatal, symptoms can be serious and last for months or in some cases, years. People who contract this disease may suffer varying degrees of lethargy plus flu and arthritic like symptoms.

In the case of mosquito bites, prevention is certainly better than cure. So try these tips:

- Stay inside around sunset or sunrise when mosquitoes are about.
- Make sure all caravan flyscreens are intact.
- When camping, make sure it is a mosquito-proof tent.
- If outside during evening and at night, wear long loose-fitting clothing to cover most skin area. Light colours are supposed to be less attractive to mossies.
- Use repellent on exposed skin.

Sand Flies

Although tiny, sand flies (also known as midges) really pack a punch. The itch caused by the bite can be enough to make you go practically insane. Some victims suffer an allergic reaction and come out with painful sores that can become infected. Coastal regions, especially near mangroves are sand-fly hotspots, especially after recent rain. Grassy areas also seem to be hot spots for sand flies.

Spiders

Spiders are common throughout Western Australia, but bites are usually rare. Several species of spider can inflict a painful bite and in rare cases cause a nasty infectious reaction. The **redback spider** (*Latrodectus hasselti*) is one of Western Australia's more common poisonous spiders. It is often found in urban areas as well as under rocks and logs in drier bushland. The rarely seen **trapdoor spider** certainly can inflict a very painful bite that may be toxic. They are ground dwellers, so avoid bare feet when outdoors, especially at night. A large **huntsman spider** may bite when provoked, but an ice pack is usually all the treatment that is required. Other spiders are generally too small to be of any consequence to humans.

Nevertheless, it's best not to get bitten so follow these hints:

- Don't walk around the campsite in bare feet at night.
- Shake out clothing left hanging out overnight.
- Check boots left outside the tent before wearing them.

Dangerous Marine Life

Jellyfish

There are two dangerous species of jellyfish, also called stingers, found in tropical waters south to Exmouth – **chironex box jellyfish** (*Chironex fleckeri*) and **irukandji jellyfish** (*Carukia barnesi*). Both are transparent, thus virtually invisible. Chances are you won't know they are there until you feel the pain that indicates you've made contact with the stinging cells in their tentacles. Box jellyfish are usually found in waters close to the coast while irukandji jellyfish are often found in deep water although they can be washed inshore.

Trapdoor spider, Shark Bay

Generally speaking, stingers are most prevalent in summer months (early October to late April), although not exclusively so. Avoid swimming where there are warning signs. If stung, the pain is excruciating and sometimes fatal: this is one contact in the natural world that is best avoided.

If a person is stung:

- Remove the victim from the water, but don't attempt to remove any attached tentacles as this may cause more venom to be released.
- Call for medical assistance – Ph 000 or 112 from a mobile. If you are at a patrolled beach, seek help from the lifesaver.
- If necessary, provide CPR until medics arrive.
- Liberally pour vinegar on sting area for at least 30 seconds.
- The symptoms of an irukandji sting may take up to 40 minutes to appear so it is important to monitor victims for at least 45 minutes following a sting.

For more information on jellyfish and first aid for stings visit www.marinestingers.com.au.

Stonefish

Superbly camouflaged, the ugly slow-moving stonefish lays in waiting for a passing fish to eat. They feature a row of sharp barbs down the back that, if trodden on, can inflict a painful wound. They are found in shallow coastal waters north of Geraldton, including **Shark Bay**. Sometimes stonefish become stranded in rock pools at low tide and are very hard to see. When walking on reefs at low tide, wear strong boots as thongs or even sandshoes do not offer sufficient protection.

A stonefish sting causes excruciating pain and a great deal of rapid swelling. Symptoms may develop to muscle weakness, temporary paralysis and shock, which may result in death if not treated. Although bathing the area in hot water may reduce the pain being experienced you should transport the victim to medical assistance promptly. Do not attempt to restrict the movement of the injected toxin by bandaging.

Cone Shells

Beachcombing and walking on reefs at low tide is one of life's pleasures for anybody interested in nature. One of the more obvious lifeforms encountered are colourful and beautifully designed molluscs, such as cone shells. However, if you find one do not be tempted to pick it up. The cone shell packs a deadly little poisonous harpoon that can inflict an extremely painful and potentially dangerous wound on the unwary. Pain, numbness and swelling are common, and prolonged weakness of muscles and disturbance of vision, speech and hearing can also result. If stung, use pressure immobilisation with a firm bandage over the site. Seek medical treatment, as a tetanus injection may be required if the wound is contaminated.

Coral Cuts

Coral formations are sharp and rigid, and accidental contact can result in a cut with a small amount of animal protein and calcareous material in the wound. Without proper treatment, a small harmless-looking cut can quickly develop into an infected wound. Scrub the cut with soap and water, and flush with fresh water. If the wound stings, rinse it with vinegar. Flush the wound with a 50/50 mix of water and peroxide. Rinse daily and apply antibiotic ointment.

Leave station gates as you find them.

PELUSEY PHOTOGRAPHY

Heat Exhaustion & Heatstroke

Northern Western Australia has a hot climate and even winter daytime temperatures sometimes reach the mid-thirties. Every year countless visitors to the north suffer varying degrees of heat-related stress from mild dehydration to potentially fatal heatstroke. The effect of high temperatures is magnified under exertion, such as when hiking or bushwalking. Even on relatively mild days, temperatures in gorges can reach levels that are dangerous for the unprepared. Try timing your hike for the earlier cooler part of the day, and always wear a hat and loose, cool clothing, and use sunscreen.

Most importantly however is to take plenty of water when exploring these places. At least two litres per person should be carried for a day hike, even if it's only for a few hours.

If one of your party succumbs to the heat, keep them still under shade, be reassuring and apply wet towels or clothing to create cooling. If their condition is serious, seek immediate medical assistance.

Station Etiquette

Entering some of the locations mentioned in this book requires going through pastoral stations. Station owners are quite within their rights to close access if visitors do the wrong thing. Always showing common courtesy helps keep tracks and roads in station country open.

- Always **ask permission** from the station manager to be on the property. While some stations allow through traffic, permission may be required. That also goes for camping.
- Driving through stations often involves going through **gates**. It is very important to leave gates as you find them. The rule is: if it is open leave it open; if it is closed, shut the gate after going through.
- **Obey signs** – no shooting means just that.
- **Drive slowly**. This is important for several reasons: it keeps dust down around homesteads and outstation buildings; it reduces stock stress and decreases the chance of collisions with stock.
- Avoid camping near **watersources** such as drinking troughs and windmills. Human presence will spook stock and using soap in troughs is definitely not allowed.
- **Stay on designated tracks** to avoid pasture damage.
- Calculate your **fuel** needs carefully. Unless otherwise stated, pastoral stations are not there to provide their precious fuel to careless travellers.
- **No campfires** without permission. If it is okay, make your campfire small and controlled. During periods of high fire danger, use gas stoves only.

Security

It may seem obvious in the city – lock the car, don't openly display valuables such as cameras while leaving the car unattended etc, but it also applies in the bush. Whenever you leave the vehicle, carry valuables with you in a daypack. Consider taking out travel insurance.

Shopping

Big centres such as Geraldton, Carnarvon, Exmouth, Karratha and Port Hedland are well stocked with almost everything you can possibly need. Away from these centres, services can run somewhere between basic to nonexistent. Roadhouses do carry basic grocery lines, but due to high transport costs are generally expensive places to shop. The answer is to simply stock up while you are in major centres, especially any hard to get pharmaceuticals and prescribed medications. EFTPOS facilities are widely available, but take some cash anyway, just in case.

Where to Stay

For anybody seeking an outback holiday experience, heading north has the lot. With that in mind, there are plenty of accommodation options to match. Most towns have at least one caravan park and hotel or motel. Smaller but more 'touristy' destinations such as Kalbarri, Denham and Exmouth have plenty of accommodation types available because of their popularity. Major centres such as Geraldton, Carnarvon, Karratha and Port Hedland are well served with accommodation options, including multiple caravan parks. During peak holiday seasons, make sure you book well in advance in popular tourist locations – for example Coral Bay.

Free Camps

There are some designated 24-hour rest areas scattered about the inland and northern regions. Facilities at these rest areas are usually limited to a toilet or drinking water. These areas attract campers who are reluctant to pay caravan park fees every night and those who like getting away from the crowds. Ironically, many campers outstay that 24-hour limit resulting in congestion not dissimilar to what can be experienced in a caravan park.

Tents

National parks in the area have some of the State's most popular campsites, including Cape Range, Karijini and Kennedy Range. (See Hema's *Camping Atlas of Western Australia* for more information on campsites.)

First Aid Heat-Induced Conditions

Signs & Symptoms of Heat Exhaustion

- Feeling hot, exhausted and weak.
- Persistent headache.
- Thirst and nausea.
- Giddiness and faintness.
- Fatigue.
- Rapid breathing and shortness of breath.
- Pale, cool, clammy skin.
- Rapid, weak pulse.

First Aid for Heat Exhaustion

- Lie casualty down in a cool place with circulating air.
- Loosen tight clothing and remove unnecessary garments.
- Sponge with cold water.
- Give fluids to drink.
- Seek medical aid if the casualty vomits or does not recover promptly.

Signs & Symptoms of Heatstroke

- High body temperature.
- Flushed and dry skin.
- Irritability and mental confusion may progress to seizure and unconsciousness.
- Dizziness and visual disturbances.
- Headache, nausea and/or vomiting.

First Aid for Heatstroke

- Follow the St John DRABCD plan – danger, response, airway, breathing, CPR, defribillator.
- Apply cold packs or ice to neck, groin and armpits.
- Cover with a wet sheet.
- Call 000 for an ambulance.
- If casualty is fully conscious, give fluids.

WARNING: Heatstroke is a potentially lethal condition.

[Information supplied by St John Ambulance – visit www.stjohn.org.au.]

The main thing to look for in a tent is plenty of ventilation. You also need to make sure the insect mesh is fine enough to keep out the smallest mosquito. Strong winds are not uncommon throughout this region, so plenty of strong pegs and ropes are essential too. Good sand pegs are a must in coastal locations. **One tip**: Try to avoid camping under a tree. At the least, dropping seed pods and bird droppings are annoying and at worst, a falling branch could be catastrophic.

Caravans & Trailers

Go anywhere north of Perth in the cooler season and you could be excused for thinking that caravans, motorhomes and camper trailers are the only way people travel. While towing, most caravanners only experience off-road conditions when going through road works. This is probably a good thing, as even so-called off-road caravans are not necessarily suitable for all outback conditions. The motto here is: if in doubt take a tent and leave the van behind. Off-road camper trailers, on the other hand, are generally more suitable for the rough stuff, but not in all cases. Tracks such as the Canning Stock Route claim expensive camper trailers every year. If you are 'first timer' when it comes to caravanning, we strongly suggest doing a caravan confidence course. The one we did was through Global Gypsies, www.globalgypsies.com.au.

Another great idea is to join one of the many caravanning clubs throughout Australia. Their group trips are very educational and lots of fun too.

Hotels and Motels

The towns in this area have a range of hotels and motels, ranging from the swanky resorts to basic donger-type rooms. The range of accommodation depends mainly on the number of tourists and what mining industry is nearby.

Station Stays

Some traditional cattle and sheep stations are diversifying into tourism by offering accommodation to travellers. A few of these stations provide additional services such as 4WD tours into scenic areas on their properties. By staying on these stations, tourists can get a rewarding insight into station life. Local visitor centres have details about station stays in their areas.

Getting There

The obvious starting point is Perth, where you simply get in the car and head north either on the more inland Great Northern Highway or the coastal Brand and North West Coastal highways. Better still – go up one and down the other and get the best of both worlds. If you are exploring the Goldfields, then head east of Perth along the Great Eastern Highway. For visitors entering WA by crossing the Nullarbor, the obvious target is the Goldfields.

Our suggestion is, in order to see the best bits, leave the highways occasionally and take the back roads. Be adventurous, but in a responsible way taking into consideration the capability of your vehicle and experience of the driver.

Serious corrugations

PELUSEY PHOTOGRAPHY

PELUSEY PHOTOGRAPHY

24-hour free camping at Galena Bridge

Getting Around

Driving

There is only one real way of exploring this vast region, and that is to drive. Most major roads that travellers are likely to drive on are sealed and suitable for caravans. However those who stick just to the main roads are missing a lot. Numerous unsealed roads and tracks criss-cross the area, particularly in station country, and many lead to scenic highlights.

However, unsealed roads vary a lot, with some as smooth as any bitumen you are likely to come across. Although the temptation may be to put the foot down this is fraught with danger, especially for inexperienced outback travellers. Dirt roads are unpredictable and potholes, uneven surfaces and clouds of dust can appear from nowhere. Not to mention the possibility of stock on the road or wild animals crossing.

After rain, particularly in the summer season, many of the unsealed roads are closed or only suitable for 4WD vehicles. Never drive on 'closed' roads. (See *Road Reports* below for contact details.)

Corrugations

Even for the seasoned outback traveller, driving on corrugated roads is a pain in the proverbial. Most unsealed roads in the Goldfields, Gascoyne and Pilbara have some degree of corrugation, the least being a gentle shudder, the worse a bone and car shattering test of endurance. The big question is. What speed should you travel at to keep this problem to a minimum? The answer depends of the severity of corrugations. Generally, you will endure agonising bumps at really slow speeds of say 20kph. On the other hand, at high speeds the ride might be more comfortable but you have less control over the vehicle as it skids across the top. At high speeds, wear and tear on the tyres and suspension is magnified and the chances of a puncture are increased. A speed of around 70kph is probably a good compromise, but be aware that there's a fine line between comfort and putting yourself and the vehicle at risk.

Driver Training & Tag-along Tours

The big tip for four-wheel driving is to know your vehicle. The best way to learn about driving your vehicle off-road is the under controlled conditions of a recommended and accredited 4WD course. Four-wheel driver trainers usually take course participants to a range of terrains, such as sand, mud and rocky ascents. You learn about what safety and recovery gear is needed and most importantly, how to use it. In these situations if you get into trouble, an experienced and well-equipped expert is there to assist. The other way to learn your limits is to go on trips with experienced friends or 4WD clubs. (For a list of 4WD clubs, see the WA 4WD Association website: www.wa4wda.com.au.)

- *Eureka 4WD Training*, Armadale (Ph 08 9497 5655, www.eureka4wd.com.au)
- *Global Gypsies*, Scarborough (Ph 08 9341 6727, www.globalgypsies.com.au)

- *Pilbara Iron Country Tours*, Newman (Ph 08 9175 1715, www.pilbaraironcountrytours.com)
- *Tumblagouda 4WD Tag-along Tours*, Murchison House Station, Kalbarri (Ph 08 9937 1998, www.murchisonhousestation.com.au)
- *WA 4WD Training*, Perth (Ph 08 9306 8278, www.wa4wdtraining.com.au)

Road Reports

Road conditions change rapidly so visitors should always obtain up-to-date information and seek local advice before travelling. See www.mainroads.wa.gov.au for the current status of roads or Ph 1800 131314. Local visitor centres and councils can also be a good source of information. For roads within national parks contact the relevant district DEC office or check the DEC website (see p21).

Communications

When travelling in the outback, having the ability to keep in contact with others is not only reassuring, it could save your life. The key thing to realise is that common old mobile phones, even those on Next G networks, are next to useless away from populated areas.

UHF Radio

UHF radios are excellent for communication between vehicles in convoy situations. In good conditions you can get a range of up to five or more kilometres, but in hilly or dusty situations it will be a lot less. You can increase the range up to about 20km by installing an outside aerial.

Most caravanners use channel 18 and motorhomers use channel 20. Listen into channel 40 for truckie conversations, which are sometimes useful for knowing about upcoming road conditions. Those with sensitive natures should be warned that some truckie conversations may be on the 'blue' side. Keep in mind that idle chitchat can clog up channels that may otherwise be used by local pastoralists and other workers. So if you start getting outside activity, try finding a less busy channel.

HF Radio

If you plan a lot of remote outback travelling, then think about a HF radio. Although the equipment is much more expensive than UHF, it has a much greater range.

The Australian National 4WD Network, with a call sign of VKS737, is a non-profit organisation that covers most of mainland Australia. It took over the radphone service once provided by the Royal Flying Doctor Service. Many a life has been saved by a volunteer picking up an emergency call through this network. (To find out more, Ph 08 8287 6222 or visit www.vks737.on.net.)

Satellite Telephone

With more reliable satellite phones available these days, this orm of communication is becoming popular with remote area travellers. However, due to scarily high call charges, it's best to use satellite phones with discretion. Satellite phones, and EPIRBS for that matter, can be hired if you don't want to outlay big bucks for something you may not use that often. Check the Yellow Pages or internet for companies that hire this equipment. ■

WARNING
NO- FOOD, WATER OR FUEL AVAILABLE BEYOND THIS POINT
BEFORE YOU PROCEED -
1. HAVE YOU CHECKED ROAD CONDITIONS ?
2. IS YOUR VEHICLE SUITABLY EQUIPPED ?
3. DO YOU HAVE SUFFICIENT FOOD, WATER AND FUEL ?
4. DO YOU KNOW THE AREA YOU ARE ENTERING ?
5. HAVE YOU NOTIFIED NULLAGINE POLICE OF YOUR INTENDED MOVEMENTS ?
IF IN DOUBT, DO NOT PROCEED BEYOND THIS POINT!
INSTEAD, SEEK ADVICE FROM THE POLICE AT NULLAGINE
DO NOT- BE NUMBERED AMONGST THOSE WHO HAVE PERISHED IN THIS AREA DUE TO THE LACK OF PREPAREDNESS

PELUSEY PHOTOGRAPHY

When on outback roads like this, taking an EPIRB, satellite phone or HF radio is essential.

Driving Safety

For travellers used to driving in more populous places, such as coastal locations in eastern Australia or even Europe, touring around the wide open spaces of WA can be rather daunting. However, if you follow a few basic rules, your trip should be an enjoyable one.

- Make sure the vehicle and whatever you are towing is in **sound mechanical condition**. A comprehensive service is a good idea before departing. Workshop facilities are usually available in towns, but lengthy delays are possible due to the availability of spare parts. For this reason it's a good idea to take some basic spares such as fan belts, fuses and radiator hoses.
- If going off road, take **two spare wheels.**
- **Do not overload the roof rack** beyond its specifications. Besides risking roof rack breakage, overloaded roof racks can alter the vehicle's centre of gravity making cornering more hazardous.
- Crossing **flooded creeks and rivers** are an occasional hazard when travelling in the outback. Thunderstorms and cyclone activity can cause potentially life threatening flash flooding. If approaching a flooded waterway, observe depth indicators. Anything around the bottom of the door level is getting into dangerous territory for conventional vehicles, especially if the water is flowing fast. High-clearance 4WDs are better suited, but driver judgement and experience is critical. If you are unsure, don't do it. Creeks often rise and fall rapidly so it's better to play it safe and wait a while if necessary.
- **Speeding**, even if it is only up to the legal speed limits is a major cause of crashes on unsealed roads. Driving to the conditions is the key here.
- **Driver fatigue** is a major cause of death on country roads. It is a good idea to change drivers every couple of hours or at least regularly take breaks and stretch the legs. Yawning is a telltale sign that you are entering the danger zone.
- **Dust clouds** kicked up by passing traffic are another potential killer on unsealed roads. If you are travelling in a convoy, allow plenty of space between vehicles so the person behind is not eating dust. Dust clouds can create zero visibility, so pull over until an oncoming vehicle has passed by and the dust has settled enough to safely continue.
- Large **animals** such as kangaroos and livestock are common hazards on outback roads: both sealed and unsealed. If possible, reduce the chances of a disastrous encounter by not driving near sunset, sunrise and at night when animals such as kangaroos are most active. If night driving is unavoidable, reduce speed accordingly.

A victim of poor judgement when crossing a flooded creek.

PELUSEY PHOTOGRAPHY

chapter three

What to Do

Aboriginal Culture

No touring in Western Australia is complete without gaining some insight into indigenous culture. For tour operator details, make enquiries at the local visitor centre. Some Aboriginal tours are mentioned in the appropriate chapters in this book.

- **Geraldton** – *Marra Aboriginal Art Gallery* at the Bill Sewell Complex, cnr Chapman Rd & Bayley St; Ph 08 9965 3440
- **Geraldton** – *Yamatji Cultural Trails*, offer tours around the Geraldton area with the chance to sleep under the stars; Ph 08 9956 1126
- **Laverton** – *Laverton Outback Gallery*, 4 Euro St; sells authentic Aboriginal art on behalf of the people of the Laverton and Western Desert area; Ph 08 9031 1395
- **Monkey Mia** – *Wula Guda Nyinda Aboriginal Cultural Walks*, for local indigenous dreaming and bushtucker trips; Ph 08 9948 1320, 0429 708 847
- **Paynes Find** – *Ninghan Station*, farm stay accommodation and activities; Ph 08 9963 6517
- **Port Hedland** – *Port Hedland Courthouse Gallery*, 16 Edgar St; Ph 08 9173 1064, www.courthousegallery.com.au

Driving up Mount Nameless, Tom Price PELUSEY PHOTOGRAPHY

Kayaking is popular at Monkey Mia

STEVEN DAVID MILLER, NATURAL WANDERS

PELUSEY PHOTOGRAPHY

Walking above Yardie Creek, Cape Range

- **Roebourne** – *Roebourne Art Group*, 27 Roe St; sales and exhibition of contemporary Australian Aboriginal art from the West Pilbara; Ph 08 9182 1396, www.roebourneart.com.au
- **Tom Price** – *Pebble Mouse Studio Art Gallery*, Shop 9, cnr Stadium & Central Rds; sells Aboriginal arts and crafts; Ph 08 9189 3051
- **Yanchep National Park** – the *Aboriginal Experience* showcases Nyoongar culture with traditional dance, music, and bushtucker and cultural tours; the program is available weekends and public holidays (subject to availability and weather conditions), book at the McNess House Visitor Centre; Ph 08 9561 1004, www.dec.wa.gov.au
- **Wiluna** – the *Tjukurba Art Gallery*; located behind the Wiluna Shire office; has many pieces of local art available for sale (Open 8am-4.30pm Mon-Fri)

Visit the Western Australian Indigenous Tourism Operators' website for more information on the experiences available – www.waitoc.com.

Land-Based Activities

Bushwalking

Unless you are physically restricted, bushwalking is one of the best ways to experience the places described in this book. All walks undertaken should be on designated trails to reduce environmental impacts, as well as for the safety of walkers. Off-trail hiking into wilderness areas should be only undertaken by walkers who are very experienced, physically fit and well equipped. Permission from relevant authorities may also be required.

For bushwalking enthusiasts, Karijini National Park is one of the best locations in Australia. There are trails for all levels of fitness and experience, and anybody who puts in at least a little effort will be richly rewarded. One of our favourites is the Dales Gorge Rim Walk because it offers a tremendous variety of unique ecosystems, wonderful scenery, surprising sights and good swimming. This trail made the **WA Top Trails List** (see boxed text p32).

Other national parks with good walking trails are Cape Range, Chichester-Millstream, Mount Augustus, Kennedy Ranges and Kalbarri, to name just a few.

Trail Grades

Walks trails are graded according to the level of difficulty. Some trails are simply short strolls from the car park to a local scenic or historic landmark, and these are not necessarily graded unless there's some distance or difficulty involved. Please follow the trail grade signage which is usually located at trail heads.

Class 1

These are generally short trails of even surfaces and level, or nearly level, gradients. They are suitable for all ages and minimal fitness levels.

Class 2

These trails are generally well marked with even surfaces and gentle gradients. Some steps may be uncounted. No experience is required, but walkers should use commonsense.

Class 3

Users need to be of moderate fitness and have some bushwalking experience. Trails, although normally well marked, may be uneven and potentially unstable in nature and have possible steep sections. Adverse weather could also affect personal safety.

Class 4

Generally, these trails, although usually marked, can be indistinct from surrounding terrain in places. Surfaces are often very uneven and unstable, and sections can be steep and fairly demanding. Walkers need to be fit, well prepared and experienced in the more demanding forms of bushwalking. Weather conditions will affect personal safety.

Class 5

These trails are indistinct and often follow undisturbed natural terrain. They are inherently dangerous for the inexperienced as they can be very steep, unstable under foot and physically demanding. A high level of physical fitness is mandatory. Users must be well prepared and experienced, or at least with an experienced guide. Adverse weather conditions can make conditions dangerous to life and limb.

Class 6

Do NOT use these trails unless you are qualified and prepared, with the necessary safety equipment to abseil and rock climb, or you are instructed by a DEC licensed operator. (See *Gorge Safety* p75.)

Organised Walking Tours

Darwin-based **Willis' Walkabouts** offers extended guided bushwalks in Karijini National Park a couple of times a year from Tom Price. Occasionally they also run walks in the Chichester Range. (Ph 08 8985 2134, www.bushwalkingholidays.com.au)

If you want to experience the highlights of the Pilbara region, while staying in motel-style accommodation, then **InterNational Park Tours** have a trip that may suit you. It starts and ends at Perth and includes Karijini, Cape Range, Kalbarri and Nambung national parks, as well as Monkey Mia. (Ph 07 5533 3583, www.parktours.com.au)

Another extended walking tour is offered by **Environmental Encounters**. Their 15-day walking and camping tour starts at Broome and travels through the Kennedy Ranges, Mt Augustus and Karijini national parks to finish at Perth. (Ph 08 9364 3781, www.environmentalencounters.com.au)

To explore Kalbarri National Park's gorges, ask about the treks through **Kalbarri Adventure Tours**. (Ph 08 9937 1667, www.kalbarritours.com.au)

Other Land-Based Tours

- **Coastal Adventure Tours**, Coral Bay – self-drive ATV adventures (Ph 08 9948 5190, www.coralbaytours.com.au)
- **Kalbarri Abseil** – full- and half-day abseiling tours suitable for beginners to experienced (Ph 08 9937 1618, www.abseilaustralia.com.au)
- **Kalbarri Safari Tours** – 1, 2 and 3 hour quad-bike safaris (Ph 08 9937 1011, 0407 371 011 www.kalbarrisafaritours.com.au)
- **Kalbarri Sandboarding** – sandboarding from 'nursery' dunes to the more extreme (Ph 08 9937 2377, www.sandboardingaustralia.com.au)
- **Luxury 4x4 Adventures** – take you in their 4WD to some of the harder to access places, including Yardie Creek via the real back roads (Ph 0427 180 568)
- **Ningaloo Safari Tours** – tour from Exmouth to Cape Range National Park and Ningaloo Reef (Ph 08 9949 1550, www.ningaloosafari.com)
- **Outback Coast Safaris** – run a range of tours from half-day foodie tours to three-day Mount Augustus trips (Ph 08 9941 3448, www.outbackcoastsafaris.com.au)
- **Shark Bay Camel Safari** – beach and bush rides available (Ph 08 9948 3136)
- **Wagoe Beach Quad Bike Tours** – see sand dunes and wildlife along Wagoe Beach, 20km south of Kalbarri (Ph 08 9936 6067, www.wagoe.com.au)

WA's Top Trails

- **Camel Trail** – moderate 6hr return walk in Millstream-Chichester National Park featuring the view from the top of Mt Herbert (see p78)
- **Gorge Rim Walk**, Dales Gorge – moderate 1.5hr walk along the rim of Dales Gorge in Karijini National Park (see p75)
- **Loop Walk** – a moderately challenging 3-4hr walk in Kalbarri National Park which includes Nature's Window (see p56)
- **One Mile Jetty** – easy 1hr walk from Carnarvon town centre along the Gascoyne River (see p64)
- **Summit Trail**, Mt Augustus – difficult 6-7hr walk to the top of the world's biggest rock (see p94)
- **Yardie Creek** – moderate 1hr walk in Cape Range National Park to the top of Yardie Creek Gorge for views over the creek and out to the Ningaloo Reef (see p71)

See www.toptrails.com.au for more information.

View from the north face of Mount Augustus

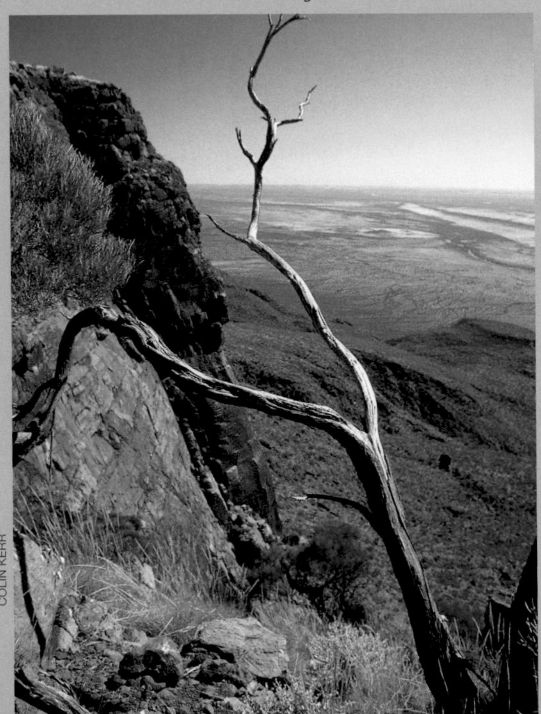

COLIN KERR

Watching Wildlife

One of the main attractions of touring from Perth to the Pilbara is the opportunity to see wildlife in its natural environment. To improve your chances of spotting elusive wildlife, try being patient for starters.

Go bushwalking and take binoculars. Getting out of the car and quietly walking sharpens the observation skills as well as putting you right amongst it.

When walking, occasionally sit down for a while and quietly observe. It's amazing how creatures reveal themselves when it seems at first that nothing is around.

In dry regions, wildlife, especially birds, gather around waterholes for a drink. Near sunrise and sunset are the best times, but please keep your distance and observe with binoculars to decrease disturbance.

Stash a few animal guidebooks in the car so you can identify what you are looking at.

For a different perspective, check out the nightlife by walking around camp with a torch.

To increase your chances of spotting wildlife, go to known hot spots. A sure bet for good wildlife observing is to visit national parks where natural habitats and their residents are protected.

10 Wildlife Hot Spots

- The marine environment of the **Abrolhos Islands** is a veritable nature lover's paradise. As well as fish, marine mammals, turtles, whales and sea snakes, there are huge colonies of nesting seabirds on the flat rocky islands.
- Turtles nest at rookeries along the **Dampier Archipelago** from September to April and humpback whales are seen between July and September. Dugong, bottlenose dolphins and 26 species of seabirds can also be seen.
- **Eighty Mile Beach**, between Port Hedland and Broome, features tidal flats that attract migratory waders and birds of prey such as sea eagles.
- In the **Goldfields and Gascoyne-Murchison regions**, keep your eye on the skies to spot wedge-tail eagles or flocks of tiny zebra finches.
- June to December is the best time to spot whales off the coast from **Kalbarri**. There are numerous vantage points around the area and tours operate too. The town is also home to the Seahorse Sanctuary, Oceanarium and Rainbow Jungle Parrot Breeding Centre.
- The varied habitats in **Karijini National Park** attract numerous bird and reptile species.
- The permanent water and tall paperbarks in **Millstream National Park** make it an ideal place to see freshwater fish, birds and insects.
- With whale sharks, whales, manta rays, prolific fish life, seabirds and marine reptiles in abundance, **Ningaloo Reef** should be a 'must-see' for nature lovers. From December to February you can also see turtles when they come ashore at night to lay their eggs. The adjoining Cape Range National Park has black-footed wallabies and other marsupials.
- **Shark Bay** has it all: birds, whales, dugongs, dolphins, turtles and reptiles of all kinds. Although the Monkey Mia dolphins may be the most famous, in this area it is nearly impossible to avoid contact with wildlife. **Project Eden** (see p15) has certainly increased your chances of seeing different species of marsupials. The Ocean Park is also a great place to learn about the marine environment.
- Flocks of crested pigeons, corellas and galahs, and the odd kangaroo, get amongst patrons staying at the **Tom Price** caravan park.

Walk Safety

The number one rule for bushwalking is to stay within your capabilities. The grading system (see p32) is an easy way to work out which walk or walks are suitable for your levels of fitness and experience. Take into account that even on short walks, heat can be a serious problem. Daytime winter temperatures can be hot, especially in the Pilbara and Gascoyne regions.

- **Don't overdo it:** choose walks within your personal fitness levels and capabilities.
- **Dress appropriately** for the conditions. That means loose comfortable clothing and good walking boots with ankle support. Also, start out with a liberal application of sunscreen and a shady hat. One tip: long cotton pants minimise the discomfort inflicted by that prickly spinifex.
- Avoid walking during the middle of the day, when the **heat** is at its most intense. (See p27 for information on Heat Exhaustion and Heatstroke.)
- Never set out on even a short walk without sufficient **water**.
- It's a good idea to take a small but comprehensive **first aid kit**, just in case.
- If it is possible, **talk to rangers** before setting out on a walk if you are unsure about what to expect.
- Although walking alone can be a pleasurable experience, the old saying, **safety in numbers** is worth considering. Two or three companions is a nice compromise.
- At some trail heads, **walker registration books** should be filled in with the appropriate information such as time of starting and importantly time of completion. Failure to do the last bit may prompt a fruitless search.
- **Stick to the trail** to lessen the risk of becoming lost. If you do suddenly become disoriented, don't panic and stay where you are. Most trails in popular national parks are fairly well used, so help shouldn't be too far away. Straying away from the trail in an attempt to take a shortcut is highly risky and foolhardy, not to mention environmentally unsound.

Euros being photographed, Tom Price

PELUSEY PHOTOGRAPHY

Bridled terns, Abrolhos Islands

PELUSEY PHOTOGRAPHY

Organised Wildlife Tours

- **Coral Bay Adventures** – swim with whale sharks or manta rays, or go whale watching (Ph 08 9942 5955, www.coralbayadventures.com.au)
- **Jurien Charters**, Jurien Bay – see Australian sea lions in Jurien Bay Marine Park (Ph 08 9652 1109, www.juriencharters.com)
- **King's Ningaloo Reef Tours**, Exmouth – snorkel with whale sharks from late Mar to late July (Ph 08 9949 1764, www.kingsningalooreeftours.com.au)
- **Monkey Mia Yacht Charters**, Denham – see dolphins, dugongs and other marine creatures in Shark Bay (Ph 1800 030 427, www.monkey-mia.net)
- **Ningaloo Blue Dive**, Exmouth – snorkel with whale sharks from Apr to July (Ph 1800 811 388, www.ningalooblue.com.au)
- **Ningaloo Experience**, Coral Bay – snorkel with manta rays and whale sharks from late Mar-Jun (Ph 08 9942 5877, www.ningalooexperience.com)
- **Ningaloo Reef Dreaming**, Exmouth –eco cruises to see whale sharks, manta rays, turtles or humpback whales (Ph 1800 994 210, www.ningaloodreaming.com)
- **Ningaloo Whaleshark-n-Dive**, Exmouth – snorkel with whale sharks, including an option to overnight onboard (Ph 08 9949 1116, www.ningaloowhalesharkndive.com.au)
- **Ocean Eco Adventures**, Coral Bay & Exmouth – see whale sharks and manta rays on the Ningaloo Reef, or marinelife in Coral Bay; Apr-Oct (Ph 0427 425 925, 0409 374 550, www.oceanecoadventures.com.au)
- **Reefwalker Adventure Tours**, Kalbarri – whale watching and dolphin encounters (Ph 08 99371356, www.reefwalker.com.au)
- **Sea Lion Charters**, Green Head – experience marinelife up close (Ph 08 9953 1012)
- **The Specialists Ocean Safaris**, Kalbarri – whale watching (Ph 0417 912 901, www.thespecialists.com.au)
- **Three Islands Marine Charters**, Exmouth – snorkel with whale sharks Apr to early July (Ph 1800 138 501, www.whalesharkdive.com)
- **Turquoise Coast Enviro Tours**, Cervantes – in-depth tours of the Pinnacles (Ph 08 9652 7047, www.thepinnacles.com.au)

Also see *Fishing Charters* (pp36-37) and *Cruises* (pp37-38) as most tourist companies with boats offer wildlife viewing too.

Water-Based Activities

Fishing

Fishing is the main game for most visitors to coastal parts of this region, and there are several good reasons fishing on the west coast is so popular. Unlike the more populated eastern seaboard, there is still plenty of fish about, although dhufish and baldchin groper are under fishing pressures. The other main reason is that Western Australia's coastline covers a huge and varied range of marine habitats ensuring a great diversity of fish species. The upshot of all this is some of the best fishing in Australia, and arguably the world.

Having said that, to be successful, there's more to it than just putting bait on a hook and chucking it in. You need to know where they are biting and how to catch them. There are plenty of books and magazines targetting fishing in WA, so our suggestion is to read up before starting out (see p22 for suggestions). For an outline of what to expect to catch we have divided fishing into main tourist regions where fishing is possible.

Coral Coast

The main quarry for beach anglers in the area just north of Perth to Geraldton, is **tailor**. In summer, anglers target tailor by casting a mulie or pilchard into a gutter or deep hole on any number of suitable beaches. Most fish caught in summer are under 30cm and are called choppers. They bite best in the late afternoon and after dark when there is a good sea breeze blowing. In winter, when conditions allow, bigger tailor are about but they are fewer in numbers. Yanchep reef area, Guilderton and beaches near Jurien are good spots. North of Geraldton, Shark Bay and Carnarvon, tailor up to a whopping 8kg are sometimes landed and fish around 4kg are quite common. Tailor are voracious predators and do hit and run raids on hapless bait fish. When on the bite, the action is often short, but exciting as they fight hard.

Offshore, the main trophy fish is without doubt the **Western Australian dhufish**. A species prized for its firm white and flavoursome flesh, the dhufish grows to over 20kg. They inhabit offshore reefs in deeper water, so boat fishing is the go, although some are taken from shore locations off rocks. Heavy handlines or boat rods, with sinkers and various fish baits are used. Octopus is also popular as bait. These fish are found in patches and don't move around much, therefore are very prone to overfishing. Strict rules apply on bag limits and size limits.

Other offshore species targeted are **pink snapper**, **Rankin cod**, **baldchin groper**, **coral trout**, **trevally** and numerous **emperor** species, especially north of Kalbarri. The Exmouth and Ningaloo

A goanna in Hancock Gorge, Karijini National Park

PELUSEY PHOTOGRAPHY

A classic pink snapper, Shark Bay

PELUSEY PHOTOGRAPHY

PELUSEY PHOTOGRAPHY

The threadfin salmon are big at Eighty Mile Beach

Reef region offers both anglers and shore fishers superb fishing, but it's the boaties that really clean up. Fish most prized are **coral trout**, **red emperor**, various **cods**, **Spanish mackerel** and **spangled emperor**. A stout boat rod, 15kg line, medium weight sinker, and octopus or fish bait on a single hook is the favoured tackle. For gamefish chasers you head out to the continental shelf in big boats and wrestle with **marlin**, **sailfish**, **dolphin fish** and **tuna**.

Beaches and headlands offer opportunities to catch **trevally** species, **emperors**, **darts** and **queenfish** on lighter gear. Bread and butter fish such as **herring** (Tommy Ruff), **silver trevally** (skipjack), **whiting** and **garfish** are more prevalent further south. These fish are easily caught from jetties at Jurien, Cervantes and Geraldton.

You can also set a few pots and get amongst that mainstay of WA's professional fishing industry, the **Western rock lobster**. Just be warned that strict regulations apply to recreational lobster fishers. It's vitally important that would-be recreational lobster fishers contact the Department of Fisheries (www.fish.wa.gov.au). If you are caught doing the wrong thing, huge fines apply and there is the possibility the boat will be confiscated.

Pilbara Coast

The hard-hitting and great-eating narrow-barred **Spanish mackerel** is the main quarry along the Pilbara coastline. Fish of over 40kg are not uncommon, making the Pilbara one of the best spots for Spanish mackerel fishing anywhere. Voracious schools of marauding Spanish mackerel rip into schools of bait fish and the remnants attract hungry seabirds, which in turn attract observant boat fishers. The favourite method of catching these beauties is trolling fish bait or a shiny lure. Drags are set loose on reels as these fish peel off many metres of line on one or two blistering runs before tiring. Boat fishing is the preferred method of catching these species, although cliffs and rock platforms provide exciting shoreline angling for the adventurous. Other species such as spotted, shark and narrow-barred mackerels are often in the mix, along with line-busting giant trevally.

The numerous mangrove-lined creeks and muddy tidal flats that dominate much of the Pilbara coast provide shelter for juveniles. Mangroves are also haunts for good-eating **mangrove jacks**, **trevally**, **catfish** and even the odd **barramundi**. **Threadfin salmon** also come in the mix and are hard fighting and tasty in the pan as well. This most unusual predator is supremely adapted to catching its prey in even the most silted water. It has big eyes and whiskery filaments that help the fish sense its way about in near-zero visibility.

At the northern extremity of the Pilbara coast is Eighty Mile Beach with its shallow mudflats subject to massive tidal movements. On the incoming tide to about an hour after high tide, metre long

Rock Lobster Industry

The rock lobster industry on Western Australia's west coast is Australia's most lucrative single fishery industry. Depending on availability, lobsters are worth anything between $200 million to $600 million dollars a year. Most of the catch heads overseas to Japan, Asia in general and the USA. Commercial rock lobster fishing is strictly controlled to prevent overfishing. There are pot limits placed on commercial vessels and strictly enforced seasons. Females with eggs are released along with undersized lobsters. If these rules are broken, huge fines apply as well as the potential loss of commercial licences worth millions of dollars.

The history of lobster fishing is fairly recent as industries go. Nothing much happened until a factory in Geraldton opened up in 1940 to process lobster tails. By far most of the lobsters came from the Abrolhos Islands. In 1950, a co-op was formed in Geraldton to process lobster tails and export them. Prices were high and the industry expanded. The Abrolhos fishery expanded, but not to same extent as in areas where bigger boats fished. As the industry grew other settlements sprang up along the coast with their own processing plants. Places such as Green Head, Cervantes, Jurien and Leeman started from such humble beginnings. In the 1960s, overfishing was becoming a reality so strict rules were put in place to regulate the industry.

PELUSEY PHOTOGRAPHY

Rock lobsters bound for Japan

Kayak fishing in Shark Bay

PELUSEY PHOTOGRAPHY

PELUSEY PHOTOGRAPHY

Measuring a snapper caught in Shark Bay

threadfin salmon nose in and lines of anglers target them along the beach. The preferred bait is the mulie or pilchard weighted with a running sinker. These fish are most common early in the dry season. The Eighty Mile Beach Caravan Park fills up with anglers who stay long periods targetting threadfin and **mulloway**.

Rules and Regulations

A licence is required for all freshwater angling, as well as for abalone, rock lobster, marron and net fishing. The Department of Fisheries (Ph 08 9482 7333, www.fish.wa.gov.au) publishes leaflets on minimum legal size limits, bag sizes and seasonal closures. These are widely available from DEC information centres, tourist offices, post offices and tackle shops. Licence applications can be obtained at post offices and the Department of Fisheries offices in Perth, Fremantle, Geraldton, Mandurah, Albany, Broome, Esperance or Bunbury. A licence will take about 30 days to process, so allow plenty of time.

Fishing Charters

- **Aqua Jack Charters**, Dongara – visit Dongara, Abrolhos Islands, Shark Bay, Carnarvon, Exmouth & Coral Bay (Ph 08 9927 220, www.aquajack.com.au)
- **BlueSun2** – day or overnight trips to Carnarvon, Abrolhos Islands and Montebello Islands (Ph 0405 305 305, www.bluesun2.com.au)
- **Coral Bay Ocean Game Fishing Charters** – full day charters (Ph 08 9942 5874, www.mahimahicoralbay.com.au)
- **Jetwave Boat Charters**, Denham – fishing charters (Ph 08 9948 1211, www.jetwaveboatcharters.com.au)
- **Jurien Charters**, Jurien Bay – full- and half-day fishing charters (Ph 08 9652 1109, www.juriencharters.com)
- **Kalbarri Explorer** – deep sea fishing (Ph 08 9937 2027, www.kalbarriexplorer.com.au)
- **Mac Attack Fishing Charters**, Denham – half or full day trips (Ph 08 9948 3776, www.sportfish.com.au)
- **Montebellos Sport Fishing Charters**, Exmouth – 6-day live aboard charter from Oct to Mar (Ph 08 9942 5874, www.mahimahicoralbay.com.au)
- **Ningaloo Blue Dive**, Exmouth – deep sea fishing charters from the western side of Cape Range (Ph 1800 811 388, www.ningalooblue.com.au)
- **Reefwalker Adventure Tours**, Kalbarri – reef fishing for experienced, average and beginners (Ph 08 99371356, www.reefwalker.com.au)
- **Sea Force Coral Bay** – fishing tours and deep sea and sport fishing charters (Ph 08 9942 5817, www.seaforcecharters.net.au)

King Waves Kill

A sign located near the Blowholes at Quobba on the rocky coastline north of Carnarvon says it all: "King Waves Kill". What it is referring to is the odd wave that is several times bigger than the average swell of the day. These waves are totally unpredictable and can catch the unwary out, sometimes with fatal consequences. Several lives have been lost near this particular sign. Most victims are overly confident rock-fishing anglers and tourists trying to get a closer look.

To avoid being a statistic:

- Stay away from wet areas that may have indicated previous wave action.
- Stay away from ledges.
- Keep an eye on the ocean at all times – never turn your back on the sea.
- Take heed of any warning signs.

Fishing off rocks near Steep Point requires great care

PELUSEY PHOTOGRAPHY

Fishing is the main reason people go boating out of Shark Bay.

PELUSEY PHOTOGRAPHY

After a day of boating, Geraldton marina

PELUSEY PHOTOGRAPHY

- **The Specialists Ocean Safaris**, Kalbarri – deep sea and game fishing (Ph 0417 912 901, www.thespecialists.com.au)
- **West Coast Marine Fishing Charters**, Onslow – fishing charters to the Mackerel Islands from Apr to Oct (Ph 0417 176 385, 0428 124 751, www.westcoastmarine.com.au)

Boating

Fishing is a popular pastime, but boating opens up all sorts of other leisure activities as well. Boats allow scuba divers to get to the best spots on offshore locations such as Montebello Islands, Abrolhos Islands, Dampier Archipelago and Ningaloo Reef. With consistent winds blowing most of the year, sailing is an obvious pursuit along the length of coast from Perth to the Pilbara.

All this activity on the water increases environmental and safety pressures in some of the more popular locations such as Shark Bay, Ningaloo and the Abrolhos Islands. Marine animals such as turtles and dugongs are sometimes wounded or killed by inattentive boat users. Boats enable anglers to get to offshore reefs where vulnerable species come under unsustainable fishing pressures. Changeable weather conditions, strong tidal movements, freak waves, dangerous reefs and inexperienced boat handlers cause real safety concerns. Every year, boating incidents cause a number of deaths along the coast.

Rules & Regs

In Western Australia, every skipper of a registrable, recreational vessel, powered by a motor greater than 4.5kwp (6 hp) is required to hold a Recreational Skipper's Ticket (RST). A current interstate or foreign skipper's ticket, which is recognised by the WA Department of Transport and listed in their skills recognition section, is acceptable as a RTS until three months have elapsed since you entered the State. More information is available on the Department's website www.transport.wa.gov.au/imarine.

Boat Hire

- **Coral Bay Adventures** – half and full day hire (Ph 08 9942 5955, www.coralbayadventures.com.au)
- **Discovery Sailing Adventures**, Dampier – hire a boat (Ph 0408 801 040, www.discoverysailingadventures.com.au)
- **Exmouth Boat & Kayak Hire** – aluminium boats and kayaks for hire (Ph 0438 230 269, www.exmouthboathire.com)
- **Jurien Charters**, Jurien Bay – boat hire (Ph 08 9652 1109, www.juriencharters.com)
- **Kalbarri Boat Hire and Canoe Safaris** – hire powerboats for river use, canoes, kayaks, surfcats, paddle boats or a barracuda bike (Ph 08 9937 1245, www.kalbarriboathire.com)
- **Moore River Beach Houses**, Guilderton – kayak hire (Ph 0427 131 149, www.mooreriver.com.au)
- **Murchison Boat Hire**, Kalbarri – one- to seven-day boat hire (Ph 08 9937 2043, www.murchisonboathire.com.au)
- **Ningaloo Kayak Adventures**, Coral Bay – hire out kayaks, boogie boards and snorkelling equipment (Ph 08 9948 5034, www.ningalookayakadventures.com)

Coastal Cruises

Coral Bay

- **Coastal Adventure Tours** – two-, four- or six-hour catamaran trips (Ph 08 9948 5190, www.coralbaytours.com)
- **Coral Bay Charter and Glass Bottom Boats** – one or two hour glass bottom boat trips to see coral (Ph 08 9942 5932, www.coralbaywa.com)
- **Ningaloo Experience** – outer reef experiences (Ph 08 9942 5877, www.ningalooexperience.com)

Dampier

- **Discovery Sailing Adventures** – day cruises and overnighters to the Dampier Archipelago (Ph 0408 801 040, www.discoverysailingadventures.com.au)

Exmouth

- **Ocean Eco Adventures** – three-day live aboard trip to the Ningaloo Reef, Apr-Oct (Ph 0427 425 925, 0409 374 550, www.oceanecoadventures.com.au)

Guilderton

- **Moore River Cruises** – range of cruises including morning, afternoon, sunset and moonlight (Ph 08 9577 1600)

Kalbarri

- **Kalbarri Extreme** – jet-boat rides through the Murchison River mouth (Ph 0407 371 393)
- **Kalbarri Wilderness Cruises** – lunchtime and sunset cruises on the Murchison River (Ph 08 9937 2259, www.kalbarricruises.com.au)
- **The Specialists Ocean Safaris** – sunset cruises (Ph 0417 912 901, www.thespecialists.com.au)

Shark Bay

- **Aqua Rush** – speed boat cruise to Steep Point and Dirk Hartog Island (08 9949 1446, www.sharkbaysnorkel.com.au)
- **Jetwave Boat Charters** – day tours to Dirk Hartog Island from Denham (Ph 08 9948 1211, www.jetwaveboatcharters.com.au)
- **Monkey Mia Yacht Charters** – various cruise options in Shark Bay including mini, morning, afternoon, sundown and Cape Peron (Ph 1800 030 427, www.monkey-mia.net)
- **Monkey Mia Wildsights** – three daily wildlife sailing cruises (Ph 1800 241 481, www.monkeymiawildsights.com.au)

A yacht about to strike a squall off Monkey Mia.

PELUSEY PHOTOGRAPHY

A nice tailor caught off Carnarvon from a sea kayak by the author.

PELUSEY PHOTOGRAPHY

In March, **Matrix Cruises** leave Fremantle for a week-long cruise up the coast to Exmouth (Ph 08 9437 1777, www.matrixcruises.com).

Also see *Organised Wildlife Tours* (p34) and *Fishing Charters* (pp36-37) as many tourist companies with boats offer general cruises too.

Canoeing & Kayaking

The coastline and rivers such as the **Murchison** provide numerous opportunities for kayaking. The **Abrolhos Islands** and **Dampier Archipelago** are also pristine kayaking locations, but you need a bigger boat to get them there.

The main advantages of kayaking are it provides a different perspective of the landscape and intimate contact with nature. Paddling also gets you into places conventional boats cannot. This pleasurable activity has some inherent dangers so follow these basic principles:

- Make sure you take the appropriate safety equipment including a life jacket.
- Don't paddle alone.
- Good kayaking experience is required for most paddling ventures.
- If not experienced, go with a credited kayaking touring company or with an experienced paddler.
- Under no circumstances should you go out in windy rough conditions.
- Take water with you as paddling can be very dehydrating, even for short times.

Shark Bay

The marine habitats and potential marine life sightings, along with often calm conditions in winter, make Shark Bay an ideal paddling location. You can paddle anywhere in Shark Bay and have a good time, but there are a few standouts. The waters within South Passage near Steep Point offer excellent fishing for mackerel and emperors. Avoid going out in a prevailing southerly though or you could end up on Dirk Hartog Island. Paddling around the spectacular **Peron Peninsula** can be a once in a lifetime experience when it comes to marinelife contact. As well as gliding over schools of fish, you can get up close and personal with dugongs, manta rays, dolphins and seabirds. Paddling around Peron Peninsula should only be undertaken when tides and winds are favourable. **Monkey Mia**, away from the dolphin exclusion zone, also offers easy paddling.

Kalbarri & Murchison River

Kayaking near the mouth of the Murchison River at Kalbarri is popular, but stay away from the mouth where strong outgoing currents can cause problems at times. Further upstream, experienced paddlers can enjoy the gorges from a water-level perspective.

Exmouth & Ningaloo Reef

Kayaking inside the Ningaloo Reef's sheltered waters, protected from the big swells, can be paddling paradise. Crystal-clear waters, abundant marine life and easy access points for kayaks is why sea kayaking is so popular. For visitors without kayaks, tour operators can help out.

Organised Tours

- **Kalbarri Adventure Tours** – one hour canoe tours of the Kalbarri gorges (Ph 08 9937 1667, www.kalbarritours.com.au)
- **Kalbarri Boat Hire and Canoe Safaris** – canoe safaris (Ph 08 9937 1245, www.kalbarriiboathire.com)
- **Kalbarri Safari Tours** – 4WD & canoe tour (Ph 08 9937 1011, 0407 371 011, www.kalbarrisafaritours.com.au)
- **Ningaloo Kayak Adventures**, Coral Bay – two and three hour kayaking and snorkelling trips (Ph 08 9948 5034, www.ningalookayakadventures.com)
- **Ningaloo Reef Seakayaking**, Fremantle – sea kayaking expeditions to Ningaloo Reef & Shark Bay (Ph 08 6267 8059, www.capricornseakayaking.com.au)

Sea kayaking at Shark Bay PELUSEY PHOTOGRAPHY

Swimming

There are plenty of swimming spots to choose from on a coastline that stretches for thousands of kilometres. The dangers of swimming at unpatrolled beaches are obvious. In summer, Geraldton's main swimming beach is patrolled by lifesavers so swimming between the flags is the thing to do. However, most of the beaches covered by this book are unpatrolled and in many cases are also isolated. In those cases commonsense rules should be followed:

- Never swim alone.
- Don't push yourself beyond your abilities.
- Avoid murky water.
- Avoid swimming in rough weather.
- Do not swim at dusk or night as these are prime times for shark attacks.
- Be careful if swimming in Karijini National Park's gorges in winter as the water can be extremely cold.

10 Top Swimming Spots

In our opinion these are the nicest swimming locations for families:

- Coral Bay
- Crossing Pool in Millstream-Chichester National Park
- Fern Pool in Karijini National Park
- Fortescue Falls in Karijini National Park
- Gnaraloo Bay, north of Carnarvon
- Monkey Mia at Shark Bay
- River mouth at Guilderton
- South Passage at Shark Bay
- Turquoise Bay on Ningaloo Reef
- Yanchep Lagoon

Diving & Snorkelling Operators

- **Aqua Rush**, Denham – snorkelling in Shark Bay (Ph 08 9949 1446, www.sharkbaysnorkel.com.au)
- **Batavia Coast Dive Academy**, Geraldton – Abrolhos charter dives, South Tomi wreck dives and training (Ph 08 9921 4229, www.bcda.com.au)
- **Coastal Adventure Tours**, Coral Bay – half and full-day snorkel cruises (Ph 08 9948 5190, www.coralbaytours.com.au)
- **Coral Bay Adventures** – dive on the Ningaloo Reef (Ph 08 9942 5955, www.coralbayadventures.com.au)
- **Jetwave Boat Charters**, Denham – dive charters (Ph 08 9948 1211, www.jetwaveboatcharters.com.au)
- **Jurien Charters**, Jurien Bay – scuba dives in Jurien Bay Marine Park (Ph 08 9652 1109, www.juriencharters.com)
- **King's Ningaloo Reef Tours**, Exmouth – snorkel Ningaloo Reef (Ph 08 9949 1764, www.kingsningalooreeftours.com.au)
- **Mackerel Islands**, off Onslow – numerous diving sites and a snorkelling trail (Ph 08 9184 6444, www.mackerelislands.com.au)
- **Ningaloo Reef Dive**, Coral Bay – dive courses plus snorkel and dive on the inner and outer reefs (Ph 08 9942 5824, www.ningalooreefdive.com)
- **Ningaloo Reef Dreaming**, Exmouth – dive Exmouth Navy Pier and dive or snorkel Ningaloo Reef and Muiron Island (Ph 08 9949 4777, 1800 994 210, www.ningaloodreaming.com)
- **Ningaloo Whaleshark-n-Dive**, Exmouth – learn to dive and snorkelling tours (Ph 08 9949 1116, www.ningaloowhalesharkndive.com.au)

PELUSEY PHOTOGRAPHY

Moore River mouth, Guilderton

HENRY BOEGHEIM

Aerial view of Karijini National Park

Aerial Activities

For a different perspective, aerial views are hard to beat. In our opinion, the pick of the scenic flights are:

- Over **Shark Bay** to see stunning colours and patterns of the sea, the Zuptdorp Cliffs, red dunes and white beaches.
- Over the **Exmouth** region to see the absolutely stunning Cape Range and Ningaloo Reef.
- Over **Karijini National Park** and its gorges.

Scenic Flights

- **Batavia Coast Air Charter**, Geraldton – Abrolhos Islands, Pinnacles, Monkey Mia & Kalbarri gorges (Ph 1300 660 834, www.abrolhosbat.com.au)
- **Golden Eagle Airlines**, Port Hedland – scenic flights from Port Hedland (Ph 08 9191 1132, www.goldeneagleairlines.com)
- **Kalbarri Scenic Flights** – fly over Kalbarri's coastal cliffs at sunset, take a trip to the Abrolhos Islands for snorkelling or fly to Monkey Mia to feed the dolphins (Ph 08 9937 1130, www.kalbarricharter.com.au)
- **Shark Bay Air Charter**, Denham – Shark Bay, Dirt Hartog Island, Ningaloo Reef, Coral Bay, Kalbarri National Park, Mt Augustus and the Kennedy Ranges (Ph 0417 919 059, www.sharkbayair.com.au)
- **Shine Aviation Services**, Geraldton – Abrolhos Islands and Kalbarri National Park (Ph 08 9923 3600, www.tropicair.com.au) ■

chapter four

Coral Coast

The Coral Coast is the beautiful coastal strip of Western Australia from Perth to Exmouth. It is well named because the warm southward-moving Leeuwin Current in the Indian Ocean creates conditions for coral to grow as far south as Rottnest Island off Perth. The Leeuwin Current is an unusual phenomenon as it is the only warm current to flow down the west coast of any continent.

At the northern end of the Coral Coast is of course the jewel in the crown, Ningaloo Reef which is the longest fringing reef in the world. In some sections, coral outcrops are within short snorkelling distance of beautiful white beaches. What is more, these beaches are only a short walk from the car park.

The Coral Coast is also divided into smaller sections: Turquoise Coast, Batavia Coast and Outback Coast.

There is no need to ask why the section from Perth to Dongara is called the **Turquoise Coast** once you see the colour of the ocean in the many secluded bays along Indian Ocean Drive. The turquoise waters are home to the western rock lobster or, as locals still call them, crayfish. In the season, from November to June, specially designed lobster boats bring in their legal catch to the respective ports along the coast. These ports are also popular holiday locations. In spring the Mount Lesueur wildflowers are second to none. Add the fascinating history of Greenough and Dongara and you have a great area to explore.

The **Batavia Coast** covers the Dongara to Kalbarri section. *The Batavia* was a Dutch East India ship that met an untimely end on the Abrolhos Islands in the 1600s. The resulting mutiny and massacre is the stuff of legend.

The **Outback Coast**, from Shark Bay to Exmouth, includes two icons of Western Australia: Shark Bay and Ningaloo Reef. The Shark Bay World Heritage Area's vast area of unique marine and terrestrial habitats is a great attraction for visitors. The town of Carnarvon and the rugged coastline to the north, the holiday centre of Coral Bay and the world-renowned attractions of Ningaloo Reef all come together to make the Coral Coast an essential destination for any visitor. The fact that Ningaloo Reef is going to be nominated for World Heritage-listing, and Shark Bay has already made it, is testimony to that.

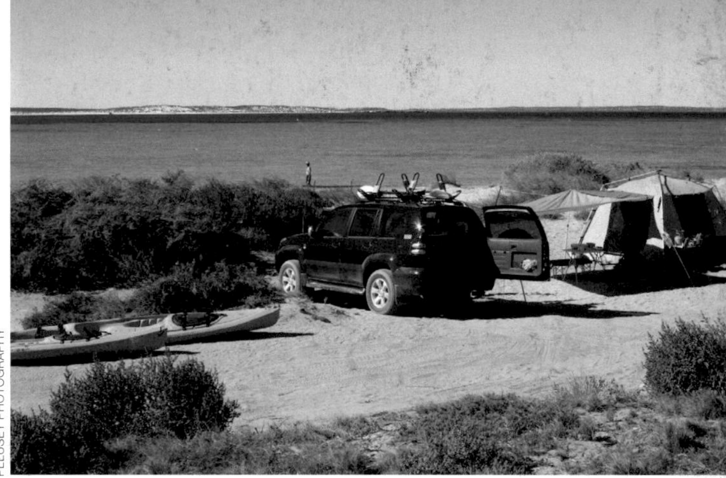

PELUSEY PHOTOGRAPHY

Camping at South Passage, Shark Bay

Not surprisingly, the main activities of the Coral Coast revolve around the water with fishing and boating major drawcards. Once finished on the top of the water, it is time go beneath by glass bottom boat, snorkelling or scuba diving. The Coral Coast has some pristine waters and beautiful underwater playgrounds. Shark Bay has the largest underwater grass beds in the world. Wreck dives on the Turquoise Coast are great in the right conditions, and Exmouth and Coral Bay have some of the best snorkels and dives in the world. Exmouth's Jetty Dive is listed in the top ten in the world. For those who don't like to get their hair wet, Coral Bay, Exmouth and Ningaloo all have glass bottom boats.

All along the Coral Coast there are also rivers that flow to the Indian Ocean, although some are restricted by sandbars, such as Moore River at Guilderton and Greenough River at Greenough. Other rivers are seemingly dry but still remain the mainstay of the community, like the Gascoyne River at Carnarvon. Powerful waterways such as the Murchison River created the amazing gorges at Kalbarri.

Murchison River, Kalbarri National Park JEFF DREWITZ

Coastal cliffs, Kalbarri on the Batavia Coast

PELUSEY PHOTOGRAPHY

Leeuwin Current

The Leeuwin Current is a narrow band of warm tropical water that flows southward from the Sunda Shelf – between northwest Australia and Indonesia – to Cape Leeuwin, then eastwards into the Great Australian Bight before petering out on the west coast of Tasmania.

As well as being warm and clear, the waters of the Leeuwin Current are low in nutrients. These conditions do not favour the production of large quantities of finfish, but are ideal for invertebrates such as crayfish. The current transports the larvae of tropical marine animals and, because it flows most strongly in autumn and winter, its warming influence makes it possible for these animals to survive much further south than would otherwise be the case.

Perth to Cervantes

Perth's northern coastline consists of long stretches of white beaches and aqua sea backed by coastal vegetation and dunes. From late autumn to early summer, hot mornings often give way to cool afternoons as the sea breeze or gale kicks in. Perth's northern beaches are virtually undeveloped with high-rise on this stretch of coast a beach shack on a sand dune. Yanchep National Park and the nearby suburbs of Yanchep and Two Rocks are popular holiday and weekend destinations because of their attractions and close proximity to Perth. Windsurfers from around the world converge on Lancelin in summer. Further north, Cervantes is the gateway to another of WA's best-known national parks: Nambung National Park.

COURTESY YANCHEP NP (DEC)

Lake in Yanchep National Park

Yanchep National Park (Map 2 G4)

Yanchep National Park features a variety of significant habitats, such as limestone caves, freshwater swamps and lakes, heath and eucalypt woodlands. This popular park also boasts a large **koala enclosure**, stunning **wildflower gardens** (in season) and grassy lakeside **picnic areas**. The Tudor-style **Yanchep Inn** has served visitors, especially honeymooners, since 1936 with its friendly old worlde feel and a pleasantly shady beer garden. Limestone caves are dotted throughout the park with **Crystal Cave** and **Yonderup Cave** open to the public. (Guided tours of Crystal Cave are conducted daily. Adventure caving is available, but only to school groups and the like.) Yanchep's caves were once unusual venues for weddings and ballroom dancing and **Cabaret Cave** is still used today for functions. At the **Wangi Mia** (talking place) Nyoongar Aboriginal culture is demonstrated in traditional dance, music and hunting, bushtucker and cultural tours. Nestled in lovely parks and bushland, **Loch McNess** provides an opportunity for a gentle punt or a lake cruise. (Row boats are available for hire from the information centre.) **Bird-watching** can also be a rewarding pastime as the park's varied habitats attract a variety of birdlife, including several WA endemics including the endangered Carnarby's black-cockatoo. In September the extensive heathlands are a fantastic sight when the **wildflowers** are in full bloom.

Walk Trails

Walkers can explore the park and its surrounds on a number of marked trails, all of which are shown on maps available from the visitor centre. They range from short (an hour or less) habitat walks to more challenging excursions.

- **Dwerta Mia Walk Trail** – easy 500m walk along the base of a limestone gorge (20min return)
- **Wetlands Walk Trail** – easy 2km walk around Loch McNess (45min return)
- **Woodlands Walk Trail** – easy 2.6km through coastal woodland of banksia, tuart, marri, stunted jarrah and sheok (1hr return)
- **Caves Walk Trail** – easy 4.5km walk to Crystal Cave (2hr return)
- **Ghosthouse Walk Trail** – medium 9.2km walk through the park's wilderness areas to the ruins of the Ghost House (4.5hr return)
- **Cockatoo Walk Trail** – medium 17.5km walk through various landscapes for impressive views (8hr return)
- **Yanchep Rose Walk Trail** – medium 19.5km walk that from early July to late August features the spectacular blooms of the Yanchep rose (9hr return)
- **Yaberoo Budjara Walk Trail** – challenging 28km trail that follows the traditional route of the local Nyoongar people with stunning views (1 day from Yanchep NP to Joondalup)
- **Coastal Plains Walk Trail** – challenging 55km trail to Melaleuca Conservation Park (3.5 days to go one way)

Ruin on the Ghosthouse Walk Trail.

PELUSEY PHOTOGRAPHY

PELUSEY PHOTOGRAPHY

Yanchep Lagoon

PELUSEY PHOTOGRAPHY

Yanchep Inn

Information & Facilities

The **McNess House Visitor Centre** in Yanchep National Park is open daily from 9am to 5pm (Ph 08 9561 1004). Book the Crystal Cave Tours, Lake Tour and Aboriginal Experience through the visitor centre. Rowboat hire is also available and there is a range of gifts and souvenirs too. Within the national park, **camping** is only permitted along the longer walk trails at sites suitable for self-sufficient backpack camping.

The **Yanchep Inn** offers meals and accommodation (Ph 08 9561 1001, www.yanchepinn.com.au) and light lunches and refreshments are also available from the **Chocolate Drops Tearooms** (Ph 08 9561 6699, www.chocolatedrops.com.au: open daily 10.30am to 4.30pm).

Two Rocks (Map 2 G3)

Just outside Yanchep National Park's boundaries is a development of more recent historical significance. In anticipation of *Southern Cross* winning the **America's Cup**, Alan Bond developed the Two Rocks area. He was planning the defence races would be held off Two Rocks after wrestling the Cup from the Americans. Alas the timing and location was out, but some years later, his persistence paid off.

Where to stay

- *Sun City Holidays* – two holiday homes (Ph 08 9561 6695, www.suncityholidays.com.au)
- *Sunset Coast B&B* (Ph 08 9561 5660, www.thesunsetcoast.net)
- *Two Rocks Harbour View Apartments* (Ph 08 9561 1469)

Yanchep (Map 2 G3)

Slightly north of Two Rocks is the Yanchep community. The sheltered waters of **Yanchep Lagoon** are protected by an encircling reef, making it a great place for **swimming**. In season it is patrolled by lifesavers. **Anglers** trying their luck can pick up good size tailor and mulloway at night.

Where to stay

- *Club Capricorn* – resort with lodge rooms, chalets & caravan and camping sites (Ph 08 9561 1106, www.clubcapricorn.com.au)
- *Yanchep Holiday Village* – self-contained apartments (Ph 08 9561 2244, www.yanchepholidays.com)

Dog beach, Guilderton

Mouth of Moore River, Guilderton

Guilderton (Map 2 F3)

Located between Yanchep and Lancelin, Guilderton is 94km north of Perth. For most of its existence, Guilderton was merely a fishing village with the mandatory fishing shacks lining the hills. Now, many of these shacks have morphed into four-bedroom holiday homes. The summer school holidays are, to say the least, busy due to the region's attractions and close proximity to Perth. The caravan park is perfectly located near the water but it gets very busy. Try out of school holidays, weekends and long weekends if you can. If not, enjoy the company.

In 1931, 40 17th century silver guilder coins were found in a sand dune. They were thought to have come from a Dutch ship, the *Gilt Dragon* that had been wrecked nearby. The **wreck** itself wasn't discovered until 1963. You can visit a 32m tall **lighthouse** near the wreck site. There is a string of 14 wrecks, dating from 1656 to 1983, along the coast from Guilderton to Lancelin. They are described in the WA Maritime Museum's excellent brochure, *Shipwrecks of the Guilderton to Lancelin Coast*.

The town is situated on the northern bank of the **Moore River**, which meets the **Indian Ocean**. The river and ocean only combine occasionally when floodwaters break through a naturally formed sandbar. This sandbar is one of the reasons Guilderton is such a good place to visit because it creates a calm inviting estuary by dividing the river from the sea. The river at its mouth is pretty shallow on the edge and popular with parents of little children. For those who like their **swimming** a bit more challenging, there are superb beaches either side of the mouth. The more northern beach is set aside for dogs and their owners.

What to do

Probably Guilderton's major attraction is **fishing**. With the hamlet's handy location near a river and open seas, there is plenty of variety to keep you interested. Moore River is a black bream hotspot, and this cagey fish can be taken near the shoreline or from a small powerboat. Fishing from a canoe or kayak is also an excellent option. Beach fishing brings in tailor, salmon, herring, skippy (silver trevally), mulloway and sharks. **Boat ramp** facilities are located near the caravan park and on an off-branch about 1km from the mouth. Bait and tackle is available from the shop and service station.

Other non-landbased activities are **kayaking** and **canoeing**. You can paddle hard for exercise or simply drift along absorbing the solitude and scenery of **Moore River**. It is possible to hire kayaks through *Moore River Beach Houses* (see *Where to Stay*). **Moore River Cruises** offer a range of cruises including morning, afternoon, sunset and moonlight (Ph 08 9577 1600).

A big dune that backs onto the caravan park can be accessed by a **boardwalk** to a **lookout** for great views out to sea and inland up the Moore River. Alternatively, stroll along **walk trails** that follow the meandering river through shady forest.

Where to Stay

- *Guilderton Caravan Park* (Ph 08 9577 1021)
- *Moore River Beach Houses* – booking agency for various holiday houses (Ph 0427 131 149, www.mooreriver.com.au)
- *Moore River Holidays* – self-contained house (Ph 0427 131 149, www.mooreriverholidays.com.au)

Gingin (Map 2 F5)

Just inland from Guilderton is the small rural town of Gingin. One of the State's oldest towns, it retains some important remnants of its pioneering days dating back to the 1850s. A **walking trail** features many historic attractions within the town's central precinct. The picturesque **Granville Scenic Park**, in the centre of town, is surrounded by preserved **buildings** of historical significance. The park is an excellent spot for a picnic or barbecue, and there's a waterwheel turned by the spring-fed **Gingin Brook**.

What to Do

The **Gravity Discovery Centre** is great fun for young and old as it focuses on the big questions about life, the universe and everything. The **leaning tower** is a great climb and has views over the Gingin sand plains. Dropping a water-filled balloon from the tower certainly gives children a dramatic insight into the effects of gravity. (Open Tue-Sun 9.30am-5pm & public holiday Mondays; Ph 08 9575 7577, www.gdc.asn.au)

At the **Gingin Observatory**, tour one of Australia's most well-equipped public observatories and stargaze through telescopes. (Ph 08 9575 7740, www.ginginobservatory.com)

While you are in the area, try the local produce from **West Coast Honey** and **Regans Ridge Olives**. Gingin is also the starting point for the **Chittering Valley Wine Trail** with **Riseborough Estate** and **Jylland Vineyard**.

Where to Stay

- *Amirage Restaurant & B&B*, West Gingin (Ph 08 9575 7646, www.amiragerestaurantbb.com.au)
- *Angela's Holiday House* – 2brm self-contained unit (Ph 0408 572 566)
- *Brookside Budget Accommodation & Chalets*, West Gingin (Ph 08 9575 7585, www.brooksideaccommodation.com.au)
- *Gingin B&B* (Ph 08 9575 2541)
- *Gingin Caravan Park* (Ph 08 9575 2258)
- *The Runners Rest* – B&B on a working cattle farm (Ph 08 9575 1414)
- *Sandy Lake Farm B&B* (Ph 0428 288 422)
- *Willowbrook Farm Tearooms and Caravan Park*, West Gingin (Ph 08 9575 7566, www.users.bigpond.com/willowbrookfarm)

Seabird & Ledge Point (Map 2 F3 & E3)

Western rock lobster is the mainstay of the tiny **fishing villages** of Seabird and Ledge Point. They are great places to cast a hook and go surf fishing, or just enjoy a quiet beach holiday. If you are game, you can also try **windsurfing** and **kite surfing**.

What to Do

Fishing for tailor on summer evenings when the sea breeze is whipping up a chop is a popular pastime for anglers. Reefs near the beach seem to be an attraction for fish, although angling can be very frustrating when seaweed comes in on the back of storms. Boat anglers can tuck into tough fighting Samson fish, dhufish and pink snapper offshore in calm conditions. If fishing isn't your game, **beach walking** could well be.

For experienced **divers**, Ledge Point is host to some of the most interesting wreck sites in the world. The wreck dives include the *JP Webb* (sunk in 1951) and the *Vergulde Draeck*, commonly known as the *Gilt Dragon*. The *Gilt Dragon* was a Dutch ship that sank on a journey from Jakarta in 1656. Other wrecks are the *Manakoora*, a stolen fishing boat that sank in 1946, and the *Key Biscayne*, a capsized oil rig, which is popular with experienced divers.

Swimming and **windsurfing** are the go along the beaches here. In summer, Ledge Point is the kickoff point for the international **Lancelin Ocean Classic** – a windsurfing race from Ledge Point to Lancelin.

Where to Stay

- *Ledge Point Holiday Park* – chalets, studios & caravan and camping sites (Ph 08 9655 2870, www.ledgepointholidaypark.com.au)

Lancelin (Map 2 E3)

The small coastal resort town and **crayfishing port** of Lancelin is about 125km from Perth at the northern end of the sealed coast road (State Hwy 60). The town is a very popular weekend escape for Perth residents and is also one of Australia's main **windsurfing** centres. The nature of the sea breezes brings windsurfers from all over the world so having a quiet drink at the Lancelin pub in summer, you are more than likely be in the company of sun-tanned Germans. For off-road bikes, quad bikes, beach buggies and 4WD thrillseekers, the huge white **dunes** are an obvious attraction. Despite being a popular tourist town, the main reason for Lancelin's existence is due to its thriving **rock-lobster industry**. Judging by the size of some of the houses around here, catching lobsters is pretty lucrative. When staying in Lancelin during the season, you can hear the boats heading out well before dawn and returning around lunchtime with their catch.

Information

Lancelin's **Visitor Information Centre** is at 102 Gingin Rd (Ph/fax 08 9655 1100). Ask here for details (including a mud map) of the coastal track to Cervantes.

What to Do

For such a quiet, unprepossessing little place Lancelin certainly has a lot of things to do in the outdoor pursuits department. The town's major attraction is **windsurfing**, which mainly takes place between mid-November and the end of April. **Werner's Hot Spot** (Ph 0407 426 469, www.windsurfwa.com) operates from the beach at the end of Hopkins St. Werner hires windsurfing and kitesurfing gear, and gives tuition. Each year in January the town hosts the **Lancelin Ocean Classic** over three days at Lancelin and Ledge Point.

Surfing is also popular, especially in winter when swells are bigger and more consistent. There are good surfing breaks on reefs in the area, the best being off **Back Beach**. From their base in Perth, **Lancelin Surf Camp** (Ph 08 9245 7341, www.surfschool.com) runs surf lessons and surfing tours – from day trips to extended camps.

Lancelin is on a sheltered bay with glorious white sand **beaches** and good **swimming** from one end to the other. Swimmers often find themselves sharing the water with **dolphins**, while **sea lions** also pop up from time to time.

There's good **snorkelling** on the reefs around **Edward Island** (best at low tide) and in the fish habitat-protected area behind

Lancelin to Cervantes track

Lancelin is the kickoff point for this challenging drive along a **4WD track** north to Cervantes and the Pinnacles. It weaves past an **army bombing range** and other fishing shack settlements such as **Wedge Island**. The track is a mixture of soft sand, beach runs and limestone rocks. The state of the beach depends on wind and ocean conditions. Sometimes the beach part is closed due to overly soft sand or weather and tide conditions. Great care and some sound four-wheel-driving experience is required, especially on the beach. Many a bogged 4WD has come to a watery end, so if in doubt, there are inland routes to take. Always stop at Lancelin Roadhouse for the latest conditions and to check if the track is closed due to bombing activity. (See Track 22 in Hema's *WA 4WD Top 50 Atlas & Guide* for more detail.)

For a long time there's been a plan in place to bituminise this stretch of track, and indeed Stage One of the Lancelin to Cervantes Road was completed in March 2008. The project should be finished by mid-2011. It would be good for tourism to join the Lancelin Road to Cervantes as a more direct route to the Pinnacles, but until then only four-wheel drivers can enjoy this route.

Granville Scenic Park, Gingin

PELUSEY PHOTOGRAPHY

Coastal tracks on the way to Cervantes

PELUSEY PHOTOGRAPHY

Lancelin Island. A string of 14 **wrecks** dating from 1656 to 1983 attracts **scuba divers** to the coast between Lancelin and Guilderton, 40km south. They are described in the WA Maritime Museum's excellent brochure, *Shipwrecks of the Guilderton to Lancelin Coast.*

Beach **fishing** isn't a huge attraction, but wetting a line can be fruitful off the jetty (squid) and in the channel between the mainland and Edward Island (herring, whiting and cobbler). In March the channel is a hot spot for tailor.

Just north of Lancelin, a series of white sand **dunes** slightly inland are a haven for four-wheel drivers and dirt bikers who like to hack around in the sand. These activities may be great fun, but they do have their dangers. If playing in the sand, remember to stick up a dune flag, keep a wary eye out for all manner of speed demons and make sure you know how steep the dune is on the other side before going over the top.

The dunes behind Lancelin also make a good venue for **sand boarding**. Boards can be hired from the **Have a Chat Supermarket** and **Lancelin SurfSports**, both on Gingin Rd near the information centre.

In spring and early summer, **bird-watching** is a rewarding pastime on Lancelin and Edward islands, both of which are wildlife sanctuaries. A number of sea-bird species including ospreys and several terns nest there – walk only on established paths to avoid stepping on the nests. **Lancelin Island** is home to a rare **red-legged skink** and also has a small colony of **sea lions**.

Where to Stay

The information centre is the booking agent for numerous short-term rental properties in Lancelin. *Lancelin Accommodation Services* (Ph 08 96551454, www.lancelinaccommodation.com.au) and *Coastal Real Estate* (Ph 08 9655 1305, www.lancelinrealestate.com) also have listings of holiday rentals.

Other options include:

- *Lancelin Caravan Park* (Ph 08 9655 1056)
- *Lancelin Motel/Hotel* (Ph 08 9655 1005)
- *North End Caravan Park* (Ph 08 9655 1115

Cervantes & The Pinnacles (Map 2 C2 & D3)

The Pinnacles is a famous Western Australian attraction that is regularly inundated with visitors by the busload. Even Scottish comedian, Billy Connolly was filmed running naked between the rocks. This series of limestone pillars that have evaded erosion, leaving behind yellow sentinels in a sea of sand, are encapsulated by **Nambung National Park (2 D2)**.

The fishing town of **Cervantes**, 17km away, has all the facilities for tourists visiting the Pinnacles. Although the town was in fact named after an American whaling ship that sank in 1844, it has a coincidental similarity to the author of *Don Quixote*, Miquel Cervantes. In true opportunism, some street names in Cervantes come from the book's characters.

Jurien Bay Marine Park stretches north along the coast from **Wedge Island** (between Cervantes and Lancelin) to **Green Head**.

Information

The **Cervantes Visitor Centre** (Ph 08 9652 7700, www.visitpinnaclescountry.com.au) is next to the shops on Iberia St. Ask here for a mud map and route information if you are taking the coastal track south to Lancelin – see the boxed text p45.

Nambung National Park is managed from the DEC office in Cervantes (Ph 08 9652 7043); contact the office in **Jurien Bay** on Ph 08 9652 1911 for information on the marine park. The new **Pinnacles Desert Discovery visitor centre** in Nambung National Park has displays and a shop. It is open 9.30am to 4.30pm seven days.

What to See & Do

A sealed road links **the Pinnacles** area with Cervantes, and there's a fee-collecting point at the end of the bitumen. From here an unsealed vehicle track does a 4km circuit of the formations. The bush book *Discovering Nambung National Park* describes 33 stops or points of interest along the drive trail through **Nambung National Park**. The pillars, which are up to four metres high, rise eerily from the shifting yellow sands. You'll get the best appreciation of this fascinating area by leaving your

The Pinnacles at sunrise.

JEFF DREWITZ

vehicle in the car park and **walking** from there. A new visitor centre, the **Pinnacles Desert Discovery**, provides interpretive information for visitors. Interactive displays teach how these fascinating landforms came to be. The 1.2km **loop walk trail** gives an insight into the unique limestone formations and tells of the local Yued indigenous group and their life in the area. A new sealed pathway leads from the centre to the **Pinnacles View Lookout**. The best time to visit the Pinnacles is either at sunrise or sunset, when they glow dramatically. Another reason for coming at those times is to avoid the crowds. For an indepth tour of the Pinnacles, contact **Turquoise Coast Enviro Tours** (Ph 08 9652 7047, www.thepinnacles.com.au).

Beach fishing is popular at **Kangaroo Point** and **Hangover Bay**, both about 1km off The Pinnacles access road. There are numerous beach-fishing options both south and north of Cervantes. Evening and night fishing in a brisk sea breeze is great for tailor as they like the choppy conditions. **Offshore boat fishing** places anglers in the realm of dhufish, Samson fish and other deeper water species. If you can't catch your own, don't despair, just head down to the **Indian Ocean Rock Lobster Factory** (Ph 08 9652 7010, www.indianoceanlobsters.com.au). They sell direct to the public with western rock lobster and marinated octopus their specialties.

Cervantes is another popular **windsurfing** spot. Each year in early December it hosts the **Slalom Windsurfing Carnival**, which attracts local, interstate and international sailors.

Also of interest are the **stromatolites** of **Lake Thetis**, a short drive from town. This is one of only five places in Western Australia where you can see these ancient living fossils. As is usual in this part of the world, **wildflowers** are also a major attraction in spring. The marine park has many good opportunities for **scuba diving** and **snorkelling**, not to mention **fishing**.

Where to Stay

See the Cervantes Visitor Centre website for a listing of the numerous holiday houses available.

Other options include:

- *Best Western Cervantes Pinnacles Resort* (Ph 08 9652 7145, www.cervantespinnaclesmotel.com.au)
- *Cervantes Holiday Homes* – 1, 2 & 3 brm self-contained units (Ph 08 9652 7115)
- *Cervantes Lodge And Pinnacles Beach Backpackers* (Ph 08 9652 7377, 1800 245 232, www.cervanteslodge.com.au)
- *Cervantes Pinnacles Caravan Park* (Ph 08 9652 7060, www.pinnaclespark.com.au)

Badgingarra (Map 2 C3)

Just north of the Cervantes turnoff on the Brand Highway, **Badgingarra** is a tiny settlement of around 250 people. The town's main attraction is the nearby **Badgingarra National Park (2 C3)**, which is a **wildflower** hotspot. A 2km **walking track** through the park leads to a **lookout** on the edge of a breakaway. The track starts opposite the Badgingarra Roadhouse, where you can park and pick up a DEC brochure. For information contact DEC's Cervantes office on Ph 08 9652 7043.

Come in spring to enjoy a plethora of wildflowers on display. Expect to see feather flowers enmasse, as well as banksias, grevillea species, paper daisies, bottlebrushes, coneflowers, leschenaultias and numerous types of ground orchids. Combine Badgingarra with Mount Lesueur and you will have sampled some of the world's richest botanical hotspots. (Badgingarra National Park is also part of the **Everlastings Trail** see p100.)

JEFF DREWITZ

Ronsard Bay, Cervantes

Indian Ocean Drive – Cervantes to Geraldton

Heading north from Cervantes, the scenic Indian Ocean Drive hugs the coast to Jurien Bay, Green Head and Leeman before ending at the junction with the Brand Hwy, just south of Port Denison.

Jurien Bay (Map 7 K7)

Jurien Bay is a vibrant holiday and fishing town of 1200 people situated on a wide sweep of coastline. Parts of these turquoise waters are protected by the **Jurien Bay Marine Park (7 K7)**, that extends from Cervantes to Green Head. The marine park is home to **sea lions**, **seals**, **seabirds**, **western rock lobsters** and a huge variety of **fish**. Although a small part of the park is a no-fishing sanctuary, most of it is accessible for **swimming**, **snorkelling** and **fishing**. Signs explain acceptable and prohibited activities.

A short drive north is **Sandy Cape Recreation Park**, a beachfront **campsite** for rough camping and **four-wheel driving**. Campsites at Sandy Cape will regularly be full during peak times, such as school holidays and long weekends. No bookings are taken – sites are available on a first-in basis. (For more information see the Shire of Dandaragan website, www.dandaragan.wa.gov.au, or contact the ranger on Ph 08 9652 0800.)

Information

- The **Jurien Bay Visitor Centre** (Ph 08 9652 0800, www.dandaragan.wa.gov.au) is on Bashford St.

What to Do

Being the major centre along this part of the coast, Jurien Bay has numerous facilities to entice **anglers** who like to get out in boats. A **marina** offers great public access with excellent boat launching facilities and boat ramps. Therefore, Jurien Bay is possibly the best location for targeting **offshore species** along this part of the Coral Coast. Bigger boats can get amongst dhufish, Samson fish, pink snapper, baldchin groper and tuna. Spanish mackerel are often caught in late summer and autumn by trolling lures and fish baits. The **jetty** at Jurien Bay and the rock walls of the marina allow anglers to target silver trevally or skippy, tailor, whiting and herring during the day. At night, patient anglers may catch a big tailor, tangle with a shark or tuck into some calamari. (Please be aware that special fishing regulations apply within the Jurien Bay Marine Park. For more information see www.fish.wa.gov.au, contact the DEC Jurien Bay office on Ph 08 9652 1911 or visit www.dec.wa.gov.au for a map outlining the zones.)

To explore the **Jurien Bay Marine Park**, take a tour with **Jurien Charters**, to see **Australian sea lions** and other marine creatures (Ph 08 9652 1109, www.juriencharters.com). They also offer **scuba diving** and **fishing charters** as well as **boat hire**.

Mount Lesueur & Stockyard Gully

Located just north of Jurien Bay, and slightly inland, is a region of world botanical importance that was nearly lost to mining. **Mount Lesueur (8 K8)** was named after a French artist onboard the *Naturaliste* that sailed by this coast in 1801. The *Naturaliste* and her French sister ship, the *Geographe* were mapping the coastline of Australia not covered by Captain James Cook. Subsequent visits by botanists, such as **Charles Gardner**, recognised the Mount Lesueur region as of great **botanical importance**. Under threat from possible coal mining, 26 987 hectares were put aside as a national park in 1992. Just walking through the low scrub, you will notice many different plant species. In spring this is even more obvious as each plant comes into flower and the area is a sea of colour. Over 900 species, or about 10% of WA's known plants are found here, despite poor soil. In plant diversity terms **Lesueur National Park (8 K8)** comes third after Fitzgerald National Park and the Stirling Ranges in WA. This diversity of flora means 122 species of **birds** also live in this varied bushland ecosystem.

The roads around here used to be 4WD only, but increasing visitors in **wildflower** season have led to DEC bituminising a loop road through the park. At the 7km mark on the loop road is a car park for the **Mount Lesueur climb**. Mount Lesueur itself is a flat-topped hill, 313m above sea level. Signs at the trailhead explain the park's biodiversity and range of wildflowers. The first part of the trail, that is wide and bituminized, leads to a lookout. A sandy trail that leads toward the flat top hill is initially flat but then there is a climb up the slope of Mount Lesueur, although it does switchback up the slope. The view is of the surrounding bushland, farmland and the Indian Ocean in the distance. The summit of the hill is across the top on the other side to the trail. (Lesueur National Park is also part of the **Everlastings Trail** see p100)

Almost adjacent to Lesueur National Park is **Stockyard Gully Nature Reserve (8 J8)**. You need a 4WD with moderate clearance to tackle this diversion. The **caves** were created by an underground river system, and in the past provided overnight shelter for drovers on cattle drives bound for Perth. There are two caves within a few hundred metres of each other along a gum tree-lined riverbed. The **walking circuit** is well described on prominent information boards at car parks at either end. To explore the cave system properly, take sturdy shoes and a big torch with adequate batteries. The entrances to the caves have some fallen rocks to climb over. If it has been raining recently, sand on the cave floor can act like quicksand, so tread carefully. Flood-level indicators give a sobering warning not to take on these caves if heavy rain is in the area. Look out for beehives hanging like stalactites from the entrance of both caves.

Grass trees near Mt Lesueur

PELUSEY PHOTOGRAPHY

Where to Stay

- *The Heights B&B* (Ph 08 9652 1100)
- *Jurien Bay Motel Hotel* (Ph 08 9652 1022)
- *Jurien Bay Tourist Park* (Ph 08 9652 1595, www.jurienbaytouristpark.com.au)
- *Jurien Bayview Realty*, Professionals – range of holiday accommodation (Ph 08 9652 2055, www.jurienbayholidays.com)
- *Jurien Beachfront Holiday Units* (Ph 08 9652 2400)
- *Top Spot Jurien Cottages* (Ph 08 9652 1290)

Green Head & Leeman (Map 7 K7 & J7)

The two small fishing towns of **Green Head (7 K7)** and **Leeman (7 J7)** are located close to each other on the **Turquoise Coast** section. They have populations of 244 and 539 respectively. Their specialty is the lucrative **rock lobster-industry**, although Leeman also claims to be the home of the much-prized **dhufish**.

Information

For more information on the townships of Green Head and Leeman, contact the Leeman administration centre of the **Shire of Coorow** at 20 Morcombe Rd (Ph 08 9953 1388, www.coorow.wa.gov.au).

What to Do

These villages are perfect for anyone who likes to **fish** and stroll along quiet white **beaches**. **South Bay** is a long crescent-shaped beach, while **Anchorage and Billy Goat bays**, just north of Green Head, offer protected beaches, good fishing and **windsurfing**. **Dynamite Bay** is almost circular in shape and protected from open sea swells so provides a good spot for families to swim.

Fisherman's Island and **Beagle Island** south of Green Head and north of Leeman are home to **Australian sea lion** breeding colonies. Nearly 300 Australian sea lions breed on Beagle Island, which makes it the largest breeding colony of these marine mammals in Western Australia. To see these amazing creatures up close, take a tour with **Sea Lion Charters** in Green Head (Ph 08 9953 1012).

These islands and neighbouring offshore **reefs** are also superb locations for **scuba divers**. The warm **Leeuwin Current** (see p41) results in prolific tropical and temperate marinelife, including soft corals, hard corals and colourful sponges. **Sea lions** are often seen swimming in the bays and even basking on beaches. Don't approach these animals as they can sometimes become aggressive. Ask at **Beagle Island Diving** in Leeman about arranging a dive charter (Ph 08 9953 1190).

Fishing is better from boats around offshore reefs as the beaches are quite shallow. Nevertheless, tailor, whiting and herring are fairly easily targeted by shore anglers. Try for dhufish, snapper and Samson fish from small boats when sea conditions are good.

The foreshore at the small fishing town of Leeman.

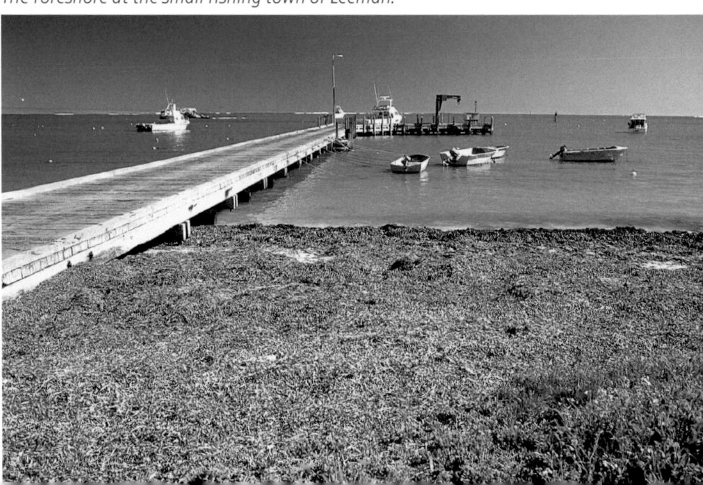

PELUSEY PHOTOGRAPHY

Where to stay

- *Coast House Guest House B&B*, Leeman (Ph 0437 900 771)
- *Green Head Caravan Park* (Ph 08 9953 1131)
- *Leeman Caravan Park* (Ph 08 9953 1080)
- *Leeman Holiday Units* (Ph 08 9953 1190, www.leemanholidayunits.com)
- *Macca's B&B*, Green Head (Ph 08 9953 1461)

Eneabba (Map 8 J8)

The Eneabba Coolimba Rd that joins Leeman and Eneabba is spectacular for **wildflowers** in spring. Eneabba itself is a mining town for **mineral sands**, and the sandy soil is also the reason for the huge variety of wildflowers.

Along the Eneabba Coolimba Rd is **Lake Indoon (8 J8)**, an A-class reserve and freshwater lake where people like to **swim**, **sail** and **picnic**. The **camping** area has toilets and a water tank. The lake is also a fine habitat for an assortment of **waterbirds**. (Lake Indoon is also part of the **Everlastings Trail**, see p100.)

Just north of Eneabba, the **Western Flora Caravan Park** is situated on 160 acres of prime wildflower country. In spring, there is a **guided wildflower walk** at 4.30pm that is included in the tariff. **Birds** also accumulate here to get the nectar from the flowers and catch insects.

If you continue east to Carnamah you'll pass **Tathra National Park (8 J9)** that also has sandy wildflower displays.

Information

For more information contact the **Shire of Carnamah** in MacPherson St Carnamah or Eneabba Dr Eneabba (Ph 08 9951 7000 or 08 9955 1058, www.carnamah.wa.gov.au).

Where to Stay

- *Eneabba Travellers Rest* – one-room accommodation (Ph 08 9955 1194)
- *Lake Indoon camping area* (Ph 08 9951 1055)
- *Lake Indoon B&B* – self-contained cottage on a working farm (Ph 08 9955 6035)
- *Western Flora Caravan, Camping and Tourist Park* – chalets, on-site vans, & powered and unpowered sites (Ph 08 9955 2030)

PELUSEY PHOTOGRAPHY

A wildflower talk at the Western Flora Caravan, Camping and Tourist Park

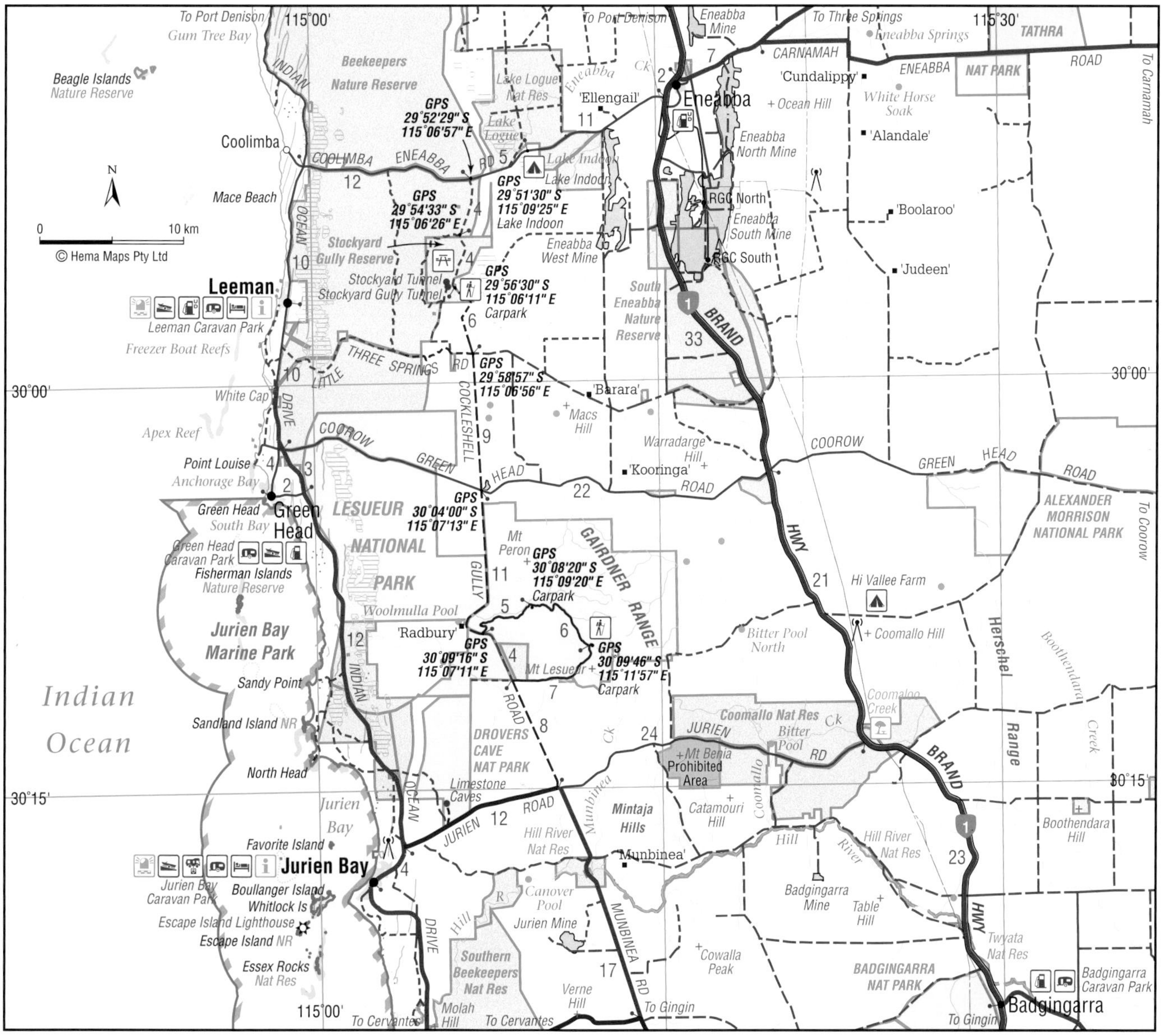

Dongara & Port Denison (Map 7 G7)

Dongara and Port Denison are twin towns located 65km south of Geraldton on the Brand Highway. **Dongara** is an historic town, going back 150 years to when the early pastoralists found good wheat and sheep country. Just under 100 years later, Dongara became a hub for another industry – **western rock lobster** – and this was the real birth of Port Denison. Today these vibrant communities have 3500 residents and a growing tourism industry.

Information

The **Dongara Denison Visitors Centre** is at 9 Waldeck St, Dongara. (Ph 08 9927 1404, www.irwin.wa.gov.au)

What to do

Visit Dongara's old part of town to see many interesting buildings, including **Russ Cottage** that was built in the 1860s as a yeoman's cottage. The cottage was restored by the Irwin District Historical Society. Built in 1894, the **Royal Steam Flour Mill** is an imposing building. The **Old Police Station** has been renovated to serve as the local **museum**. A good way to see the highlights is to walk the **Heritage Trail** to 28 heritage-listed buildings. (Booklets are available at the visitors centre.) The **cemetery** also has a self-guided walk, taking in some of the old graves that date back to the 1870s.

In the summer months you can catch a film at Dongara's **drive-in cinema**.

Moreton Terrace is named because of the huge Moreton Bay fig trees that line the main street. They were planted in 1906. There are also cosy **cafes** for a meal or coffee along this charming street.

Take a leisurely stroll along the **Irwin River Nature Trail** as it meanders along the river. Some **lookouts** provide great vantage points along the way.

The view from **Fisherman's Lookout** at **Leander Point** in **Port Denison** encompasses the whole fishing boat harbour. The Port Denison foreshore has pleasant grassy **picnic** areas and parking for cars and caravans.

The **beaches** of Dongara and Port Denison have something for everyone. **South Beach** is great for **swimming** and watersports, with the Surf Life Saving Club based here too. **Seaspray Beach** is for **fishing** because swimming is dangerous because of drop-off sand banks and rips. Great for **surfing** in the right conditions, **Surf Beach** joins onto the calmer **Granny's Beach**.

Beach fishing is good along the coast north of town, but to get to the good spots a **4WD** is essential to negotiate the soft tracks through the dunes. Expect to catch tailor and mulloway.

PELUSEY PHOTOGRAPHY

Irwin River, Dongara

South of town, herring and small tailor are the main catches along the predominantly shallow beaches. The seaward side of the breakwater provides protection for **Port Denison marina**, offering good fishing for big mulloway and tailor at night. The numerous **offshore reefs** offer boat anglers endless possibilities. Dhufish are the main target, but there is plenty of samson fish and pink snapper out there too. Late summer and autumn are good times to troll for Spanish mackerel and tuna. From Dongara you can take a fishing trip to the Abrolhos Islands, Shark Bay, Carnarvon, Exmouth or Coral Bay with **Aqua Jack Charters** (Ph 08 9927 220, www.aquajack.com.au).

Where to stay

There is a large range of holiday rentals, units and B&Bs available – see the visitor centre's website for details. It's a good idea to book your accommodation, especially if you are visiting during the very busy school holidays.

- *Dongara Denison Beach Holiday Park* (Ph 1800 600 776, 08 9927 1131, www.ddbeachholidaypark.com)
- *Dongara Denison Tourist Park* (Ph 08 9927 1210, www.dongaratouristpark.com.au)
- *Dongara Hotel Motel* (Ph 08 9927 1023, www.dongaramotel.com.au)
- *Dongara Old Mill Motel* (Ph 08 9927 1200)
- *Leander Reef Holiday Park* – formerly known as the Dongara Strata Caravan Park (08 9927 1840, www.leanderreefholidaypark.com)
- *Priory Hotel* – refurbished heritage hotel (Ph 08 9927 1090, www.prioryhotel.com.au)
- *Seaspray Caravan Park* (Ph 08 9927 1165, www.seaspraybeachresort.com.au)

Moonlight over Port Denison

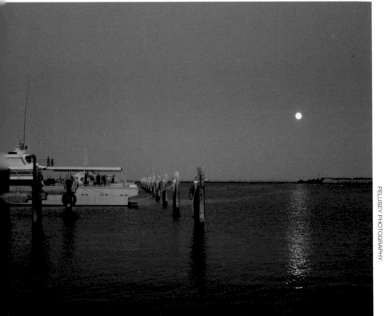

PELUSEY PHOTOGRAPHY

Shady main street of Dongara

PELUSEY PHOTOGRAPHY

Greenough (Map 7 F6)

The historic hamlet of Greenough was settled by tough pioneer farmers who established the settlement in the 1800s. Many of the buildings from this time have been preserved and become a major attraction. The **Greenough Historic Settlement** is open seven days a week for visitors to wander through. Run by the National Trust of WA, it contains 11 restored buildings including a gaol, courthouse, police station and churches. A café also serves lunches, coffee and cakes.

Separated by the Brand Highway is another aspect of Greenough: the superbly restored **Hampton Arms Hotel** (1864). Murder mystery dinners are held at the hotel and the owner also has a spectacular display of rare and secondhand books for sale. Browsing through the books, followed by a drink or meal is a great way to spend a few hours. Nearby is the **Greenough Pioneer Museum** (Ph 08 9926 1058), which is in a homestead built in the 1860s. The old homestead has an eerie feeling, especially the room supposedly haunted by 'grandma'.

Further up the road is another small settlement, at the **Greenough River**. The river itself is great for gentle **boating** and the **Greenough River Nature Trail** is a 17km loop that follows both sides of the scenic **Devlin Pool**. This scenic trail is open to walkers and mountain bikers, with a shorter section open

PELUSEY PHOTOGRAPHY

Greenough coastline

to 4WD vehicles. Part of Devlin Pool is open to **water-skiing**. The mouth of the river is usually covered by a sandbar. **Walk trails** also lead to the sandbar and onto the beach, and 4WDs also drive along here to get to good fishing spots.

When heading toward Geraldton look out for **leaning trees**, a testament to the prevailing winds that windsurfers love so much.

Information

For information contact the **Greenough Visitor Centre** at the Greenough Hamlet. (Ph 08 9926 1084)

Where to stay

- *Rock of Ages B&B* (Ph 08 9926 1154, www.members.westnet.com.au/rockofages)
- *Greenough River Resort* (Ph 9921 5888, www.members.westnet.com.au/grenor)
- *Greenough Rivermouth Caravan Park* (Ph 1800 800 580, 08 9921 5845)
- *S-Bend Caravan Park* (Ph 08 9926 1072)

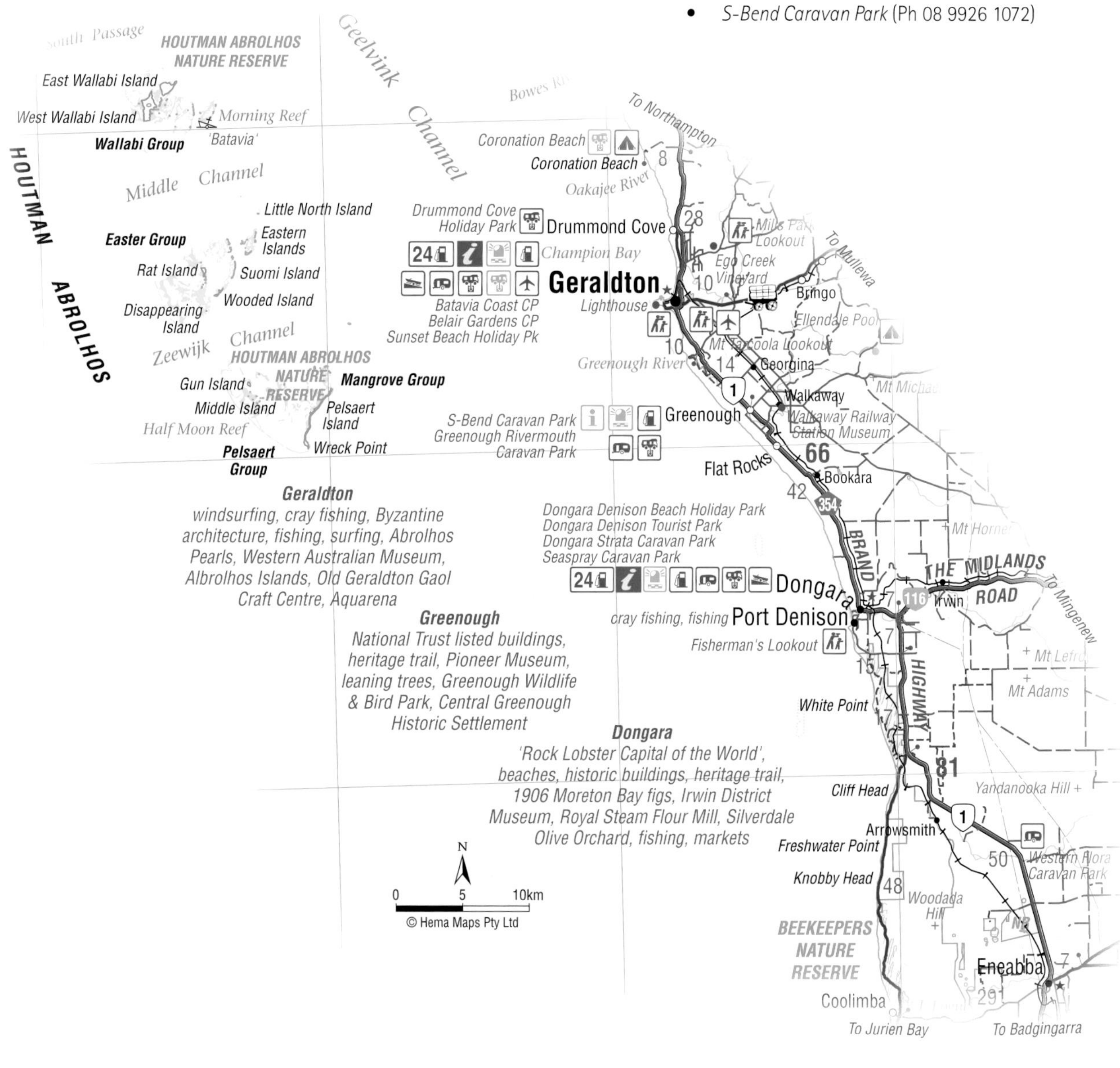

HOUTMAN ABROLHOS NATURE RESERVE
East Wallabi Island
West Wallabi Island
Morning Reef
'Batavia'
Wallabi Group
Middle Channel
HOUTMAN ABROLHOS
Little North Island
Easter Group
Eastern Islands
Rat Island
Suomi Island
Wooded Island
Disappearing Island
Zeewijk Channel
Gun Island
Middle Island
Mangrove Group
Pelsaert Island
Half Moon Reef
Wreck Point
Pelsaert Group
Geelvink Channel
Coronation Beach
Oakajee River
To Northampton
Drummond Cove Holiday Park
Drummond Cove
Champion Bay
Geraldton
Batavia Coast CP
Belair Gardens CP
Sunset Beach Holiday Pk
Lighthouse
Greenough River
Mills Park Lookout
Ego Creek Vineyard
To Mullewa
Bringo
Ellendale Pool
Mt Tarcoola Lookout
Georgina
Walkaway
Walkaway Railway Station Museum
S-Bend Caravan Park
Greenough Rivermouth Caravan Park
Greenough
Flat Rocks
Bookara
Dongara Denison Beach Holiday Park
Dongara Denison Tourist Park
Dongara Strata Caravan Park
Seaspray Caravan Park
Dongara
THE MIDLANDS ROAD
Irwin
To Mingenew
cray fishing, fishing Port Denison
Fisherman's Lookout
BRAND HIGHWAY
Mt Adams
White Point
Cliff Head
Yandanooka Hill
Arrowsmith
Freshwater Point
Western Flora Caravan Park
Knobby Head
Woodada Hill
BEEKEEPERS NATURE RESERVE
Eneabba
Coolimba
To Jurien Bay
To Badgingarra

Geraldton
windsurfing, cray fishing, Byzantine architecture, fishing, surfing, Abrolhos Pearls, Western Australian Museum, Albrolhos Islands, Old Geraldton Gaol Craft Centre, Aquarena

Greenough
National Trust listed buildings, heritage trail, Pioneer Museum, leaning trees, Greenough Wildlife & Bird Park, Central Greenough Historic Settlement

Dongara
'Rock Lobster Capital of the World', beaches, historic buildings, heritage trail, 1906 Moreton Bay figs, Irwin District Museum, Royal Steam Flour Mill, Silverdale Olive Orchard, fishing, markets

N
0 5 10km

Houtman Abrolhos Islands

The Abrolhos Islands is one of the most significant natural and historic landmarks in Western Australia. These 122 islands, and many more coral outcrops, are scattered over 80km of Indian Ocean. There are three separate groups of islands: the **Wallabi Group**, **Easter Group** and **Pelsaert Group**. At the closest point, the Abrolhos Islands is 60km west of Geraldton. With the exception of **North Island**, most of these islands are barely above sea level. Early explorers must have found these treacherous reefs and islands a nightmare to navigate. Just 10 years after the islands' discovery by Dutch navigator **Frederick Houtman**, Australia suffered its second oldest shipwreck when the *Batavia* went down (see p8). The islands are a haven for nesting **seabirds**, and thus attracted **guano miners** in the 1880s. In the 1940s, **rock lobster fisherman** started utilising the bountiful seas and built a few shacks. These shacks gradually grew in number as more families took up residence during the lobster-fishing season, from mid-March to the end of June. For the other nine months, the islands are largely left to the seabirds.

The Abrolhos also boasts an incredible range of tropical and temperate **marinelife** thanks to the Leeuwin Current. Warm ocean temperatures, strong currents and plenty of sunshine provide a perfect cocktail for luxuriant **coral** growth. Over 180 species of staghorn, plate and brain corals thrive in the clear, unpolluted waters. Attracted to this coral and nutrient-rich waters are numerous tropical species of **fish** including angel fish, Moorish idols, parrot fish, butterfly fish, anemone fish, cod and baldchin groper. On the deep outer edges of islands wait predators such as Spanish mackerel, tuna, sharks and trevallies. Southern species also congregate around the islands including big tailor, dhufish and pink snapper. Amongst the coral reef ledges hide **rock lobsters**, the mainstay of a multi-million dollar industry off Geraldton. All this richness adds up to magnificent **scuba diving, snorkelling** and **fishing**.

Being isolated from mainland predators, the Abrolhos is also one of Western Australia's most important **seabird-breeding** areas. Over a million birds nest on these islands, including the **lesser noddy** – its only Australian breeding location. Landing on these islands is strictly controlled to avoid disturbing nesting birds.

Rock lobster shacks, Abrolhos Islands

PELUSEY PHOTOGRAPHY

Hooked into a Spanish mackerel at the Abrolhos Islands

PELUSEY PHOTOGRAPHY

Geraldton (Map 7 E6)

With a population of 33 000, Geraldton is the largest centre in the State north of Perth. Today it's a major port and administrative centre for the region, but Geraldton began as an outpost for convicts in the 1850s. Many of the early buildings were constructed by these convicts. Geraldton is the major port for the surrounding agriculture areas, particularly wheat, as well as the main centre for the rock lobster industry. With a new port planned at nearby Oakajee to service inland iron-ore mines, Geraldton looks set to continue to grow.

Information

The **Geraldton-Greenough Visitor Centre**, in the Bill Sewell Complex cnr Chapman Rd & Bayley St, can help with accommodation bookings. (Ph 1800 818 881, 08 9921 3999, www.geraldtontourist.com.au)

What to Do

Don't miss the **HMAS Sydney Memorial**, a moving tribute to the sailors who died in Australia's greatest maritime disaster. In November 1941, during a WWII battle, 645 Australian sailors were lost. The memorial features a silver dome of 645 seagulls, each representing one of the sailers lost on the *HMAS Sydney*. A bronze statue of a 1940s woman looks out to sea, representing grief, and a nearby structure signifies the bow of a ship. Every day at 10.30am there is a **free tour** of the memorial where volunteers explain the significance. (For customised tours contact Brian Clausen on Ph 08 9965 4978.) In May 2008, the wrecks of the *HMAS Sydney* and *Kormoran* were found off the Western Australian coast.

Walk the **boardwalk** at the **Batavia Coast Marina** and visit the state-of-the-art **WA Museum of Geraldton** where you'll be enthralled by Geraldton's tempestuous maritime history. This extension of the Perth Maritime Museum has a great display of the *Batavia*, a Dutch East India Company ship that ran aground at the Abrolhos Islands in 1629. The survivors made it to land only to face a bloody mutiny and over 100 were killed. The whole gruesome story is depicted in the museum with fascinating displays including the stone portico that was found on the ship. (Ph 08 9921 5080, www.museum.wa.gov.au/oursites/geraldton: open 9.30am - 4.30pm, excluding Wednesdays)

One of Geraldton's unique architectural gems is the **Cathedral of St Francis Xavier**. The cathedral is one of many designed by **Monsieur Hawes**, who built religious buildings with an interesting combination of Gothic and Romanesque styles across the Wheatbelt. He was a successful architect in England before he changed direction and became an Anglican missionary, and then

HMAS Sydney Memorial in Geraldton

COLIN KERR

Geraldton Cathedral

PELUSEY PHOTOGRAPHY

Fishing near Geraldton

PELUSEY PHOTOGRAPHY

converted to Catholicism. Monsignor Hawes arrived in Australia in 1916 to become the parish priest in Mullewa, and he left his mark by building distinctive houses of worship from chapels to cathedrals. To get the full atmosphere of this trail pick up the *Monsignor Hawes Heritage Trail* booklet in the Geraldton visitors centre.

Another point of architectural interest is the distinctively red and white striped **Point Moore Lighthouse**. Built in the 1870s, it was the first steel tower ever constructed in Australia.

The **Marra Aboriginal Art Gallery**, at the Bill Sewell Complex, displays a variety of work by artists from the Yamaji region (Ph 08 9965 3440; open 10am-2pm Mon-Fri or by appt).

Fishing

Geraldton has a large fishing fleet, with western rock lobster boats and fishing boats. Fresh produce can be bought from the **Geraldton Fish Market**. If you happen to be visiting between mid-November and the end of June you'll have a chance to see Geraldton's major rock lobster fishing industry in action. Lobster boats unload their catches at **Fishermen's Wharf** and you can tour the **Geraldton Fishermen's Co-operative processing facilities**. (Ph 08 9965 9000, www.brolos.com.au; or contact the visitor centre for times and dates.)

Needless to say, Geraldton is a major centre for **recreational fishing** too. For boats, the **Abrolhos Islands** is the ultimate destination. But this destination is not for everyone because seaworthy boats and skilled boat handling are prerequisites for fishing these potentially treacherous islands. If in doubt, go on a charter – there are plenty available. Bottom fishing rewards anglers with pink snapper, dhufish, coral trout, baldchin groper, cod and many others. Trolling will lure Spanish mackerel, tuna, amberjacks and yellowtail kingfish. Further out, the game fishers get amongst marlin, dolphin fish and sailfish. Many of these species are also caught around reefs in waters off other parts of Geraldton.

Beach fishing is popular, with tailor and mulloway the big targets. Places such as **Coronation Beach**, **Sunset Beach** and **Drummonds Cove** are the busiest spots, especially on summer evenings when the tailor are running. The **Geraldton harbour** and breakwater are good for herring, silver trevally and whiting, with the odd mulloway at night.

Beaches

Geraldton is famous for its beaches, but also its wind. So there is a no doubt wind sports, such as **windsurfing** and **kitesurfing**, are big here. Some beaches, like **Town Beach**, are better for swimming.

Organised Tours

- *Batavia Coast Dive Academy* – Abrolhos charter dives, South Tomi wreck dives and training (Ph 08 9921 4229, www.bcda.com.au)
- *Batavia Coast Air Charter* – Abrolhos Islands, Pinnacles, Monkey Mia & Kalbarri gorges (Ph 1300 660 834, www.abrolhosbat.com.au)
- *Shine Aviation Services* – Abrolhos Islands and Kalbarri National Park (Ph 08 9923 3600, www.tropicair.com.au)
- *Yamatji Cultural Trails* – offer tours around the Geraldton area with the chance to sleep under the stars (Ph 08 9956 1126)

Where to Stay

There are many accommodation options available, so check with the Geraldton Visitor Centre or book online at their website.

Some of the more inexpensive options include:

- *Batavia Coast Caravan Park* (Ph 08 9938 1222, www.bataviacoastcp.com.au)
- *Belair Gardens Caravan Park* (Ph 08 9921 1997, www.belairgardenscaravanpark.com.au)
- *Foreshore Backpackers* (Ph 08 9921 3275)
- *Sunset Beach Holiday Park* (Ph 08 9938 1655, 1800 353 389, www.sunsetpark.com.au)

Chapman Valley

The **Chapman River** meanders through the Chapman Valley, which is now the location of the State's most northerly wineries. Wine is a fairly new product for the region, and you can follow the **Chapman Valley wine-tasting trail** to sample the local vintages.

In winter and spring, touring around the surprisingly green flat-topped hills of the **Moresby Range** and its valleys is a pleasurable experience. Follow one of the **day trips** around the Chapman Valley to experience the scenery and **wildflowers**. (For more information on these day trips see the Shire of Chapman Valley website, www.chapmanvalley.wa.gov.au.)

Point Moore lighthouse

PELUSEY PHOTOGRAPHY

Northampton (Map 7 D6)

Northampton is a historic town that was registered with the National trust in 1993. First settled in 1848, it is one of WA's oldest settlements and has a myriad of heritage buildings from the early farming times. There is also plenty of **wildflower** colour in spring, including the lovely feather flowers and pink everlastings.

Information

The **Northampton Visitor Centre** is in the Old Police Station, in Hampton Rd. (Ph 08 9934 1488, www.northamptonwa.com.au)

What to Do

To see the town's **heritage buildings**, follow the **Hampton Road Heritage Walk Trail** (a brochure is available from the visitor centre). The buildings include **Chiverton House** (1895) and the visitor centre, which was the old police station. During the September/October school holidays the historic buildings are draped with the spectacular craftwork of quilters for the annual **Airing of the Quilts**.

The first public railway in Western Australia ran from Geraldton to Northampton in 1879. A static display of railway memorabilia is now on display at the **Northampton Railway Station** (1913).

The **St Mary's in Ara Coeli Church** (1936) and **Sacred Heart Convent** (1919) next door were both designed by Monsignor Hawes. To see all the buildings he was responsible for throughout the Mid West, follow the **Monsignor Hawes Heritage Trail** (see p53).

Between Geraldton and Northampton you will find the 1860 **Oakabella Homestead and Tearooms (7 D6)**.

North of Northampton, visit the **Independent Principality Of Hutt River (7 C5)**. In 1970 Prince Lennard and Princess Shirley seceded from the rest of Australia to become a new principality. They even have their own money and stamps. Visitors are welcome daily between 10am and 4pm, and basic camping/caravan sites are available (www.principality-hutt-river.com).

Where to Stay

- *Coronation Beach camping area* – on the coast between Geraldton and Northampton (Ph 08 9920 5011)
- *Hampton Rose B&B* (Ph 08 9934 1244)
- *Jidamya B&B* (Ph 08 9934 1024, http://members.westnet.com.au/jidamya/)
- *Ninghan Park Farmstay* – at Isseka, between Geraldton and Northampton (Ph 08 9934 2550, 0488 695 451, www.ninghanpark.com)
- *Northampton Caravan Park* (Ph 0439 979 489, www.northamptoncaravanpark.com)
- *The Old Convent* – budget accommodation (Ph 08 9934 1692)
- *Old Miners' Cottages* (Ph 08 9934 1864, 0429 312 031, www.starlightcouple.com)
- *Railway Tavern* – also known as Northampton's 'Bottom Pub' (Ph 08 9934 1120, www.railwaytavern.com.au)

Northampton history

PELUSEY PHOTOGRAPHY

Horrocks (Map 7 D5)

The popular holiday and fishing village of **Horrocks** is located just 22km from Northampton. Early Aboriginal cave paintings, and some interesting rock formations, can be seen at the **Bowes River mouth** (see the Northampton Visitor Centre for information). The other main feature is beautiful **Three Mile Beach**, which is protected by an outer reef.

What to Do

Horrocks offers great **swimming**, **fishing**, **surfing**, **diving**, **windsurfing** and other beachside activities. From June to around November you also have a good chance of seeing migrating **humpback whales** – the whale-watching lookout is the best vantage point.

Horrocks is one of those places where dinghy **anglers** can safely fish within protected water inside an expansive reef. Tailor, whiting and silver trevally are the main fare. For a more leisurely fishing experience, the town jetty is quite good for herring and tailor, and worth a go at night for lovers of squid. Anglers wishing to get amongst big tailor, mulloway and sharks can try more exposed beaches with gutters. However, the best spots are only accessible by 4WD. Good launching facilities make it easy for owners of small boats to access deeper water for the usual prized species common along this stretch of coastline.

Where to Stay

- *Horrocks Beachside Cottages* – 12 self-contained cottages (Ph 08 9934 3031)
- *Horrocks Beach Caravan Park* (Ph 08 9934 3039, www.horrocksbeachcaravanpark.com.au)

Port Gregory (Map 7 C5)

An easy 47km drive from Northampton, **Port Gregory** only has a population of about 50 but it does swell with visitors during school holidays. Heading to Port Gregory from Horrocks, you cannot help but notice the appropriately named **Pink Lake**. And yes, it really is pink most of the time.

What to Do

Like, Horrocks, Port Gregory has a protective outer reef that provides a safe playground for families on holiday. Beachside barbecues and shelters add to make it a good location to enjoy a nice day by the beach. All this means Port Gregory is all about **fishing**, **diving** and **boating**.

Port Gregory offers good fishing for small species inside the reef in calm waters and off the town jetty. Boat anglers can get out deep when conditions are good to get amongst dhufish, snapper, baldchin groper and Spanish mackerel in autumn. Heading north, before Kalbarri, you will notice a sign pointing to **Wagoe Beach**. In a 4WD you can find gutters along this sensational stretch of coastline where sharks, giant tailor, mulloway and any number of other species are regularly caught. This is beach fishing at its most exciting. (See the Kalbarri section below for details of the accommodation and quad bike tours at Wagoe Beach.)

Just before entering Port Gregory, you will notice a curious assortment of stone buildings. Established in 1853 the **Lynton Hiring Station** employed convicts to work at the local Geraldine Mine and nearby pastoral stations.

Where to Stay

Port Gregory Caravan Pk (Ph 08 9935 1052, www.portgregory.com)

Kalbarri (Map 13 K5)

Kalbarri didn't become a town until the 1950s when it was discovered that the fishing was pretty good. Soon other delights became apparent and hardy tourists began braving the rough unsealed road into town. Now it is a thriving town of over 2000 lucky souls, with fishing and tourism the biggest industries.

At 590km north of Perth, Kalbarri is far enough north to enjoy a mild winter climate with an average daytime temperature of 22°C. Summer temperatures sometimes top 45°C.

Kalbarri means edible seed in the local Aboriginal language, so when you drive into town in spring it is not surprising there is an amazing amount of bushtucker. The land is also ablaze in flowers.

Information

The **Kalbarri Visitor Centre** is at 70 Grey St in the Allen Community Centre. (Ph 1800 639 468, www.kalbarriwa.info)

What to Do

The question should be what is there not to do? Many visitors spend their whole annual leave here, and for good reason.

Kalbarri National Park River Gorges

Driving along the river road into Kalbarri it is hard to imagine there is much out there, however that is because you can't see the great eroded landscape the river has created in the relatively flat plain. The **Murchison River** is a permanent and gently flowing river most of the time but occasionally cyclonic rains transform it into a raging flood of rare force. Over the millennia these forces of nature have carved deep meandering gorges into the ancient colourful sandstone. Places to view the gorges and

Hawks Head is one great place to view Kalbarri National Park's gorges.

COLIN KERR

Nature's Window in the early morning light.

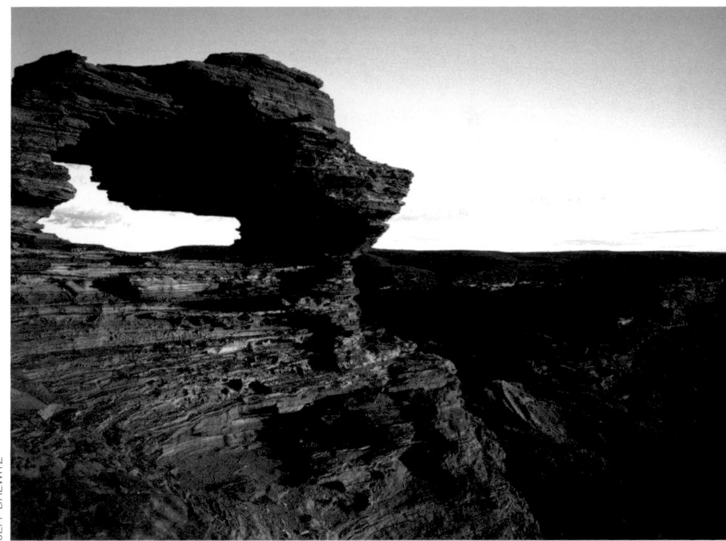

JEFF DREWITZ

The Loop, Kalbarri National Park

PELUSEY PHOTOGRAPHY

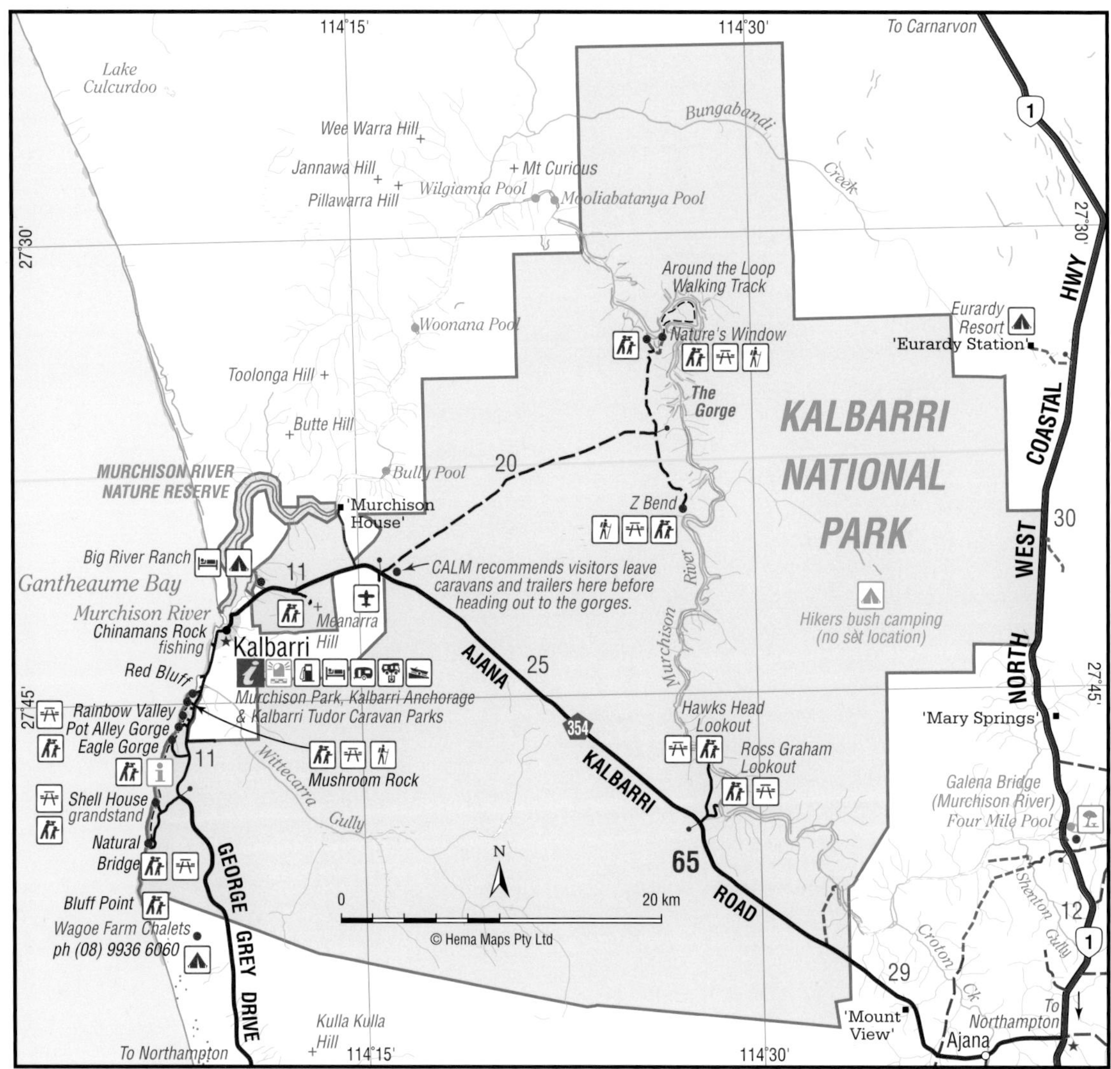

river are **Nature's Window**, **Z Bend**, the **Loop** and **Hawks Head**. **Walking** and **kayaking** are the major activities in these gorges. Add some ropes and there is **rock climbing** and **abseiling** for the adventurous. The Loop, which is challenging in places, is for experienced walkers and is one of WA's Top Trails (see p32). It is 8km with some rock scrambling, but you can cool off with a swim in the river.

To explore Kalbarri National Park's gorges, ask about the treks through **Kalbarri Adventure Tours**. (Ph 08 9937 1667, www.kalbarritours.com.au)

Kalbarri National Park Coastal Gorges

Kalbarri's spectacular coastal gorges are actually the southern extremity of the **Zuytdorp Cliffs** that continue all the way to Shark Bay. Evocative names like **Red Bluff**, **Pot Alley**, **Blue Holes**, **Eagle Gorge**, **Mushroom Rock** and **Natural Bridge** describe the rock formations that were forged by the sea. The best way to see this spectacular coastline, where cliffs rise up to 100m above the ocean, is to drive to the designated **lookouts**, then get the boots on and go for a walk. For a short amble, Mushroom Rock is a beauty but for a longer walk there is the **Bigurda Trail** (8km one-way).

For a great spot to see the sun set over the Indian Ocean, head to **Eagle Gorge Lookout** where the coastal cliffs light up in a rainbow of colours. When not looking at the cliff colour, don't forget to keep an eye out for the telltale spray of water that signifies the migration of **humpback whales**. This is usually between June and November.

Fishing

It is hard to know where to start when summing up Kalbarri as a fishing location because this place offers almost every type of fishing available to the angler.

The **coastal cliffs** and **reef platforms** make for exciting rock fishing for catches of big fish. When winds blow offshore, keen anglers can get amongst Spanish mackerel and tuna using the ballooning technique. Otherwise heaving out weighted mulies or pilchards can land you some of the biggest tailor caught anywhere in Australia, along with snapper and mulloway. The cliffs near **Red Bluff** are a popular rock-fishing hot spot.

Warning: Do not fish if there is a swell about as you could end up in the water. These rocks are prone to king waves. For safety, never fish alone.

If you are fishing in the **estuary**, black bream and whiting are the target species inside the mouth of the **Murchison River**. Upstream the bream are bigger and cagier. **Chinaman Rock** at the entrance to the river is a good spot for mulloway and tailor. On the northern side of the river mouth is **Oyster Reef**, where tailor up to 6kg are caught along with snapper and mulloway. You need a dinghy or kayak to get to the other side of the estuary and then you need to lug the gear across the sandbar. Walk further north a bit to the well-named **Frustration Rock**, but make sure you take plenty of spare tackle as the rocky terrain gobbles it up. The rewards are big tailor and big mulloway. Although lugging back a 30kg mulloway seems like hard work.

The rewards for getting out into the deep blue on a **boat** are the stuff of legends. Negotiating the particularly tricky river mouth however, can be a problem. If there is any swell about, wait for a lull then go for it. Rock lobster professionals do this all the time, but even they draw the line if it's rough out there and so should you. Once out there it's a smorgasbord: you can troll for Spanish mackerel, tailor and tuna, or go deep to get stuck into dhufish, coral trout, baldchin groper, pink snapper and other bottom feeders. The fun and games continue when you have to run the gauntlet back through the mouth again. If you haven't got a boat, don't despair as **charter fishing companies** do operate from Kalbarri.

Fishing Charters

- **Kalbarri Explorer** – deep sea fishing (Ph 08 9937 2027, www.kalbarriexplorer.com.au)
- **Reefwalker Adventure Tours** – reef fishing for experienced, average and beginners (Ph 08 99371356, www.reefwalker.com.au)
- **The Specialists Ocean Safaris** – deep sea and game fishing (Ph 0417 912 901, www.thespecialists.com.au)

Boat Hire

- **Kalbarri Boat Hire and Canoe Safaris** – hire powerboats for river use, canoes, kayaks, surfcats, paddle boats or a barracuda bike (Ph 08 9937 1245, www.kalbarriiboathire.com)
- **Murchison Boat Hire** – one- to seven-day boat hire (Ph 08 9937 2043, www.murchisonboathire.com.au)

Coastal Cruises

- **Kalbarri Extreme** – jet-boat rides through the Murchison River mouth (Ph 0407 371 393)
- **Kalbarri Wilderness Cruises** – lunchtime and sunset cruises on the Murchison River (Ph 08 9937 2259, www.kalbarricruises.com.au)
- **The Specialists Ocean Safaris** – sunset cruises (Ph 0417 912 901, www.thespecialists.com.au)

Fishing at Red Bluff, Kalbarri

PELUSEY PHOTOGRAPHY

Rainbow Jungle

PELUSEY PHOTOGRAPHY

PELUSEY PHOTOGRAPHY

Jacques Point on an average day.

Surfing

- **Jacques Point** is an institution for local surfers, and on big days it can take your breath away. The surf break rolls in alongside a rocky point, so spectators get up close and personal as the surfers pass.

Kayaking & Canoeing

Kayaking near the mouth of the **Murchison River** at Kalbarri is popular, but stay away from the mouth where strong outgoing currents can cause problems at times. Further upstream, experienced paddlers can enjoy the gorges from a water-level perspective. You can take a tour or hire a canoe or kayak and head out on your own.

Organised Tours

- **Kalbarri Adventure Tours** – one hour canoe tours of the Kalbarri gorges (Ph 08 9937 1667, www.kalbarritours.com.au)
- **Kalbarri Boat Hire and Canoe Safaris** – canoe safaris (Ph 08 9937 1245, www.kalbarriiboathire.com)
- **Kalbarri Safari Tours** – 4WD & canoe tour (Ph 08 9937 1011, 0407 371 011, www.kalbarrisafaritours.com.au)

Watching Wildlife

June to December is the best time to spot **whales** off the coast from Kalbarri. There are numerous vantage points around the area and tours operate too. The town is also home to the Seahorse Sanctuary, Kalbarri Oceanarium and Rainbow Jungle Parrot Breeding Centre. At 8:45am on the river foreshore, prepare for a flapping experience when the local Kalbarri **pelicans** glide in for a feed.

At the world-class **Rainbow Jungle Parrot Centre**, the wonderful free-flight areas are a great way to see the rare and endangered parrots. A breeding centre for Australian and exotic parrots, this facility is set in beautifully landscaped gardens making it a 'must-visit' for bird lovers or garden lovers alike. (Ph 08 9937 1248, www.rainbowjunglekalbarri.com; open 9am-5pm Mon-Sat, 10am-5pm Sun, last admission 4pm)

At the **Seahorse Sanctuary**, seahorses are breed for the aquarium market. Take a self-guided tour through the breeding stable and relax afterwards with a Devonshire tea. (Ph 08 9937 1124, www.seahorsesanctuary.com.au; open 10am-4pm Tue-Sun, 10am-4pm 7 days in school holidays & closed Feb)

See a huge variety of fish and other marine life in large aquariums and touch pools at the **Kalbarri Oceanarium**. It's a great way to see the region's marine life without getting wet! (open 10am-4pm daily)

Organised Wildlife Tours

- **Reefwalker Adventure Tours** – whale watching and dolphin encounters (Ph 08 99371356, www.reefwalker.com.au)
- **The Specialists Ocean Safaris** – whale watching (Ph 0417 912 901, www.thespecialists.com.au)

Coral Coast

Wildflowers

In spring, from August to October, the Kalbarri region is aglow with the myriad of colours from wildflowers. As Kalbarri is nestled in sandplain country, the soil quality is poor so no one species of flora can dominate. Therefore diversity is the name of the game and flowering plants come in all sorts of colours and shapes. The tall yellow grevilleas that line the road into Kalbarri is a sight to behold, and then there are numerous banksia species, smokebushes, featherflowers and red kangaroo paws too.

Scenic Flights

Fly over Kalbarri's coastal cliffs at sunset with **Kalbarri Scenic Flights** for a different view of the region. They also operate a trip to the Abrolhos Islands for snorkelling and one to Monkey Mia to feed the dolphins. (Ph 08 9937 1130, www.kalbarricharter.com.au)

Other land-based tours

- **Kalbarri Abseil** – full- and half-day abseiling tours suitable for beginners to experienced (Ph 08 9937 1618, www.abseilaustralia.com.au)
- **Kalbarri Safari Tours** – 1, 2 and 3 hour quad-bike safaris (Ph 08 9937 1011, 0407 371 011, www.kalbarrisafaritours.com.au)
- **Kalbarri Sandboarding** – sandboarding from 'nursery' dunes to the more extreme (Ph 08 9937 2377, www.sandboardingaustralia.com.au)
- **Wagoe Beach Quad Bike Tours** – see sand dunes and wildlife along Wagoe Beach, 20km south of Kalbarri (Ph 08 9936 6060, www.wagoe.com.au)

Where to Stay

As a popular holiday and tourist destination, Kalbarri has a wide range of accommodation available including resorts, apartments, villas and holiday houses. See the visitor centre website to book.

Caravan Parks

- *Kalbarri Anchorage Caravan Park* (Ph 08 9937 1181)
- *Kalbarri Tudor Holiday Park* (Ph 08 9937 1077, www.tudorholidaypark.com.au)
- *Murchison Park Caravan Park* (Ph 08 9937 1005, www.murcp.com)

Farm Stays

- *Big River Ranch* – accommodation & camping, also offer horse riding (Ph 08 9937 1214, www.bigriverranch.net)
- *Eurardy Resort* – north on the North West Coastal Hwy (Ph 08 9936 1038)
- *Riverside Sanctuary* – northeast of Kalbarri, off the highway (Ph 08 9936 1021, www.riversidesanctuary.com.au)
- *Wagoe Farm Chalets* – between Port Gregory and Kalbarri, bookings required (Ph 08 9936 6060, www.wagoe.com.au)

Caravan park, Kalbarri

PELUSEY PHOTOGRAPHY

PELUSEY PHOTOGRAPHY

Shark Bay

The Outback Coast

The most northerly part of the Coral Coast, the Outback Coast is where the dry Golden Outback region meets the Indian Ocean. Places like Carnarvon rarely see much rain, with thunderstorms or the occasional cyclone filling the ephemeral rivers inland. To see the mighty Gascoyne River in flood is an unforgettable experience. The Outback Coast includes Shark Bay, Carnarvon, Exmouth and Ningaloo Marine Park, and the contrast in coastline is remarkable. Heading north, the Zuytdorp Cliffs make way for white sandy beaches, then mangrove-filled bays with muddy tidal flats, and finally the white sand of Ningaloo plunges into the crystal blue seas with coral reef.

The Outback Coast is a great place to wet a line with a wide range of fish species thanks to the southward flowing Leeuwin Current. Tropical species mingle with more southern species around Shark Bay and Carnarvon, while Ningaloo is truly tropical in its richness. This, together with the warmer weather, means the area becomes very busy in the winter months with people from the south looking for some sun.

Shark Bay (Map 13 E4)

In 1991 Shark Bay was declared a World Heritage site, and it is one of the few that are recognised for all four natural criteria. The **Shark Bay World Heritage Area** covers two peninsulas that protrude into the warm waters of Shark Bay, and those waters are home to the biggest **underwater grass beds** in the world. Aboriginal people have lived in the area for the last 30 000 years, so there are over 130 registered **heritage sites** too. Shark Bay is also recognised as one of the first places in Australia where Europeans landed. The Dutch landed on what is now called Dirk Hartog Island in 1616, and the French claimed sovereignty of the west coast of Australia here in 1772. English explorer **William Dampier** named the area 'The Bay of Sharks'.

The Shark Bay region covers a huge area of varied ecosystems, so for the visitor there is an endless range of possibilities. As soon as you turn off the North West Coastal Highway you are immersed in a series of unique natural phenomena. The World Heritage listing was given because of the world's largest seagrass beds, high saltwater tolerant species such as the cockle shells at Shell Beach and the amazing stromatolites at Hamelin Pool. Add the friendly dolphins at Monkey Mia and this place could easily keep you entertained for weeks.

Information

The **Denham & Monkey Mia Visitor Centre** is at 27 Thornbill Loop in Denham (Ph 1300 135 887, www.sharkbaywa.com.au). Information is also available from the **Shark Bay World Heritage Discovery Centre** at 29 Knight Terrrace in Denham (Ph 08 9948 1590, www.sharkbayvisit.com or www.sharkbayinterpretivecentre.com.au).

Several websites are also are good sources of information, including the **DEC's website** www.sharkbay.org.au and the **Shire of Shark Bay** site www.sharkbay.wa.gov.au/tourism.

Fishing

Shark Bay's huge area and many marine ecosystems make the region an angler's paradise. It is one of those places where tropical and temperate waters mix, ensuring a rich choice of fish species to target. There are several main angling regions, including Zuytdorp Cliffs and Steep Point, Henri Freycinet Harbour, and Dirk Hartog Island.

Just a reminder, **fishing regulations** for the Shark Bay area are complex and changeable so it's essential to get the latest information before you give fishing a go. (Contact the Shark Bay District Office at 89 Knight Terrace in Denham, Ph 08 9948 1210. See Regulations p36 for more details.)

The protected and shallow waters of **Henri Freycinet Harbour (13 E3)** are a big pink snapper hotspot. These snapper can be caught using light gear because the terrain is fairly open. A half pilchard, single hook on a short trace and a small running sinker is all you need. Fishing for pink snapper in the Shark Bay region is governed by strict regulations as they are very vulnerable to exploitation. There are minimum and maximum size limits for snapper and strict catch restrictions. A blue tag system is

PELUSEY PHOTOGRAPHY

Beach fishing in Shark Bay

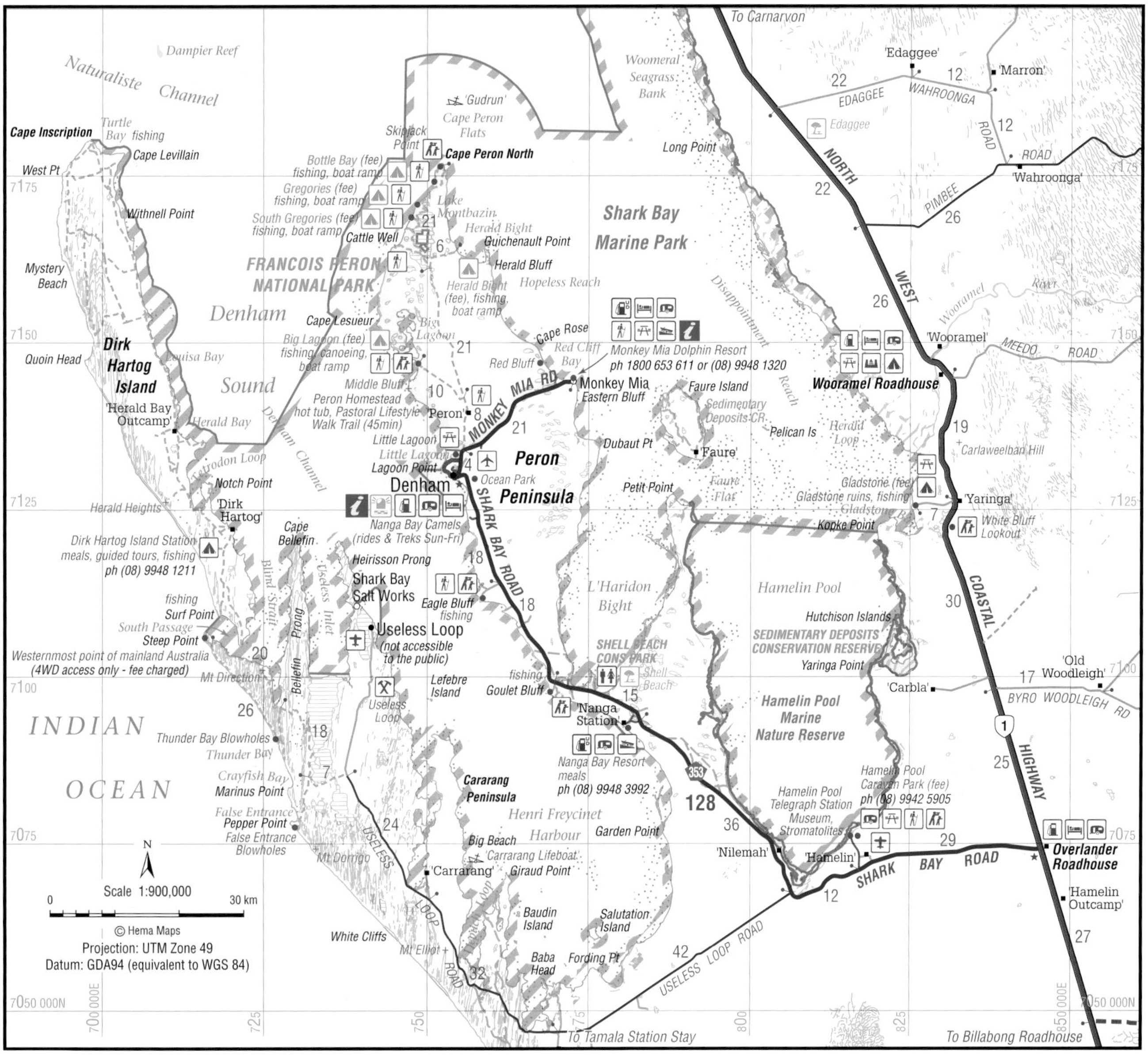

strictly enforced in Henri Freycinet Harbour, so if you are thinking of fishing for snapper here you must purchase these tags. **Tamala Station (13 F3)** offers camping and a few basic bungalows near the beach and you can launch dinghies from the shore. On the **Peron Peninsula** side of the harbour, camping, powered caravan sites and boat launching ramps are located at **Nanga Station (13 E4)**, another snapper hotspot.

The deep waters off **Shark Bay**, **Dirk Hartog Island** and **Zuytdorp Cliffs** offer magnificent fishing for experienced boat anglers when the sea and weather conditions are conducive. Deep-sea species include cod, Spanish mackerel, tuna, yellowtail kingfish, cobia, marlin, sailfish and snapper. Anglers flicking out lures or fish baits often tackle giant tailor and other pelagic fish from boats close to the cliffs. This method is seriously dangerous and certainly not to be undertaken when swells are up.

Zuytdorp Cliffs

PELUSEY PHOTOGRAPHY

Stromatolites, Hamelin Pool

PELUSEY PHOTOGRAPHY

Shell quarry

PELUSEY PHOTOGRAPHY

Hamelin Pool (Map 13 E5)

In 1884, a telegraph station was built at **Hamelin Pool** as a repeater station between Geraldton and Roebourne. Later it was also a pastoral station. It wasn't until 1956, that scientists discovered the wonder that lives in the warm shallow water of Hamelin Bay when what was thought to be rocks in the bay, turned out to be **stromatolites**. These strange rock-like lumps are actually slow-growing living microorganisims that are believed to be the earliest forms of life on Earth. Shark Bay's stromatolites are only 2000 to 3000 years old, but they are similar to lifeforms found on Earth up to 3.5 billion years ago. The stromatolites that live in these warm, shallow and very salty waters are the centrepiece of the unique **Hamelin Pool Marine Nature Reserve (13 D4)**. Walk out along the boardwalk for easy viewing.

As well as seeing the stromatolites, visitors can see a shell block quarry near the shoreline and the historic **Flint Cliff Telegraph Station**. The Station is now a museum. While camping isn't allowed on the Reserve's beach, the adjacent **Hamelin Pool Caravan Park** offers camping and caravan sites.

Where to stay

- *Hamelin Pool Caravan Park* – on Shark Bay Rd, 29km from the North West Coastal Hwy (Ph 08 9942 5905)

Steep Point (Map 13 D2)

A 4WD track leads out along the **Cararang Peninsula** to the most westerly spot on the Australian mainland – **Steep Point**. It is a legendary **fishing** spot but even if fishing is not your thing, just the scenery and abundant marine life make it worth the trip. Steep Point is situated on a series of sheer drops, part of the **Zuytdorp Cliffs**. You can **4WD** along the top of the cliffs which plunge 170m to the pounding sea below, **camp** on the pristine beaches of the **Inside Passage** and go exploring to **Thunder Bay**. Just around the corner from Steep Point are the sheltered white beaches and aqua waters of **South Passage**.

The camping is 'BYO everything' and remember to take plenty of drinking water and fuel. If you don't have your own 4WD you can take a tour from Denham. A permit, entry fee, camping fees and refundable environment levy apply for Steep Point, see www.steeppoint.com.au for details or contact the ranger on Ph 08 9948 3993. The area is in transition to becoming **Edel Land National Park**. Contact the ranger for the latest access information.

The salt-mining operation township of **Useless Loop (13 D3)**, which exports high-grade industrial salt around the world, is not accessible to the public.

Fishing

Although **Steep Point (13 D2)** is the westernmost location on the Australian mainland, it's the fishing that is the big attraction. Although some may argue the point, the rock platform near Steep Point is Australia's premier onshore **game-fishing** location. However, you need to know what you are doing. Hardcore anglers using heavy rods, big side cast and overhead reels float fish baits dangling below balloons. Offshore winds blow the balloon rigs out into deep water well beyond casting range. Spanish mackerel and tuna are the main targets, although marlin and sailfish strikes can add moments of intense excitement. Fishing with heavy rods with fish bait or squid off the bottom near the cliff base produces pink snapper, emperors, trevallies, mulloway and line-busting yellowtail kingfish. Long gaffs or fly gaffs are essential for landing any big fish off the cliffs. Steep Point is heavily fished, so some anglers try cliff platforms to the south along the spectacular **Zuytdorp Cliffs**. Although the rewards can be spectacular, this form of fishing is dangerous and not for the fainthearted.

The huge **Dirk Hartog Island (13 C1)** has endless fishing possibilities, with similar rock-fishing locations to those at Steep Point but far less busy. The rewards are high but so are the risks as this is very dangerous coastline for rock fishing. On the leeside, sheltered shallow waters produce whiting, flathead, dart and the highly acclaimed bonefish. Light gear is the go here. Boat fishing off the western side is only limited by your imagination and the weather, of course.

Where to stay

- *Dirk Hartog Island Station – self-sufficient camping & shearers' quarters accommodation (Ph 08 9948 1211, www.dirkhartogisland.com)*
- *Steep Point* – along the Cararang Peninsula, self-sufficient camping only (Ph 08 9948 3993, www.steeppoint.com.au)
- *Tamala Station Stay* – off Useless Loop Rd, has campsites around the bays (Ph 08 9948 3994)

Denham (Map 13 D3)

Once just a sleepy fishing village, **Denham** still has that 'small town feel' although it can be very busy with tourists exploring the wonders of Shark Bay. Denham sits on the western side of the **Peron Peninsula**. As the service town for all the stations, and remoter tourist places in Shark Bay, it has a couple of shopping centres, tourist offices, tour operators, restaurants and accommodation.

Henry Mangles Denham was the first to survey Shark Bay in 1858 for the English Royal Navy who were looking for places to locate convicts. In the late 1800s, many camps were springing up around the bays, so in 1895 a township was mapped out. This is the Denham of today. Denham was always a fishing village until a caravan park was built and the Geraldton to Carnarvon Road was bituminised in the 1960s. The bitumen road from Denham to the Overlander Roadhouse wasn't completed until 1985.

The most westerly town in Australia, Denham is an ideal base from which to explore the entire Shark Bay region. Sightseeing tours and fishing charters can be arranged, and you can even book a safari trip out to **Steep Point** or **François Peron National Park** if you don't have your own 4WD. The **Shark Bay World Heritage Discovery Centre** should be your first stop in town, and you can also learn about the marine life at **Ocean Park** (7km south).

What to Do

There is family-friendly **jetty fishing** in Denham that produces squid at night, occasional black snapper, mulloway and whiting, while small boat anglers target tailor, snapper, mulloway and mackerel species in deep channels that run through those massive seagrass beds.

On the way up the Shark Bay Road from the **Overlander Roadhouse** to Denham are some interesting places to stop, including Project Eden, Shell Beach, and Goulet and Eagle bluffs.

Nanga Station (13 E3) is 'the place' to **fish** with a boat ramp ready for you to launch your dinghy or charter boats available to hire. While you are there, have a dip in the **hot artesian spa** or a meal at the 'Bull Pit' or restaurant.

Just north of Nanga Station is **Shell Beach** – one of only two beaches of its type in the world. Instead of sand, the beach is made up of billions of small shells compacted to many metres deep. These shells are unique to the area because the critter in the shell has adapted to the high saline water of Hamelin Pool. These shells eventually compact down to make the blocks quarried at Hamelin Pool and used in buildings in Denham. Wind down the windows as you pass the quarantine grid because recordings of barking dogs are used to keep feral cats out of the Peron Peninsula. This is part of **Project Eden**, a scheme to rid Peron Peninsula of feral cats and foxes, and introduce rare species in a relatively safe habitat. Following construction of the fence, a widespread and ongoing cat and fox extermination was conducted, with reasonable success. As a result, rare **malleefowls** and **bilbies** are now breeding in numbers. Introduced **woylies, banded-hare wallabies** and other endangered marsupials are hanging on despite cats remaining in the area – albeit in smaller numbers. In the future, more rare mammals will be introduced with the aim of increasing their numbers.

On the way to Denham, don't forget to stop in at **Goulet Bluff (13 D3)** and **Eagle Bluff (13 D3)** for great views over **Henri Freycinet Harbour**. The rock formations and cliffs glow gold in the late afternoon, and when the water is still the reflections are spectacular. **Camping** at these spots can be pre-arranged through the Shire of Shark Bay.

Tour Operators

There are many and varied tours in the Shark Bay Area. For a full list contact the Denham and Monkey Mia Visitor Centre.

- **Aqua Rush** – snorkelling in Shark Bay and speed boat cruise to Steep Point and Dirk Hartog Island (08 9949 1446, www.sharkbaysnorkel.com.au)
- **Jetwave Boat Charters** – day tours to Dirk Hartog Island and dive charters (Ph 08 9948 1211, www.jetwaveboatcharters.com.au)
- **Mac Attack Fishing Charters** – half or full day trips (Ph 08 9948 3776, www.sportfish.com.au)
- **Monkey Mia Yacht Charters** – see dolphins, dugongs and other marine creatures in Shark Bay, also various cruise options in Shark Bay including mini, morning, afternoon, sundown and Cape Peron (Ph 1800 030 427, www.monkey-mia.net)
- **Monkey Mia Wildsights** – three daily wildlife sailing cruises (Ph 1800 241 481, www.monkeymiawildsights.com.au)

Denham Bay

STEVEN DAVID MILLER, NATURAL WANDERS

COLIN KERR

Cape Peron offers great views down to the clear water below.

- **Shark Bay Air Charter** – flights over Shark Bay, Dirt Hartog Island, Ningaloo Reef, Coral Bay, Kalbarri National Park, Mt Augustus and the Kennedy Ranges (Ph 0417 919 059, www.sharkbayair.com.au)
- **Shark Bay Camel Safari** (Ph 08 9948 3136)
- **Wula Guda Nyinda Aboriginal Eco Adventures** – local indigenous dreaming and bushtucker trips (Ph 0429 708 847)

Where to stay

Denham has various accommodation options available, see the websites listed earlier for more information (pp58-59).

- *Bay Lodge*, Denham – budget accomm (Ph 08 9948 1278)
- *Blue Dolphin Caravan Park*, Denham (Ph 08 9948 1385)
- *Denham Seaside Tourist Village* (Ph 1300 133 733, www.sharkbayfun.com)
- *Eagle Bluff, Fowlers Camp, Whalebone & Goulet Bluff camping areas* – free bush camping areas run by the Shire of Shark Bay (for permission contact the Shark Bay World Heritage Discovery and Visitor Centre Ph 08 9948 1590)
- *Heritage Resort*, Denham (Ph 08 9948 1133, www.heritageresortsharkbay.com.au)
- *Nanga Bay Resort* – at Nanga Station 77km along Shark Bay Rd from the North West Coastal Hwy and 51km from Denham (Ph 08 9948 3992, www.nangabayresort.com.au)
- *Oceanside Village*, Denham (Ph 1800 680 600, www.oceanside.com.au)

François Peron National Park (Map 13 C3)

Heading north from Denham, on the way to Monkey Mia, the first turnoff is to **François Peron National Park**. The French claimed Western Australia in 1722, but it wasn't until the early 1800s that they returned to do some mapping. Two ships, the *Geographe* and the *Naturaliste*, with captains **Nicolas Baudin** and **Jacques Hamelin**, explored the area. **François Peron** was a naturalist on the *Geographe* and his name, along with that of shipmate **Louis de Freycinet**, is now well known around Shark Bay and the southern coastal parts of WA.

What to Do

Pastoralists raised sheep in the area until **Peron Station** was taken over by the government and turned into a national park in 1993. The **Peron Homestead** is still there and is the only part of the park that can be visited by 2WD. You can take a dip in a spa-like **'hot tub'** fed by a hot artesian bore near the homestead, but make sure you observe the warning signs to avoid ending up like a cooked lobster. The homestead is now the location of a modern **visitor centre**, and signboards on the **Station Life Walk Trail** tell the history of the property.

Just beyond the homestead, the track turns sandy and is definitely only suitable for high clearance **4WDs**. Remember to lower the tyre pressures too. The track passes by a series of **birridas** or **salt pans**. The hard-looking smooth surface of a birrida may tempt the inner hoon, but avoid the temptation. Take warning signs seriously as a thin crust hides slimy salty mud underneath that will swallow up your car in no time. On the way north to the tip of the peninsula there are **camping** areas with toilets and gas barbecues at **Bottle Bay**, **Gregories**, **South Gregories**, **Herald Bight** and **Big Lagoon**. (No fires are permitted in the park.)

At **Cape Peron**, rich red sand dunes meet white sandy beaches before entering the blue waters of Shark Bay. As a marine park, these waters are home to an incredible range of **marine life**. In winter the vegetation is a sea of colourful **wildflowers**. Once at Cape Peron, take the 1.5km **Wanamalu Trail** along the cliffs to **Skipjack Point** with views down the cliff face to the clear water below. One of the great **wildlife encounters** we have experienced

Sunset over Shark Bay COILIN KERR

was standing here gazing in awe at a passing parade of shovel-nose rays, schools of fish, shy and rare dugongs, and vast flocks of feeding seabirds. Peron Peninsula is included in the **Shark Bay World Heritage Area**, which recognises the unique environment contained in the region.

WARNING: Beware of stonefish in the ocean waters and always wear shoes in rocky areas along the coast. See p26 for more information on stonefish.

Where to stay

Francois Peron National Park camping areas at Bottle Bay, Gregories, South Gregories, Herald Bight & Big Lagoon – park entry and camping fees apply, 4WD access only (Ph DEC Shark Bay District Office Ph 08 9948 1208)

Monkey Mia (Map 13 C3)

One of WA's tourism icons, **Monkey Mia** is just 23km by sealed road from Denham. For more than 30 years, **bottlenose dolphins** have been visiting the beach at Monkey Mia Reserve daily. Indeed Monkey Mia is so famous for its friendly dolphins that people sometimes call the whole Shark Bay area Monkey Mia. It all began in 1964 when a lady began hand-feeding a dolphin from a boat, and pretty soon other members of the dolphin community joined in for the easy feed. Wild dolphins began visiting the beach and small jetty where fisherman threw them the odd fish. This tradition continued and prospered into a mutually beneficial partnership – the dolphins get a feed every day and the resulting tourism brings in millions of dollars. Today the visiting animals span three generations, with the habit handed down from mother to offspring.

What to Do

The DEC operates an excellent **Visitor Information Centre** with a theatrette and interpretive displays as well as regular slide and information nights (Ph 08 9948 1366). To interact with the dolphins, stay close to the beach in the mornings and be aware when people start moving to the water's edge as this probably means the DEC rangers are coming down to the beach with a bucket of fish. These dolphins are wild animals that come to the beach of their own free will, and while they are hand fed each day between 8am and 1pm, rangers monitor closely the amount fed to each dolphin to ensure that hunting remains their primary source of food. Listen to the DEC rangers because there are behaviour no-nos for observers to follow. Don't wear sunscreen on your legs, because that irritates the dolphins' eyes, and never stand any more than knee deep in the water. If you are lucky, the ranger will pick you to wade out and feed a dolphin.

The **beach** and **sunsets** make Monkey Mia a lovely spot, regardless of the dolphins. Sightseeing **boat tours** enable visitors to observe dugongs, turtles, manta rays and sharks in the Shark Bay Marine Park. Fishing and pearl farm tours are also available, as well as **scenic plane flights**. The 2km **Wulyibidi Yaninyina Trail** is an easy one to two hour walk through the coastal sand plain. Go early in the morning to increase your chances of seeing some interesting wildlife.

Camping is not allowed within the Reserve but the adjacent **Monkey Mia Dolphin Resort** has a variety of accommodation, from camping and caravan sites to cabins and units. Other facilities include a campers' kitchen, laundry, tennis court, children's playground, pool, spa, restaurant, bar and small supermarket.

Where to stay

- *Monkey Mia Dolphin Resort* – includes backpackers accomm (Ph 08 9948 1320, 1800 653 611, www.monkeymia.com.au)

COLIN KERR

Monkey Mia Resort

STEVEN DAVID MILLER, NATURAL WANDERS

Dolphins at Monkey Mia

PELUSEY PHOTOGRAPHY

Sea Kayaking off Peron Peninsula

Birdlife, Monkey Mia

PELUSEY PHOTOGRAPHY

Carnarvon to the Ningaloo Coast

Carnarvon

They say **Carnarvon** is where the outback meets the ocean. Located on the coast, near the mouth of the **Gascoyne River**, Carnarvon is the commercial centre of the Gascoyne Region. Even though the river looks dry as you drive over the Gascoyne River Bridge, water still flows under all that sand. The dry riverbed actually covers a continually flowing underground stream and it is from here, metres below the sand, that water is pumped for irrigation. This water provides irrigation for local **plantations**. The plantations extend for around 16km along the banks of the Gascoyne River. Periodically after heavy rain the river flows very strongly so levee banks have been built to protect the low-lying areas during major floods. Occasionally a cyclone sweeps in and flattens these plantations as well as causing major floods. It is hard to believe that when the Gascoyne River is in flood the bridge, which is so high above the normally dry riverbed, can be under water.

The rich irrigated soils of the river flats are well known for the production of millions of dollars worth of **fruit** and **vegetables** such as mangoes, paw paws, bananas, pineapples, melons, tomatoes and beans. Other important local industries are **wool production**, **prawn and scallop processing**, **commercial fishing** (including pink snapper) and the large **Lake Macleod Salt Mining Operation**. Tours can be arranged of the **Norwest Seafood's prawn processing factory** and the salt production operation – contact the Carnarvon visitor centre.

Information

The **Carnarvon Visitor Centre** is in Robinson Street (Ph 08 9941 1146, www.carnarvon.org.au).

What to do

Carnarvon started out as a port, so the first step is to go to the **Carnarvon Heritage Precinct**. Built in 1897, the **One Mile Jetty** has been saved from demolition on a number of occasions because of its historical significance to the town. Fire has affected the jetty but restoration plans are in place to return it to its original glory. A little tram called the **Coffee Pot** travels down the jetty or you can walk. The jetty is also a great spot to see the sun set or go fishing. The **old lighthouse keeper's cottage**, which is now a museum, is worth a visit. Also in the precinct are the **Railway Museum** and **Shearers Hall of Fame**. A lifeboat from the German raider the *HSK Kormoran*, which sunk the *HMAS Sydney* during WWII, is also on display. Carnarvon is one of the closest towns to where the *HMAS Sydney* went down. The **HMAS Sydney Memorial Drive** has 645 plaques and palm trees representing the sailors that died when the ship sank.

Fascine means a bunch of sticks, which is what was used to try to prevent flood waters from the Gascoyne River inundating the town. Today the Fascine is a beautifully landscaped foreshore where an excellent **walk trail** leads to the heritage precinct across the mangroves of **Babbage Island**. If you walk or cycle this trail, you may see egrets fishing in the mangroves and mullet jumping on the incoming tide. There is even an outdoor gym if you wish to get a little physical.

Plantations are an integral part of Carnarvon and you can stop at various stalls as you drive along the South and North river roads. Tours of a plantation are available at **Bumbak's Plantation**, at 449 North River Road. The tours explain how they grow bananas, table grapes, mangoes and ground crops in Carnarvon (Ph 08 9941 8006, tours 10am Mon-Fri). The **Rivergum's Café** is also in a plantation on the banks of the Gascoyne River. Mango and banana smoothies are their specialty, all served in a delightful garden setting. At certain times of the year, these gardens teem with butterflies. Between May and November you can try the local produce at the **Gascoyne Growers' Markets** on Saturday mornings outside the visitor centre. It starts at 8am and you can choose anything from fresh tropical fruits and vegetables to an assortment of jams, chutneys and other products.

Another stand out feature in town is the **'Big Dish'**. Now no longer used, the OTC dish was part of the strategic global communication network used during the space race of the 60s and 70s. It was decommissioned after tracking Halley's Comet in 1987.

Fishing

In winter, Carnarvon is inundated with retired folk searching for warm sunshine and fishing. The focus for most anglers, whether they are locals or visitors, is the massive **One Mile Jetty**. When the mulloway are biting there's action a plenty with bent rods, busted lines and big flapping fish on deck alongside beaming anglers. A heavy line is the go here and rope gaffs to haul the big ones up the big drop. Mackerel and trevally species add spice to what is on offer on the end of Carnarvon's best-loved attraction. Big tailor go on hit and run raids on an incoming tide. Off the jetty near the shoreline and nearby beaches are good for whiting, tailor and bream. Fishing on a high tide off the **Fascine** may produce the odd small fish.

One Mile Jetty is the focus for most anglers in Carnarvon

STEVEN DAVID MILLER, NATURAL WANDERS

Miaboolya Beach (19 H3), north of Carnarvon, is a mulloway and tailor hotspot. Night fishing on a rising tide will reward those who are patient.

It goes without saying that the tropical waters off Carnarvon team with mackerel, tailor, trevally, cod, emperor, cobia, tuna and pink snapper. Further out, the deep waters off **Bernier and Dorre islands** are havens for the real big ones, but don't try it in a small boat.

If you do miss out on catching the big one, head to **Small Fishing Boat Harbour** to see what the professionals pull in. You can purchase fish, crabs and prawns from local businesses.

Organised Tours

- **BlueSun2** – day or overnight trips to Carnarvon, Abrolhos Islands and Montebello Islands (Ph 0405 305 305, www.bluesun2.com.au)
- **Outback Coast Safaris** – run a range of tours from half-day foodie tours to three-day Mount Augustus trips (Ph 08 9941 3448, www.outbackcoastsafaris.com.au)

Where to Stay

Carnarvon has a range of accommodation from caravan parks to backpackers and motel units. In the busy season, between May and October, caravan parks get full with travelling grey nomads and backpackers looking for picking work.

- *Best Western Hospitality Inn* (Ph 08 9941 1600, www.hospitalityinncarnarvon.com.au)
- *Capricorn Holiday Park* (Ph 08 9941 8153, www.capricornholidaypark.com.au)
- *Carnarvon Caravan Park* (Ph 08 9941 8101, www.carnarvonpark.com.au)
- *Coral Coast Caravan Park* – the closest to town (Ph 08 9941 1438, www.coralcoasttouristpark.com.au)
- *Fascine Lodge* (Ph 08 9941 2411, www.carnarvonmotel.com.au)
- *The Fish and Whistle Backpackers and Motel Accommodation* (Ph 08 9941 1704)
- *Gateway Motel* (Ph 08 9941 1532, www.carnarvonmotel.com.au)
- *Marloo Retiree and Senior Tourist Park* (Ph 08 9941 1439)
- *Norwesta Caravan Park* (Ph 08 9941 1277)
- *Plantation Caravan Park* (Ph 1800 261 166, 08 9941 8100, www.plantation-caravanpark.com.au)
- *Wintersun Caravan and Tourist Park* (Ph 1300 555 585, 08 9941 8150, www.wintersuncaravanpark.com.au)

Rocky Pool

PELUSEY PHOTOGRAPHY

Around Carnarvon

Kingsford Smith Mail Run

Carnarvon is the start or finish of the **Kingsford Smith Mail Run** (see p98) that links to **Meekatharra**. The first/last plaque is in the main street of Carnarvon opposite the old post office restaurant.

Rocky Pool (Map 19 G4)

About 59km east of Carnarvon, **Rocky Pool** is a deep freshwater billabong on the Gascoyne River that's popular for **bushcamping, swimming** and **picnicking**. The Pool is on the Kingsford Smith Mail Run and has lovely natural rocky platforms. Birdlife is prolific, especially around sunset when cockatoos come in for a drink.

Wooramel Coast

To the south of Carnarvon are several popular **bushcamping** locations situated right on the coast.

The turnoff to **Gladstone Camping Area (13 C5)** is 145km south of Carnarvon, or 55km north of the Overlander Roadhouse. The basic facilities include composting toilets and a boat ramp. (Camping fees apply.) There are some ruins of a causeway and jetty that are relics of a port facility from the early 1900s. **Fishing** is a popular pastime here, but be aware that restrictions apply because of the **Gladstone Special Protection Zone**. Waters south of the Gladstone boat ramp are closed to boating 1 Sep to 15 Jan and the waters north of the ramp are closed between 1 Dec and 31 Mar. Just north of Gladstone, the Disappointment Reach Special Protection Zone is closed to fishing all year. The **White Bluff Lookout**, just south of the turnoff to Gladstone, gives good views towards Hamelin Pool.

About 40km south of Carnarvon, an access road leaves the highway for the bushcamping spots of **Bush Bay (19 J3)** and **New Beach (19 J4)**. There are no facilities at either site and only campervans with chemical toilets are allowed to camp.

All three sites are administered by the Shire of Carnarvon (Ph 08 9941 0000, www.carnarvon.wa.gov.au).

The Blowhole Coast

North of Carnarvon is a coastline of contrasts: one end is a rugged rocky coast and the other has the calm waters of Gnaraloo Bay. This is pastoral station country in a land blessed with stunning coastline, making it a compelling attraction for tourists. The result is these stations are starting to diversify into accommodating visitors. Even though these stations have provided some services, such as toilets and kiosks for visitors, they are still running sheep and therefore station etiquette applies. Roads on these stations range from good gravel to soft sand at the Gnaraloo Bay end.

WARNING – This part of the coastline is notorious for freak or king waves that can appear suddenly out of calm seas. Take great care around rocks and observe warning signs as deaths have occurred.

Quobba Station (Map 19 F2)

The first part of the drive to **Point Quobba (19 G2)** from Carnarvon, is via a sealed road across tidal flats to the coast. If the swell is up at Point Quobba, several **blowholes** blast a geyser of spray up to 20m into the air every few seconds. Be very careful of king waves and don't ever turn your back on the **Indian Ocean**. There are also **memorial cairns** along the coast which relate to the story of the *HMAS Sydney* and the German raider *Kormoran* which both sank off the coastline in 1941.

Around the corner is a **fishing village** made up of old shacks and a few caravans. Many people bring their caravans to this serene bay and **camp** here during winter. (Camping fees apply and there is an onsite ranger. Contact the Shire of Carnarvon Ph 08 9941 0000, www.carnarvon.wa.gov.au).

Although **Quobba Station (19 F2)** is popular for **fishing**, it is a place for experienced anglers who are used to rocky headlands. (See their website for a map of fishing locations.) Also keep your eyes peeled for **humpback whales** as you may catch the huge mammals in full breach. The Station has a range of **accommodation** options, including chalets, cottages, shacks and shearing quarters as well as caravan and camping sites. The Station Store has some grocery and souvenir items. (Ph 08 9948 5098, www.quobba.com.au)

Dampier Salt exports salt from their operation at **Lake Macleod**, just south of **Cape Cuvier**. These cliffs are also the location of the wreck of the *Korean Star*. For a while, the wreck became a bit of a tourist destination, but powerful waves put paid to that and it is no longer visible.

Heading north, the now unsealed road hugs a dramatic coastline with small tracks branching off to vantage points. A detour to **Red Bluff (19 E2)** – world renowned for its monster left-hand break – is a must. Coming over the hill, you are greeted by a spectacular beach and 100m bluff protecting the bay. The coastline between Red Bluff and Gnaraloo has almost legendary status amongst the **surfing** community. Big waves and the rocky terrain mean that surfers should be experienced, although anybody can watch the action from a safe vantage point. When you see perfect waves peeling off Red Bluff, with **dolphins** jumping around on a warm winter's day you can see why surfers have been making the pilgrimage for years. When the area first became popular with surfers in the 1970s, it was basic camping to say the least but now it is more like an **eco retreat**. Four eco tents rest on the top of the cliff overlooking the spectacular bay while down below at surfing level are some campsites. Caravans are welcome, but off-road versions are more appropriate. (Ph 08 9948 5001, www.quobba.com.au)

Gnaraloo Station (Map 19 D3)

Further north you cross the boundary into **Gnaraloo Station**, passing by **Three Mile Camp (19 D2)**, another **surfing** hotspot. Being on the southern end of the **Ningaloo Reef**, **Three Mile Lagoon** and **Gnaraloo Bay** are popular spots for **snorkelling**. Surfing is an institution at Gnaraloo with classic waves such as **Tombstones** attracting surfers from all over the world. (Why do they give surf breaks such funny names?) Another common pastime is **fishing**, or you can opt to help out around the station under the **WWOOF system** – Willing Workers On Organic Farms. Most importantly, just chill out because that is the true essence of Gnaraloo.

Gnaraloo is still a working sheep station but has a range of **accommodation** from campsites to limestone-built cabins. Three Mile Camp offers beachside camping, with toilets, hot showers, laundry facilities and a shop with basic supplies. The Homestead has a range of self-contained accommodation options. There is no camping at Gnaraloo Bay and it is not possible to drive through Warroora Station north to Coral Bay. (Ph 08 9315 4809, www.gnaraloo.com.au)

Point Quobba blowholes

STEVEN DAVID MILLER, NATURAL WANDERS

PELUSEY PHOTOGRAPHY

Camping at Red Bluff

Fishing

This coastline is **rock fishing** nirvana, but it can come at a huge cost as inattentive anglers fishing too close to the water, or when there's a swell about, put their lives at risk. So called **king waves** can come out of a deceptively calm sea. If you are washed into the ocean, your best hope is a passing boat or the ability to tread water until help arrives as clambering back up the oyster-encrusted rocks is not a viable option. You might wonder why anglers take the risk, and the answer is possibly the best rock fishing in Australia: for those who know what they are doing.

The first type of fishing is **bottom fishing** off reef platforms, where species such as baldchin, snapper, emperor, trevally and cod dwell. Heavy gear and plenty of it is required in this snaggy country.

The second, more adventurous, method is **balloon fishing** in favourable offshore breezes for Spanish mackerel, other mackerel species, tuna and pesky sharks.

There are plenty of fishing vantage points along the coast of varying degrees of difficulty, and danger for that matter. Some of these locations require steep descents and ascents, made more difficult when loaded down with fish, so good fitness and care are required. Popular locations are **Camp Rock**, **The Caves**, **High Rock** and **Garth's Rock**. The last spot was named after Max Garth, a legendary character who fished the area back in the 1970s.

Coral Bay (Map 19 B3)

The **Coral Bay** area first came to European notice in 1884 with the landing of the schooner *Maud*. The bay where it landed is still known as **Maud's Landing (19 B3)**. The original settlement, a little to the north of the current township, was established in the 1870s as a port. With trucks and better road access in the early 1900s, the need for the port rapidly diminished and today there is scarcely any evidence of this once important facility. Today Coral Bay is a very busy tourist community, especially in the winter months with people drawn to the warm weather, crystal-clear water, underwater life and fishing. In fact, many families come year after year for their annual holidays.

What to Do

Coral Reef Viewing

The Coral Bay tourist hub exists because of its strategic location at the southern end of the **Ningaloo Reef**. The best way to see the myriad of coral and fish is to get out there and get wet. **Snorkelling** and **scuba diving** are very popular ways to see the wonders of the reef, so is a **glass-bottom boat** if you want to stay dry. The inner reef of the bay provides protection for **swimmers** off the beautiful white beach. The outer reef is deeper, exposed and subsequently rougher.

Wildlife Interaction

Whale sharks would be the number one interaction on the Ningaloo Reef. Luckily, although whale sharks are the biggest fish in the sea, those big toothless mouths only eat plankton. They arrive around the end of March and leave by the middle of June, and spotter planes are used to find the sharks. Once the boats find the sharks snorkellers can jump in and swim with them for an amazing experience. Rules apply to the snorkellers and boat operators, so times can be limited.

Manta rays are found in the Ningaloo area all year round while **humpback whales** on their migration arrive after the whale sharks in June and stay until November. **Loggerhead turtles** lay their eggs on the beaches in the hotter months of February and March.

Organised Water-Based Tours

There are many options for snorkelling, diving, and whale shark and manta ray trips, as well as kayaking and cruising the coast.

- **Coastal Adventure Tours** – half and full-day snorkel cruises; two-, four- or six-hour catamaran trips (Ph 08 9948 5190, www.coralbaytours.com.au)
- **Coral Bay Adventures** – swim with whale sharks or manta rays, or go whale watching; dive on the Ningaloo Reef (Ph 08 9942 5955, www.coralbayadventures.com.au)
- **Coral Bay Charter and Glass Bottom Boats** – one or two hour glass bottom boat trips to see coral (Ph 08 9942 5932, www.coralbaywa.com)
- **Ningaloo Experience** – snorkel with manta rays and whale sharks from late Mar-Jun; outer reef experiences (Ph 08 9942 5877, www.ningalooexperience.com)
- **Ningaloo Kayak Adventures** – two and three hour kayaking and snorkelling trips (Ph 08 9948 5034, www.ningalookayakadventures.com)
- **Ningaloo Reef Dive** – dive courses plus snorkel and dive on the inner and outer reefs (Ph 08 9942 5824, www.ningalooreefdive.com)
- **Ocean Eco Adventures** – see whale sharks and manta rays on the Ningaloo Reef, or marinelife in Coral Bay; Apr-Oct (Ph 0427 425 925, 0409 374 550, www.oceanecoadventures.com.au)

Fishing

Judging by the number of small trailer boats being launched in the area, this form of fishing is exceptionally popular. Calm conditions for boaties are more likely to occur between April and August. On the outer side of the **Ningaloo Reef** you can troll for Spanish mackerel, tuna, cobia, sailfish and dolphin fish. The calmer, more shallow waters teem with smaller species. Fish like dart and queenfish are possibilities from the **beach**, where fishing is allowed. No fishing sanctuary zones are signposted and must be obeyed. For non-boat owners who want to get amongst the big ones, taking a trip on a **charter boat** is a great option. They know the good spots and a good catch is almost guaranteed.

On the beach at Coral Bay

COLIN KERR

Coral Coast

Boat Hire

- **Coral Bay Adventures** – half and full day hire (Ph 08 9942 5955, www.coralbayadventures.com.au)
- **Ningaloo Kayak Adventures** – hire out kayaks, boogie boards and snorkelling equipment (Ph 08 9948 5034, www.ningalookayakadventures.com)

Fishing Charters

- **Coral Bay Ocean Game Fishing Charters** – full day charters (Ph 08 9942 5874, www.mahimahicoralbay.com.au)
- **Sea Force Coral Bay** – fishing tours and deep sea and sport fishing charters (Ph 08 9942 5817, www.seaforcecharters.net.au)

Land-Based Tours

- **Coastal Adventure Tours** – self-drive ATV adventures (Ph 08 9948 5190, www.coralbaytours.com.au)
- **Luxury 4x4 Adventures** – take you in their 4WD to some of the harder to access places, including Yardie Creek via the real back roads (Ph 0427 180 568)

Where to stay

- **Bayview Coral Bay** – powered and unpowered sites, cabins, cafes and resort style features (Ph 08 9942 5935, www.coralbaywa.com)
- **Ningaloo Beach Resort** (Ph 1800 795 522, www.ningalooreefresort.com.au)
- **Ningaloo Club** – backpacker accommodation (Ph 08 9948 5100, www.ningalooclub.com)
- **Peoples Park Caravan Village** (Ph 08 9942 5933, www.peoplesparkcoralbay.com.au)
- **Warroora Station** – south of Coral Bay, off the Minilya Exmouth Rd; cottage, old homestead and shearers and stockmans quarters accommodation plus camping areas (Ph 08 9942 5920, www.warroora.com)

Exmouth (Map 25 F4)

Exmouth is situated near the end of the **North West Cape**, 1260km north of Perth. Although Europeans sighted the Cape as early as 1618, it wasn't until the 1960s that the town of Exmouth actually came into existence. In 1963 an agreement was signed between the Australian and US governments for the establishment of the **Harold E Holt Naval Communication Station**. It includes the world's largest very low frequency transmitters and **Tower Zero**, which at 387.6m is the second tallest structure in the Southern Hemisphere. Exmouth was originally established as a support town for the communication station. Before that, **Learmonth**, to the south, served as an airforce base during WWII. Located between the **Exmouth Gulf** and the **Indian Ocean**, today Exmouth is the base for exploring the delights of **Ningaloo Marine Park** and **Cape Range National Park**.

Information

The **Exmouth Visitor Centre**, on Murat Road, is on the main road as you enter town. (Ph 1800 287 328, www.exmouthwa.com.au)

What to Do

Visiting the **Vlamingh Head Lighthouse (25 E4)**, 19km north of Exmouth, can be a sublime experience. Drive up to the top of the hill and set up your camp chairs to watch the **whales** breaching in the Indian Ocean as the sun sets. The views are superb, and early risers can also opt to see the sun rise over the gulf. Built in 1912, the lighthouse has been restored to its original working condition.

The **Exmouth Gulf** is the home to a large **prawn-fishing fleet**. During the prawn-catching season, from April to November, the **MG Kailis group** open their factory to the public to purchase

GAVIN JAMES

Sunset over the North West Cape.

fresh prawns. Head south out of town for 23km and look for the giant prawn – you can't miss it.

The big new **boat harbour and marina** is a work in progress. It was born out of the destruction wreaked upon Exmouth during the grade five **Cyclone Vance**. Bedsides providing safe anchoring and launching facilities for small boats, the harbour is a good place to view the big prawning fleet when they are in port.

The **Potshot Memorial (25 G4)**, about 30km south of Exmouth, commemorates Operation Potshot (1942-1945) when US submarines used the area as an advanced refuelling base. In 1943 the *MV Krait* set out from this coastline on its famous undercover mission to destroy enemy shipping in Singapore Harbour. Nearby is the **Learmonth RAAF base (25 G4)**, originally established as a support for Operation Potshot, which is also the main domestic air terminal for the Exmouth region.

Ningaloo Reef

The best way to see the myriad of coral and fish on the Ningaloo Reef is to go **snorkelling** or **scuba diving**. If you prefer to stay dry, then take a tour on a **glass-bottom boat**. While whale sharks are a major drawcard, manta rays, humpback whales and loggerhead turtles can also be seen in the region. **Whale sharks** arrive around the end of March and leave by the middle of June, while **humpback whales** on their migration arrive after the whale sharks in June and stay until November. **Manta rays** are found in the Ningaloo area all year round and **loggerhead turtles** lay their eggs on the beaches in the hotter months of February and March.

Glass-bottom boats run from Tantabiddi and Bundegi boat ramps. Various operators can take you coral viewing, snorkelling and whale watching.

Organised Wildlife Tours

- **King's Ningaloo Reef Tours** – snorkel with whale sharks from late Mar to late July (Ph 08 9949 1764, www.kingsningalooreeftours.com.au)
- **Ningaloo Blue Dive** – snorkel with whale sharks from Apr to July (Ph 1800 811 388, www.ningallooblue.com.au)
- **Ningaloo Reef Dreaming** –eco cruises to see whale sharks, manta rays, turtles or humpback whales (Ph 1800 994 210, www.ningaloodreaming.com)
- **Ningaloo Whaleshark-n-Dive** – snorkel with whale sharks, including an option to overnight onboard (Ph 08 9949 1116, www.ningaloowhalesharkndive.com.au)
- **Ocean Eco Adventures** – see whale sharks and manta rays on the Ningaloo Reef; three-day live aboard trip to the Ningaloo Reef; Apr-Oct (Ph 0427 425 925, 0409 374 550, www.oceanecoadventures.com.au)
- **Three Islands Marine Charters** – snorkel with whale sharks Apr to early July (Ph 1800 138 501, www.whalesharkdive.com)

The big prawn, Kailis processing factory

PELUSEY PHOTOGRAPHY

Snorkelling & Diving

The **Navy Pier** is touted as the one of the top ten scuba dives in the world. The **marine life** on the pylons is luxuriant and **fish-life**, including giant cod, prolific. Scuba divers come in their droves, especially in late summer to see the **coral spawning** in the Ningaloo Marine Park.

Diving & Snorkelling Operators

- **King's Ningaloo Reef Tours** – snorkel Ningaloo Reef (Ph 08 9949 1764, www.kingsningalooreeftours.com.au)
- **Ningaloo Reef Dreaming** – dive Exmouth Navy Pier and dive or snorkel Ningaloo Reef and Muiron Island (Ph 08 9949 4777, 1800 994 210, www.ningaloodreaming.com)
- **Ningaloo Whaleshark-n-Dive** – learn to dive and snorkelling tours (Ph 08 9949 1116, www.ningaloowhalesharkndive.com.au)

Kayaking

Kayaking inside the Ningaloo Reef's sheltered waters, protected from the big swells, can be paddling paradise. Crystal-clear waters, abundant marine life and easy access points for kayaks is why sea kayaking is so popular. Visitors without kayaks can hire one through **Exmouth Boat & Kayak Hire** (Ph 0438 230 269, www.exmouthboathire.com).

The Fremantle company, **Ningaloo Reef Seakayaking**, runs sea kayaking expeditions to Ningaloo Reef (Ph 08 6267 8059, www.capricornseakayaking.com.au).

Fishing

The waters of **Exmouth Gulf** are generally shallow and warmer than the western side. Although the Gulf is generally sheltered from the big Indian Ocean swells, it is still prone to strong winds that whip up nasty chop. The winter months are generally less windy than the spring and early summer months. In good conditions, small **boat anglers** enjoy catching coral trout, emperor, trevally and queenfish. Further out and you are in the world of Spanish mackerel and even sailfish. **Beaches** fish well for nice whiting and other small species such as bream. **Mangrove creeks** at the southern end of the Gulf shelter mud crabs and snag-loving mangrove jacks. The jetties at **Bundegi Beach** and near **Learmonth** are good for trevally and queenfish with the odd mackerel if bait fish are about. The big Naval Jetty is out of bounds to anglers, which probably accounts for the rich fishlife seen around the pylons. Inside the **marina**, flicking a lure around the boats may produce a mangrove jack or trevally. You can hire aluminium boats from **Exmouth Boat & Kayak Hire** (Ph 0438 230 269, www.exmouthboathire.com).

Fishing Charters

- **Montebellos Sport Fishing Charters** – 6-day live aboard charter from Oct to Mar (Ph 08 9942 5874, www.mahimahicoralbay.com.au)
- **Ningaloo Blue Dive** – deep sea fishing charters from the western side of Cape Range (Ph 1800 811 388, www.ningalooblue.com.au)

Where to Stay

- *Best Western Sea Breeze Resort* (Ph 08 9949 1800, www.seabreezeresort.com.au)
- *Exmouth Cape Holiday Park* (Ph 1800 621 101, www.aspenparks.com.au)
- *Ningaloo Caravan Park and Holiday Resort* (Ph 08 9949 2377, www.exmouthresort.com)
- *Ningaloo Lighthouse Caravan Park* (Ph 08 9949 1478, www.ningaloolighthouse.com)
- *Novotel Ningaloo Reef* (Ph 08 9949 0000, www.novotelningaloo.com.au)
- *Pot Shot Resort* – includes Osprey Holiday Apartments and Excape (Ph 08 9949 1200, www.potshotresort.com)
- *Ningaloo Lodge* (Ph 1800 880 949, www.ningaloolodge.com.au)
- *Sal Salis Ningaloo Reef* – bush camping luxury (Ph 1300 790 561, www.salsalis.com.au)
- *Yardie Creek Homestead Caravan Park* – on the west side of the cape near Ningaloo Marine Park (Ph 08 9949 1389)

Cape Range National Park (Map 25 F4)

The **Cape Range National Park** encompasses the land and gorge area of the **North West Cape**. The landscape is one of hills, gorges and unusual rock formations (see p12) for geological details).

Information

The **Milyering Visitor Centre** in the Cape Range National Park is open daily from 9am to 3.45pm (Ph 08 9949 2808). Further information is also available from the **DEC Exmouth District Office** at 20 Nimitz St in Exmouth (Ph 08 9947 8000).

Eastern Side

There are two sides to Cape Range and the best places to view the eastern side are at **Charles Knife Gorge (25 F4)** and **Shothole Canyon (25 F4)**. Charles Knife Road climbs up onto the top of the hills with wonderful views to the gulf seas and deep gorges below. Shothole Canyon Road follows the creekline at the base of one canyon. If you are fit you can do the 8km **Badjirrajiia Trail** from Charles Knife Road. Extreme heat during summer makes trekking in Cape Range an exceptionally unpleasant experience, so go in the cooler months. **Rock climbing** and **abseiling** trips can be arranged through the Exmouth Visitor Centre.

Shothole Canyon Road

PELUSEY PHOTOGRAPHY

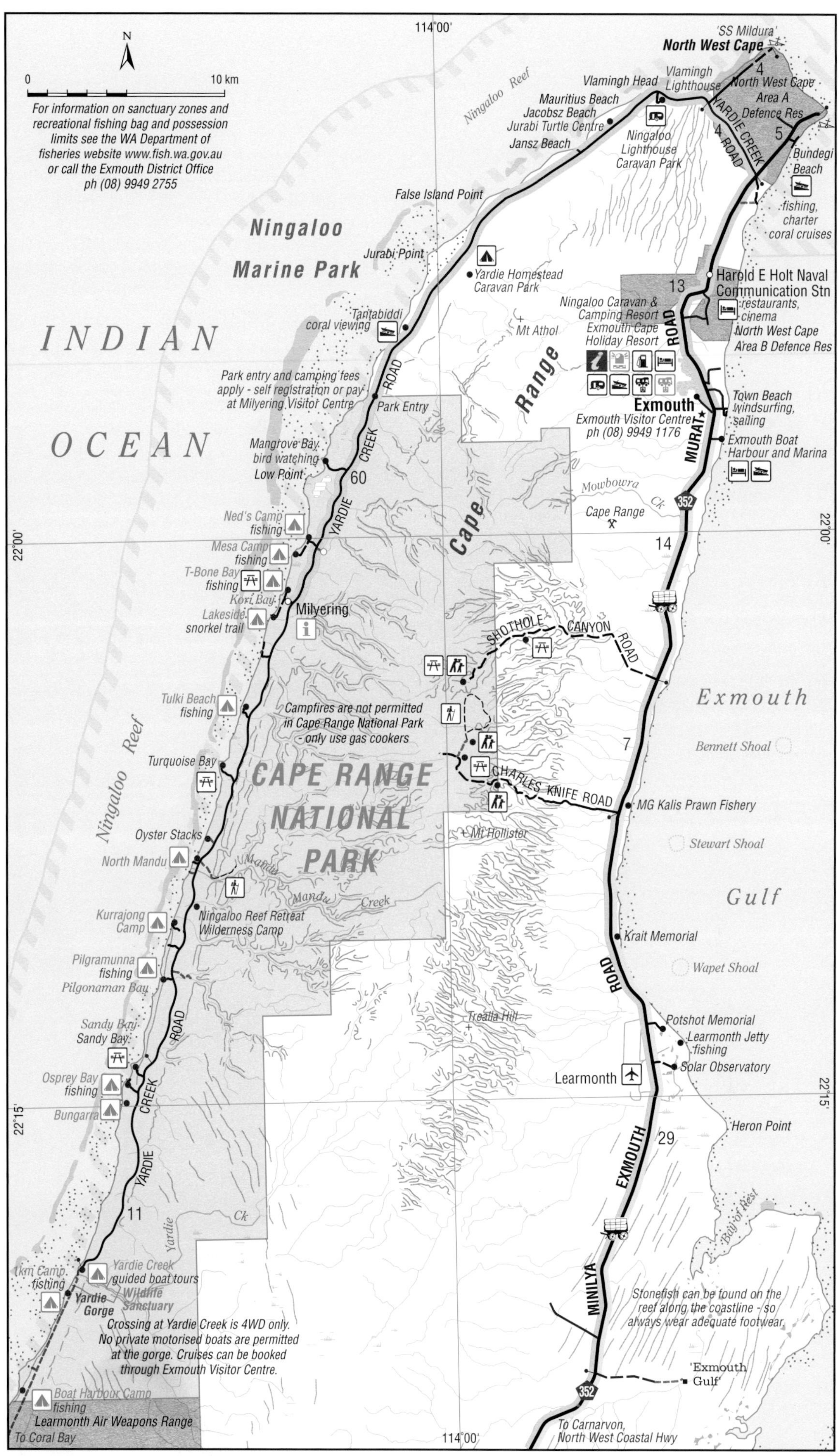
N
0
10 km
For information on sanctuary zones and recreational fishing bag and possession limits see the WA Department of fisheries website www.fish.wa.gov.au or call the Exmouth District Office ph (08) 9949 2755
114°00'
'SS Mildura'
North West Cape
Vlamingh Head
Vlamingh Lighthouse
North West Cape Area A Defence Res
Mauritius Beach
Jacobsz Beach
Jurabi Turtle Centre
Jansz Beach
Ningaloo Lighthouse Caravan Park
YARDIE CREEK ROAD
Bundegi Beach
fishing, charter coral cruises
False Island Point
Ningaloo Reef
Ningaloo Marine Park
Jurabi Point
Yardie Homestead Caravan Park
Harold E Holt Naval Communication Stn
restaurants, cinema
North West Cape Area B Defence Res
Ningaloo Caravan & Camping Resort
Exmouth Cape Holiday Resort
Mt Athol
Tantabiddi
coral viewing
INDIAN
OCEAN
Park entry and camping fees apply - self registration or pay at Milyering Visitor Centre
Park Entry
Range
Exmouth
Exmouth Visitor Centre
ph (08) 9949 1176
Town Beach windsurfing, sailing
MURAT ROAD
Exmouth Boat Harbour and Marina
Mangrove Bay bird watching
Low Point
60
Mowbowra Ck
Cape Range
352
Ned's Camp fishing
Cape
Mesa Camp fishing
T-Bone Bay fishing
Kori Bay
Milyering
Lakeside snorkel trail
22°00'
14
SHOTHOLE CANYON ROAD
Exmouth
Gulf
Tulki Beach fishing
Campfires are not permitted in Cape Range National Park - only use gas cookers
Bennett Shoal
7
Turquoise Bay
CAPE RANGE NATIONAL PARK
CHARLES KNIFE ROAD
MG Kalis Prawn Fishery
Mt Hollister
Stewart Shoal
Oyster Stacks
North Mandu
Mandu Mandu Creek
Kurrajong Camp
Ningaloo Reef Retreat Wilderness Camp
Krait Memorial
Pilgramunna fishing
Pilgonaman Bay
Wapet Shoal
Trealla Hill
Potshot Memorial
Learmonth Jetty fishing
Solar Observatory
Sandy Bay
Learmonth
Osprey Bay fishing
Bungarra
22°15'
Heron Point
29
EXMOUTH
MINILYA
11
Yardie Ck
Bay of Rest
1km Camp fishing
Yardie Creek guided boat tours
Wildlife Sanctuary
Yardie Gorge
Crossing at Yardie Creek is 4WD only. No private motorised boats are permitted at the gorge. Cruises can be booked through Exmouth Visitor Centre.
Stonefish can be found on the reef along the coastline - so always wear adequate footwear.
'Exmouth Gulf'
Boat Harbour Camp fishing
Learmonth Air Weapons Range
To Coral Bay
To Carnarvon, North West Coastal Hwy
13
4
5

Western Side & Ningaloo Marine Park

On the western side, the rugged rocky gorges and hidden caves of Cape Range meet the glorious blue seas, coral reef and sandy beaches of **Ningaloo Reef** and the **Ningaloo Marine Park**. The rammed-earth **Milyering Visitor Centre (25 F4)** is the place to visit for information on Cape Range National Park and the Ningaloo Marine Park. North of the national park boundary, the **Jurabi Turtle Centre** explains the lifecycle of the marine turtles on Ningaloo Reef.

What to Do

With its aqua water and white beaches, **Ningaloo Marine Park** is the jewel in the crown for this region. The **Ningaloo Reef** is one of WA's greatest natural wonders, with over 200 species of **corals** and over 500 species of **fish**. The reef varies from 200m to 7km from the shoreline. In fact, in some places, visitors can see abundant marinelife within walking and snorkelling distance of the parked car.

The Ningaloo Reef's most famous inhabitant is the majestic **whale shark**, which migrates to the area between March and June. Specially licensed **tour boats** take snorkellers and divers to swim with these harmless giants (see p68). Whale sharks are nearly always sighted but not always, so most charters offer a chance to come back the next day and not a refund. To ensure you don't miss out, allow at least a few days stay in Exmouth. Other interesting sealife includes **manta rays**, **turtles** and **dugongs**. **Humpback whales** are often seen breaching on the seaward side of the reef on their migrations up and down the west coast.

Snorkelling at **Turquoise Bay** is a must if you are a confident swimmer. It is best to enter the water off the beach and drift over the coral, carried by the strong current. Look out for turtles and small reef sharks as you drift past a vast array of coral and fish. After a few hundred metres a sandbar appears, and this is the best point to get off the ride and paddle hard to shore. Be warned: this activity is not for weak swimmers, especially children. There are other snorkelling spots that can be easily reached from the shore, such as **Oyster Stacks**. All these snorkelling spots are strictly look only and take nothing! For those who don't wish to get wet, there is a **glass-bottom boat** at Tantabiddi, north of the national park boundary.

Turquoise Bay

STEVEN DAVID MILLER, NATURAL WANDERS

Mandu Mandu Gorge has a great 3km walk that allows you to explore **Cape Range** up close. The walk travels along the creek bed, then climbs up onto the escarpment before heading west with views to Ningaloo Reef. Rare **black-footed rock wallabies** can occasionally be seen hiding on rock ledges. Gorges in Cape Range are blisteringly hot in summer, with temperatures over 50°C, so go in the cooler months.

Unlike Mandu Mandu Gorge, **Yardie Creek** has permanent water. A **boat trip** is the best way to see this popular gorge from ground level, and there is a **walk trail** to view the gorge from above. The view from the top of this vividly coloured gorge to the distant blues of Ningaloo Reef is well worth the effort. Again, **black-footed rock wallabies** are frequently seen in this area, especially on the boat tour. (The one-hour boat trips can be booked through the Exmouth and Milyering visitor centres.)

For the four-wheel driver with an adventurous streak, the trek south from Yardie Creek to Coral Bay is a must. (For details see Track 31 in Hema's *WA 4WD Top 50 Atlas & Guide*.)

Ningaloo Safari Tours offer a tour from Exmouth to Cape Range National Park and Ningaloo Reef (Ph 08 9949 1550, www.ningaloosafari.com).

Fishing

Fishing is very popular along this coast, but before hitting the water check out the **regulations** because the marine environment comes under the protection of the **Ningaloo Marine Park**. Size and bag limits are strictly policed here, see p36 for where to get the latest information. Tide charts and fishing advice are available from the Exmouth and Milyering visitor centres. Be aware that there are sanctuary zones within the marine park, including areas where fishing is banned entirely. There are two main fishing areas to consider: inside the reef and outside the reef.

Inside the reef, which can be as close as 100m from the shore in places, is prime country for trevally species, spangled emperors, queenfish and numerous other species. Small dinghies or sea kayaks are ideal, as big boats may get into problems in some places. Small boats can be launched from the beach at **Neds Camp**, **Pilgramunna** and **Osprey Bay**. Shore fishing is also worth a go, but make sure you stay away from those sanctuary zones.

Outside the reef, the water deepens dramatically toward the continental shelf. If you can get out beyond the reef, big fish are the name of the game, including Spanish mackerel, tuna, cobia, sailfish, wahoo, big trevally, barracuda and even marlin. See p70 for details of *Fishing Charters* from Exmouth.

Where to stay

Camping is the only option in the national park, but you'll be spoilt for choice with numerous oceanfront sites offering easy access to clean beaches and the sparkling sea. Our favourite site is **North Mandu**. Most of these DEC campsites have bush toilets and allocated campsites. In the tourist season – May to October – the park is very busy and to get a spot you'll need to get to the DEC gate early and get in the queue. For information contact the Exmouth or Milyering visitor centres, or the DEC district office in Exmouth. ■

chapter five

Pilbara

The Pilbara is one of Australia's most beautiful places, and also one of the wealthiest. Extending from Onslow to south of Broome on the coast, the Pilbara also includes inland outback areas towards the deserts of central Australia. The size of Victoria, the Pilbara lies about 1200km north of Perth and is about as far away from the populated east coast as you can get. Within the Pilbara are areas of striking contrasts, from the rich diversity of the coast and sea to the red gorges inland.

Offshore there are a myriad of islands such as the Montebellos, Dampier Archipelago and Mackerel Islands. Some of these islands have white sandy beaches while others are rocky outcrops covered in ancient indigenous petroglyphs. However, the seas surrounding all teem with marine life of extraordinary diversity so the fishing is spectacular. Try some deep-sea fishing off Onslow and Karratha, or fish for thread fin salmon and mulloway at high tide at Eighty Mile Beach.

In contrast, red gorges filled with clear cool water fringed with maiden hair ferns await in Karijini National Park and the still waters of Millstream are a marvellous sight after all the red soil and dust. More remote areas, like Rudall River National Park, require complete self-sufficiency as there are no facilities. The Karijini, Millstream Chichester and Rudall River national parks also have strong links to their traditional owners. Karijini is co-managed by the Gumala Aboriginal Corporation.

However, the Pilbara is bountiful in ways other than its stunning scenic attractions. It is also the money-making machine of Western Australia with iron ore mined near Tom Price, Pannawonica, Paraburdoo and Newman. These are amongst the largest deposits of iron ore found anywhere in the world. The ore is then transported by the longest trains in the world to the two busiest ports in regards to tonnage: Dampier and Port Hedland. Huge bulk carriers take the red ore to Japan and China. But the natural riches don't end here as there is also gold near Marble Bar and the North West Shelf Venture out to sea off Karratha that pipes natural gas to the Burrup Peninsula for refining into liquefied natural gas. The mining towns are always busy with workers and in some towns if you aren't wearing an orange safety shirt and steel-capped boots you may feel left out. For insights into these massive industrial ventures, tours are available or you can stop at the informative visitor centres.

One of the best ways to get around the Pilbara is to follow the Warlu Way (see boxed text p74). Warlu is the Aboriginal term for snake. This trail offers travellers a tourist drive of great scenic and natural beauty, combined with fascinating Aboriginal culture.

As you enter the area your biggest problem will be to decide what to do first, particularly if you have come in a 4WD, because there are many off-road adventures in store. However you come, make sure that you are well prepared, and above all avoid the scorching heat of the summer months unless you decide to stay close to the cool water of the Indian Ocean.

The Grotto, Karijini National Park
STEVEN DAVID MILLER, NATURAL WANDERS

PELUSEY PHOTOGRAPHY

Chichester Ranges at sunset

STEVEN DAVID MILLER, NATURAL WANDERS

Wildflowers in Karijini National Park

Karijini National Park (Map 27 H5)

Some people say **Karijini National Park** in the **Hamersley Range** is their favourite spot in Western Australia, even Australia. When you first drive in, it is hard to believe in all this relatively flat country there is something spectacular hidden away. That's because instead of creating mountains, here the water has etched deep gorges in a landscape of spinifex and white snappy gums. What seems superficially a dry, harsh region has many hidden micro-ecosystems featuring freshwater pools of waterlilies and luxuriant ferny nooks. The water in some gorges offers refreshing, if sometimes chilly, respite from the heat and after a long walk there is not much better. This landscape has taken more than two billion years to create, so allow plenty of time to explore. WA's second largest national park is bound to leave its imprint on your mind long after you leave, with its ever-changing scenery of deep red rock, sheer cliffs and spinifex-clad rolling hills.

Some roads within the park are unsealed and visitors in a 2WD may find them a little on the rough side, especially the corrugated sections. However, don't let that put you off as any discomfort is well worth the effort. If you wish to stay on the seal, you can still visit Mt Bruce and the visitor centre, as well as the Dales day use section, which includes Dales Gorge, Fortescue Falls and Circular Pool. One word of warning: make sure you have at least a near full tank before entering the park as there are no fuel facilities. Many people underestimate the distances involved. You should also take plenty of drinking water.

Information

The **Karijini National Park Visitor Centre**, off Banjima Dr, is a splendid building constructed of rusted-brown steel to blend in with the surrounding landscape. It features interpretive displays and information about the area's early geological and human history, as well as a theatre. (Ph 08 9189 8121)

What to Do

Lookouts

One of the big attractions of Karijini is that its scenery is so accessible – you can literally pull into a car park and walk 50m to a lookout to peer into 100m gorges.

Oxer Lookout is one of those spectacular views that leave visitors with a sense of awe at nature's grandeur. At this vertigo-inducing spot, people gaze into the junction of four gorges: Hancock, Red, Weano, and Joffre. From **Joffre Lookout**, peer deep into Joffre Gorge at the unusual curved wall that forms a natural amphitheatre.

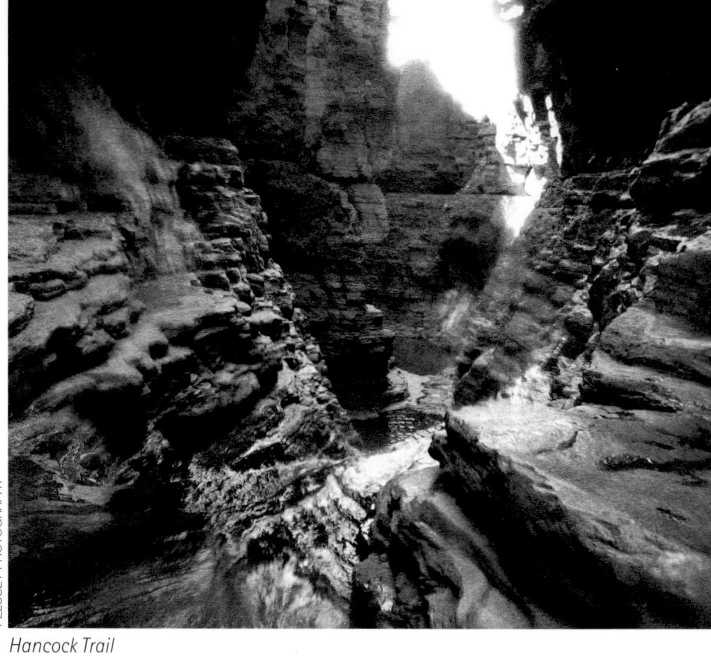

PELUSEY PHOTOGRAPHY

Hancock Trail

Warlu Way

The **Warlu Way** encompasses some of northern WA's most iconic locations, including the Ningaloo Reef, Karijini National Park and Broome. The whole drive revolves around the Aboriginal Warlu, or serpent, that is believed to inhabit the area and there are strong indigenous links through traditional stories, and ancient and modern art.

The snake is an important feature in indigenous dreaming stories throughout Australia. In Western Australia's Pilbara region the snake is called the Warlu, while in the South West it is called the Waugal. In other states it is known as Yingarna, Almudj and Kalseru, to name just a few.

The Warlu Way snakes through the Pilbara, mostly away from Highway One. The route links the rich diversity of Aboriginal culture in the region with the ancient landscape. This is more than just a 'pretty tourist trail' as indigenous communities are actively involved.

The Warlu Way passes though Exmouth, Tom Price, Karijini National Park, Millstream-Chichester National Park, Karratha, Cossack, Point Samson and Port Hedland on its way to Broome. There are side-road detours to the towns of Coral Bay, Onslow, Newman and Marble Bar.

The Warlu Way also connects some of **WA's Top Trails** (www.toptrails.com.au) including the Dales Gorge Walk in Karijini National Park and the Camel Trail in the Millstream-Chichester National Park.

Warlu Way, Chichester Ranges.

PELUSEY PHOTOGRAPHY

Bushwalking

As good as the gorges look from above, the real magic begins when you go down into them. Karijini National Park is such a bushwalker's delight that there are almost too many tracks to mention. Even the trails that are reasonably short often involve some rock hopping, and climbing up and down rocks. Great care is required when negotiating slippery rocks and steep, sloping surfaces. There is a great map available in the park that explains the difficulty grading of each trail. (See *Trail Grades* on p32.)

Walking in gorges requires extra consideration, and some trails within Karijini National Park are Class 6. With its steep and slippery sides, the bottom end of Weano Gorge near Handrail Pool is a case in point. Statistically, Karijini National Park has one of the highest rates of accidents of any national park in Australia. But it is also one of the most beautiful places, so don't let that stop you tackling the class 5 and 6 trails if you are experienced and qualified.

Walks at Mt Bruce

The **Hamersley Range** has WA's two highest mountains. In comparison to other states, and indeed the world, these are but pimples but that doesn't detract from their magnificence. **Mount Meharry** (1245m) and **Mount Bruce** (1235m) are WA's number one and two highest mountains respectively.

A series of challenging walks allow visitors to experience the rooftop of Karijini National Park from Mount Bruce:

- **Honey Hakea** – 4.6km, 3hr return (Class 3)
- **Marandoo View** – 500m, 30 min return (Class 2)
- **Summit** – 9km, 6hr return (Class 4)

Walks at the western end of Banjima Drive

- **Hancock Gorge** – 135m, 10 min return (Class 4 to the top of the ladder)
- **Handrail Pool** – 1km, 1.5hr return (Class 3, then Class 5 as gorge narrows)
- **Kermit's Pool** – 200m, 45 min return (Class 5 from the top of the ladder at Hancock Gorge)
- **Joffre Falls** – 3km, 2hr return (Class 4)
- **Joffre Lookout** – 100m, 10 min return (Class 2)
- **Knox Gorge** – 2km, 3hr return (Class 4 – return at the 'Gorge Risk Area' sign)
- **Oxer & Junction Pool lookouts** – 800m, 30 min return from the Weano Recreational Area (Class 2, then Class 3 beyond Junction Pool Lookout)

Walk along Banjima Drive

- **Kalamina Falls** – 3km, 3hr return (Class 3)

Walks at Dales Gorge

Dales Gorge has a variety of different trails from the easy to moderately challenging, and an incredible variety of scenery and ecosystems.

If you can, walk along the **Gorge Rim trail** which is easy, and offers stupendous views into the gorge (2km, 1.5hr return, Class 2). You can start the Gorge Rim walk from either end where there are car parks. Walking the Gorge Rim trail from Fortescue Falls to the Circular Pool end is a good option if you are reasonably fit and sure-footed.

Then follow a steep but well-marked descent into **Dales Gorge** to walk the length, taking in an entirely different perspective (2km, 3hr return, Class 4).

After admiring the vertigo-inducing views of **Circular Pool** from a lookout with a safety railing, you can take the steep trail down to the gorge floor (800m, 2hr return, Class 4). There are steps and a ladder that makes it an easier descent than it might otherwise be. At ground level the fern-lined crystal clear pool, trickling waterfall and sheer rock face backdrop make Circular Pool sublimely beautiful.

The sweaty walk to **Fortescue Falls** is well rewarded with a swim at the permanently flowing waterfall (800m, 1hr return, Class 3). Carefully negotiate the rocks above the falls and follow a shady trail for a 300m detour to **Fern Pool** (Class 4). A tranquil swimming hole, Fern Pool is spiritually important to the local indigenous people so treat it with great respect. Retrace your steps back to Fortescue Falls, then climb steps up the gorge to the car park.

Walks at Hamersley Gorge

Around on the western edge of Karijini National Park, **Hamersley Gorge** is just off Munjina Rd. A 400m walk (1hr return, Class 3) leads to the **Hamersley Waterfall**. The 1km (3hr return, Class 4) **Hamersley Gorge** walk leads into the less steep, but pretty, gorge.

Gorge Safety

'Gorge Risk Area' signs are located in the gorges to indicate a Class 6 trail. This classification means the route involves rock climbing and abseiling.

Do not proceed beyond a 'Gorge Risk Area' sign, unless you:

- Have a nationally recognised accreditation to abseil and climb on natural surfaces.
- Are under the supervision of a qualified leader that has nationally recognised accreditation to abseil and climb on natural surfaces.
- Are using Standards Australia/International Standards approved abseil and climb equipment.

When exploring these potentially dangerous places:

- Always stick to designated trails or markings.
- Stay away from edges that may be loose underfoot.
- Wear good walking boots with good ankle support.
- Take plenty of water.
- Take special care in areas with potentially slippery water-smooth rock and loose surfaces.
- Water in gorges that receive little sunlight in winter can be seriously cold, so take care if swimming. Do not ever jump or dive into any pools of water.
- Tell others before setting out on a hike.
- Observe all warning signs.

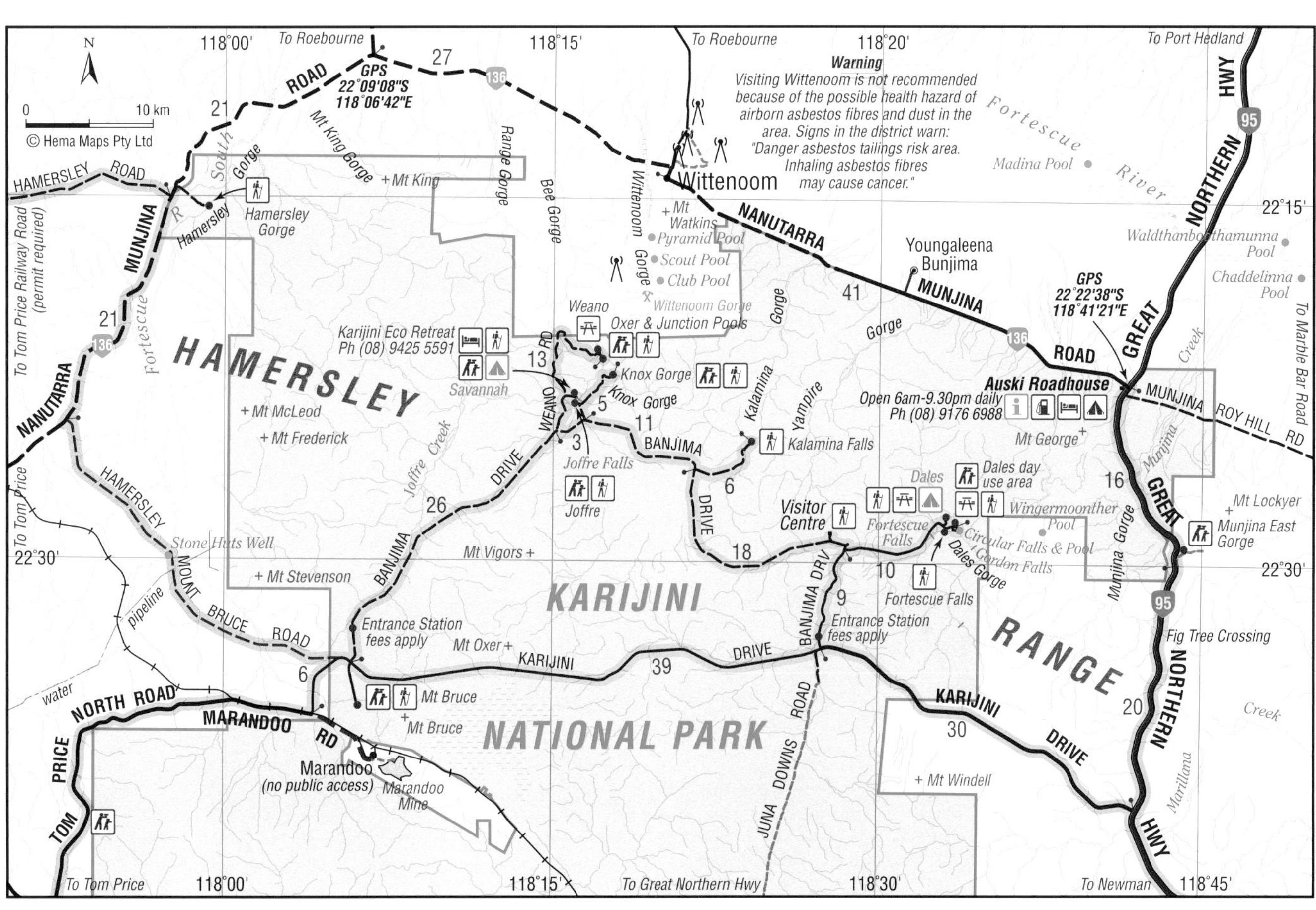

Where to Stay

Karijini Eco Retreat has luxury eco tents and unpowered camping sites with lots of facilities (Ph 08 9425 5591, www.karijiniecoretreat.com.au). The Retreat is 100% owned by the Gumala Aboriginal Corporation.

The *Dales Gorge Campground* is a DEC-run area operating on a first-in, best-dressed system. There are generator and non-generator camps, as well as spots for big groups. The area has bush toilets and showers, picnic tables and gas barbecues.

On the eastern edge of Karijini National Park, the *Auski Roadhouse* provides caravan and camping sites (Ph 08 9176 6988).

Along the Roebourne Wittenoom Rd, about half way between Millstream-Chichester and Karijini national parks, *Mount Florance Station* offers camping and caravan sites between April 1 and September 30 (Ph 08 9189 8151).

Tour Operators

Karijini Eco Retreat work in partnership with various operators to offer some tours. **REMTREK** have trekking and astronomy tours (Ph 0409 087 677, www.remtrek.com.au), with **West Oz Active** you can access Class 6 gorges (Ph 0438 913 713, www.westozactive.com.au) and **Pilbara Gorge Tours** save your car with a half- or full-day tour (Ph 08 9188 1534, www.pilbaragorgetours.com.au). Bookings for all tours can be made with Karijini Eco Retreat (Ph 08 9425 5591, www.karijiniecoretreat.com.au).

Based in Tom Price, **Lestok Tours** provide full-day tours of Karijini National Park on an air-conditioned coach or bus (Ph 08 9189 2032, www.lestoktours.com.au).

Darwin-based **Willis' Walkabouts** offers extended guided bushwalks in Karijini National Park a couple of times a year from Tom Price (Ph 08 8985 2134, www.bushwalkingholidays.com.au).

Jindawurrunha (Chinderwarriner) Pool

STEVEN DAVID MILLER, NATURAL WANDERS

Millstream-Chichester National Park

(Map 27 D3)

Really two parks in one, **Millstream-Chichester National Park** is the combination of sections of both the **Chichester Range** to the northeast and the mighty **Fortescue River** in the southwest. These two special spots are separated by a 20km drive. A **natural spring**, from an underground aquifer fed by the Fortescue River, the oasis of Millstream is made up of permanent pools that are important to the Yinjibarndi people. Later, pastoralists also prized this water supply when the area was an early sheep-grazing property. After the Millstream pastoral station was acquired by the government as a water supply and national park, the homestead became the visitor centre. Today, the park is jointly managed by Aboriginal rangers.

The park is fairly isolated and you'll have to plan your trip well because the nearest supplies and fuel are 132km away. There is now a sealed access road from Karratha to the intersection with the Roebourne Wittenoom Rd (an access permit is no longer required). Other roads into and through the park are gravel, but suitable for a 2WD vehicle. The condition of the roads depends on how recently the grader went through, and the uneven grids need to be taken with care. It is best to visit during the winter months (April to October) when the daytime temperatures are lower and there is little rain.

Information

The **Visitor Centre** in the Old Millstream Homestead has information about the park and displays on Aboriginal culture and pastoral history (Ph 08 9184 5144). The **DEC's Pilbara Regional Office** is in Anderson Rd Karratha (Ph 08 9143 1488).

The **Karratha Visitor Centre** can also provide information (Ph 08 9144 4600, www.pilbaracoast.com).

For a greater understanding of the park's significance to the area's traditional landowners, pick up a copy of *Ngurra Wardurala Buluyagayi: Exploring Yindjibarndi Country*. The book can be ordered through the Juluwarlu Aboriginal Corporation's website, www.juluwarlu.pilbara.net.

What to Do – Millstream section

Walking

The wheelchair-accessible **Homestead Walk** (750m, 30 min return) leads from the Homestead to a crystal-clear pool that is carpeted with lily pads and shaded by huge paperbarks and introduced date palms. **Jindawurrunha (Chinderwarriner) Pool** is very special to the Yinjibarndi people, and was also important as a water source for the coastal town of Dampier. The walk trail has interpretive signage explaining the lives of the people who lived at this outback oasis.

The easy **Murlunmunyjurna Track** (5km, 1.5hr return) also starts near the Homestead. Walk this track to see the very rare and native **Millstream palm** (*Livistona alfredii*) that grows along the banks.

Swimming

The **Fortescue River** has permanent pools of water at Millstream that are fed by the natural spring. **Crossing Pool** and **Deep Reach** are popular spots for **swimming**, **canoeing** and **windsurfing**. The facilities at these sites include safety railings and steps to get in and out of the pools. A full loop along **Snappy Gum Drive** passes both Crossing Pool and Deep Reach Pool.

Lookout

Gazing across the landscape from **Cliff Lookout** is a 'must do', especially near sunset when the rocks overlooking the **Fortescue River** glow vibrant red. Below lies a beautiful sweep of river lined

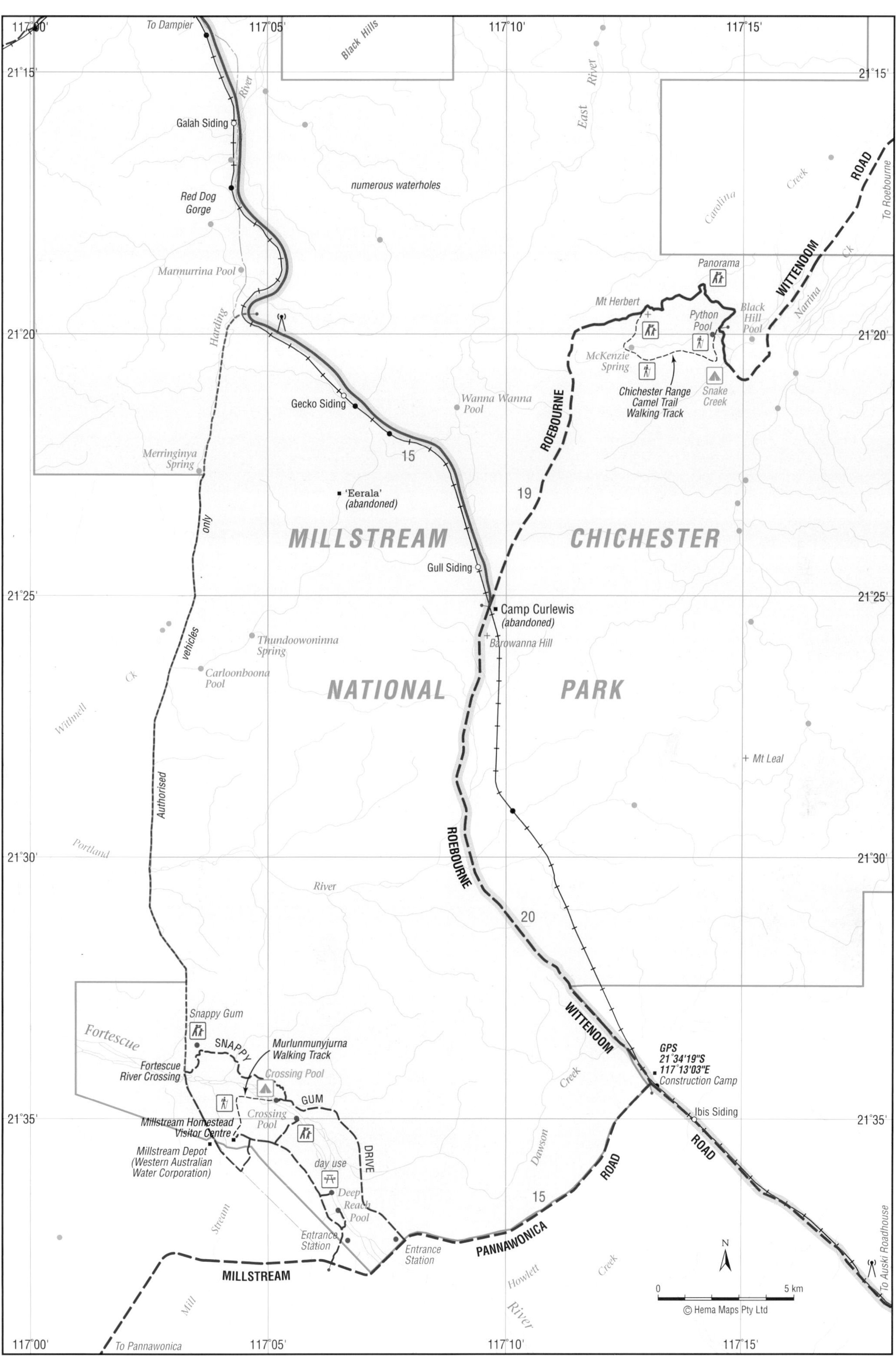
MILLSTREAM CHICHESTER
NATIONAL PARK
To Dampier
Black Hills
Galah Siding
Red Dog Gorge
numerous waterholes
Marmurrina Pool
Harding River
East River
Carolina Creek
To Roebourne
Panorama
Mt Herbert
Python Pool
Black Hill Pool
Narrina Ck
McKenzie Spring
Chichester Range Camel Trail Walking Track
Snake Creek
WITTENOOM ROAD
ROEBOURNE
Gecko Siding
Wanna Wanna Pool
Merringinya Spring
'Eerala' (abandoned)
Gull Siding
Camp Curlewis (abandoned)
Barowanna Hill
Thundoowoninna Spring
Carloonboona Pool
Authorised vehicles only
Withnell Ck
Mt Leal
Portland River
Snappy Gum
Fortescue
Fortescue River Crossing
SNAPPY GUM DRIVE
Murlunmunyjurna Walking Track
Crossing Pool
Millstream Homestead Visitor Centre
Millstream Depot (Western Australian Water Corporation)
day use
Deep Reach Pool
Entrance Station
Dawson Creek
GPS 21°34'19"S 117°13'03"E
Construction Camp
Ibis Siding
ROEBOURNE WITTENOOM ROAD
PANNAWONICA ROAD
MILLSTREAM
Mill Stream
Howlett River
Creek
To Pannawonica
To Auski Roadhouse
0 5 km
© Hema Maps Pty Ltd
117°00' 117°05' 117°10' 117°15'
21°15' 21°20' 21°25' 21°30' 21°35'
15 19 20

with palms and gums. Near sunset is also the time to see flocks of **corellas** swoop through searching for a roost for the night. Then the **white cockatoos** start to come in pairs until there are great mobs of them too.

Where to Stay – Millstream section

Camping is at the DEC-run *Crossing Pool campsite*, where there are pit toilets and gas barbecues.

Along the Roebourne Wittenoom Rd, about half way between Millstream-Chichester and Karijini national parks, *Mount Florance Station* offers camping and caravan sites between April 1 and September 30 (Ph 08 9189 8151).

What to Do – Chichester Range section

Driving between the Millstream section of the park and the Chichester Range, the road meanders through rounded dome hills dusted in spinifex and snappy gums with spectacular views at every turn. Although the Chichester Range could be considered the little sister when compared with the Hamersley Range, they are a spectacular place in their own right. Though extremely rugged, the Chichester Range has rolling spinifex hills, spectacular escarpments and winding tree-lined watercourses. There are fewer facilities than at Karijini National Park, but that also means less visitors.

Swimming

Python Pool is the most visited place in the Chichester Range. A sheer drop plunges into a permanent freshwater pool eroded over millions of years that is a popular place for a **swim**. The pool is surrounded by sheer, red-rock walls. (Camping was allowed here once, but it isn't anymore.)

Walking

The walk trails are generally graded Class 4 so you need to be fairly fit to attempt them. Heat is a real issue too, even in winter, so don't leave the car without suitable clothing and plenty of drinking water. The **Chichester Range Camel Trail** is a total of 16km return, so should be undertaken early in the day when the temperatures are lower.

The **Python Pool Track** (100m, 20 min return) leads from the car park along the creek bed to Python Pool.

The **Chichester Range Camel Trail** (8km, 3hr one way) leaves from Python Pool. The first part of the track is known as the **Cameleer Trail** as it climbs up the escarpment to a lookout over the spectacular vista below. The trail up the escarpment is narrow and that Pilbara spinifex can get a bit scratchy. At the top of the escarpment, it is simply a matter of following an old 4WD track over the rolling spinifex and termite mound-covered hills. About 5km in is the permanent **McKenzie Spring**, a pretty waterhole that feeds down to Python Pool. Following the old camel trail, it is not difficult to imagine back to the times when Afghan camel drivers slaved to blast their way through the hills to build the camel trails over which their teams carried bales of wool to the ports on the coast.

Crossing the pool on flat water-eroded rocks begins the **Mount Herbert Track** (600m, 45 min return from the Camel Trail). The mountain is one of the taller peaks in the area and the trail is single file in width. Once again the view over the plain below is spectacular.

Other than the views, these walks offer an opportunity to see some iconic Pilbara **wildflowers** in the winter months, including the Sturt pea and *Grevillea wickhami*.

Scenic Drive

The **Chichester Drive** is one of WA's great drives. For safety this section of the narrow road has been sealed, so it is safe for all combinations of rigs if undertaken slowly. The driver needs to concentrate though because the scenery is spectacular and the road snakes steeply up to heights of over 360m. To resist the rubbernecking there is a series of **lookout** car parks, the last being the car park at **Mount Herbert**.

Where to Stay – Chichester Range section

Camping is at the DEC-run *Snake Creek campsite*, where there are pit toilets but no other facilities. (No camping fee applies.) It's worth camping a night here just to see the setting sun light up the ranges with an unbelievable hue of glowing red.

View from the Cameleer Trail

PELUSEY PHOTOGRAPHY

PELUSEY PHOTOGRAPHY

Cleaning crabs, Onslow

Onslow to Point Samson Peninsula

Onslow (Map 25 D7)

A coastal town between Exmouth and Karratha, **Onslow** is an 80km detour off the North West Coastal Highway. The original town of Onslow, which was located at the mouth of the **Ashburton River**, was proclaimed in 1883. It was established as a port for the newly expanding pastoral industry, but the low, exposed position made it very vulnerable to rampaging cyclones. Around 1925 Onslow was moved to its present site next to **Beadon Point** and many of the buildings from the old town site were relocated. Despite the move, Onslow is still regarded as one of the most cyclone-prone towns in Australia. If you happen to be in town between December and April, learn about what to do in a cyclone and heed warnings.

Information

The **Onslow Tourist Centre** is located in Second Avenue (Ph 08 9184 6644). The Centre is only open from May to October (closed Sundays).

Information is also available from the **Shire of Ashburton's Onslow office** (Ph 08 9184 6001, www.ashburton.wa.gov.au).

What to Do

From the turnoff through to Onslow, be amazed at the thousands of **termite mounds** that stand tall beside the road. Perfectly adapted to this extreme climate, the termites use the red dirt to create tall multi-storey mounds.

One of the few places where the sun both rises and sets over water, Onslow is a popular place to see the phenomenon known as the **'Staircase to the Moon'** – during the winter months. At any time of year, a wander along the **Ian Blair Boardwalk** to see the sunrise or sunset is a popular activity.

Visitors can also follow the **Heritage Trail** or browse through the **Goods Shed Museum** to read about the town and look through the vast collection of machinery, bottles and memorabilia.

Fishing is a popular pastime and during the winter months the sleepy town fills up with keen fishers. There are numerous excellent spots locally, or visitors can head offshore to the **Mackerel Islands** group. On the right tide, **Four Mile Creek** is good for mangrove-loving fish and **mud crabs**. Other popular spots include the **Groyne** and **Ashburton River**. The Mackerel Islands are paradise for boat anglers seeking Spanish mackerel, trevally, coral trout, red emperor, tuna, sailfish, marlin and many other tropical species. A holiday resort is located on **Thevenard Island**, a coral atoll that is 6km long and 1.5km wide. Jump aboard the local dive operator charter to explore the colourful marine wonderland. The island offers accommodation with a dining room, bar and pool, plus a general store. If you have good boating skills and are looking to really get away from it all, then try **Direction Island**. You need to be self-sufficient as there are no facilities on the island, except a cabin that sleeps up to six.

Most **four-wheel driving** around Onslow centres on finding the good fishing spots. The nearby **Back Beach** has a soft-sand run to **Four Mile Creek**. There are also tracks in various states of drivability around **Old Onslow** and the nearby **Ashburton River**. The Ashburton River is tidal and lined with mangroves towards its mouth. It also forks into two branches near the ocean, making it hard to reach the true mouth.

The largest remains at **Old Onslow (25 E7)** are the police complex, built of brick and stone, which are well worth a look. An informative trail brochure of the ruins, complete with a mud map, is available from the Onslow Tourist Centre.

Low tide at Onslow

PELUSEY PHOTOGRAPHY

PELUSEY PHOTOGRAPHY

Beach fishing near Onslow

PELUSEY PHOTOGRAPHY

Road to Paraburdoo

Organised Tours

- **Mackerel Islands**, off Onslow – a snorkelling trail and many diving sites (Ph 08 9184 6444, www.mackerelislands.com.au)
- **West Coast Marine Fishing Charters**, Onslow – fishing charters to the Mackerel Islands from Apr to Oct (Ph 0417 176 385, 0428 124 751, www.westcoastmarine.com.au)

Where to Stay

- *Beadon Bay Village* (Ph 08 9184 6007)
- *Onslow Mackerel Motel* (Ph 08 9184 6586, www.onslowmackerelmotel.com.au)
- *Onslow Ocean View Caravan Park* (Ph 08 9184 6053)
- *Onslow Sun Chalet* (Ph 08 9184 6058, www.onslowsunchalets.com.au)

Camping

Away from the coast, the *Ashburton River* is lined with shady river gums that make it a pleasant spot for camping. There have been reports of a wayward saltwater crocodile in various locations along the Ashburton River, so check with the tourist centre about current conditions.

Mackerel Islands

- *Direction Island* – one beach cabin that sleeps up to six people (Ph 08 9184 6586 or 08 9184 6444, www.mackerelislands.com.au)
- *Thevenard Island* – Club Thevenard Accommodation Village & 2, 3 & 5 brm beach cabins; Club Thevenard is closed from Nov to Mar (Ph 08 9184 6444, www.mackerelislands.com.au)

Mangrove Islands
Salt mine tours, museum, heritage trail, fishing
Fuel : 7am-6pm Mon-Fri, 7am-1.30pm Sat & Sun
Service Station Ph (08) 9184 6113
Onslow
Onslow Ocean View Caravan Park
Onslow Solar Saltfield
To Fortescue Roadhouse
Mining town, limited accommodation
Fuel : 7.30am-5pm Mon-Fri, 8am-1pm Sat
Service Station Ph (08) 9184 1017
Pannawonica
GPS 21°35'31"S 115°56'14"E
MILLSTREAM PANNAWONICA ROAD
To Karratha
Millstream Homestead Visitor Centre
NORTH WEST COASTAL HWY
ONSLOW ROAD
HAMERSLEY
Cane River Conservation Park
GPS 22°30'16"S 115°31'08"E
NANUTARRA MUNJINA ROAD
Nanutarra Roadhouse
Ph (08) 9943 0521
Open 6.30am-10pm daily
GPS 22°39'51"S 116°13'28"E
GPS 22°58'10"S 117°04'54"E
Barlee Range Nature Reserve
To Minilya Roadhouse
© Hema Maps Pty Ltd

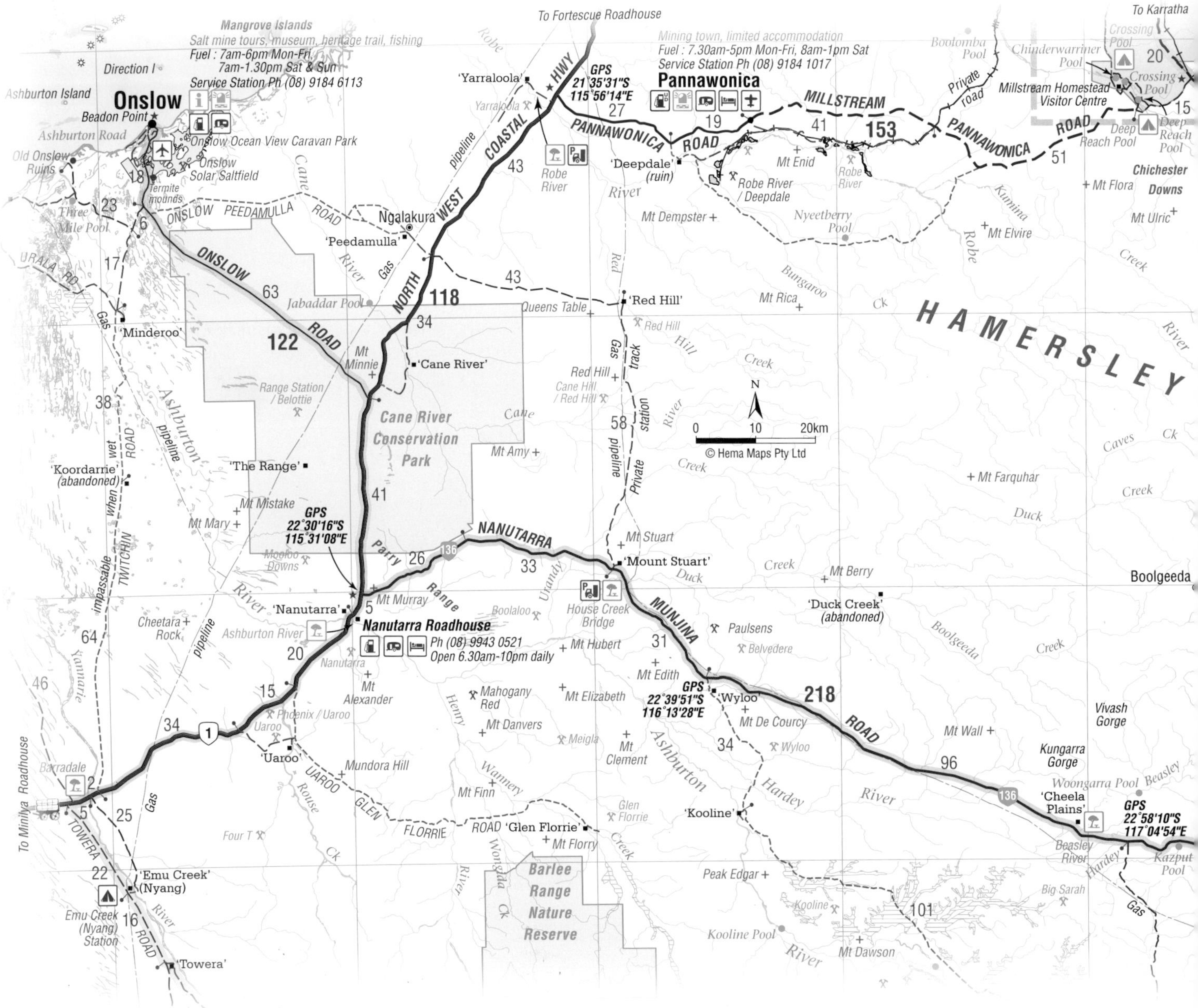

Pannawonica (Map 26 D11)

The sealed road from the North West Coastal Highway to **Pannawonica** – or Panna to the locals – passes through spectacular countryside of tabletop mesas and eroded ranges. Keep an eye open for the **'Boot Tree'**. Pannawonica is a handy spot to stop if you're heading inland to explore **Millstream-Chichester National Park** (see p76). Be warned, the Millstream-Yarraloola Rd is only recommended for 4WDs and is not suitable for caravans or trailers. Pannawonica is a true mining town, basically just there to service the mine workers. An **open-air cinema** that is free (yes, actually free) is an added attraction in an otherwise purely functional town. Things get lively in September when the **rodeo** hits town.

Information

Information is available from the **Shire of Ashburton's Pannawonica office** (Ph 08 9184 1038, www.ashburton.wa.gov.au).

Where to stay

- *Pannawonica Caravan Park* (Ph 08 9184 1038)
- *Pannawonica Tavern* – motel-syle units (Ph 08 9184 1073)

Paraburdoo (Map 27 K3)

Built by Pilbara Iron (a subsidiary of Rio Tinto) in 1970, the township of **Paraburdoo** is now part of the Shire of Ashburton. With a population of less than 1000 people, the town's sole purpose is to provide services for the huge mining operations in the area. Great views of the mining operations are possible from **Radio Hill Lookout**, 5km south of the town.

For tourists, the town's proximity to **Karijini National Park** is its major asset – although most people choose Tom Price as their base. If you are flying in or out of this region, you'll be doing so from Paraburdoo as Tom Price doesn't have an airport. Be warned, it is a busy airport too because of all the 'fly-in fly-out' mine workers. (The airport is owned and maintained by Pilbara Iron.)

Paraburdoo derives its name from the Aboriginal name Pirupardu, which means 'meat feathers', because of the abundance of corellas in the area.

Information

Contact the **Shire of Ashburton's Paraburdoo office** (Ph 08 9189 5402, www.ashburton.wa.gov.au).

Where to Stay

- *Paraburdoo Inn* (Ph 08 9189 5303)

Tom Price (Map 27 H3)

The gateway to **Karijini National Park**, Tom Price is also a destination in itself. Whichever way you approach the town, nestled deep in the **Hamersley Range**, you will be rewarded with beautiful scenery. A relatively new town, Tom Price sprang up with the discovery of iron ore in the region in the 1960s. It is named for an American, **Thomas Moore Price**, who came to the area in the 1960s to assess the iron ore. He lobbied the governments to allow the mines and export of iron ore to go ahead.

Tom Price is situated at the base of **Jarndrunminhna (Mount Nameless)**, which is 1128m above sea level. As mountains go in Western Australia, it's a big one. Tom Price itself is already 747m above sea level, making it Western Australia's highest town.

Information

The **Tom Price Visitor Centre** in Central Rd can assist with tour and accommodation bookings (Ph 08 9188 1112, www.tompricewa.com.au/centre.asp).

What to do

The spectacular **Jarndrunminhna (Mount Nameless)** typifies the Pilbara with its red rock covered by green spinifex and white trunks of snappy gums. There are two ways of getting up to the top of Jarndrunminhna: by 4WD or foot. There is a steep **4WD track** up the hill, but you'll have to leave the caravan behind. This is the highest 4WD track in WA. If you really want to be energetic then climb the **walk trail** to the top from the Nameless Valley Road or Tom Price Tourist Park. Whichever way you ascend, the views from the top over the massive open-cut mine and surrounding countryside are stupendous.

After seeing the **Pilbara Iron Ore Mine** from the top of Jarndrunminhna (Mount Nameless), you will probably have an urge to see it up close and personal. **Tours** run from the visitor centre to allow you to do just that. Once you have donned your safety helmet and glasses (wear long sleeves,

Summit of Mount Nameless after rain

PELUSEY PHOTOGRAPHY

PELUSEY PHOTOGRAPHY

Driving down Mount Nameless

GAVIN JAMES

Woodside Visitor Centre on the Burrup Peninsula

long pants and closed-in shoes) it is off to the mine site in a bus. The first time a haul pack drives past the window you will be in awe of their incredible size.

Of course Tom Price is only a 45 minute drive from **Karijini National Park** (see p73), which makes it the perfect base from which to explore, whether you drive yourself or jump aboard a local day tour.

Where to Stay

- *Tom Price Tourist Park* (Ph 08 9189 1515)
- *Tom Price Hotel Motel* (Ph 08 9189 1101)
- *Windawarri (Karijini) Lodge* (Ph 08 9189 1110)

Along the Roebourne Wittenoom Rd, about half way between Millstream-Chichester and Karijini national parks, *Mount Florance Station* offers camping and caravan sites between April 1 and September 30 (Ph 08 9189 8151).

Tour Operators

Lestok Tours offer tours of the Pilbara Iron Ore Mine and full-day tours of Karijini National Park on an air-conditioned coach or bus (Ph 08 9189 2032, www.lestoktours.com.au).

Wilanah Walkabouts provide an indigenous cultural bush walk (contact the Tom Price Visitor Centre Ph 08 9188 1112).

Various operators work in partnership with **Karijini Eco Retreat** to offer some tours in Karijini National Park. **REMTREK** have trekking and astronomy tours (Ph 0409 087 677, www.remtrek.com.au), with **West Oz Active** you can access Class 6 gorges (Ph 0438 913 713, www.westozactive.com.au) and **Pilbara Gorge Tours** save your car with a half- or full-day tour (Ph 08 9188 1534, www.pilbaragorgetours.com.au). Bookings for all tours can be made with Karijini Eco Retreat (Ph 08 9425 5591, www.karijiniecoretreat.com.au).

Dampier & the Dampier Archipelago

Overlooking Hampton Harbour, **Dampier (26 A12)** was built in 1966 by Hamersley Iron (now called Pilbara Iron) to house the port facilities where iron ore is stockpiled and loaded onto gigantic ships for export. Today the town is still a buzz with the mining boom. The massive **North West Shelf Gas Project**, situated on the nearby **Burrup Peninsula**, is managed by Woodside Energy. The Pilbara also boasts Australia's largest **solar salt fields**, including one at Dampier. Dampier Salt is WA's principal salt producer.

English buccaneer **William Dampier** discovered the **Dampier Archipelago (26 A11)** in 1699, but what he saw of the barren coastline near Dampier did not impress him much. Dampier, in command of the *Roebuck*, was the first European known to have stepped onto the islands of the Dampier Archipelago. School children from Dampier have built a memorial where he landed. The region's indigenous history goes back long before Dampier's 'discovery' though and is still evident today through the **petroglyphs** that can be found on the islands.

Further west are the **Montebello Islands** that are prized for fishing, snorkelling and diving.

Information

For information on Dampier contact the **Karratha Visitor Centre** (Ph 08 9144 4600, www.pilbaracoast.com) or the **Shire of Roebourne** in Karratha (Ph 08 9186 8555, www.roebourne.wa.gov.au).

What to Do

The Karratha Visitor Centre can organise tours of the **Pilbara Iron port facilities** in Dampier. Visitors can't help but be impressed by the enormity and complexity of these projects. Don't miss the memorial to **'Red Dog'** on the way into town.

Burrup Peninsula (Map 26 A13)

Nearby, the **Burrup Peninsula** is a testament to the 30 000-year-old history of the Aboriginal people in the Pilbara. The most prolific **rock engraving (petroglyphs)** site in the world, it was national heritage listed in 2007. The Pilbara's petroglyphs are considered to be among the earliest examples of art in Australia. Massive piles of jagged red rocks dominate the spinifex-studded landscape. Many of these rocks feature a variety of up to one million carved images. A walk around this amazing site reveals engravings of turtles, kangaroos, other animals and human parts. It is thought these petroglyphs were the work of the Jaburara people who once lived in this region. Scientific dating techniques have revealed these petroglyphs range from 6000 to 30 000 years old. Much of Burrup Peninsula's rock art is under protection by the DEC and local Aboriginal custodians. Due to its close proximity to the industrial areas of Dampier and Karratha, the site is considered to be potentially under threat by industry and pollution. It is also under threat from the expanding nature of the North West Shelf Venture. To see the petroglyphs, get a map from the Karratha Visitor Centre. The easiest site to reach is off the Hearson's Cove road. When you wander into the site at first you may not be able to see anything. Just take your time because you will start to see shapes and shadows on the rocks. Once you can see a few petroglyphs, more and more seem to pop up.

Visitors can also check out the **Woodside Visitor Centre** for an interesting insight into the amazing world of gas exploration and production (Ph 08 9158 8292). Natural gas was discovered 130km west of Dampier in the 1970s, and the **North West Shelf Venture** is one of the biggest projects operating in Australia. The visitor centre overlooks part of the huge Woodside Gas Plant.

Near the Woodside Visitor Centre is a **lookout** with views of the Burrup Peninsula, North West Shelf onshore operations and surrounding West Pilbara coast. The sight is particularly stunning at night. To get there, take the unmarked track at the junction of the Burrup and Dampier roads. It gets a little bumpy towards the top of the hill, but is accessible with a 2WD vehicle if you drive with care.

Hearson's Cove Beach provides the perfect vantage point to view the phenomenon known as **'Staircase to the Moon'** during the full moon dates of winter.

Burrup Fertilisers is also located on the Burrup Peninsula – they are the world's largest single-train ammonia plant.

COLIN KERR

West Lewis Island, Dampier Archipelago

Fishing & Boating

The major attractions and activities for locals and visitors alike revolve around one thing – water.

The **mangrove creeks** that dominate the tidal flats around Dampier offer good fishing for mangrove jack, threadfin salmon, mud crabs, bream and catfish. An incoming tide to high tide is the best time. Check with the tackle or sports shops in Karratha for the latest information. But for the real action, get a **boat** or go on a **fishing charter** and head out to the islands.

Fishing and boating go hand in hand, so it may be no great surprise that both Dampier and Karratha have one of the highest rates of boat ownership per capita in Australia. Besides fishing, people use boats to get to the islands where the sheltered beaches and snorkelling and diving on the beautiful coral reefs are the major attractions.

Dampier Archipelago (Map 26 A11)

Of the 42 islands that make up the beautiful, unspoilt Dampier Archipelago, 25 are classified as **nature reserves**. These islands have a fascinating history of shipwrecks, whaling and pearling.

The waterways around the islands are rich in marine life and are popular **fishing** grounds, including game fishing. You can use lures to catch big trevally, dart and queenfish almost anywhere. Trolling bait or lures behind a boat can tempt hard-hitting Spanish mackerel, tuna, cobia, trevally and sailfish. Anglers chasing bottom fish are well served with red emperor, coral trout, cod, several emperor species and big trevally, just to name a few.

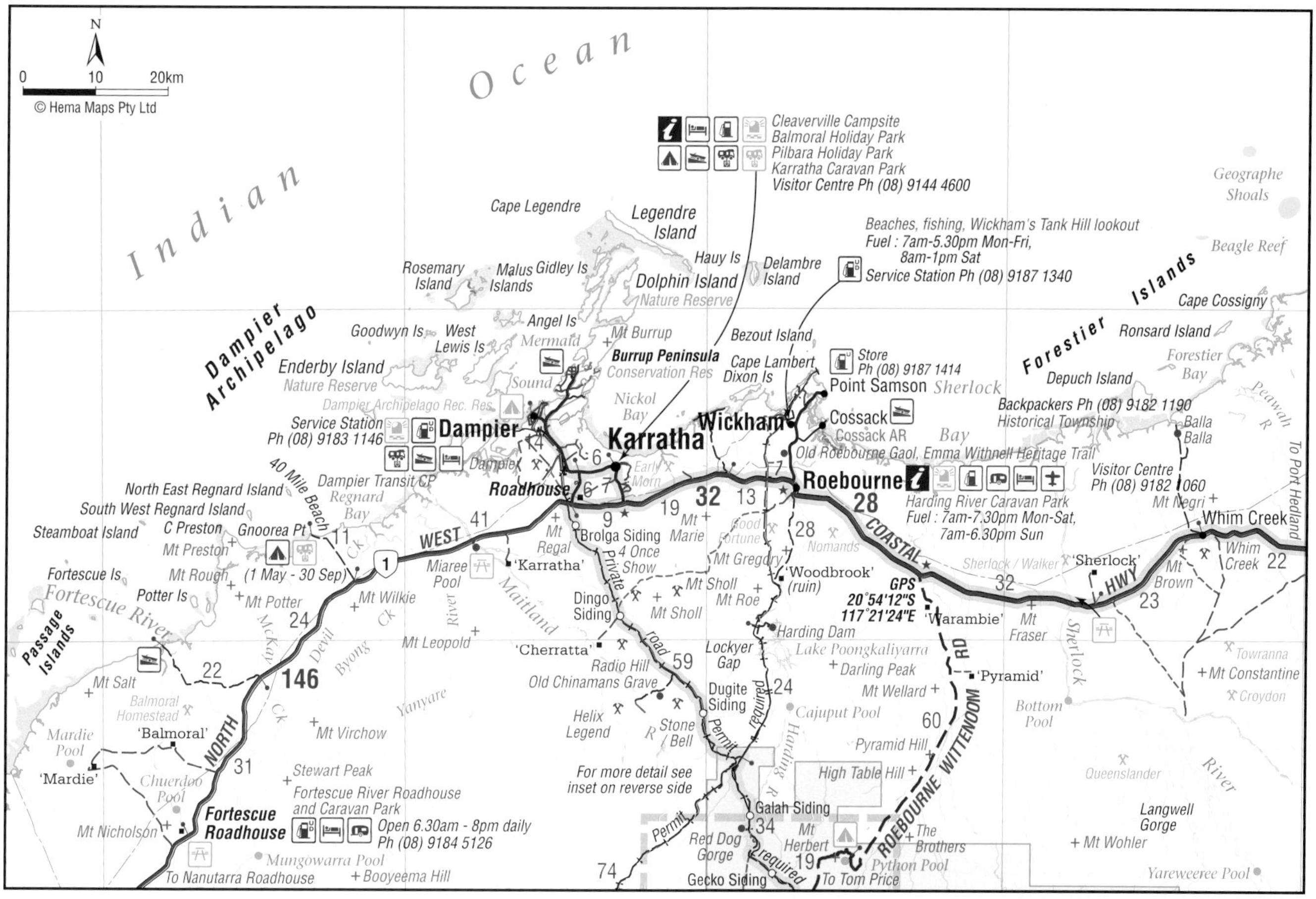

Many visitors also **dive** on the **coral reefs** around the islands where turtles, dugongs, bottlenose dolphins and whales are often seen. **Turtles** nest at rookeries along the Dampier Archipelago from September to April and **humpback whales** are seen between July and September. The islands are also the place to see 26 species of **seabirds**. Over 200 species of **corals** have been classified in waters surrounding the Dampier Archipelago. The best diving sites are located in reef country off the outer islands such as **Rosemary Island**.

Visitors wishing to go snorkelling, diving or fishing amid the islands can either hire a boat or go on a charter cruise.

Early Aboriginal communities inhabited a number of these islands, and on those with extensive areas of granite, dolerite and basalt rocks there are many excellent examples of **rock engravings (petroglyphs)**.

On a number of the islands **camping** is allowed up to 100m inland of the highwater mark, but no facilities are provided. Islands such as **East Lewis** and **Rosemary** have DEC-run shacks. It can get windy out here but the islands do offer some sort of shelter on their leeside. (Full details on camping are available from the DEC's Karratha office.)

Montebello Islands (Map 26 A9)

The **Montebello Islands** are further out and therefore require bigger boats that are suited to more open sea conditions. Fish species are similar to what you might expect to catch in the Dampier Archipelago, but there are more of them due to its isolated location. The **Montebello Islands Marine Park** was created to protect areas of unique reef and island ecosystems. Whales, dugongs and turtles are frequently seen in the area. In season, trips operate to the Montebello Islands.

Where to Stay

- *Dampier Mermaid Hotel & Motel* (Ph 08 9183 1222, www.dampiermermaid.com.au)
- *Dampier Transit Park* – three night limit (Ph 08 9183 1109)

View of the expanding Karratha

PELUSEY PHOTOGRAPHY

Dampier Archipelago

PELUSEY PHOTOGRAPHY

Camping

Bush camping is permitted on many of the islands of the *Dampier Archipelago*, 100m inland of the highwater mark. Contact the DEC's Karratha office for details (Ph 08 9143 1488).

Bush camping is also permitted at *40 Mile Beach campsite*, on the coast south of Dampier, from 1 May to 30 September each year. Maximum three month stay. The site is 4WD access and there is a boat ramp. Contact the Shire of Roebourne in Karratha for more information (Ph 08 9186 8555, or ranger service 08 9186 8528, www.roebourne.wa.gov.au).

Tour Operators

- **Aqualand Charters** (Ph 08 9183 1885, www.aqualand.com.au)
- **Discovery Sailing Adventures** – take day cruises and overnighters to the Dampier Archipelago, or hire a boat if you have a skipper ticket (Ph 0408 801 040, www.discoverysailingadventures.com.au)
- **Pilbara Sea Charters** – fishing, whale watching and custom cruises; operate from Point Samson too (Ph 08 9144 4600)

Karratha (Map 26 A13)

The youngest and fastest growing town in the Pilbara, **Karratha** is the administrative centre for the Shire of Roebourne. Aptly named for the Aboriginal word meaning 'good country', Karratha owes its existence to a shortage of land for housing in Dampier and the major mining and gas projects around it. While Dampier was originally a closed town, owned by the mining companies, Karratha was the service town for the people brought in by the mining industry. Natural gas discoveries on the North West Shelf provided another booming industry for the towns. Trains from the mines around Tom Price deliver their ore to the port at **Cape Lambert**. The boom of the early 2000s saw a hive of activity to provide housing, roads and facilities for the growing population. Karratha is a busy town and well served with facilities, including major shopping centres, which makes it a good place to stock up before entering the Pilbara's more isolated areas.

Information

For information contact the **Karratha Visitor Centre** in Karratha Rd (Ph 08 9144 4600, www.pilbaracoast.com). The **Shire of Roebourne** in Karratha can also provide help, including road conditions and cyclone information (Ph 08 9186 8555, www.roebourne.wa.gov.au).

What to Do

The Jaburara, the indigenous people of the Karratha region, were massacred in the early days of European exploration. However, some evidence of the Jaburara being in the area can be found in the range of hills just behind the Karratha township. The **Jaburara Heritage Trail** has been established to highlight the Jaburara's history. The trail begins at the Karratha Visitors Centre and initially involves a short walk uphill to the water tanks on a rough dirt road. There are good views from here over the town and out to sea.

If you have your own boat then ask about **Back Beach** where you can explore the tidal area's mangroves and try **fishing** for barramundi.

With its good facilities and range of accommodation, Karratha makes a handy base for day trips to attractions such as Point Samson, Roebourne, Cossack and the Burrup Peninsula.

Tour Operators

- **Adventure Sports** – diving (Ph 08 9185 1957)
- **Norkat Boat Charters** – fishing and eco tours to the Dampier Archipelago and Montebello Islands (Ph 08 9144 4922)
- **Oceanus Sport Fishing Charters** – fishing and eco tours to the Dampier Archipelago; sport and game fishing charters (Ph 08 9144 4322)

Where to Stay

- *All Seasons Karratha* (Ph 08 9159 1000, www.allseasons.com.au)
- *Balmoral Holiday Park* – minimum three month stay (Ph 08 9185 3628, www.aspenparks.com.au)
- *Best Western Karratha Central Apartments* (Ph 08 9143 9888, www.karrathacentral.bestwestern.com.au)
- *Comfort Inn and Suites* (Ph 08 9144 0777, www.choicehotels.com.au)
- *Karratha Apartments* (Ph 08 9143 9222, www.karrathaapartments.com.au)
- *Karratha Caravan Park* (Ph 08 9185 1012)
- *Karratha International Hotel* (Ph 1800 099 801, www.karrathainternational.com.au)
- *Pilbara Holiday Park* (Ph 1800 451 855, www.aspenparks.com.au)

Camping

Bush camping is permitted at *Cleaverville campsite*, from 1 May to 30 September each year. Maximum three month stay. The site is 4WD access and there is a boat ramp. Contact the Shire of Roebourne in Karratha for more information (Ph 08 9186 8555, or ranger service 08 9186 8528, www.roebourne.wa.gov.au).

Port Samson Peninsula

Information

The **Roebourne Visitor Centre** is in the Old Goal in Queen St (Ph 08 9182 1060, www.pilbaracoast.com). The **Shire of Roebourne** in Karratha can also provide assistance on what there is to see and do in the region, including road conditions and cyclone information (Ph 08 9186 8555, www.roebourne.wa.gov.au).

Roebourne (Map 27 A2)

Gazetted as a town in 1866, **Roebourne** was the administrative centre for the whole area north of the Murchison River for many years. The town was named for **John Septimus Roe**, who was the first surveyor general in Western Australia. For some meteorological reason, Roebourne gives Marble Bar a run for its money in summer as a WA hot spot.

What to Do

A number of old **stone buildings** remain from the time Roebourne was an important administrative centre for the region, including the **old Roebourne gaol**. Other solid heritage buildings include the old **Holy Trinity Church** (1895), **old hospital** (1887) and the **post office** (1887). Nearby on **Mount Welcome** is a view over the town to the coast and hills inland.

The old gaol is now home to the Roebourne Visitor Centre, **historical museum**, and local arts and crafts. It's also the starting point for the **Emma Withnell Heritage Trail**, a 52km driving and walking route that heads from Roebourne to explore Cossack, Wickham and Point Samson. Emma Withnell is known as the 'first lady of the Pilbara'. She was the first female settler in the Pilbara when she arrived with two children and some livestock to live in the first house built in Roebourne.

Roebourne is a hot bed of talented people with two **art groups** operating to support the indigenous artists of Roebourne and the North West. The work of the **Yinjaa-Bardi Art Group** has been exhibited in the Cossack Art Award and Port Hedland Art Award. Senior artists also have work in the Art Gallery of Western Australia. The gallery, in the historic Dalgety House next to the old gaol, is open for sales in the tourist season. The **Roebourne Art Group** represents indigenous artists in the West Pilbara. The gallery has paintings, carvings and weavings for viewing and sale.

To tour the **Cape Lambert iron ore facility** near Wickham and the old town of **Cossack**, ask at the visitor centre about the **Port to Port Tour**.

Roebourne is a great base from which to head inland to explore the **Millstream Chichester National Park** (see p76).

Where to Stay

- *Harding River Caravan Park* (Ph 08 9182 1063)

Cossack (Map 27 A2)

The historic township of **Cossack**, founded in 1863 when it was called **Tien Tsin Harbour**, is just 12km from Roebourne. It was first used as a port after **Walter Padbury** charted the harbour, and throughout its early history the township had a few unofficial names. In 1871 the name Cossack was decided on for the *Cossack*, the ship that brought Western Australian Governor Sir Frederick Weld to the Pilbara. In 1872, the townsite was declared and by 1887 a horse-drawn tramway connected Cossack and Roebourne. Cossack grew and prospered due to a thriving pearling industry that, like Broome, attracted immigrants from many Asian backgrounds. Factors such as over-fishing of pearl shell and Point Samson's increasingly important role as a port resulted in Cossack's ultimate demise in the early 1950s. Today Cossack is a popular destination for tourists because several of the original buildings have been fully restored, offering an insight into the region's colonial past.

What to Do

Explore the **old town** where the solidly constructed old buildings, which mostly date from the 1890s, have been faithfully restored. These include the post and telegraph office, courthouse, customs house/bond store, police station and gaol. Cossack's colourful history is richly on show at the local **museum**.

The historic **Customs House** has an art studio displaying works from local artists. Cossack is also home to the **Cossack**

Mudflats near Cossack

PELUSEY PHOTOGRAPHY

Photographs in the Old Gaol in Roebourne

GAVIN JAMES

Art Award, which has turned into an event of national recognition from what was merely a local art competition. The competition is held in August each year.

For an opportunity to interact with local **Bujee Nhoor Phu Aboriginal artists**, wander down to **Galbraith's Store** to see the array of artwork on display.

Just out of town, is an **old cemetery** registered with the National Trust. The cemetery is the final resting place of many Asian pearl divers who flocked to the Pilbara coast in the 1870s.

Cossack Adventure Cruises operate a range of tours to explore sites such as the old town of Cossack, Jarman Island lighthouse and Settler's Beach. (Ph 08 9187 0296, www.cossackcruises.com.au)

Where to stay

- *Old Police Barracks* – budget accommodation (Ph 08 9182 1190)

Wickham (Map 27 A1)

The massive 170 tonne haul truck on display at the entrance to **Wickham** is a reminder of the importance of mining in the Pilbara region. Wickham was established to service the mining industry and still mainly houses the workers from **Cape Lambert**. Pilbara Iron is responsible for the massive port facilities at Cape Lambert.

At sunset, Wickham's **Tank Hill Lookout** provides a view like no other and the secluded sandy beaches around **Port Walcott** have ideal **fishing** spots. For a different view of the area, try taking to the air with **Wickham Skydivers** (Ph 0417 180 064, www.australianskydivingadventures.com).

The town was named after **Captain John Clements Wickham**, who was in command of the *HMS Beagle* when it surveyed the area in 1840. *Grevillea wickhamii*, a red grevillea common in the Pilbara, is also named after Wickham.

Point Samson (Map 27 A2)

Roebourne's original port was at Cossack, but in 1904 a long jetty that could serve bigger ships was built at **Point Samson**. Eventually Point Samson took over from Cossack as the main port (see p85). Point Samson was in turn superseded by the township of Dampier, which was built in the 1960s. Port Samson then became a quiet fishing village until the boom period of the early 2000s when people of the surrounding communities realised its potential as a beach playground. Only 20 years ago the town consisted of little more than a hotel, caravan park and some fishing shacks, but today there are a few resorts, two caravan parks and some large houses. Some people even choose to live here and commute the 55km to Karratha and Dampier.

While the iron ore from Paraburdoo goes to Dampier, Tom Price's ore comes to Cape Lambert, virtually next to Point Samson. The trains arrive laden with ore that is then dumped onto a conveyor belt and transported along one of the highest and longest open ocean wharves in Australia. It stretches 2.5km out to sea where giant ore carriers lay waiting. A **lookout** reveals it all to the visitor.

Point Samson's beautiful sandy **beaches** are protected by fringing **coral reefs**, making them perfect for enjoying **swimming** and **snorkelling** all year round. **Samson Reef** lies just offshore and on a calm day at high tide it is nice to snorkel here. (Take care though, as the tides can be strong.) Rocky outcrops provide shelter from the winds in the secluded bays, one of which is romantically named **Honeymoon Cove**.

Fishing is a favourite pastime too, either off the beaches or on a charter boat. Anglers often try their luck off a small **causeway** just out of Point Samson. On a high or rising tide mangrove jack, trevally, queenfish and the odd barramundi can be caught there. Similar species can be found in many of the **mangrove creeks** in the area. Offshore, expect to tuck into the big ones such as Spanish mackerel, barracuda, cobia, huge trevally, a variety of emperors, coral trout and many others. For the real hardcore, further out there are tuna, marlin and sailfish. **Pilbara Sea Charters** offer fishing charters as well as whale watching cruises (Ph 08 9144 4600).

PELUSEY PHOTOGRAPHY

Caravan Park, Point Samson

A major **fishing fleet** also operates out of Port Samson with prawns, blue swimmer crabs and fish caught by a fleet of over 20 boats. The annual catch is one of the biggest in Western Australia. To try the local produce, head to the **seafood restaurants** on the Point or go to **Westmore Seafood's Factory**, on Bill Miller Dr off Honeymoon Rd, to buy fresh and frozen seafood.

Just 2km off the shore sits **Jarman Island** and its **lighthouse**. The original lighthouse for the port was built here in 1888, and it is still standing, although the lighthouse keeper's residence is a ruin. (You can visit Jarman Island on a cruise with Cossack Adventure Cruises – see above.)

Where to Stay

- *Amani Cottage* (Ph 08 9187 1085)
- *Cove Caravan Park* (Ph 08 9187 0199, www.thecovecaravanpark.com.au)
- *Delilah's B&B 'On the Beach'* (Ph 08 9187 1471)
- *Point Samson Resort* (Ph 08 9187 1052, www.pointsamson.com)
- *Samson Beach Chalets & The Round House* (Ph 08 9187 0202)
- *Samson Beach Tavern and Caravan Park* (Ph 08 9187 1414)
- *Samson Hideaway* (Ph 08 9187 0330)

Port Hedland to Broome

Port Hedland (Map 31 H6)

Port Hedland is a place for big transport as well as big piles of red and white dirt: the red is **iron ore** and the white is actually **salt**. And as for the transport, some of the longest and heaviest trains pull into Port Hedland regularly and iron-ore super tankers ease their way in and out of the harbour.

Gazetted in 1892, Port Hedland was named for **Captain Peter Hedland**, who made landfall at **Mangrove Harbour** in 1863. The first jetty was completed in 1899 with another built in 1908. In its early days, Port Hedland served as a port for Marble Bar, where gold had been discovered, and a railroad was built to facilitate the movement of goods between the two centres. Pearling luggers also used the port, as problems with berthing at Cossack increased. In the sixties, the population grew tenfold as Port Hedland became a transport hub for the fledgling, but rapidly growing, iron-ore industry. In the coming decades, Port Hedland's port facilities became one of the world's biggest in respect of tonnage handled. In that regard, Port Hedland vies with Dampier for the honour, but plans are afoot to increase the tanker capacity. Today, Port Hedland has a population of around 15 000.

Just 18km inland from Port Hedland, **South Hedland (31 H6)** is a modern satellite town with plenty of facilities.

Information

Port Hedland Visitor Centre,13 Wedge St (Ph 08 9173 1711).

What to Do

Trainspotters and lovers of big **ships** can drop into the Visitor Centre for the daily timetables. (Usually the times are written on a board outside.) Each day, long trains filled to the brim with iron ore chug along the tracks to the port. A good vantage point is **Redbank Bridge** on the way into town, just park the car and walk onto the bridge walkway. Trains pass under the bridge. In 2001, three world records were set for train transport when a BHP Billiton train lumbered into port with 682 cars loaded with iron ore, dragged along by eight locomotives. This feat set world records for: longest train, at 7.4km; heaviest total weight at 99 732 tonnes; and net mass of ore carried, at 82 262 tonnes.

When wandering around Port Hedland, you might also notice a huge cargo ship heading into town. The centrally located **Marapikurrinya Park** is an ideal viewing spot to watch tug boats manoeuvre the huge, but empty, bulk carriers into port. After loading up with ore, the ships leave – this time much lower in the water. This up close and personal view of the huge ships is sure to enthral.

Getting away from the mining focus, visitors can take a dip at **Pretty Pool**. The nearby **Cooke Point** and **Cemetery Beach** come alive during the winter months for the **'Staircase to the Moon'** phenomenon, and again during summer when **flatback turtles** nest and then hatchlings emerge.

Port Hedland has been pro-active in putting together some interesting **walks**, and brochures are available from the Visitor Centre. The *Walk-it Hedland* brochure has walks in both Port Hedland and South Hedland, including the **Turtle Walk** and **Point Cooke Walk**. The **Port Hedland Cultural and Heritage Trail** is a walk around the city centre and then a drive trail further down the road following 44 interpretive signs. Sign number 17 is **Dalgety House**, which is now a great little museum. They have imaginative audio displays and you can sit back in one of the old chairs and listen to some oral history from previous generations.

The **Harbour** offers great **fishing**, as do isolated spots at **Twelve Mile Creek**, **Tichilla** and **Cape Keraudren**.

The **Port Hedland Courthouse Art Gallery** is a beautiful centre with amazing changing exhibitions, culminating in the **Port Hedland Art Award**. There is always something interesting to see in here, and it is a great place to linger for a while away from the heat of the outside world.

For great views of the area, head to either **Koombana Lookout** or the **Town Observation Tower** (behind the visitor centre).

The outback and remote communities and stations in the region receive their mail from the flying postman. The **RASS Mail Run** leaves for a Port Hedland round trip on Wednesday. This is a great way to experience the really remote places of Western Australia. (The mail run also runs from Newman.) Other interesting insights into the region can be gained from a visit to the **Royal Flying Doctor Service** and the **School of the Air** at the Port Hedland international airport.

Where to Stay

- *All Seasons*, Port Hedland (Ph 08 9173 7000, www.allsesaons.com.au)
- *Beachfront*, Port Hedland (Ph 08 9173 2000)
- *Black Rock Tourist Park*, South Hedland (Ph 08 9172 3444)
- *The Esplanade Hotel*, Port Hedland (Ph 08 9173 1811)
- *Cooke Point Holiday Park*, Port Hedland (Ph 1800 459 999, www.aspenparks.com.au)
- *Hospitality Inn*, Port Hedland (Ph 08 9173 1044, www.porthedland.wa.hospitalityinns.com.au)
- *The Lodge Motel*, South Hedland (Ph 08 9172 2188)
- *Pier Hotel*, Port Hedland (Ph 08 9173 1488)
- *Port Hedland Caravan Park*, Port Hedland (Ph 08 9172 2525)
- *Port Hedland Walkabout Hotel*, Port Hedland (Ph 08 91721222)
- *South Hedland Motel*, South Hedland (Ph 08 9172 2888)

Off the Great Northern Highway south of Port Hedland, *Indee Station* offers accommodation (Ph 08 9176 4968).

Rock pool on Indee Station, off the Great Northern Hwy south of Port Hedland

COLIN KERR

Sunset Eighty Mile Beach

Early morning, Eighty Mile Beach

Port Hedland to Eighty Mile Beach

The 600km trip from Port Hedland to Broome is often completed in one very long day, and the countryside is pretty dull. However, if you get off the Great Northern Highway and take some side roads to the coast, there is a lot to see and do. Less than 20km off the highway is a series of beautiful beaches, including the famous Eighty Mile Beach. The **Pardoo and Sandfire roadhouses** also provide welcome breaks along the highway, especially if you are continuing your journey right to Broome.

About 84km from Port Hedland, there is a popular **camping** and picnic area on the **De Grey River (32 H9)**.

Pardoo Station (32 G9), about 120km from Port Hedland, offers rooms as well as powered and unpowered caravan sites. They also have a shop with basic supplies. (Ph 08 9176 4930)

Cape Keraudren Coastal Reserve (Map 32 G10)

Marking the southern end of **Eighty Mile Beach**, **Cape Keraudren** has white sands, aquamarine waters and fabulous **fishing**. A coastal reserve, the area is a haven for marine and terrestrial animals, including the **migratory birds** that visit the area every year. The **'Staircase to the Moon'** phenomenon is visible during winter (full moon dates) and **turtle nesting** takes place during the summer months.

Cape Keraudren also has good **fishing** for threadfin, golden snapper, trevally and barramundi. There are good launching facilities for small boats where the usual offshore species hang out. *Be warned*: small boats are vulnerable to the strong winds that frequently occur in the dry season.

Self-sufficient **camping** is permitted in designated areas along this special part of the coast. Vehicle entry and camping fees are payable to the on-site ranger. For information on fees and other regulations, see the Shire of East Pilbara website www.eastpilbara.wa.gov.au.

Eighty Mile Beach (Map 32 F12)

The magnificent **Eighty Mile Beach** is an incredible paradise of pristine coastline with kilometres of open beach perfect for high-tide fishing, fossicking for shells or sitting back and enjoying the breathtaking sunsets. Remember to be careful when taking your **4WD** near the water's edge as many vehicles have become stuck in the soft sand on a quickly rising tide. **Walking** along Eighty Mile Beach at sunrise or sunset is beautiful, and the further away from the caravan park you are the more shells you will see.

Despite the water being shallow here, **fishing** is a big drawcard. Before high tide, anglers start to wander down to the beach and by high tide the place is wall-to-wall fishers. The quarry is big threadfin salmon and mulloway with small sharks thrown in for good measure. Don't expect to have the place to yourself in the dry season!

Birdlife is prolific along this whole stretch of coastline with wading birds such as plovers, sandpipers, dotterels and stints often seen combing the tidal edge for microorganisms (see p16). Many of these birds are migratory having come from as far away as Siberia. A common sight along this part of the coast is the striking-looking pied oystercatchers. Egrets, herons, bitterns and kingfishers are not uncommon amongst the dense thickets of mangroves.

The **Eighty Mile Beach Caravan Park**, which has plenty of sites within 200m of the beach, is the perfect stopover halfway between Port Hedland and Broome. Facilities are excellent for such a remote location with a small shop that is quite well stocked with the basics, especially bait.
(Ph 08 9176 5941)

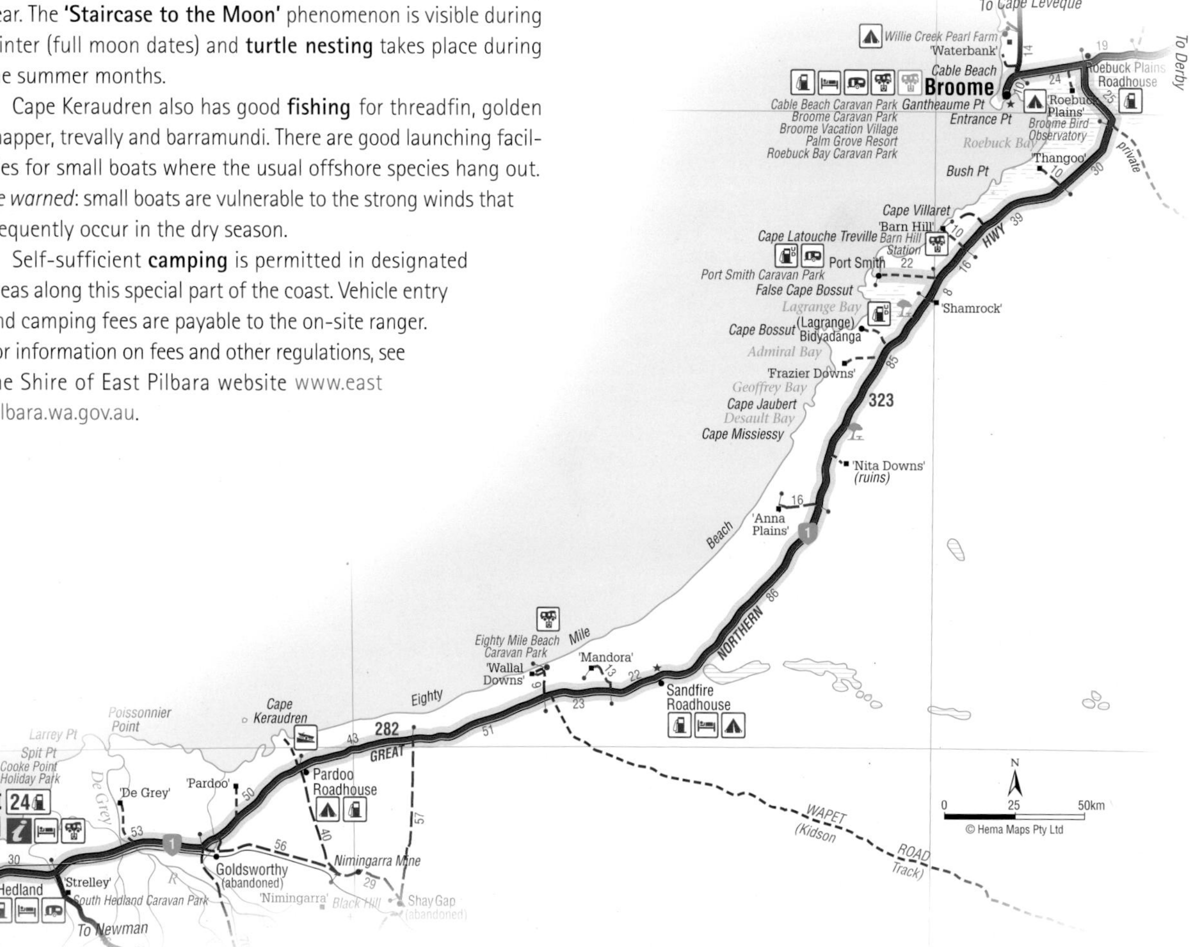

Great Northern Highway to Broome

Port Smith

Port Smith has a caravan park and bird park. The **Port Smith Bird Park & Gardens** has an extensive collection of Australian and exotic parrots, pigeons and cockatoos. About 1km before the **lagoon** is **Port Smith Caravan Park** (Ph 08 9192 4983). The lagoon is popular for **fishing**, with common catches in the sheltered estuary environment including mangrove jack, whiting, trevally, queenfish and mud crabs. Sandy **4WD tracks** take you around the lagoon to its entrance, where there's good beach and reef fishing. The lagoon mainly dries up at low tide, leaving pools and channels.

Barn Hill Station

The coastline of red cliffs and unusual rock formations at **Barn Hill** is a stunning sight, especially near sunset. **Fishing** is the main attraction at this popular spot, but there's also good potential for **bird-watching** and beach **walks**, while a small **bowling green** provides an unexpected focus for social activities.

Visitors can stay at the **working cattle property** in a **camping** area, near the homestead, which has basic amenities just a short walk from a stunning stretch of coast. The shady powered sites and cabins are at the end of an unsealed but well maintained track: make sure you close the gates as instructed. (Ph 08 91912 4975)

Broome

The casual atmosphere in **Broome** today makes it difficult to imagine the fervour that existed at the height of the pearling industry boom, when over 400 luggers operated. There's plenty of history in Broome, including **Chinatown**, the historic **Streeters Jetty** and **Sun Pictures**, which still shows the latest movies under the stars. Of course no visit to Broome would be complete without seeing **Cable Beach**. This 22km stretch of beautiful beach has become renowned for its sunsets and the camel rides. A myriad of **tours** operate from Broome, including: 4WD adventures, fishing and dive charters, pearl farm tours, scenic flights, and Kimberley coast wilderness cruises and charters. At **Gantheaume Point**, just 6km south of Broome, see dinosaur footprints at extremely low tides, and cement casts of the impressions at the cliff's top. The **Broome Bird Observatory** is recognized as one of the world's top five locations for watching wading birds.

For more information on Broome see Hema's *The Kimberley Atlas & Guide*.

Marble or Jasper

A unique rock feature 4km out of town on the **Coongan River** is a colourful **jasper bar** that the town was named after. If you are a little confused, that's because the early settlers of the new town were too. They thought they were living near a large deposit of marble, but it turned out to be jasper. Even though it isn't marble, the jasper bar is still very pretty, just wash the rock down with water to see the surreal colours come to life. According to geologists, this colourful, banded rock dates back to about 350 million years ago. **Warning:** Don't be tempted to souvenir a sample as big fines apply!

Jasper rock at Marble Bar

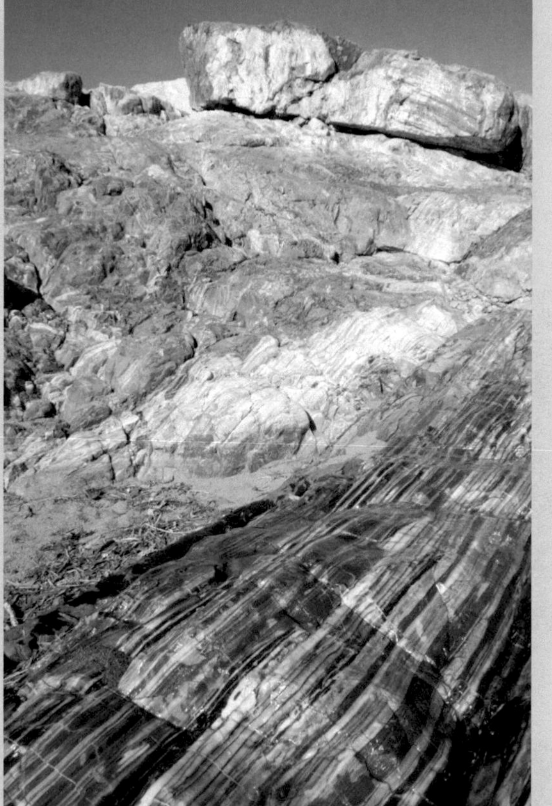

PELUSEY PHOTOGRAPHY

East Pilbara

Although it is the least visited part of WA's northwest, the East Pilbara is a special place. Those looking for quiet, starry skies and lovely winter weather will find what they are searching for in the East Pilbara. Marble Bar frightens some with its 'hottest town in Australia tag'. That is in the summer months, and you should avoid it then, but in the winter months Marble Bar has great weather with cool nights and warm days with clear blue skies. This is a more remote part of the state, so be prepared for your trip with a serviced car and drinking water, and tell someone where you are going.

Marble Bar (Map 28 C10)

Located 203km inland from Port Hedland (see p86), **Marble Bar** has a population of less than 400. Said to be **Australia's hottest town**, Marble Bar consistently records day time temperatures of over 38°C in summer. The town's reputation however comes from a record set in the summer of 1923/1924. Admittedly Marble Bar is shatteringly hot in summer, but averaged out over a whole year, places such as Wyndham, Fitzroy Crossing and Kununurra in the Kimberley are hotter. If you visit Marble Bar in winter, you will find near perfect weather with cool to cold evenings and gloriously sunny days with maximums just less than 30°C.

Information

The Marble Bar office of the **Shire of East Pilbara** in Francis St can help with information on the area. (Ph 08 9176 1008, www.eastpilbara.wa.gov.au)

Fishing at Barn Hill coastline

PELUSEY PHOTOGRAPHY

What to See & Do

One of the oldest mining towns in the west, Marble Bar has some very **historic buildings** including the police station, warden's court, mines department, post office and Poinciana House. The most solid structure in Marble Bar is the **Government Building**, which was built with local stone in 1895. It holds most of the government departments.

Of course you should also stop for a beer at the famous **Iron Clad Hotel**, because being in the 'hottest' town in Australia deserves a beer. Having a coldie and chatting to locals and bar staff in the air conditioning is a great way to experience outback hospitality too.

Gold was discovered in the region back in 1891, and for an interesting insight into the area's mining history you can visit the old **Comet Gold Mine**. The Comet Gold Mine, which began in 1936, has some ruins left to see including the 75m high chimney. In its heyday, Comet produced nearly 4000kg of gold, mostly over a period of two decades up to the 1950s. Today the mine has a fascinating display of minerals, historical information and attractions.

If you wish to **fossick**, there is a somewhat remote possibility of finding **gold** but there's a treasure trove of colourful **agates** and **jasper** to be found. Remember to bring a mining licence and a map as many areas are under leases. Although the jasper in the Marble Bar is not to be taken, there is an area called the **Jasper Deposit** where it is okay to take a souvenir.

Another interesting diversion is to see the **old Corunna airbase** on **Corunna Downs Station (28 D10)**. Marble Bar was the location of a WWII airbase, and if you drive about 35km from town you will come across the remains of the Corunna Downs Airbase. For the child at heart it's fun driving along the runway pretending you are a landing Liberator bomber.

If you have a little more time, a good **4WD day trip** is to head out to **Coppin Gap (28 B11)** and **Kitty's Gap**. Coppin Gap is a tranquil and scenic gorge lined in red jasper, with a pool of water that is fed by an underground spring. (For more information on this drive see Track 38 in Hema's *Western Australia 4WD Top 50 Atlas & Guide*.)

From **Doolena Gap (28 B10)** you can take a short sidetrip to see **Doolena Gorge**. There is a short 1.5km stretch along a rocky track to the banks of the usually dry **Coongan River**. At this point the riverbed is wide, with impressive gorge walls lining both sides.

There are impressive walls lining both sides of Doolena Gorge.

COLIN KERR

Coppin Gap is a good 4WD trip from Marble Bar.

COLIN KERR

Carawine Gorge & Running Waters

Although many people think the Nullagine and Marble Bar region is flat and featureless, this part of the Pilbara is surprisingly hilly and scenic. The region features spinifex-covered ranges divided by mainly dry rivers that occasionally flood with rain from passing cyclones. The **Oakover River** passes close to the hills, cutting a deep pool and sheer cliff at **Carawine Gorge (28 D14)**. There is a good dirt track to Carawine Gorge that is accessible by AWD. Above the higher than normal waterline is a stony riverbed that can be driven on in 4WD. Look closely at the riverbed and you'll notice that the river stones contain some pretty agates. You can **camp** here, but extra padding will help on the stony riverbed. This large body of water is not surprisingly a haven for **birdlife.**

Further down the road, on the way to Nullagine, is another beautiful part of the Oakover River called **Running Waters (28 E14)**. Here a rough, high-clearance and low-range **4WD track** leads to a crystal clear pool of water that bears no resemblance to Carawine Gorge. Although it is only 3.7km in to the pool, expect it to take 30-45 minutes. When popping in a toe, it becomes apparent that it's not your normal river water. A permanent **warm spring** keeps the Running Waters pool somewhere between 27 and 30°C. This hard-to-get-to location makes a lovely **campsite**, shaded by huge paper barks, but there is limited space. If you are **swimming,** be aware that there are catfish in the pool with spines that could inflict a very painful sting.

This region is extremely hot in summer. If you are planning on going out here, regardless of time of year, heed the signs and take extra fuel, water and food. Notify someone as to where you are going and avoid summer. Always remember that people have died out here doing the wrong thing. For more information contact the Shire of East Pilbara (Ph 08 9175 1924) or see Track 39 in Hema's *Western Australia 4WD Top 50 Atlas & Guide* for more details of this drive.

Carawine Gorge

PELUSEY PHOTOGRAPHY

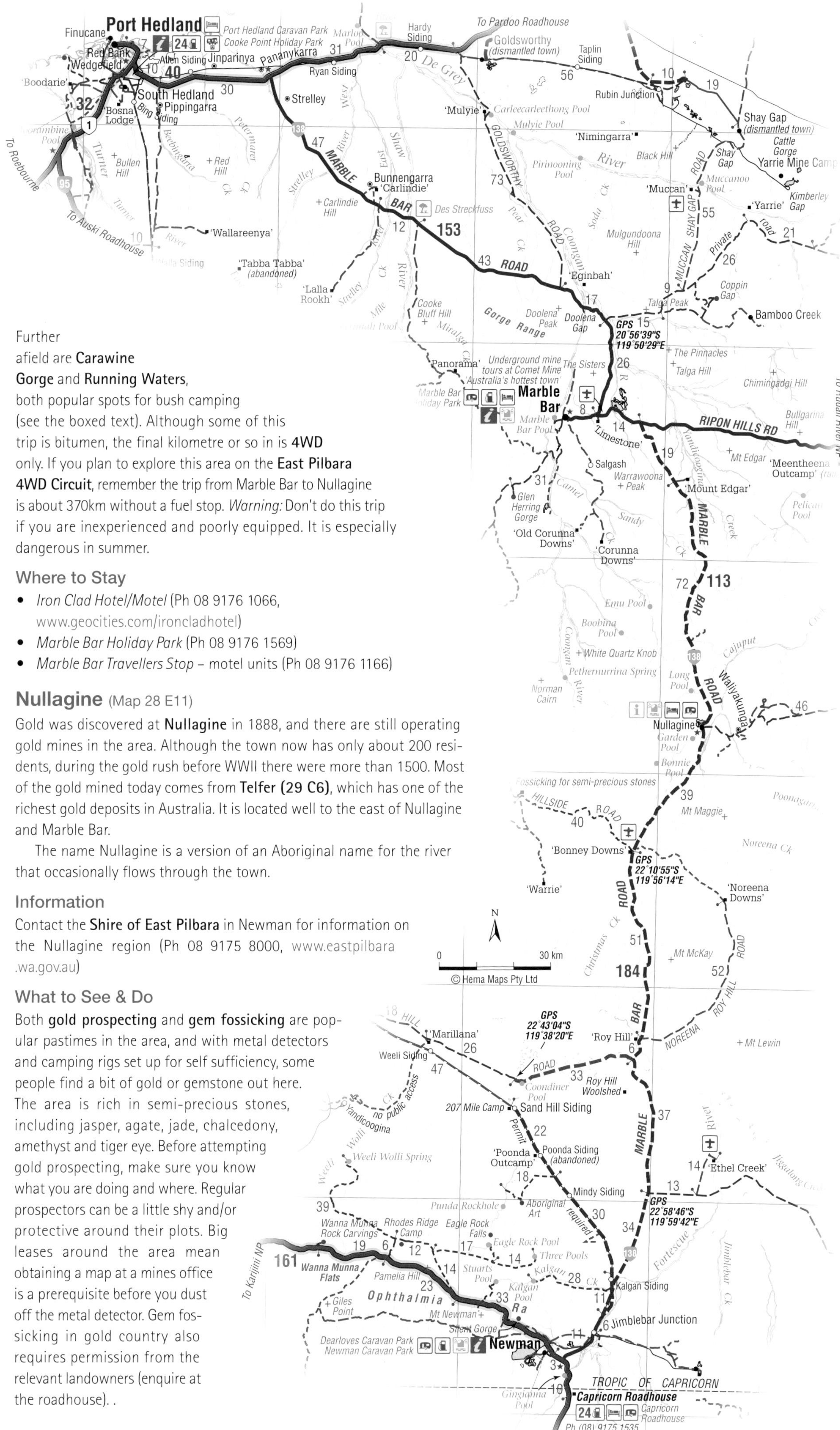

Further afield are **Carawine Gorge** and **Running Waters**, both popular spots for bush camping (see the boxed text). Although some of this trip is bitumen, the final kilometre or so in is **4WD** only. If you plan to explore this area on the **East Pilbara 4WD Circuit**, remember the trip from Marble Bar to Nullagine is about 370km without a fuel stop. *Warning:* Don't do this trip if you are inexperienced and poorly equipped. It is especially dangerous in summer.

Where to Stay

- *Iron Clad Hotel/Motel* (Ph 08 9176 1066, www.geocities.com/ironcladhotel)
- *Marble Bar Holiday Park* (Ph 08 9176 1569)
- *Marble Bar Travellers Stop* – motel units (Ph 08 9176 1166)

Nullagine (Map 28 E11)

Gold was discovered at **Nullagine** in 1888, and there are still operating gold mines in the area. Although the town now has only about 200 residents, during the gold rush before WWII there were more than 1500. Most of the gold mined today comes from **Telfer (29 C6)**, which has one of the richest gold deposits in Australia. It is located well to the east of Nullagine and Marble Bar.

The name Nullagine is a version of an Aboriginal name for the river that occasionally flows through the town.

Information

Contact the **Shire of East Pilbara** in Newman for information on the Nullagine region (Ph 08 9175 8000, www.eastpilbara.wa.gov.au)

What to See & Do

Both **gold prospecting** and **gem fossicking** are popular pastimes in the area, and with metal detectors and camping rigs set up for self sufficiency, some people find a bit of gold or gemstone out here. The area is rich in semi-precious stones, including jasper, agate, jade, chalcedony, amethyst and tiger eye. Before attempting gold prospecting, make sure you know what you are doing and where. Regular prospectors can be a little shy and/or protective around their plots. Big leases around the area mean obtaining a map at a mines office is a prerequisite before you dust off the metal detector. Gem fossicking in gold country also requires permission from the relevant landowners (enquire at the roadhouse). .

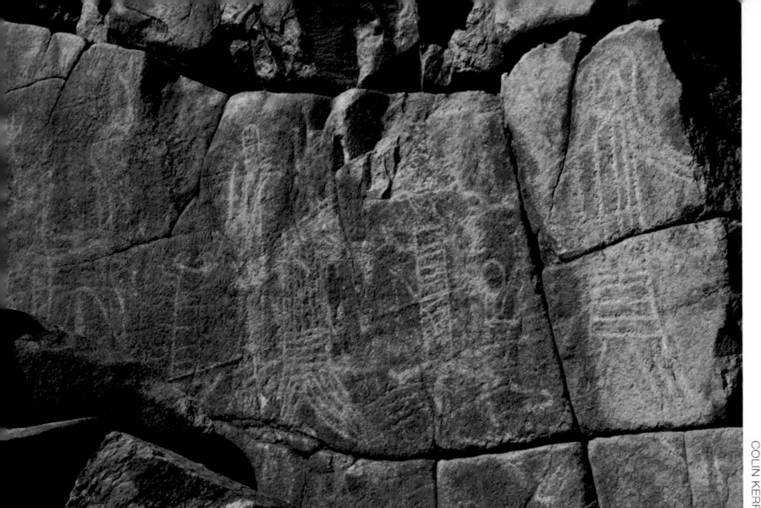

COLIN KERR

Indigenous rock carvings at Wanna Munna

COLIN KERR

Kalgan Pool can be visited in a 4WD

Rudall River National Park

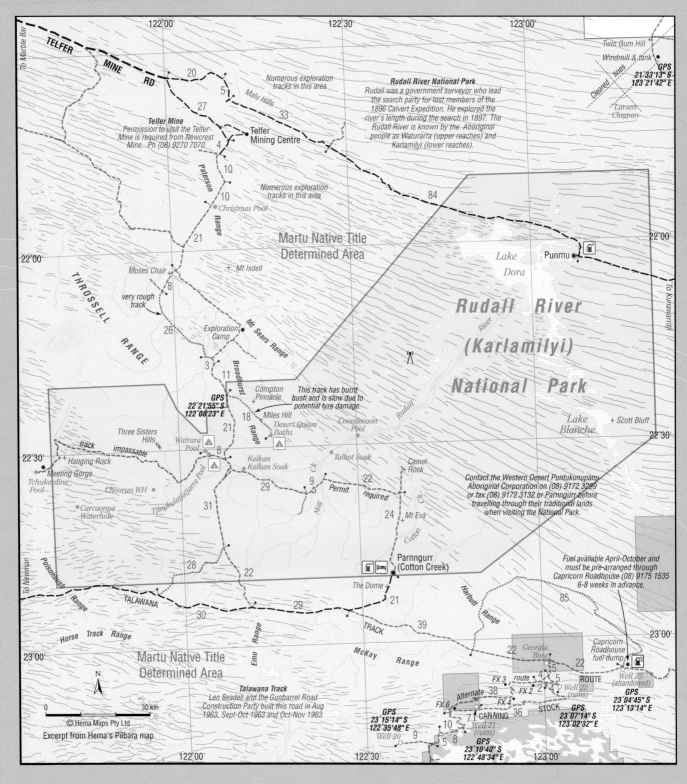

Rudall River National Park
Rudall was a government surveyor who lead the search party for lost members of the 1896 Calvert Expedition. He explored the river's length during the search in 1897. The Rudall River is known by the Aboriginal people as Waturarra (upper reaches) and Karlamilyi (lower reaches).

Telfer Mine
Permission to visit the Telfer Mine is required from Newcrest Mine. Ph (08) 9270 7070.

Numerous exploration tracks in this area

This track has burnt bush and is slow due to potential tyre damage.

Contact the Western Desert Puntukunupanu Aboriginal Corporation on (08) 9172 3299 or fax (08) 9172 3132 or Parnngurr before travelling through their traditional lands when visiting the National Park.

Fuel available April-October and must be pre-arranged through Capricorn Roadhouse (08) 9175 1535 6-8 weeks in advance.

Talawana Track
Len Beadell and the Gunbarrel Road Construction Party built this road in Aug 1963, Sept-Oct 1963 and Oct-Nov 1963.

Rudall River (Karlamilyi) National Park

Martu Native Title Determined Area

Telfer Mine Rd · Telfer Mining Centre · Paterson Range · Christmas Pool · Mt Isdell · Moses Chair · Throssell Range · very rough track · Exploration Camp · Mt Sears Range · Broadhurst Range · Compton Pinnacle · Miles Hill · Desert Queen Baths · Coondecoon Pool · Three Sisters Hills · track impassable · Watrara Pool · Hanging Rock · Meeting Gorge · Tchukardine Pool · Choorun WH · Carcoonya Waterhole · Tingkulatjatjarra Pool · Kalkan Kalkan Soak · Talbot Soak · Camel Rock · Permit required · Mt Eva · Cotton Ck · May Ck · Parnngurr (Cotton Creek) · The Dome · Lake Dora · Punmu · Lake Blanche · Scott Bluff · Twin Gum Hill · Windmill & tank · Cleared lines · Larsen Claypan · Malu Hills · Poisonbush Range · Talawana Track · Horse Track Range · Emu Range · McKay Range · Harbutt Range · Georgia Bore · Capricorn Roadhouse fuel dump · Well 23 (abandoned) · Well 22 (ruins) · Well 21 (ruins) · Well 20 · Canning Stock Route · Alternate route · FX 2 · FX 3 · FX 4 · FX 6

GPS 21°33'13" S 123°21'42" E · GPS 22°21'55" S 122°08'23" E · GPS 23°04'45" S 123°13'14" E · GPS 23°07'14" S 123°02'32" E · GPS 23°10'40" S 122°48'34" E · GPS 23°15'14" S 122°35'48" E

To Marble Bar · To Kunawarritji · To Newman

0 — 30 km

© Hema Maps Pty Ltd

Excerpt from Hema's Pilbara map

COLIN KERR

Desert Queen Bath is a feature of Rudall River National Park.

Rudall River National Park

Western Australia's biggest national park, at 1.5 million hectares, **Rudall River (30 D8)** is also probably the most remote. The river and park was named after **William Rudall**, a government surveyor who searched the region around 1897 for lost members of the Calvert Expedition.

The national park is located in the middle of the **Great Sandy Desert** and **Little Sandy Desert**, so rainfall is extremely unreliable. However, the odd decaying cyclone can bring flooding rain that tops up soaks, waterholes and billabongs which provide oasis conditions for plants, animals and the occasional human visitor. **Wallabies, birds** and a plethora of **reptiles** thrive under these conditions so it is little wonder that the Martu Aborigines have inhabited this region for thousands of years. The indigenous landowners call this place **Karlamilyi**. Feral **camels** also inhabit the area, and although they make an arresting sight these animals are pests as they cause damage to watercourses.

The landscape around Rudall River is remarkably varied: red sand dunes up to 40m high drift across the spinifex and desert oak studded plains while outbreaks of sandstone and quartz date back more than 200 million years ago, a result of ancient glacial activity. Looking at the landscape today, it is hard to believe that glaciers were ever a feature around here. In stark contrast, rocky outcrops, rugged gorges and colourful cliffs stand abruptly within the **Broadhurst and Fingoon ranges**. Coolabah trees and river gums line pristine pools in Rudall River and other watercourses. The elegant-looking desert oak likes to grow on the sandplains along with spinifex.

Rudall is also very close to the **Canning Stock Route**, which passes just 90km to the east, so it is often included in Canning Stock Route publications. (See p110)

The park is 260km east of Newman, consequently it is a very remote area without facilities. You have to be well prepared and self sufficient with a high clearance **4WD** vehicle to attempt this journey. It is preferable to travel with at least one other vehicle. If you are inexperienced, go on a tag-along tour.

Contact the **Western Desert Puntukunupana Aboriginal Corporation** (Ph 08 9172 3299) before travelling through their traditional lands when visiting the park. For more detailed information see Track 40 in Hema's *Western Australia 4WD Top 50 Atlas & Guide.*

Even if you are not into prospecting, its still worth taking your time and exploring the region around Nullagine. Just 5km south of town is a pretty little picnic spot by a permanent and shady pool, appropriately named **Garden Pool**. The **Nullagine Roadhouse** (Ph 08 9176 2012) can also provide information and mud maps of other scenic locations such as **Daylight Pool** and **Beatons Creek Gorge**.

Where to Stay

- *Conglomerate Hotel* (Ph 08 9176 2265)
- *Nullagine Caravan Park* (Ph 08 9176 2090)

Newman (Map 22 B9)

Mount Newman was named in 1896 for explorer **Aubrey Newman**, although he actually died of typhoid and didn't see the mountain himself. In 1957 veteran prospector **AS 'Stan' Hilditch** discovered a massive iron ore deposit at **Mt Whaleback** (5km southeast of Mt Newman). Mining began in 1969 and Mt Whaleback is now the largest single open-cut iron ore mine in the world. The mine is still the mainstay of the community and it is likely to be that way long into the future. With nearly 800 million tonnes of high-grade iron ore, Mt Whaleback has the largest deposit in the Pilbara. Today, the mountain looks more like a giant hole rather than a whale-shaped mountain, which is not surprising really. **Tours** of BHP Billiton's Mt Whaleback Mining Operation can be booked at the Visitor Centre. (Remember to wear long pants, long-sleeve shirts and enclosed shoes.)

Information

- The **Newman Visitor Centre** is on the corner of Fortescue Ave and Newman Dr. (Ph 08 9175 2888 www.newmanwa.org)

What to See & Do

Once just a mining town, Newman is now the **administrative centre** for the East Pilbara Shire. As you would expect in a thriving mining town, Newman has all the facilities you'll need including shopping centres and mechanical repairs. This makes Newman the ideal place for stocking up and vehicle maintenance before setting out on more remote journeys, to say Rudall River.

The **Newman Visitor Centre** is worth a look itself as it has a great range of **art pieces** that reflect the colours of the Pilbara. They also sell model CAT trucks – miniatures of the ones working in the Mount Whaleback mine. There are good views over the town and mine from **Radio Hill Lookout** and **Ophthalmia Dam** is a popular picnic spot that's a great vantage point at sunset.

The outback and remote communities and stations of this region get their mail from the flying postman. The **RASS Mail Run** leaves Newman at 8.30am every Tuesday and flies to Jigalong, Cotton Creek, Well 33, Punmu and Balfour Downs before returning to Newman. This is a great way to experience the really remote places of Western Australia. (For details Ph 08 9173 1711)

In the surrounding district there are a number of rock art sites and waterholes that can be visited in a **4WD** including **Weeli Wolli Spring** (see p19), **Kalgan Pool**, **Wanna Munna** indigenous rock engravings and **Eagle Rock Falls**. Many of these locations are fairly hard to get to, so grab a map from the Visitor Centre and fill out a permit as you will pass over mining company land.

For the adventurous, Newman is also the kick off point for the **Rudall River National Park** (see boxed text).

Where to Stay

- *Dearloves Caravan Park* (Ph 08 9175 2802)
- *Mia Mia Hotel* (Ph 08 9175 8400, www.miamia.com.au)
- *Newman Caravan Park* (Ph 08 9175 1428)
- *Newman Hotel Motel* (Ph 08 9175 1101)
- *Seasons Hotel Newman* (08) 9177 8666, www.seasonshotel.com.au) ■

chapter six

Gascoyne and Mid West

While most tourists hug the coastline, to really discover what epitomises the Australian outback you must go inland and explore WA's Gascoyne and Mid West regions. The Murchison extends from the northern wheatbelt to the edge of the Gascoyne, which is pastoral station country.

Most tourists visit both the Murchison and Gascoyne to see the famous spring wildflowers that carpet the landscape. Pick up a wildflower drive brochure from the towns you drive through as each town has its own specialty. Rocky outcrops that dot the countryside are the best place to see wildflowers because the rainfall that runs off the rocks concentrates the multitude of flowers that grow at the base.

Many drive trails criss-cross the region, offering a mix of history and some of the more scenic spots of the Mid West and Gascoyne. The region's three Outback Pathways trails are the Kingsford Smith Mail Run, Miners Pathway and Wool Wagon. Another interesting drive trail is the Monsieur Hawes Heritage Trail.

Wherever you go in the Mid West and Gascoyne there are also opportunities to go for a short stroll or head off on a full-on hike. Whether it's a heritage trail around a town, a wander through the bush looking at wildflowers or climbing the magnificent Mount Augustus and Kennedy Range, the true way to experience the outback is to get out of the car and take a walk.

Gascoyne

Mount Augustus National Park (Map 20 F13)

Mount Augustus has been called the world's largest monocline and the world's biggest rock. Whatever the technicality, it is twice the size of Uluru (Ayers Rock). Mount Augustus rises 1106m above sea level, is about 8km long, covers an area of 4795 hectares and is roughly 1700 million years old. Unlike Uluru, Mount Augustus does have vegetation growing on it.

The local Wadjari Aboriginal people call the rock **Burringurrah** and they have dreaming stories explaining the massive rock. Today the Wadjari people live in the nearby community of **Burringurrah (20 G13)**.

Information

The **DEC office in Carnarvon** can provide information on the park (Ph 08 9941 3754).

For the latest road conditions in the area contact the **Shire of Upper Gascoyne** in Gascoyne Junction (Ph 08 9943 0988).

What to Do

Mount Augustus is a big rock so it deserves viewing from many different angles. Firstly, drive around the rock on the 49km **Burringurrah Drive**. This circuit drive provides excellent views of the rock's changing faces and access to all feature sites.

Although you can drive around the park on the Burringurrah Drive, to really explore you'll need to follow the numerous walk/climb trails to gorges, pools, Aboriginal art sites and a lookout.

- **Cave Hill Trail** – 4km return (2hr) from Goordgeela
- **Edney's Trail** – 6km return (2.5hr) from Ooramboo picnic area
- **Kotke Gorge Trail** – 2km return (1hr) from Warrarla (Gum Grove) picnic area
- **Petroglyph Trail** – an easy 300m return walk to the Mundee rock wall
- **Saddle Trail** – 2km return (1hr) from The Pound
- **Summit Trail** – 12km return (6hr): one of WA's Top Trails, see p32

Wildflowers near Paynes Find
COLIN KERR

There are great views of Mount Augustus from Burringurrah Drive.

COLIN KERR

Taking a break on the Mount Augustus Summit Trail.

PELUSEY PHOTOGRAPHY

After all that physical activity, it is time for a cool dip at **Cattle Pool (Goolinee)**. This permanent waterhole on the **Lyons River** is a popular spot for a **swim** and picnic. There is plenty of **birdlife** around the water's edge too.

Finally, spend a sunset at the **Emu Hill Lookout (20 E13)** where you can see Mount Augustus, like Uluru, change into vivid colours.

Emus, bustards, goannas and red kangaroos are common on the surrounding plain, and permanent pools on the Lyons River attract large numbers of birds, including waterbirds.

Where to stay

There is strictly no camping within the park, but the nearby **Mt Augustus Outback Tourist Resort** is just a short drive on the northern side. This lovely grassy caravan park and camping area also provides some basic rooms.

- *Cobra Bangemall Station* – 37km from Mt Augustus; has ensuite, station rooms and a caravan park (Ph 08 9943 0565)
- *Mt Augustus Outback Tourist Resort* (Ph 08 9943 0527)

Kennedy Range National Park (Map 19 F7)

Although small in size, the **Kennedy Range National Park** makes up for it in spectacular scenery. The Kennedy Range was in pastoral lease until 1977, but as there was limited water in the area the cattle did not overgraze the vegetation. The whole park still retains a wilderness feel that offers visitors a truly remarkable experience.

The Kennedy Range was part of the old seabed 250 million years ago, and the park protects an ancient eroded plateau with cliffs rising up to 100m above the surrounding plain. On the eastern side of the range a maze of steep-sided canyons lead back into the mesa where ancient marine fossils can be found embedded into the sandstone cliffs. The top of the range is a waterless red dunefield, dominated and stabilised by spinifex and small shrubs.

What to Do

Drive tracks on the eastern side lead into several gorges and, depending on rainfall, the area can have a colourful array of **wildflowers** in late winter and early spring.

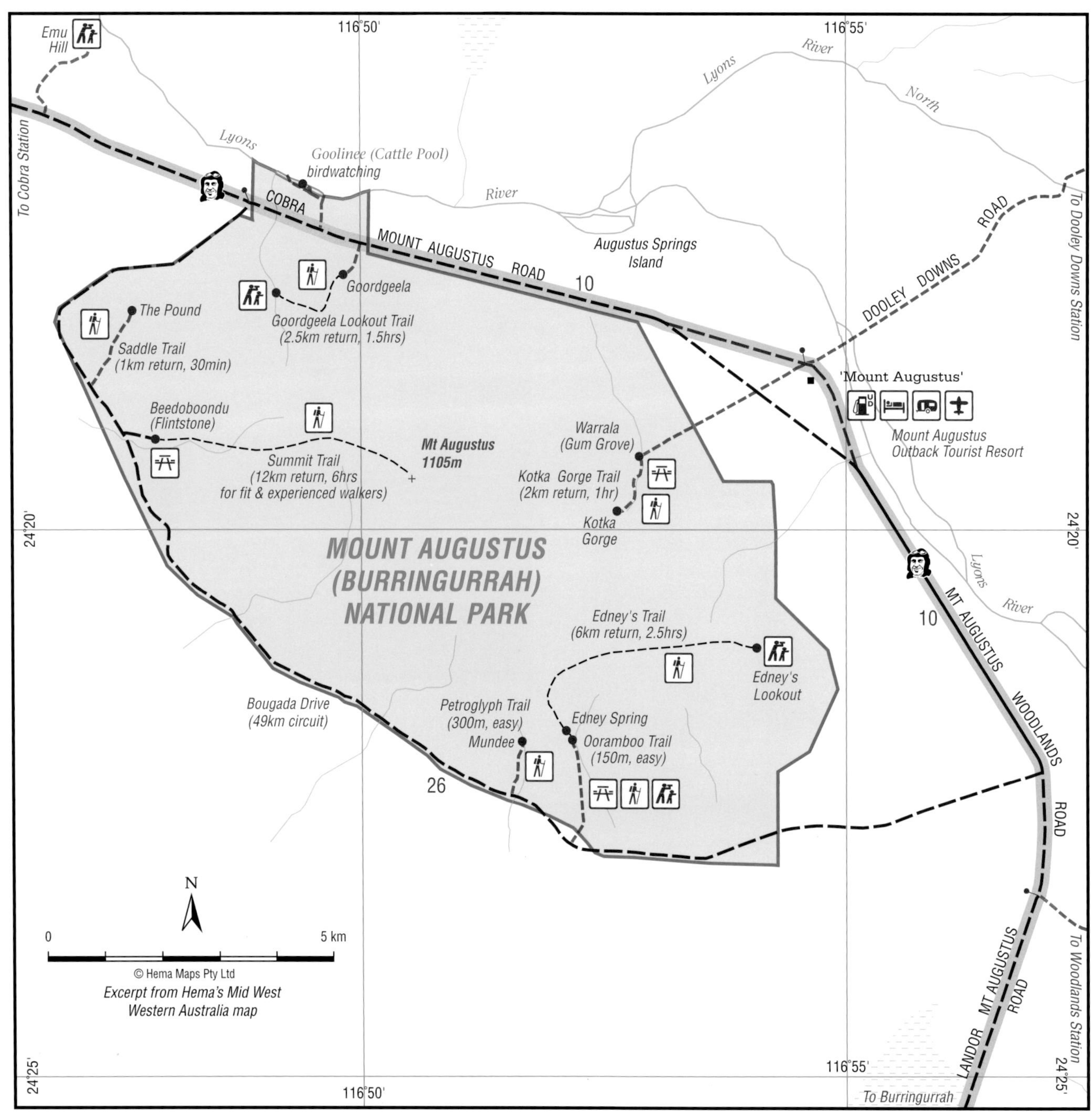

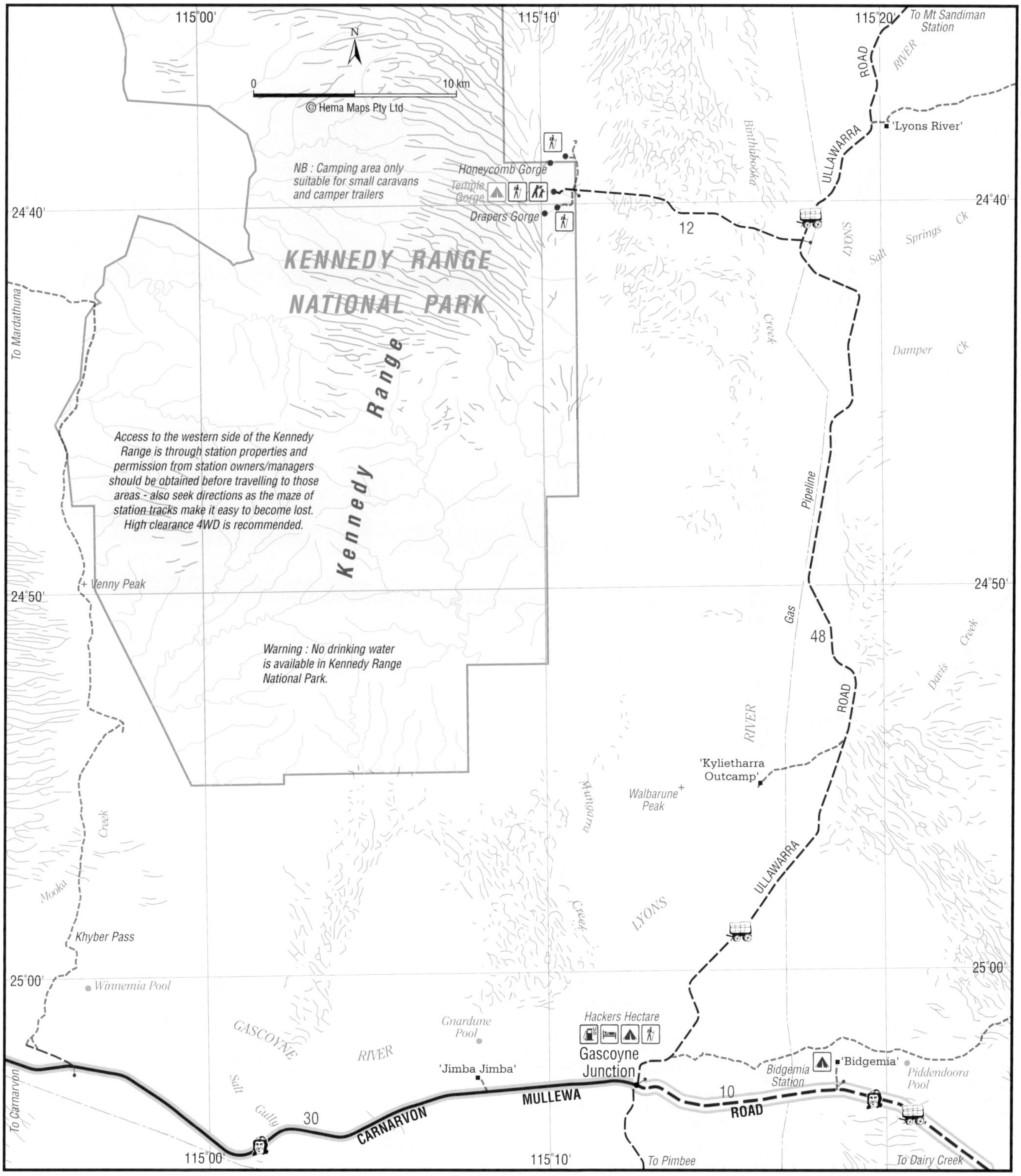

115°00' 115°10' 115°20'

To Mt Sandiman Station

0 10 km

NB : Camping area only suitable for small caravans and camper trailers

Honeycomb Gorge

Temple Gorge

Drapers Gorge

24°40'

12

ULLAWARRA ROAD

'Lyons River'

LYONS RIVER

Binthubooka Creek

Salt Springs Ck

Damper Ck

KENNEDY RANGE NATIONAL PARK

Kennedy Range

To Mardathuna

Access to the western side of the Kennedy Range is through station properties and permission from station owners/managers should be obtained before travelling to those areas - also seek directions as the maze of station tracks make it easy to become lost. High clearance 4WD is recommended.

Gas Pipeline

Venny Peak

24°50'

48

Davis Creek

Warning : No drinking water is available in Kennedy Range National Park.

'Kylietharra Outcamp'

Walbarune Peak

Mungarra Creek

LYONS

Mooka Creek

Khyber Pass

25°00'

Winnemia Pool

Gnardune Pool

GASCOYNE RIVER

Hackers Hectare

Gascoyne Junction

'Jimba Jimba'

Bidgemia Station

'Bidgemia'

Piddendoora Pool

Salt Gully

30

CARNARVON MULLEWA 10 ROAD

To Carnarvon

To Pimbee

To Dairy Creek

115°00' 115°10'

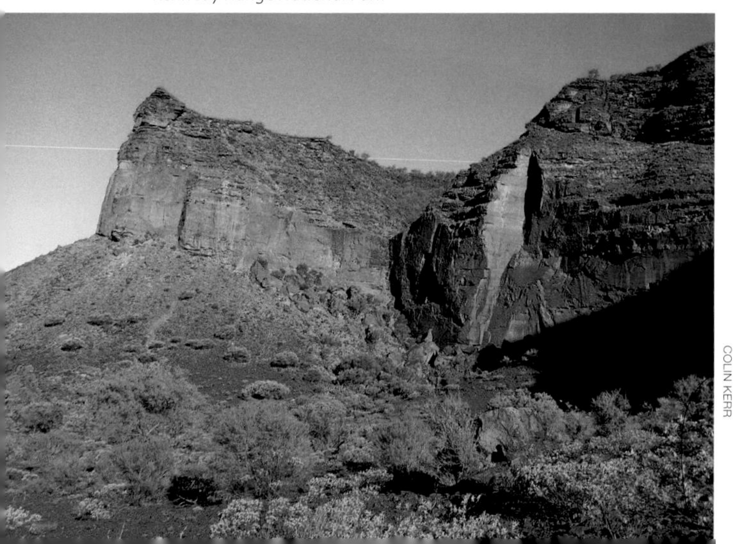

Kennedy Range National Park

COLIN KERR

Kennedy Ranges near sunrise

PELUSEY PHOTOGRAPHY

Kingsford Smith Mail Run

© NATIONAL LIBRARY OF AUSTRALIA

Charles Kingsford Smith

It is a fascinating but little known fact that the famous Australian aviator **Sir Charles Kingsford Smith** set up a transport company in 1924. One contract was a mail run between **Carnarvon** and the **Bangemall goldfields** near Cobra Station. This outback trail follows the great aviator's footsteps. (Or should that be wheel ruts?) Heritage interest aside, this trail takes tourers through rugged and spectacular outback scenery.

Along the trail are 19 **interpretive sites** that not only provide informative stops, but also make interesting breaks for the kids. The trail starts (or ends, depending which way you wish to tackle it) in **Meekatharra** – an interesting outback centre (see p107). Highlights are **Mt Augustus, Mount Gould lockup (15 B2)** and a 120km return detour to **Kennedy Range National Park. Carnarvon** offers coastal respite to the arid interior (see p63). On the whole, the roads along the trail are pretty good but corrugations in parts and sandy patches would make it tough for caravans, unless of the 'off road' variety.

The *Gascoyne Murchison Outback Pathways* book is a useful guide to have if you wish to do this trail, and other pathways in the Murchison and Gascoyne. Information is also available on the Outback Pathways website, www.outbackpathways.com.au, and from the **Gascoyne Junction Visitor Centre** (Ph 08 9943 0880).

Fuel and facilities are available along the trail at Meekatharra, Burringurrah, Mount Augustus Resort, Cobra Bangemall Station, Gascoyne Junction and Carnarvon. However, Meekatharra and Carnarvon are the only centres for major supplies and there is no fuel at all on the 302km between Meekatharra and Burringurrah.

There are caravan parks at Meekatharra (p107), Mount Augustus Resort (p96), Cobra Bangemall Station (p96) and Carnarvon (p63). Additionally, near Gascoyne Junction there are camping sites at **Bidgemia Station (20 H8)** and **Hackers Hectare (19 J7)**.

Mount Gould Lockup

PELUSEY PHOTOGRAPHY

Honeycomb Gorge

PELUSEY PHOTOGRAPHY

PELUSEY PHOTOGRAPHY

Camping in the Kennedy Range

One special spot is **Honeycomb Gorge**, where after a 300m ramble from the car park you will find yourself in an amphitheatre of, well, honeycombed rock. The formations are quite fascinating. While there try to imagine what the normally dry **waterfall** would be like after a rare big downpour.

It is also possible to walk or scramble to the end of **Temple Gorge**. Walkers follow a creekbed festooned with big boulders. Another **walk trail** from the campsite leads to the top of the cliffs. Be very careful as the rocks can be loose and it is a long way down.

Further south is **Drapers Gorge** – another walk into the spectacular landscape where some ancient **rock art engravings (petroglyphs)** can be seen.

The only **camping** permitted in the national park is at Temple Gorge. Although it has very basic facilities, just a drop toilet, we rate it one of the most spectacular campsites in Western Australia. The camping area has a limited turning circle, so is more suitable for small caravans and camper trailers. Remember to bring all your drinking water, as there is no water available in the park. DEC brochures are available at the information shelter near Temple Gorge, and camp hosts are stationed here during the cooler months – May/June to Sep/Oct.

Access to the Kennedy Range is via a 50km gravel road from **Gascoyne Junction (20 J8)**. Although the roads are accessible to conventional vehicles in dry weather, after heavy rain they are often impassable. Just out of Gascoyne Junction take note of the boat sitting on top of a station building – it graphically shows flood levels.

Wool Wagon Pathway

This 1332km trail takes the traveller deep into the heart of sheep and wool country. Although the trail starts and ends on the coast, **Geraldton** to **Exmouth**, it travels through the real outback of the Murchison and Gascoyne. This is a vast arid landscape that hides many scenic and historic gems. It's hard to imagine a trail with more contrasting sights, from the coral-studded and beach-lined coastline to the red dirt and stark rocky landscapes of the inland. The **Kennedy Range** is just one of the trail's highlights. Like other designated tourist trails in the region, there many informative **interpretive sites** along the way to enrich the journey.

The *Gascoyne Murchison Outback Pathways* book is a useful guide to have if you wish to do this trail, and other pathways in the Murchison and Gascoyne. Information is also available on the Outback Pathways website, www.outbackpathways.com.au, and from the visitor centres along the trail.

Fuel and facilities are available at Geraldton, Mullewa, Yalgoo, Murchison Roadhouse, Gascoyne Junction and Exmouth. However, the major supply points are either end – Geraldton and Exmouth. Ensure you have enough fuel for the 497km leg between Gascoyne Junction and Exmouth.

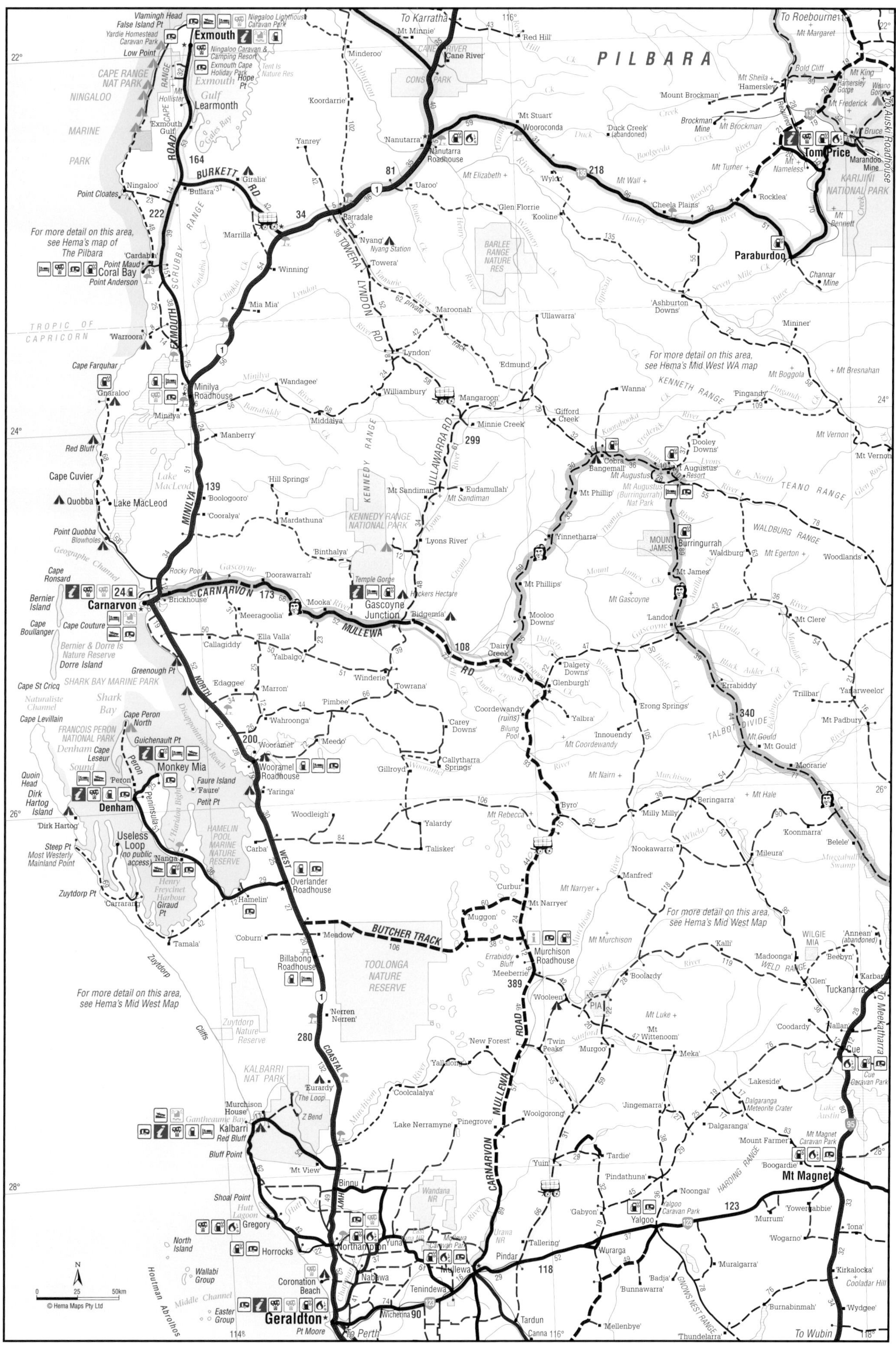
To Karratha
To Roebourne
PILBARA
Exmouth
Vlamingh Head
False Island Pt
Low Point
CAPE RANGE NAT PARK
NINGALOO MARINE PARK
Exmouth Gulf
Learmonth
BURKETT RD
Point Cloates
For more detail on this area, see Hema's map of The Pilbara
Coral Bay
Point Maud
Point Anderson
TROPIC OF CAPRICORN
Cape Farquhar
Minilya Roadhouse
Red Bluff
Cape Cuvier
Quobba
Lake MacLeod
Point Quobba Blowholes
Cape Ronsard
Bernier Island
Carnarvon
Cape Boullanger
Cape Couture
Bernier & Dorre Is Nature Reserve
Dorre Island
Greenough Pt
Cape St Cricq
SHARK BAY MARINE PARK
Naturaliste Channel
Shark Bay
Cape Levillain
Cape Peron North
FRANCOIS PERON NATIONAL PARK
Denham Sound
Guichenault Pt
Cape Leseur
Monkey Mia
Quoin Head
Dirk Hartog Island
Denham
Faure Island
Petit Pt
Useless Loop
Steep Pt
Most Westerly Mainland Point
HAMELIN POOL MARINE NATURE RESERVE
Henry Freycinet Harbour
Overlander Roadhouse
Zuytdorp Pt
Hamelin
BUTCHER TRACK
TOOLONGA NATURE RESERVE
Billabong Roadhouse
For more detail on this area, see Hema's Mid West Map
Zuytdorp Nature Reserve
Zuytdorp Cliffs
KALBARRI NAT PARK
Kalbarri
Red Bluff
Bluff Point
Binnu
Shoal Point
Hutt Lagoon
Gregory
North Island
Horrocks
Wallabi Group
Northampton
Coronation Beach
Nabawa
Easter Group
Geraldton
Pt Moore
To Perth
Houtman Abrolhos
Middle Channel
© Hema Maps Pty Ltd
Cane River
Nanutarra Roadhouse
Barradale
TOWERA LYNDON RD
Wooroconda
Paraburdoo
Tom Price
KARIJINI NATIONAL PARK
Mt Brockman
Hamersley
Mt Bruce
Marandoo Mine
BARLEE RANGE NATURE RES
For more detail on this area, see Hema's Mid West WA map
KENNETH RANGE
KENNEDY RANGE NATIONAL PARK
ULLAWARRA RD
Gascoyne Junction
CARNARVON MULLEWA RD
Mt Augustus
Mt Augustus Resort
Mt Augustus (Burringurrah) Nat Park
Cobra Bangemall
Burringurrah
TEANO RANGE
WALDBURG RANGE
Mt Gascoyne
TALBOT DIVIDE
For more detail on this area, see Hema's Mid West Map
Murchison Roadhouse
WILGIE MIA
WELD RANGE
Tuckanarra
Cue
To Meekatharra
Dalgaranga Meteorite Crater
Mt Magnet
Yalgoo
Pindar
Mullewa
Tenindewa
Wurarga
Tardun
Canna
Wichenna
HARDING RANGE
GNOWS NEST RANGE
To Wubin
To Auski Roadhouse

Everlastings Trail

PELUSEY PHOTOGRAPHY
Mural in Moora

From Perth the **Everlastings Trail** heads north along the Brand Highway before detouring off to **Badgingarra National Park** (see p47), **Lesueur National Park** (see p48) and **Lake Indoon** (see p49). From here it heads north-east to **Mingenew** and **Mullewa** (see p101) before turning south through **Morawa, Perenjori, Wubin, New Norcia** and **Bindoon** back to **Perth.** Before you head off on this trail, ring around the visitor centres to make sure the wildflower season is underway, as drought can limit the flowering.

Near **Mingenew (8 F9), Depot Hill** is a flora reserve with a colourful variety of wildflowers in spring, as well as a natural pond and bird sanctuary.

South of Mullewa, **Coalseam Conservation Park (8 F9)** also has spectacular spring wildflower displays, especially the prolific pink, gold and white everlastings. It lies between two distinct botanical zones, and as a result, is one of the most diverse bush areas in the region. There is a camping area with toilets and barbecues, as well as another bush camping area with no facilities.

A busy wheat and sheep farming district, **Morowa (8 G10)** also has a wide range of wildflowers. Everlasting daisies and flowering shrubs are abundant during August and September and there is a wildflower walk near the old iron ore mine. Nearby, **Bilya Rock** and **Koolanooka Springs** are worth a visit too.

Perenjori (8 G11) also comes alive in a blaze of colour every spring with endless vistas of pink, yellow and white everlastings from July to October. The unique **wreath leschenaultia** can also be seen in September and October. The **Perenjori Tourist Centre and Pioneer Museum** has great information about the best wildflower and orchid locations.

A small wheatbelt town, **Wubin (8 K12)** has colourful wildflowers along the roadsides between July and September and a large variety of wattles east of Wubin on the Great Northern Highway. The town's old-style **wheat bins** are classified by National Trust.

Another wildflower hotspot is **Dalwallinu (2 C7)**, where there is the biggest concentration of **wattle** species in the world within a 100km radius of the town. If you are in the region around September and October, look for the spectacular and rare **wreath leschenaultia**. Flowering for this species is patchy so seek advice from the town's visitors centre. The town has one of the best-maintained shire **caravan parks** we have ever had the pleasure of staying at.

An interesting diversion from the trail is to head through **Walebing** to **Moora (2 D5)**. The biggest town between Perth and Geraldton, Moora is located on the floodplain surrounding the **Moore River**. Moora is situated on the Midlands Road, an alternate drive route that takes in towns such as Watheroo, Coorow, Carnamah, Three Springs and Mingenew. All these towns are located near areas known for their wildflower displays in spring. Near Watheroo, the **Watheroo National Park (2 B4)** is noted for its fine wildflower displays in spring.

PELUSEY PHOTOGRAPHY
Superb New Norcia architecture

New Norcia (2 E5) is a monastic community that has buildings that look like they belong in 14th century Spain rather than the Australian bush. Back in 1846 a group of Benedictine monks set about converting Aboriginal people to Christianity. From these humble beginnings, New Norcia became an established village with grand places of worship, education facilities including a boarding school for boys, a flour mill and other service buildings. Today, there are 27 **buildings** classified by the National Trust, making New Norcia one of the most important religious sites in Australia. The buildings are beautifully preserved and, what's more, still run by Benedictine monks. Daily **walking tours** provide visitors with a valuable insight into the history and daily life of this remarkable place (www.newnorcia.wa.edu.au).

From New Norcia you can take a diversion east through **Calingiri** to **Wongan Hills (2 E7)**. This neat and tidy town is set amongst the largest remaining remnant of natural vegetation in the northern Wheatbelt. As a result, Wongan Hills is a wildflower enthusiast's paradise. In fact an incredible 24 species of flowering plants are only found in the Wongan Hills region. One of the reasons there is so much bush is that much of the land is unsuitable for farming, due to its rocky, hilly terrain. Several **walk trails**, such as **Mount Matilda**, offer great views and delightful insights into the region's flora and fauna. Wongan Hills has called itself Australia's first RV friendly town, so drop in and see for yourself. There is a well-maintained **caravan park** and a classic Wheatbelt pub.

On your way back in to Perth, you drive through the little town of **Bindoon (2 F5)** located in scenic hills and farmland in the **Chittering Valley region.** Winter rains transform this region into lush green pastures, making it a great contrast from the landscape further north.

See www.wildflowerswa.com for more information on the Everlastings Trail.

PELUSEY PHOTOGRAPHY
Superb New Norcia architecture

PELUSEY PHOTOGRAPHY
Historic Berkshire Valley settlement near Moora

PELUSEY PHOTOGRAPHY
Old Yalgoo pub

Geraldton to Mullewa

If you start this trail in **Geraldton** (see p52) then simply begin by following the Geraldton Mt Magnet Rd for 90km to **Mullewa (8 D9)**. The heart of the **Wildflower Way**, Mullewa is also one of the state's most productive grain-growing districts. The colourful and unusual **wreath flowers** (*Leschenaultia macrantha*) – the Mullewa Shire's botanic symbol – are unique to the area around Mullewa, **Pindar (8 D10)** and **Tardun (8 E9)**. Mullewa is also part of the **Everlastings Trail** (see boxed text for more information).

Ask at the information centre for details of **walks** in the area including the Wildflower Walk, Bushland Trail, Town Heritage Trail and Railway Heritage Loop. The **Wildflower Walk** showcases the stunning flora that come alive in late winter, especially the dramatic carpets of pink, yellow and white everlastings. The **Bushland Trail** highlights the area's natural features, and provides panoramic views across the scrub into Mullewa. The **Railway Heritage Loop** displays Mullewa's once-expansive rail precinct, that dates back to a time when the town was a hub for trains travelling between Geraldton and Perth via Morawa, to the outback town of Wiluna. The Town Heritage Walk allows visitors to enjoy a leisurely stroll about town among the original buildings of the early 1900s.

The town's National Trust-listed **Our Lady of Mt Carmel Church** was built by **Monsignor John Hawes** in 1927. The Reverend was an architect who built religious buildings with an interesting combination of Gothic and Romanesque styles across the Wheatbelt. He was a successful architect in England before he changed direction and became an Anglican missionary, and then converted to Catholicism. He arrived in Australia in 1916 to become the parish priest in Mullewa. You can also visit the Reverend's former home (1929/30), which is now the **Priest House Museum**. To really get the full atmosphere of the **Monsignor Hawes Heritage Trail**, pick up a booklet at the Geraldton Visitor Centre.

North of Mullewa some old wells, watering holes and other historic sites have been identified along the old **Mullewa-De Grey Stock Route**. There is also an **old glacier bed** off the Tenindewa-Yuna Road.

Information

The **Mullewa Tourist Information Centre** is in Jose St. (Ph 08 9961 1500, www.mullewatourism.com.au)

Where to Stay

- *Coalseam Conservation Park* – 45km south of Mullewa; Miners Camp & Breakaway bush camping area; camping fees apply (DEC Geraldton office, Ph 08 9921 5955)
- *Mullewa Caravan Park* (Ph 08 9961 1161)
- *Mullewa Hotel* (Ph 08 9961 1950)
- *Pindar Guest House* – 30km east of Mullewa (Ph 08 9962 3024, www.pindarguesthouse.com)
- *Railway Hotel Motel* (Ph 08 9961 1050)
- *The Ranch* – s/c, 2brm house (book through the Mullewa Tourist Information Centre)
- *Wandina Station* – 65km north of Mullewa (Ph 08 9962 9597)
- *Warrakatta Farm Stay* – 55km south of Mullewa, near Canna (Ph 08 9972 2040)

Yalgoo (Map 8 C12)

Affectionately known as 'The Goo', **Yalgoo** was once a quite busy mining centre but the snail on the 'Goo Crossing' sign is a sure sign things have really slowed down. It is at the junction of two Outback Pathways – **Wool Wagon Pathway** and **Miners Pathway**. The **Courthouse Museum** has interesting displays, as well as some Aboriginal weaponry and implements. To learn more about the town's early days, follow the **Yalgoo Heritage Trail**. Another interesting colonial building is the **Chapel of St Hyacinth**, another architechtural delight from **Monsignor John Hawes** (see above). As well as designing the building, Monsignor Hawes actually worked on the construction as well. In good wildflower seasons, colourful carpets of everlasting daisies can be seen right through the area.

The fuel depot is near the railway station – be aware this is a self-serve, unmanned set of fuel pumps. As there are no attendants you will need either a credit or debit card to get fuel. (When we went through our bank's link was down – therefore no fuel. Luckily we had people with us who could pay...)

Just 10km south of town, walk the 100m-long **Joker's Tunnel (8 D12)** – a testament to prospectors' determination to find that yellow metal. Gold fever drives prospectors to do strange things, and when some miners staked out the Joker's Mining Lease they decided to find gold the hard way. They dug into unyielding rock and created a 100m tunnel, but their back-breaking gamble turned to folly and the tunnel was abandoned. Enter at your own risk and watch out for snakes and bats.

About 100km north of Yalgoo is the **Dalgaranga Meteorite Crater (8 A14)**, on Dalgaranga Station. A 100 tonne meteorite hit the earth here, creating a crater 25m in diameter and 5m deep.

Information

The **Yalgoo Shire Council** office is at 37 Gibbons St. (Ph 08 9962 8042, www.yalgoo.wa.gov.au)

Where to Stay

- *Tardie Station Stay* – 51km north of the Geraldton Mt Magnet Rd (Ph 08 9963 7980)
- *Yalgoo Caravan Park* (Ph 08 9962 8033)
- *Yalgoo Hotel* (Ph 08 9962 8031)

Our Lady of St Carmel Church, Mullewa

PELUSEY PHOTOGRAPHY

Everlasting daisies, near Mullewa

COLIN KERR

COLIN KERR

The round-roof woolshed is just one of the features of Wooleen Station.

PELUSEY PHOTOGRAPHY

Mulla Mulla, station country near Murchison River

PELUSEY PHOTOGRAPHY

Murchison River at sunrise in winter.

Bilung Pool is a pleasant picnic spot

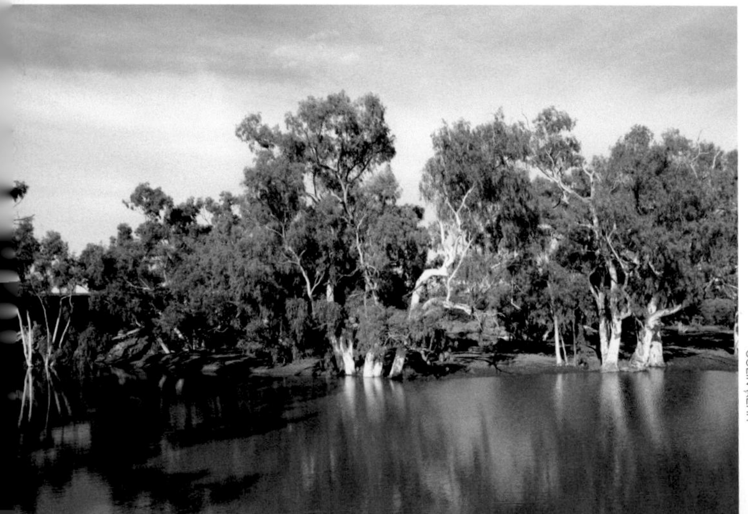
COLIN KERR

Mullewa to Murchison

North of **Mullewa** you are entering the real outback, so make sure you have enough fuel. No mechanical repairs are available, so it is a good idea to bring a range of spares and tools. The **Murchison Roadhouse** may provide some assistance in emergency situations. All roads in the Murchison shire are unsealed – check with the council office for the latest road conditions before travelling.

A popular picnic spot along the Carnarvon Mullewa Rd, between Mullewa and Murchison, is the historic concrete **Ballinyoo Bridge (14 J10),** which was built in 1932.

The tiny settlement of **Murchison (14 G10)** has fuel available at the roadhouse, as well as takeaway food and basic grocery lines. Murchison is famous for being the only shire without a town in it. The shire encompasses 26 stations and a population of – wait for it – 160, all in an area of about 50 000 square kilometres. Both the shire and service settlement are named after the **Murchison River** that has its source nearby. The Murchison is often dry, unless the tail end of a cyclone passes by or a severe thunderstorm strikes. After significant rain, the river closes roads and floods down to the sea at Kalbarri. To see the Murchison River in flood is an amazing, and rare, experience.

The **rammed-earth museum** provides a fascinating insight into the local Yamatge Aboriginal people and the district's pastoral and family histories. A 1.7km rangeland **botanical walk trail** is another point of interest. Every July 23 teams congregate on the **polocrosse** fields for an annual carnival.

For a truly authentic outback experience, stay at **Wooleen Station (14 G11)**. Just 37km southeast of Murchison, the National Trust-listed **Wooleen Homestead** features an old round-roof woolshed, shearers' quarters and a cookhouse. There is also an extensive indoor/outdoor **museum**. Wooleen was established as a sheep station in 1878, and the Pollock family took over in 1990 when they turned it into the special place it is today. **Accommodation** ranges from rooms in the homestead and guesthouses, to a campground with sites for camping and caravans. With its excellent **cellar**, Wooleen is also one of the very few stations in Australia with a liquor licence. There are **tours** available around the station, which include a trip to **Wooleen Lake** and its Ramsar-listed **wetlands**. The lake is often dry but does have water on average once every four years. When full, the lake attracts a variety of **birdlife**. Visitors can also explore the station on the 2.3km **Wooleen Walk Trail**. The station is only open during the tourist season – 1 April to 31 October.

Just 1km past the Murchison settlement is the turnoff to **Errabiddy Bluff (14 G9)**. A splendid breakaway outcrop, Errabiddy Bluff offers panoramic views over the remote semi-desert countryside.

About 150km north of Murchison, **Bilung Pool and Waterfall (14 C10)** is a pleasant picnic spot. This deep permanent pool in the **Wooramel River**, surrounded by colourful cliffs, is a tranquil spot where river gums are mirrored in the water.

Information

The **Shire of Murchison** office is open on weekdays from 8am to 5pm. (Ph 08 9963 7999, www.murchison.wa.gov.au)

Where to Stay

- *Murchison Oasis Roadhouse and Caravan Park* – sites for camping and caravans, as well as some onsite caravans; phone ahead if you plan to stay (Ph 08 9963 7968)
- *Wooleen Station Stay* – accommodation & campground (Ph 08 9963 7973, www.wooleen.com.au)

Murchison to Exmouth

Have a break at the pub in **Gascoyne Junction (20 J8)**, which was built in 1911. The only town in the Shire of Upper Gascoyne, Gasoyne Junction is a tiny settlementon the banks of the **Gascoyne River**, near the junction with the **Lyons River**. The surrounding district has a number of very large sheep stations. Also make time to drop in to the **Gascoyne Junction Museum**.

Only a 12km detour off the route is **Kennedy Range National Park** (see p96). If you stay overnight in the park you'll have the chance to see this rugged country turn vibrant red at sunset.

The region around Gascoyne Junction often tops the maximum temperature in the state on weather reports, with temperatures near 50°C not uncommon. So, if you can, you should avoid travelling in summer. On the other hand, winter and early spring are delightful, with warm sunny days although the nights may still be cold. Before you leave Gascoyne Junction, make sure you have enough fuel for the 497km leg to Exmouth.

On the way in to Exmouth, take sidetrips into **Cape Range National Park** to see Shothole Canyon and Charles Knife Canyon (see p70). **Exmouth** (see p68) is the main tourist centre for visitors to the **Ningaloo Reef**.

Station stays along the route offer varying levels of accommodation and the chance to learn a little more about station life (see *Where to Stay* below).

Information

The **Gascoyne Junction Visitor Centre** can help with information on the region (Ph 08 9943 0880). For the latest road conditions in the area contact the **Shire of Upper Gascoyne** in Gascoyne Junction (Ph 08 9943 0988).

Where to Stay

- *Barradale rest area* – overnight rest area at the junction of the North West Coastal Hwy & Towera Rd
- *Bidgemia Station* – 10km east of Gascoyne Junction; accommodation and camping sites (Ph 08 9943 0501, www.bidgemia.com)
- *Bullara Station* – 90km southeast of Exmouth, along Burkett Rd; accommodation & unpowered sites for campers and caravans; open 1 Apr - 31 Oct (Ph 08 9942 5938, www.bullara-station.com.au)
- *Emu Creek Station (formerly Nyang Station)* – 25km south of North West Coastal Hwy, along Towera Rd; accommodation and camping sites (Ph 08 9943 0534)
- *Giralia Pastoral Station* – 123km southeast of Exmouth, along Burkett Rd; accommodation & camping and caravan sites (Ph 08 9942 5937)
- *Hackers Hectare* – bush camping area near Gascoyne Junction (Ph 08 9943 0988)
- *Kennedy Range National Park* – 60km northwest of Gascoyne Junction; Temple Gorge campsite (DEC Carnarvon office Ph 08 9941 3754)

Miners Pathway

By following the Miners Pathway you are exploring in the footsteps of prospectors from a bygone era and gaining an insight into their hardships in an inhospitable but starkly beautiful land. The trail is essentially a bow-tie – passing through Mount Magnet twice on its loop. Start the journey in **Paynes Find**, then head north to **Mount Magnet**, **Cue** and **Meekatharra** before turning southeast to **Sandstone**. From Sandstone, it's back 158km to Mount Magnet (see p105) and then a further 123km to **Yalgoo** (p101). To complete the journey, return southeast to Paynes Find.

There are 22 interpretive signs along the trail that give travellers an excuse to get out of the car and be informed while stretching their legs. This trail is full of highlights in an area of Western Australia often ignored by tourists.

The *Gascoyne Murchison Outback Pathways* book is a useful guide to have if you wish to do this trail, and other pathways in the Murchison and Gascoyne. Information is also available on the Outback Pathways website, www.outbackpathways.com.au, and from the visitor centres along the trail.

Fuel, supplies and accommodation are available at Paynes Find, Mount Magnet, Cue, Meekatharra, Sandstone and Yalgoo.

An unsealed section of the Miners Pathway

PELUSEY PHOTOGRAPHY

PELUSEY PHOTOGRAPHY

Unusual rocks on Mount Singleton, Ninghan Station

Paynes Find (Map 9 G3)

The recommended start of the Miners Pathway is **Paynes Find**, where an old gold battery is located. This tiny settlement owes its existence to gold, and about 1km out of town is the **battery** and adjacent **museum**. The battery crushed ore for gold from 1912 to 1986. (For opening hours and appointments, Ph 08 9963 6513.)

Today the town consists of little more than a tavern, dating back to the 1900s, a fuel stop and small shop. A cellar, cut out by hand from solid rock, is a feature at the historic **Paynes Find Tavern**.

If there has been winter rain, visit in early spring to see colourful **everlastings** right through Paynes Find. The Paynes Find Yalgoo Rd can be particularly appealing.

Where to Stay

- *Paynes Find Tavern & Roadhouse* (Ph 08 9963 6111)

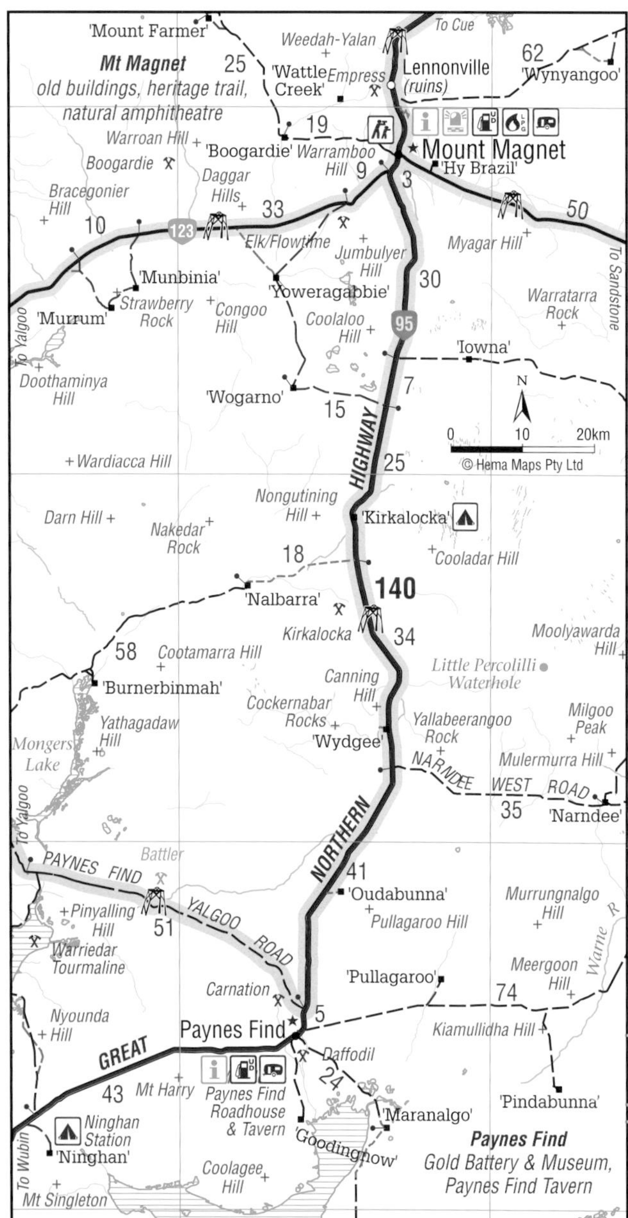

PELUSEY PHOTOGRAPHY

Outback at dusk, Wogarno Station, southwest of Mount Magnet

Ninghan Station – Magnificent wildflowers on a working station

Ninghan Station (9 G2) is an outback experience on a working station with wildflowers in abundance. About 54km south of Paynes Find, the station is situated in a hot spot for **wildflowers** between August and October. The station is in the process of being de-stocked so it will be a nature lover's paradise.

Ninghan Station is dominated by **Mount Singleton,** which was named by explorer AC Gregory back in the 1840s. For anybody game enough, **four-wheel driving** up Mount Singleton is a worthy challenge. The views of **Lake Moore** are quite good from the summit, but better as you climb slowly up or down.

On the other side of the station, **Warrdagga Rock** is reached by following the fenceline road. Warrdagga Rock is a large granite outcrop that, in season, can be surrounded by magnificent yellow, pink and white everlastings and blue cornflowers. Warrdagga Rock is a good climb with fine views, but don't climb in slippery wet weather.

This is a **working pastoral station** and therefore private property, so please see Don and Leah at the homestead before driving around the station. They can give you up-to-date information about the best places to go and the track conditions. (Also see Track 25 in Hema's *Western Australia 4WD Top 50 Atlas & Guide* for more details on the 4WD tracks on the property.) The facilities at the **shearers' quarters camping** area are fairly basic but there are hot showers, toilets and power while the station has the generator on. Other campsites have no facilities at all, so its BYO water, fuel, and food. Bookings are essential for camping, Ph 08 9963 6517.

Camping at Ninghan Station

PELUSEY PHOTOGRAPHY

Mount Magnet (Map 9 C4)

The oldest surviving town in the Murchison region, **Mount Magnet** dates back to 1854. It was named after an ironstone hill, 5km from today's township. The hill was made of iron, but it was gold that really boosted Mount Magnet's fortunes in the 1890s. The discovery of gold in 1891 saw the town develop and it continues to survive because of the detection of large underground deposits. Gold mining is still important today with two open-cut mines operating in the area.

Information

The **Mount Magnet Tourist Information Centre** in Hepburn St is open weekdays from April to October. (Ph 08 9963 4172, www.mtmagnet.wa.gov.au)

What to See & Do

The town still has a 'wild west' character and the 37km drive along the well-marked **Mt Magnet Tourist Trail** takes in some popular local landmarks and historic locations. This trail includes the drive up **Mount Warramboo** for a view of the town and current mining activity. The drive also includes an impressive rock formation called **The Granites**. This 15m breakaway really comes alive near sunset, and sunrise, when the rocks glow red in the outback light. Another great geological phenomenon is what locals fondly call the **Amphitheatre**, which has long been a popular picnic spot. The trail also takes in some of the old diggings, huts and houses from the gold rush era, including the ruins of **Lennonville (9 B4)**.

As with many areas in the Murchison and Gascoyne, add rain and you get **wildflowers** in abundance – particularly between July and September.

Visit the **Mining & Pastoral Museum** to learn more about the town's colourful past, and if that gives you a little gold fever, then pick up a **prospecting licence** in town and try your luck. You can buy a permit for a small fee at the Mining Registrar's Office, and they will give you a map showing areas that are not already controlled by claims.

Further afield is the **Dalgaranga Meteorite Crater (9 A2)**. Although it is not exactly spectacular, the crater is one of the youngest authenticated meteorite craters.

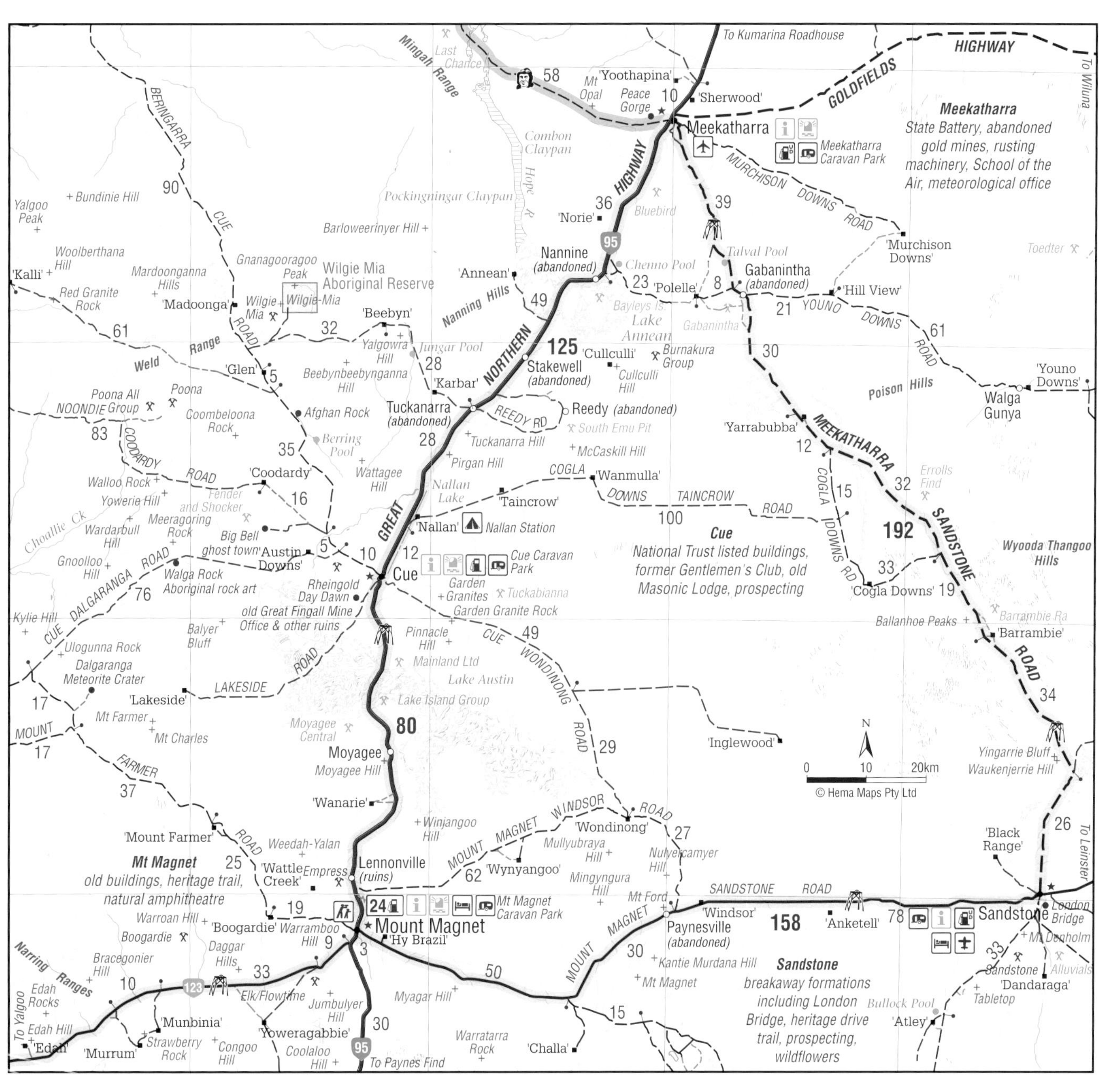

PELUSEY PHOTOGRAPHY

Masonic Lodge, Cue

Where to Stay

- *Commercial Club Hotel* (Ph 08 9963 4021)
- *Grand Hotel* (Ph 08 9963 4110)
- *Greengate Cottage* (Ph 0408 996 346)
- *The Little House* (Ph 08 9963 4061)
- *Miners Rest Units* (Ph 08 9963 4380, 0408 996 346)
- *Mount Magnet Caravan Park* (Ph 08 9963 4198)
- *Mount Magnet Hotel* (Ph 08 9963 4002)
- *Outback Gold Accommodation* (Ph 08 9963 4433)
- *Swagman Roadhouse and Motel* (Ph 08 9963 4844)

Station Stays

- *Kirkalocka Station Stopovers* – 60km south of Mount Magnet; accommodation & caravan and camping sites (Ph 08 9963 5827)
- *Wogarno Station* – 55km southwest of Mount Magnet; accommodation & caravan and camping sites (Ph 08 9963 5846, www.wogarnostation.com)
- *Wondinong Station* – 62km northeast of Mount Magnet; accommodation & caravan and camping sites (Ph 08 9963 5865)

Cue (Map 15 H4)

Dubbed the 'Queen of the Murchison', **Cue** is one of our favourite gold towns. It got this tag in the 1890s gold rush, and the title remains as the name of an annual festival held on the June long weekend. Today walking down the main street of Cue is like taking a step back in time, and there is enough here to occupy you for at least a three-day stay. In the gold rush era, Cue was the hub for all the surrounding gold-mining townships – many of which later became ghost towns. With the resurgence of gold prices in the 2000s, many of the old gold mines are now operational again.

Information

The **Cue Tourist Centre** is at the Municipal Chambers in Robinson Street. (Open Apr to Nov only; Ph 08 9963 1041, www.cue.wa.gov.au)

What to See & Do

Many of Cue's more substantial **buildings** were classified by the National Trust, and it is worth taking a drive to see them. Cue's incredible heritage buildings include the **Old Gaol**, **courthouse** and **police station**, **Cue Shire offices** and the quirky **Masonic Lodge**. The rather spooky looking Masonic Lodge is now closed to public access, but the post office, courthouse and police station are still used for their original purposes. By staying at the **Cue Caravan Park** you are sampling accommodation that hosted the inmates of the local gaol between 1896 and the 1930s. To see images of the area from the late 1800s, visit the **Historical Photograph Collection** at the Cue shire building. Another point of historic interest is the ruins of the **old hospital**, south of Cue. Built of local stone, the ruins date back to 1895.

At **Big Bell (15 H3)**, northwest of Cue, see what is left of the once-thriving 1930s gold-mining town. The remains of the grandiose art deco hotel alone are worth the drive. For years many people scavenged around the ghost towns of Big Bell and Day Dawn. The old **Great Fingall Mine Office** and a few other ruins are all that remain of Cue's once-booming sister town, **Day Dawn (15 H4)**.

Cue is also popular with **prospectors**, and as a base for exploring the surrounding district. Get local information from the tourist centre and remember you will need a licence.

This area also has a strong Aboriginal heritage, with two sites in the district. A 47km drive southwest of Cue, **Walga Rock (15 H3)** is a massive formation with plenty of indigenous art and a curious image of a sailing ship (origins unknown). **Wilgie Mia (15 F3)** is a mine for red ochre that is used for body painting in Aboriginal ceremonies. The Sinosteel Midwest Corporation runs a mining operation in the Weld Range area, but has an agreement with the Wajarri Yamatji people to protect the range's important sites.

Where to Stay

- *Cue Caravan Park* (Ph 08 9963 1107)
- *Murchison Club Hotel* (Ph 08 9963 1020)
- *Nallan Station* – just off the Great Northern Hwy, 12km north of Cue; accommodation & caravan and camping sites (Ph 08 9963 1054)
- *Queen of the Murchison Hotel B&B* (Ph 08 9963 1625)

Sunset over Nallan Lake, north of Cue

COLIN KERR

Breakaway country, near Cue

COLIN KERR

COLIN KERR

Peak Hill wasn't as fortunate as Meekatharra – today only ruins remain.

Meekatharra (Map E6)

Meekatharra sprang up in the gold rush in the Murchison region at the turn of the 19th century. It went from a mere collection of tents in 1894 to a gazetted town by 1904. While its progress has fluctuated over the years, the continual discovery of new gold reserves, including large open-cut operations nearby, means it remains a major service and supply centre. Today, 'Meeka', as it is affectionately known, is a regional centre with headquarters for outback icons: the **Royal Flying Doctor** and **School of the Air**. Other gold towns in the area, such as **Nannine (15 F5)** and **Peak Hill (15 B6)**, weren't as fortunate however and both are now ghost towns with few or no buildings left. The word Meekatharra is Aboriginal for place of little water, and on a hot summer day there is no doubting the accurarcy of that tag. A curious fact is that in 1982 Meekatharra became the first town in Australia to be powered by solar energy.

As well as being part of the Miners Pathway, Meekatharra is also the eastern end of the **Kingsford Smith Mail Run** – an 800km dirt road drive to Carnarvon (see p98).

Information

The **Shire of Meekatharra** office in Main St can provide information for visitors. (Ph 08 9981 1002, www.meekashire.wa.gov.au)

What to See & Do

To get an idea of the town and its heritage follow the **Meeka Rangelands Discovery Trail**, which includes the Meeka Creek Trail and Meeka Lookout Trail. The **Meeka Creek Trail** is an easy 3km loop that winds its way around Meekatharra Creek, with interpretive signage to inform walkers about indigenous and settlers' heritage. The 900m **Meeka Lookout Trail** features seven interpretive signs along the way to the lookout for great views over the town.

You can gain further insight into Meekatharra's history by visiting the **Meekatharra Museum** at the shire library. (Open 8am to 4.30pm Mon-Fri) Almost in front of the caravan park is the relocated **State Battery** and some other relics that are worth a look. The **Royal Flying Doctor Service** is another point of interest (open between 9am and 2pm every day). Visitors can also experience a movie at the outdoor **Picture Gardens**.

Just 3km out of town is **Peace Gorge (15 E5)**, a stunning area of unusual rock formations. The gorge is a popular picnic spot.

Where to stay

- *Auski Inland Motel* (Ph 08 9981 1433)
- *Commercial Hotel* (Ph 08 9981 1020)
- *Meekatharra Caravan Park* (Ph 08 9981 1253)
- *Royal Mail Hotel & Motel* (Ph 08 9981 1148)

Sandstone (Map 15 K7)

The history of **Sandstone** revolves around gold. In 1894 **Ernest Shillington** discovered the precious metal some 20km from where the town now stands. As is the way with gold strikes, thousands of people flooded into the area and by 1907 over 7000 people called Sandstone home, if only for a few years. Walking around the town today, it is hard to believe that many people actually lived here. At the height of its boom, the population supported four hotels, four butchers, many cafes, stores and business houses, as well as a staffed police station and two banks. By 1919, the population had dropped to just 200 hardy souls. Many of the buildings were taken down, but the remaining few today provide a lovely streetscape. The smallest of the pubs, the **National Hotel**, is the only one that remains today. Although some local mining continues in the Sandstone area, the district also produces good quality wool. The semi-arid landscape and sparse vegetation, mean that stations need to be very extensive to be worthwhile. Despite its isolation, or perhaps because of it, Sandstone makes an interesting stopover when touring the outback Gascoyne and Murchison regions.

Information

The **Tourist Information Centre** is in the Sandstone Library. (Ph 08 9963 5061, www.sandstone.wa.gov.au)

What to See & Do

Drive the 17.9km **Sandstone Heritage Trail** to sample the region's history and natural delights. (Pick up a map from the shire office or print one from their website.) Highlights include **London Bridge**, the 1907 **National Hotel** and the **Brewery**, which was constructed out of solid rock in 1907. The old **State Battery** is another point of interest along the trail.

The most-photographed local sandstone formation is **London Bridge (16 K8)**. This 10m high and 800m long expanse of eroded basalt is believed to be 350 million years old. Although it is shaped like a bridge, don't be tempted to stand on it.

Ingenuity in the gold rush era led to the construction of a **brewery** within a sandstone breakaway. In 1907 the need for beer was great, so the Irish Mr Kearney pumped water from a well to produce the product then fed it into the dynamite-dug cellar to keep it cool. However, when the new train line was finished in 1910 the stock arriving by rail was much more sought after. So we guess Mr Kearney's 'sandstone-cooled' beer can't have been that good after all.

It's also worth a visit to the quaint **Black Range Chapel** to see the fine stained-glass windows. Built in 1908, and restored in 1995, the chapel is a picture in spring when it is surrounded by **pink everlastings**.

Where to Stay

- *Alice Atkinson Caravan Park* (Ph 08 9963 5859)
- *National Hotel* (Ph 08 9963 5801)
- *Outback Accommodation* (Ph 08 9963 5869) ■

London Bridge, near Sandstone

PELUSEY PHOTOGRAPHY

chapter seven

Goldfields

The Goldfields is part of the **Golden Outback** tourism area that stretches from Merredin in the west, to the Northern Territory border in the east, and south to Norseman. This vast area was inhabited by Aborigines for thousands of years and Europeans didn't really settle there until the discovery of gold in the 1890s. Gold was discovered in 1888 at Southern Cross, then the prospectors moved to what is now Coolgardie in 1892 and later to Kalgoorlie (1894). The rest of the surrounding towns sprouted up after finding their own gold. With the **gold rush** came a huge influx of prospectors with their supporting industries and towns. The population of many of these gold rush towns soared into the thousands. However, finding gold is a fickle, and often short-term activity, and many once bustling towns are now no more than **ghost towns**. Basically whether the gold lasted or not defined the future of the town. In some places you now can't even tell there was ever a town there. Other places though still feel the wealth of gold, particularly **Kalgoorlie** as it taps into the Golden Mile – one of the richest pieces of land in the world. The up and down **nickel** market has also had its effect on this area. Mining is still the lifeblood of this region and it is possible to do mine tours, visit old mining towns and see the big mine pits from lookouts.

Both before and during the gold rush, the Goldfields were a harsh land and simply getting there was difficult enough. Before the railway went through in 1896, prospectors had to walk. Water was worth more than beer, at least until CY O'Connor's water pipeline solved that problem. There are three drive trails throughout the region that explore the Goldfields' heritage, the Golden Pipeline Heritage Trail, Golden Quest Discovery Trail and the Holland Track.

Although this is a mining area, there is still much of the natural environment left to see. The **woodlands** in the Goldfields are possibly the largest temperate forest in the world, while rocky **granite outcrops** provide refuge for a variety of **wildlife**.

Lake Ballard, On the Golden Quest Trail near Menzies
PELUSEY PHOTOGRAPHY

Golden sunset over the Goldfields

PELUSEY PHOTOGRAPHY

Goldfields Highway to Kalgoorlie

Wiluna (Map 16 E11)

In the boom gold-mining years of the 1920s and 30s, **Wiluna** had a population of 9000. At its peak, the **Wiluna Gold Mine** is believed to have been the largest gold mine in Australia. Today, many abandoned mines and shafts can still be seen in the district. These days its position on the edge of the **Little Sandy Desert** means Wiluna is an important stop for outback travellers tackling the original **Gunbarrel Highway** to the east and **Canning Stock Route** to the north. (See boxed text p110.)

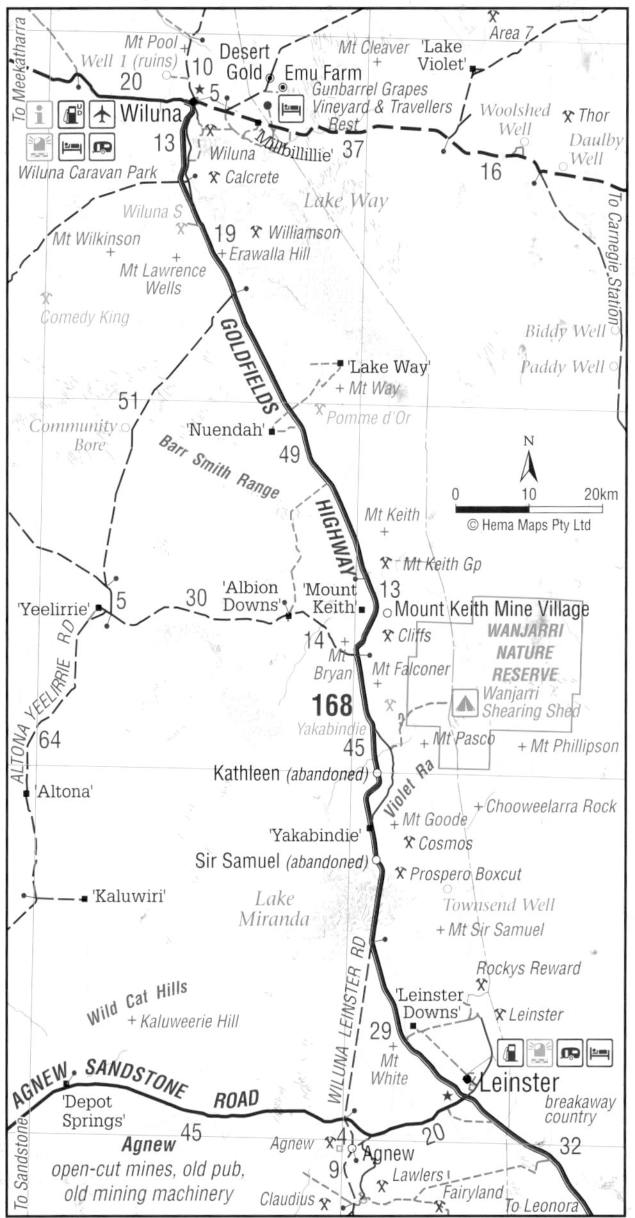

JEFF DREWITZ

Durba Hills, along the CSR

Wiluna itself is now a relatively busy multicultural community with a large indigenous population. It is also the home of the story about the "Last of the Nomads", and a **statue of Warri and Yatungka** has been erected in the town. These two members of the Mandildjara tribe were in all probability the last desert nomads living a traditional indigenous lifestyle. Indigenous law did not allow the two to marry, so they left for the desert. In 1977, people became worried about them as a severe drought was affecting the area. They were brought into Wiluna nearly starving but died two years later within weeks of each other.

Many pieces of local art are available for sale through the **Tjukurba Art Gallery** behind the shire office. (Open 8am-4.30pm Mon-Fri) Ask at the shire office for details on visiting points of interest in the district, including **Lake Violet**, **Vincenti's Pool and Rockhole**, **Red Hill** and **North Pool**.

About 160km northeast of Wiluna, the **Lorna Glen Conservation Park (17 C4)** has **camping** facilities in the old Homestead area. The Lorna Glen Station came under DEC management in August 2000, and since then the land has gradually been returned to natural reserve.

About 120km south of Wiluna along the Goldfields Highway, the **Wanjarri Nature Reserve (16 H12)** has the richest collection of native vertebrates of any nature reserve in the Western Australian arid zone. Surrounded by pastoral leases controlled by mining companies, Wanjarri plays a significant role in preserving the region's natural diversity. It was once a working station, and the shearing shed has now become the **camping** centre for an increasing number of visitors.

Canning Stock Route

Doing the Canning Stock Route is arguably Australia's greatest **4WD** challenge. It's an epic 1850km journey across vast desert tracts from Wiluna to Halls Creek in the Kimberley. Today it is a busy track: well relatively. During peak season, there can be dozens of vehicles in various states of condition scattered along its entire length. What a change from the track's first 20 years when only eight cattle teams got through.

Albert Canning was given the Herculean task of creating a cattle-droving track from the Kimberley pastoral areas to the southern region's sales yards. The isolated route was chosen to avoid cattle tick infestations in other parts. After the initial reconnoiter in 1906, Canning and his team spent the next two years digging a series of **wells** spaced about one day apart. Although there are Aboriginal waterholes, they were considered unreliable. In the end, 51 wells were built. It wasn't until the 1930s that the job was completed to its fullest potential, again by Canning who was now in his 70s.

During World War II, the track was further maintained to serve as a possible evacuation route from the north. After the war, cattle were transported by ship and the Canning Stock Route became redundant.

By the 1970s, the first adventurous four-wheel drivers began making their way along the entire route. At this time it was a serious expedition. A fuel dump was established by the Capricorn Roadhouse in the 1980s, which enabled more four-wheel drivers to have a go. The Kunawaritji community at Well 33 has further eased the fuel squeeze by pumping fuel seven days a week, along with selling some supplies.

The Canning Stock Route is covered by the National Trust and Australian Heritage Council, so do not take any souvenirs, just pictures. Sections of the CSR are also now part of the **Martu, Ngurrara** and **Tjurabalan native title areas,** so any deviation from the route without prior permission from the traditional owners is unlawful. (See Hema's *Great Desert Tracks North West Sheet* for all of the relevant contact details.)

Taking on the Canning Stock Route is well beyond the scope of this book. Track notes are provided at www.ExplorOz.com, and videos and specific publications are also available at specialty camping stores, bookshops and 4WD accessory shops.

Gunbarrel Highway

His trail-bulldozing exploits throughout the western desert region have made **Len Beadell** a legend in the world of **four-wheel driving**. Probably Len's best known trail is the 'The Gunbarrel', which runs roughly between Wiluna in WA and Uluru in NT.

The Gunbarrel was the first road built by Len Beadell to service the weapons testing grounds at Woomera in SA. As missiles launched from South Australia have no respect for state borders, the Gunbarrel and other roads were built to find them.

As a surveyor, Len Beadell had a liking for his roads to follow straight lines. Now you can see how the Gunbarrel Highway got its name. Len Beadell's sense of humour and artistic skills are also evident from his cartoons at the **Giles Weather Station**.

The Gunbarrel is for outback history buffs, so take along a history guide of the region. The track is dotted with historic plaques, marked trees and bores. The Giles Weather Station is another point of interest. It's also a perfect trip to see hardy wildlife and big night skies.

The Gunbarrel may be straight, but it's certainly not straight-forward. The track is rough and extremely remote, so vehicles need to be well prepared and carry HF radio or Satphone. Convoy support is recommended because if anything goes wrong help could take some time to arrive. (See Track 19 in Hema's *Western Australia 4WD Top 50 Atlas & Guide* or Hema's *Great Desert Tracks Atlas & Guide* for more information.)

PELUSEY PHOTOGRAPHY

Great Beyond Explorers Hall of Fame, Laverton

JEFF DREWITZ

Gwalia State Hotel, Gwalia

Information

The Shire of Wiluna office in Scotia St is open from 8.30am to 4pm Monday to Friday. (Ph 08 9981 8000, www.wiluna.wa.gov.au)

Where to Stay

- *Gunbarrel Laager – 15km east of Wiluna (Ph 08 9981 7161)*
- *Wiluna Club Hotel Motel & Caravan Park* (Ph 08 9981 7012)

Camping

- *Lorna Glen Conservation Park* – 158km northeast of Wiluna; the Homestead camping area has a barbecue, drinking water, toilets and a shower; camping fees apply (DEC Goldfields office in Kalgoorlie Ph 08 9080 5555)
- *Wanjarri Nature Reserve* – 120km south of Wiluna; the Shearing Shed camping area has a barbecue, drinking water, toilets and a shower (DEC Goldfields office in Kalgoorlie Ph 08 9080 5555)

Leinster (Map 10 B12)

Mining began in the Leinster area in 1897, but it wasn't until 1976 that the town of **Leinster** was established to support the **Agnew Gold Mining Company**. (It continues today as the Leinster Nickel Operation.) Today Leinster is a modern mining town, set up as a base for the large nickel and gold-mining operations. Sitting smack bang in the middle of the desert, Leinster provides a wide range of services and supplies. It is a town designed for the mining staff with good recreational facilities.

A popular drive is to the pub at **Agnew (10 C12)**: one of the only buildings still standing from the old town. This historic gold-mining centre is now the site for huge open-cut operations and there is an interesting display of old mining machinery.

Information

The Shire of Leonora incorporates the town of Leinster and can provide assistance. (Ph 08 9037 6044, www.leonora.wa.gov.au)

Where to Stay

- *Leinster Caravan Park* (Ph 08 9027 1388)

Leonora (Map 10 F14)

Leonora is an important goldfields **mining centre** with large local operations including gold, copper, nickel and silver. It has been a key supply and service centre for both mining and pastoral operations for more than a century. Originally there were the twin towns of Leonora and **Gwalia (10 F14)**.

Gwalia was the original town, but is now really just a museum. This was Herbert Hoover's stamping ground where he made his fortune before later becoming the President of the United States. In the early days, the Gwalia mining camp didn't have a legal pub, so sly-grog outlets thrived. In 1903, in an effort to stamp out this unsavory practice, the State Government built a **pub**, which to this day is one of finest looking buildings in the Goldfields. Many buildings are still standing and have been restored to a stage where you could really think that people from the era might still live there. One **miner's hut** is called the pink house – it's constructed of corrugated iron that has been painted pink. The **Sons of Gwalia mine** was staffed by migrant men, so there is a strong Italian heritage too. Herbert Hoover's **mine manager's house** is up on the hill overlooking the Sons of Gwalia mine pit and poppet head. Today it is a bed and breakfast, but be sure to book ahead. Next door is a great little **museum**, which if you have any interest in gold-mining history you should not miss. (The museum is open 10am to 4pm daily; closed 20 Dec to 4 Jan.)

Information

The Leonora Visitor Centre is in Tower St. (Ph 08 9037 7016, www.leonora.wa.gov.au)

Where to Stay

- *Central Hotel* (Ph 08 9037 6042)
- *Hoover House B&B* – Gwalia; open weekends only; closed 20 Dec to 20 Jan (Ph 08 9037 7122, www.gwalia.org.au/BandB.html)
- *Leonora Caravan Park* (Ph 08 9037 6568)
- *Leonora Lodge* (Ph 08 9037 7053)
- *Leonora Motor Inn* (Ph 08 9037 6444)
- *Whitehouse Hotel* (Ph 08 9037 6030)

Laverton (Map 11 C7)

Since the town's founding in 1900, **Laverton** has relied heavily on mining, and it is famous for the gold and nickel that has been found in the area. Fortunes were won, then lost, at the **Windarra Mine**: site of the Poseidon nickel-mining venture. The same mine reopened in 2006 to profit from the upswing in nickel prices, but the nickel price is always a bit of a rollercoaster. Laverton is also the kick-off spot for desert adventures such as the Outback Way (Great Central Road), Gunbarrel Highway and Anne Beadell Highway.

Information

The **Laverton Tourist Centre** is in Augusta St, in the Great Beyond Explorers Hall of Fame. (Open 8am-5pm Mon-Fri; Ph 08 9031 1750, www.laverton.wa.gov.au)

What to See & Do

The **Great Beyond Explorers Hall of Fame** features modern displays on early exploration. The centre is a tribute to the pioneers of the region, as well as explorers like **Ludwig Leichhardt**, **John Forrest** and **Ernest Giles**. You must allow plenty of time to visit this centre, and relax afterwards with a great cup of coffee.

You can also learn more about the area's history with a visit to the **old police precinct**, which includes the former station, sergeant's house and jail. (Guided tours of the complex can be arranged with the live-in caretaker – a small fee applies. Ph 08 9031 1383)

The **Laverton Outback Gallery** displays and sells authentic Aboriginal art by the people of Laverton and Western Desert areas.

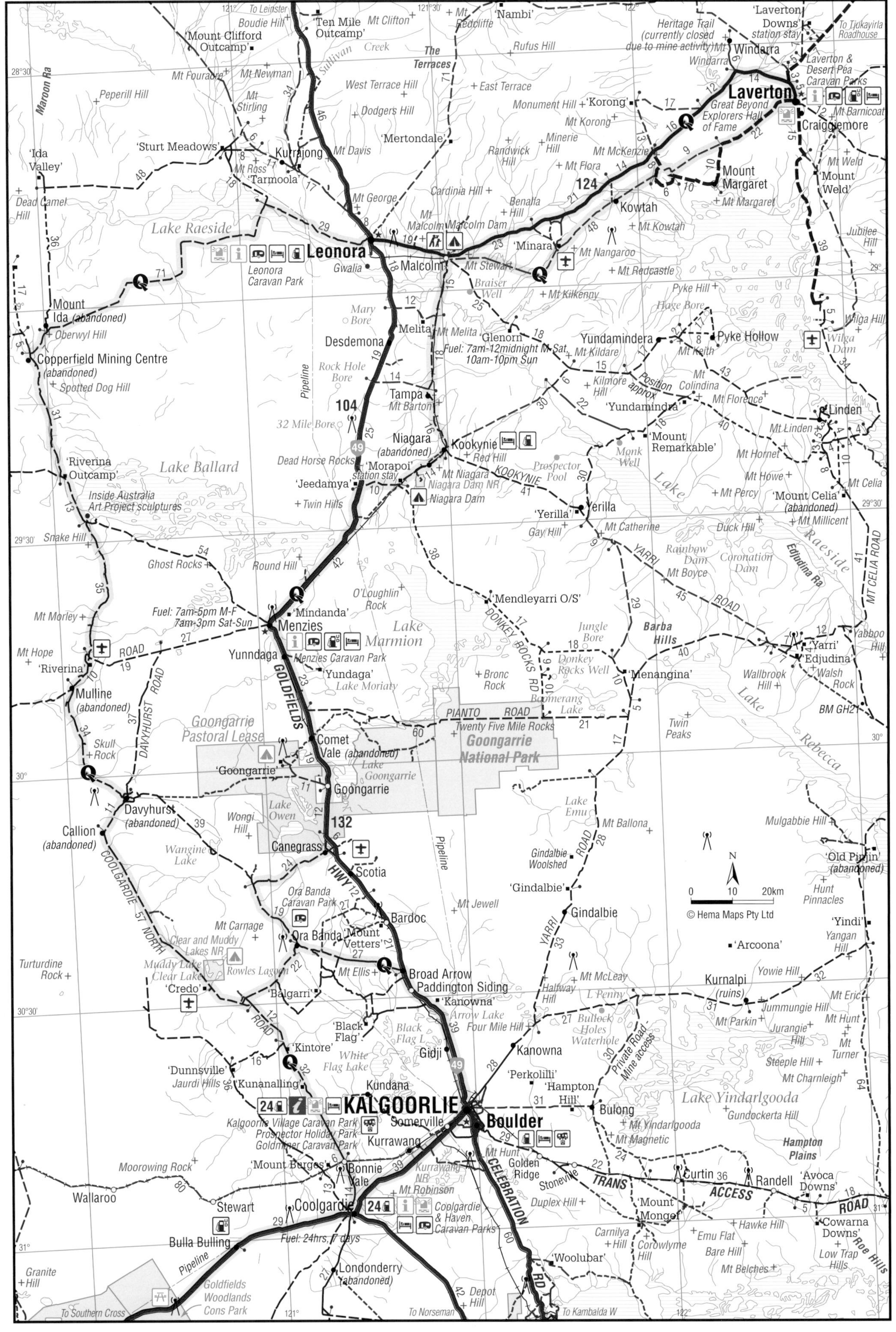
Laverton
Leonora
Menzies
KALGOORLIE
Boulder
Coolgardie
Kookynie
Kurrajong
Malcolm
Desdemona
Niagara
Yerilla
Lake Raeside
Lake Ballard
Lake Marmion
Goongarrie National Park
Goongarrie
Comet Vale
Canegrass
Scotia
Bardoc
Ora Banda
Broad Arrow
Kanowna
Kurnalpi
Bulong
Lake Yindarlgooda
Kambalda W
Norseman
Southern Cross
© Hema Maps Pty Ltd

PELUSEY PHOTOGRAPHY
Naturally dyed scarfs drying outside the Laverton Outback Gallery.

Just 13km east of Laverton, the Bandya Road provides access north into station country, and eventually the **Gunbarrel Highway** (see boxed text p110). Station stay accommodation is available 7km north of the Bandya Road at **Laverton Downs Station**.

Where to Stay

- *Desert Inn* (Ph 08 9031 1188)
- *Desert Pea Caravan Park* (Ph 08 9031 1072)
- *Laverton Chalets* (Ph 08 9031 1130)
- *Laverton Downs Station Stay* (Ph 08 9037 5998, 0429 375 998)
- *Laverton Homestyle Accommodation* (Ph 08 9031 1498)

Great Central Road (The Outback Way)

This trail offers a true **Central Desert** experience with numerous red dunes, camels, beautiful clear starry nights and wonderful desert oak trees. Starting at **Laverton** simply follow the Great Central Road to **Docker River** in the Northern Territory. (Once across the border the road name changes to Tjukkururu Rd.) From Docker River it's on to **Kata Tjuta, Uluru** and **Yulara.** From Yulara you can continue on the Outback Way through **Alice Springs** to **Boulia** and **Winton.**

There are numerous highlights along the Great Central Road, including Warburton's **Tjulyuru Art Gallery**, the **Giles Meteorological Station** and **Lasseters Cave.** A real highlight for us is seeing the tiny purple bumps on the horizon that slowly grow bigger as you approach: **Kata Tjuta (The Olgas)** is a sight to behold from the Tjukururu Road. Then you are amongst the tourist throngs at **Uluru** (Ayers Rock) and **Yulara.**

This is a true outback trail that requires some planning, as fuel can be a little unreliable. Although there are roadhouses and a couple of Aboriginal communities, travellers need to be self sufficient with food, water and extra fuel, if needed. Major supplies and fuel are available at Laverton and Yulara with more limited services at Cosmo Newberry, Tjukayirla Roadhouse, Warburton, Warakurna Roadhouse and Docker River. (Unleaded fuel is not available between Tjukayirla Roadhouse and Yulara, but the Opal substitute can be used in unleaded vehicles. Diesel is readily available.)

While other desert trails, such as the Gunbarrel Highway and Canning Stock Route, are for the hardcore four-wheel drivers the Great Central Road is kinder on vehicles, drivers and passengers. Nevertheless, it shouldn't be undertaken lightly. The trail is dirt, has corrugations in places and is sandy in patches, so it is susceptible to rain and can be closed at short notice. It is a good idea to check road conditions by contacting the Shire of Laverton (08) 9031 1202 or Main Roads on 1800 013 314.

For more information on this route, see Hema's *The Outback Way Atlas & Guide* or visit the Outback Highway website, www.outbackway.org.au.

Northern Goldfields

In the late 1800s, many people followed the gold rush to WA's Northern Goldfields to find their fortune. While some did indeed strike it rich, many died of thirst, while others died of diseases such as dysentery due unsanitary conditions. Most prospectors panned for alluvial gold in riverbeds, but it was also found as nuggets just under or on top of the ground. As these two sources of gold gradually diminished, miners dug deeper underground to find more sources. As the elusive metal ran out, many communities in the Northern Goldfields became **ghost towns.** Although the value of gold production has steadily declined since its peak in the mid-1990s, the Goldfields/Esperance region still produces about three quarters of WA's total gold production by value.

Kookynie (Map 11 F5)

In its heyday, **Kookynie** was a bustling town. Today, the corridors of the **Grand Hotel**, founded in 1894, are lined with old photographs that depict the 'high life' when the lure of gold brought people from all over the world. In the hotel's tiny, but atmospheric, public bar prospectors might even show you a couple of gold nuggets. Nearby, some broken down walls are all that remain of the **Cosmopolitan Hotel**, but old photographs show a building of considerable grace and style.

The township's immediate surrounds still have many **relics** of the gold-mining past, but be very careful around old mine shafts. You'll be surprised at some of the unusual **rock formations** too. (Ask at the bar for directions so you don't get lost.)

Where to Stay

- *Grand Hotel*, Kookynie (Ph 08 9031 3010)
- *Morapoi Station Stay* – accommodation & caravan and camping sites; indigenous cultural tours (Ph 08 9031 3380, www.morapoi.com.au)

Niagara Dam (Map 11 F5)

Although it was built in 1897 to supply water to the Goldfields, **Niagara Dam** was never actually used for that purpose. Interestingly, the dam's designed is modelled off the Mundaring Weir: where the water pipeline to the Goldfields starts.

Niagara was a mining town with large pubs and government buildings, but once the gold supply dwindled it was dismantled. Now there is barely a trace of the former community. Today, Niagara Dam is a pleasant place to **camp** or have a picnic. There's always water, so it's a popular place for a cooling dip too.

Kookynie pub

PELUSEY PHOTOGRAPHY

Mt Elvire Station Reserve

From Menzies, **Mt Elvire (10 G9)** is 194km to the east. Sandwiched between two arms of **Lake Barlee** – WA's largest salt lake – the property was formerly a harsh, remote sheep station. Today the Elvire Station homestead is run by the DEC as a nature stay.

Birdwatching is a popular pastime, and the surrounding area features granite rock outcrops such as **Elvire Rock** and **Rainy Rocks**. Within a few hundred metres of the homestead are a series of rainbow-coloured breakaways. They are particularly impressive around sunrise and sunset.

Lake Barlee is nearby whichever way you go: sidetracks to the east or west end up at the lake's edge. Resist the temptation to drive on the lake, because although it may look hard a short walk on the surface will reveal the sticky mess you may get into.

Mount Elvire is one of the bigger hills in this region, and the view from the top is worth the effort it takes to get there.

The old homestead has been set up to provide basic bunkhouse-style **accommodation**, and visitors can also **camp** around the building.

Mt Elvire homestead is generally accessible to 2WDs, but conditions can be bad following rain. You'll need a 4WD with high clearance and low range to access the mountain itself. (The reserve is also accessible from the south via Southern Cross.) For more information on the 4WD tracks within the station area, see Track 14 in Hema's *Western Australia 4WD Top 50 Atlas & Guide*.

A sculpture on Lake Ballard

PELUSEY PHOTOGRAPHY

Menzies (Map 11 G4)

Another gold-mining town that boomed in the early 1990s, **Menzies** is now virtually a ghost town. Today it is a blink-and-miss-it town with enough thirsty patrons to support one pub. However, Menzies does have an enthusiastic crew running the visitor centre, and they have restored one of the **old government buildings**. Take the time to wander around the streets, because the historic buildings give some idea of how gold transformed this town. The **cemetery**, **town hall**, **railway station** and **nursing post** are worth a look. The former **Lady Shenton Hotel** has been restored, and now houses the Visitor Centre as well as an **Aboriginal art gallery**.

Information

The **Menzies Visitor Centre**, in the old Lady Shenton Hotel, has lots of information about the area. (Ph 08 9024 2702, www.menzies.wa.gov.au/tourism)

Where to Stay

- *Menzies Caravan Park* (Ph 08 9024 2041; bookings through the Visitor Centre, Ph 08 9024 2702)
- *Menzies Hotel* (Ph 08 9024 2016)

Lake Ballard (Map 11 F3)

About 55km along a dirt road northwest of Menzies, is an interesting sight where 51 stainless steel figures are spread across the **Lake Ballard** saltpan. This surreal and dramatic artistic endeavour has become a major tourist attraction. In 2003, British artist **Antony Gormley** installed the near life-size sculptures of local Menzies people on the salt lake as part of the Perth International Arts Festival. Known as the **Inside Australia sculptures**, the dark, naked figures really stand out against the stark salt lake landscape. The sculptures were only supposed to be there for a year, but the thought-provoking display has become a permanent feature. The statues are located across an area of ten square kilometres, so seeing them all on foot takes some effort. Be warned: the saltpan surface can be wet and slippery at times, and very hot in summer.

Goongarrie & Goongarrie National Park

In 1893, gold was found in **Goongarrie (11 H4)** making it the second discovery in the region, after Coolgardie. Although the township boasted two hotels and several shops at its peak, the failure of the mine saw it abandoned.

Formerly a pastoral station, the nearby **Goongarrie National Park (11 H5)** is now a great spot to enjoy walking, camping and just observing nature. Granite outcrops and salt lakes are the chief features of the area, with diverse vegetation including gums, mulga, mallee and cypress pine. The **Goongarrie Homestead (11 H3)**, in the western section of the reserve, offers simple rustic **accommodation** and **campsites**. (Bookings are essential for Goongarrie Homestead, Ph DEC Goldfields Regional Office in Kalgoorlie 08 9080 5555. Camping fees apply.)

Broad Arrow (Map 11 K5)

The **Broad Arrow Tavern**, just 40km north of Kalgoorlie, is a classic outback pub located in a region bustling with gold-mining activity. Years ago the pub was going to be pulled down, so people started signing the walls. Many years later, the pub is still standing and the walls are entirely covered in graffiti. It makes for quite a fascinating read while you are having a drink.

Ora Banda (Map 11 J4)

A 28km detour on gravel road from Broad Arrow takes you to **Ora Banda Historic Inn**, a classic stone building originally constructed in 1911. The Inn has become an iconic relic of the Goldfields and its fascinating history continues to the present day. After being

PELUSEY PHOTOGRAPHY

Kalgoorlie's Super Pit

Golden Quest Discovery Trail

We rate the Golden Quest Discovery Trail as one of the best in WA for lovers of history, especially those interested in gold mining. There are interpretive signs dotted along the whole length of the trail that feature fascinating landmarks and provide insights into the Goldfields' history. You follow in the footsteps of the pioneers visiting once prosperous communities that are now mere ghost towns. The current mineral boom means there are a few more people moving around in this area.

The trail starts at **Coolgardie** (p116) – the start of the whole gold rush. From Coolgardie follow Coolgardie North Rd, Ora Banda Davyhurst Rd and Goldfields Hwy to **Menzies** (p114). After Menzies, continue along the Goldfields Hwy then head off via **Kookynie** (p113) to **Laverton** (p111). From Laverton head to **Leonora** (p111) and **Gwalia** (p111). Then take Leonora Mt Ida Rd to the abandoned **Copperfield (11 E2)** mining centre. Then follow Mt Ida Rd, Riverina Snake Hill Rd and Davyhurst Mulline Rd to **Davyhurst (11 J2)**. Further south, **Rowles Lagoon (11 K3)** is a popular camping and birdwatching spot. Finally, head into **Kalgoorlie** (p115) via **Ora Banda** (p114).

Although some parts of the trail are sealed, it has long unsealed sections that are prone to closure after rain. To really experience all the trail has to offer, pick up a copy of the *Golden Quest Discovery Trail Guide Book*. It is an excellent guide with maps, feature stories and goldfields yarns told on two CDs. Further information is also available on the website, www.goldenquesttrail.com.

Kunanalling town site

PELUSEY PHOTOGRAPHY

left in ruins, the building was eventually restored to its former glory. It was a great place to have a beer and a worthy addition to the Goldfields pub crawl, until a few years ago when a shooting and bomb blast reeked havoc. New owners have now taken over and renovated (again). The pub, now back to its pre-bomb-blast state, is now once more a great place to escape the heat. One wall has been left to show visitors some of the damage.

Kalgoorlie

In 1893, three Irishmen **Patrick Hannan**, **Dan Shea** and **Tom Flannigan** wandered away from the Coolgardie gold find where they weren't doing very well and stumbled across 100 ounces of alluvial gold. They had discovered the riches of the **Golden Mile** – which is the richest square mile of gold-bearing earth ever found. From that day on, **Kalgoorlie (5 C5)** and its twin town of Boulder have ridden on the back of the fluctuating gold price. Today, Kalgoorlie, or 'Kal' to the locals, is a bustling city that is the centre of gold mining in Australia. Kalgoorlie's **Super Pit** is one of Australia's largest gold mines. Since its peak in the mid-1990s, the value of gold production has steadily declined but the Goldfields/Esperance region still produces about three quarters of WA's total gold production by value.

Information

The **Kalgoorlie-Boulder Visitor Centre** is at 250 Hannan St. (Ph 08 9021 1966, www.kalgoorlietourism.com)

What to See & Do

Walks

To see Kalgoorlie's many interesting historic buildings, follow the **Inner City Trails**. (A brochure describing the 41 buildings along the trail can be downloaded from the visitor centre website.)

There are a multitude of walks around the town if you feel like stretching your legs, including the **Kalgoorlie Aboretum**, **Gribble Creek**, **Hammond Park**, **Karlkurla Bushland Park** and **Mount Charlotte Reservoir**.

Super Pit

The **Golden Mile** used to be a mass of poppet heads and mine shafts, then all the mines were combined and created the biggest mining pit in Australia: the **Super Pit**. At its biggest it will be 3.8km long, 1.5km wide and go down to a depth of more than 600m.

For an overall view of the mine, the **Super Pit Lookout** is a great vantage point from which visitors marvel at the very big hole. Blast times are available from the Visitor Centre or the Super Pit Shop in Boulder if you wish to add a bit of an edge to your visit.

Tours are available into the pit itself on Boulder Market Day (the third Sunday of each month) or with **Finders Keepers** who run 2.5hr tours (Ph 08 9093 2222, www.finderskeepersgold.com).

Mining History

The **Mining Hall of Fame** is a dedication to the people of the goldfields and the mining areas around Australia. Along with the main hall displays, it is possible to go underground into the old Hannan's North Mine. A few times a day there is a gold pour, and visitors can also try panning for gold. (Open 9am-4.30pm daily, closed Christmas, Boxing and New Years Day; Ph 08 9026 2700, www.mininghall.com)

For another more specific look at local gold-mining history, visit the **Western Australian Museum**, at the top end of Hannan St. It is the place with the big red poppet head. (Open 9.30am-4.30pm daily, except Wed; closed Xmas Day, Boxing Day, New Years Day, Good Friday, Easter Monday & Anzac Day; Ph 08 9021 8533, www.museum.wa.gov.au)

Pub Crawl

About 100 years ago in the Western Australian Goldfields, water was more expensive than beer so it's little wonder the hotels were built to last. At the turn of the century, 92 hotels quenched thirsty Kalgoorlie miners: it is said there was a pub on every corner. These days there are considerably fewer hotels, but what remain represent superb examples of Goldfields architecture. Standing at the intersection of Hannan and Maritana Sts are two of Kalgoorlie's best-known drinking establishments – the **Palace Hotel** and **Exchange Hotel**. In the foyer near the staircase of the Palace Hotel, there's a superbly ornate wood sideboard that once belonged to Herbert Hoover, an early Goldfields engineer who later became President of the United States of America. The **York Hotel**, further down Hannan St, has a wonderful Moorish art deco façade.

Brothel Tours

The so-called 'oldest profession' has been a part of Kalgoorlie pretty much since the miners first arrived. Today legal brothels, along with scantily clad bar staff and a high consumption of alcohol, are still a prominent part of life in Kalgoorlie. In 1902, Hay St was the designated location for brothels and these days several establishments run tours. **Questa Casa** (The Pink House), **The Red House** and **Langtrees** all have tours (contact the Visitor Centre for details). Questa Casa is the only brothel left from Kalgoorlie's gold rush days.

Royal Flying Doctor Service

Servicing rural and remote Australians for over 80 years, the **RFDS** is an Australian icon. To understand how the whole operation works, take a **tour** from the RFDS visitor centre at the Kalgoorlie-Boulder Airport. The tours commence on the hour and entry is a $2 donation. (Open 10am-3pm Mon-Fri, last tour at 2pm; Ph 08 9093 7595, www.flyingdoctor.net/Kalgoorlie.html)

Boulder Town Hall

The **Boulder Town Hall** (1902) is another of the area's interesting buildings. It also holds the magnificent **Philip Goatcher drop curtain** – believed to the only one like it left in the world. A stage curtain that was hand-painted with a scene of Naples, it has hung in Boulder since 1908. The Goatcher Curtain is lowered for viewing on Tuesdays, Wednesdays and Thursdays from 10am to 3pm and on every Boulder Market Day (third Sunday of every month) from 9.30am to 12.30pm.

Tour Operators

- **Finders Keepers** – prospecting tours and 2.5hr tours of the Super Pit (Ph 08 9093 2222, www.finderskeepersgold.com)
- **Goldrush Tours** – various tours around the surrounding Goldfields area, including Lake Ballard (Ph 1800 620 440, www.goldrushtours.com.au)

Where to Stay

There are a multitude of motels and hotels in Kalgoorlie – contact the Kalgoorlie Visitor Centre for more details or check the website. However, be warned that Kalgoorlie fills up quickly at certain times of the year, such as the Race Round in September and Diggers and Dealers conference in early August. It can be hard to find accommodation at these times, so be sure to book ahead.

Caravan Parks

- *Boulder Accommodation Village* (Ph 08 9093 1266, www.discoveryholidayparks.com.au)
- *Goldminer Caravan Park* (Ph 08 9021 3713, www.acclaimparks.com.au)
- *Kalgoorlie Village Caravan Park* (Ph 08 9039 4800, www.discoveryholidayparks.com.au)
- *Kalgoorlie Caravan Park* (Ph 08 9021 4855)
- *Prospector Holiday Park* (Ph 08 9021 2524, www.acclaimparks.com.au)

PELUSEY PHOTOGRAPHY

Classic Coolgardie architecture

Great Eastern Highway

Coolgardie (Map 5 D4)

In 1892, **Arthur Bayley** and **William Ford** found gold at Fly Flat – two years before it was discovered in Kalgoorlie. With a depression in the eastern states, thousands headed west excited at the thought of striking it rich. From these humble beginnings, Fly Flat developed to become the town of Coolgardie. At its peak, this bustling town had two stock exchanges, three breweries, six newspapers, 60 stores, 26 hotels and at least as many churches. Within ten years the population peaked at 16 000 making it the third biggest town in WA at the time, after Perth and Fremantle. Today, the only real evidence of the gold rush wealth is the grandeur of many of Coolgardie's **historic buildings**, especially along Bayley St.

Information

The **Coolgardie Visitors Centre** is at 62 Bayley St. (Ph 08 9026 6090, www.coolgardie.wa.gov.au/tourism)

What to See & Do

Of the 26 hotels the township boasted at its peak, only a few remain and only one still sells alcohol. Despite its very American-sounding name, Coolgardie's **Denver City Hotel** is every bit a classic Aussie pub – a two-storey building with grand balconies. It's easy to imagine sitting on the shady balcony a century ago watching the great camel trains turning around in the wide main road through town.

Coolgardie has a colourful gold-mining history that can be discovered by visiting the town's four museums. The **Goldfields Exhibition Museum**, housed in the extravagant two-storey Wardens Court Building (built 1898), has one of Australia's biggest antique bottle collections. (Open 9am-4pm Mon-Fri, 10am-3pm w/e & p/hol; Ph 08 9026 6090) **Warden Finnerty's House** is a beautiful building that was restored by the National Trust. It was constructed in 1895 of local stone for the first Mining Warden and Resident Magistrate, John Michael Finnerty. (Open 11am-4pm daily, closed Wed; Ph 08 9026 6028) The **Pharmacy Museum** has one of Australia's best pharmaceutical collections, including 18th and 19th century medicines and various advertisements and posters. (Ph 08 9026 7383) Built in March 1896, when the train finally reached the Goldfields, the Railway Station now houses the **Railway Museum**. (Ph 08 9026 6388)

Coolgardie's **historic cemeteries** have the graves of many famous people. One of the bigger tombstones is for famous explorer **Ernest Giles**, while another tells the tragic tale of one of the Afghan cameleers.

Where to Stay

- *Coolgardie Caltex Motel* (Ph 08 9026 6238)
- *Coolgardie Caravan Park* (Ph 08 9026 6009)
- *Coolgardie Motel* (Ph 08 9026 6080)
- *Denver City Hotel* (Ph 08 9026 6031)
- *The Haven Caravan Park* (Ph 08 9026 6123)

Coolgardie Esperance Highway

Kambalda (Map 5 E6)

In the gold rush of the 1890s, some **gold** was found at the edge of **Lake Lefroy**, near **Kambalda**. The rush was on until 1907 when it seemed all the gold was gone, and the town disappeared. It wasn't until the mid 1950s that the mining buzz began again when what **George Cowcil** thought was uranium turned out to be **nickel**. By 1966 the Western Mining Corporation had begun mining nickel and the town sprang to life again. Over the next 50 years the nickel price was a rollercoaster ride, seeing mines opening, closing, reopening and sometimes closing again. Just to add spice to the mineral mix, there is still gold about too.

Walk to the top of **Red Hill** for a great vista of the town and the large white-salt **Lake Lefroy** from the lookout. This salt lake is also a great surface for **land sailing**, and it really comes alive on Sundays when members of the Lake Lefroy Land Sailing Club hit the lake – weather permitting. Lake Lefroy is considered to be one of the best places for 'sailing-on-three-wheels' in the country. (If you are interested in trying out this sport, contact the Shire of Coolgardie's Kambalda office to enquire about hiring land-sailing equipment, Ph 08 9080 2100.)

Information

The **Kambalda Tourist Information Centre** is at the corner of Emu Rocks and Marianthus Rds. (Ph 08 9027 0192, www.coolgardie.wa.gov.au/tourism)

Where to Stay

- *Kambalda Caravan Park* (Ph 08 9027 1582)
- *Kambalda Motor Hotel* (Ph 08 9027 1333)

Norseman (Map 5 H6)

In 1894 a horse called Norseman kicked a rock that uncovered **gold**, and so began the town of **Norseman**. Today there are still gold mines in the area and Norseman's long gold-mining heritage is displayed at the **Norseman Historical Collection**, in the Old School of the Mines building. Fossicking for gemstones is possible if you have a permit. The very helpful staff at the Norseman Visitor Centre can help with the permit, and they also have a map that shows where various colourful semi-precious agates can be found.

A corrugated-iron sculpture of **camels** in Norseman's main street is dedicated to the Afghan cameleers and their 'Ships of the Desert' that supplied goods to the town many years ago.

Other relics of the region's gold-mining past can be seen on the **Norseman Heritage Trail** near **Lake Dundas**. Some locations have fascinating interpretive signage, and the trail includes **Dundas Rocks**, an interesting collection of rocks that is a great spot to see springtime **wildflowers**.

For expansive views over Norseman, the salt lakes and unique Goldfields woodlands, take a drive up to **Beacon Hill Lookout**.

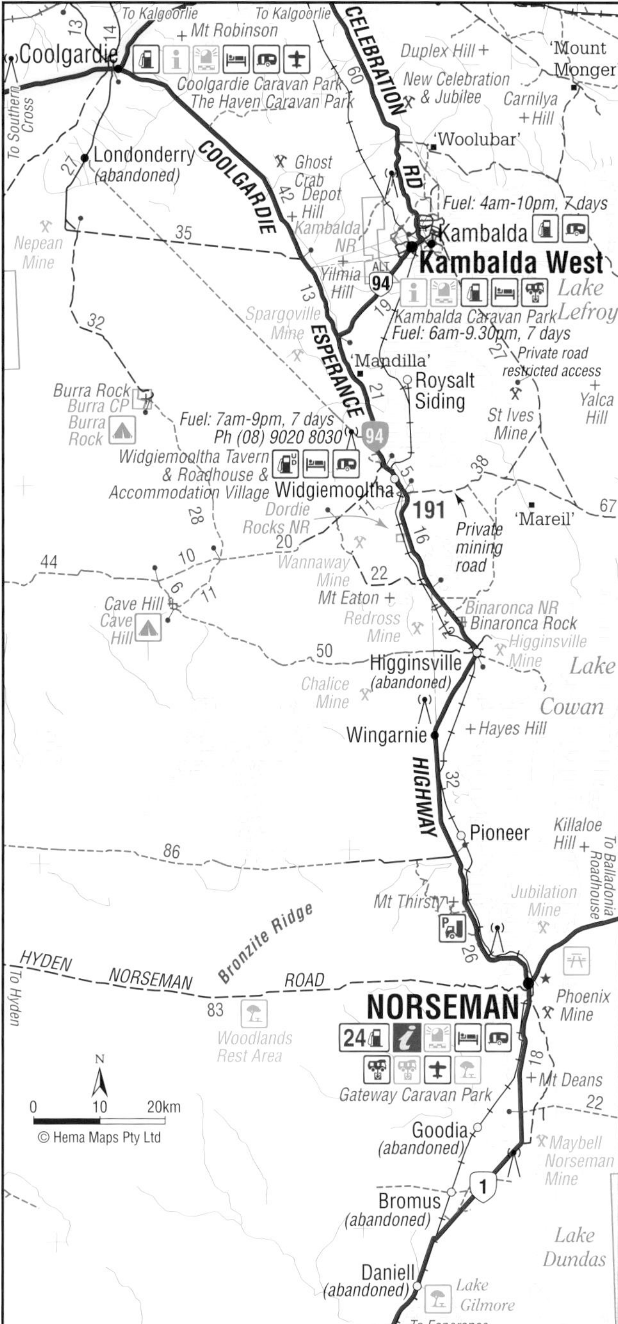

Norseman is also the kick-off spot for the iconic trip across the **Nullarbor** (see Track 20 in Hema's *Western Australia 4WD Top 50 Atlas & Guide*). About 100km east of Norseman, along the Eyre Highway, is **Fraser Range Station (6 G9)**. This sheep station was founded in 1872 and is now a wonderful place to camp or stay in accommodation in a picturesque location. Station tours are also available. (Ph 08 9039 3210, www.fraserrangestation.com.au; Check before arriving because they do close at times.)

Information

The **Norseman Visitor Centre** is in Welcome Park. (Open 9am-5pm Mon-Fri, 9am-noon & 1pm-4pm Sat, 9.30am-4pm Sun; Ph 08 9039 1071, www.norseman.info)

Where to Stay

- *Gateway Caravan Park* (Ph 08 9039 1500)
- *The Great Western Motel* (Ph 08 9039 1633)
- *Lodge 101 Guest House & Backpackers* (Ph 08 9039 1541)
- *The Norseman Eyre Motel* (Ph 08 9039 1130)
- *Norseman Hotel* (Ph 08 9039 1023)
- *The Railway* (Ph 08 9039 0003)

Part of Dundas Rocks

PELUSEY PHOTOGRAPHY

Granite Woodlands Trail

If you are looking for an alternative to the Great Eastern Highway, you may like to consider following the **Granites and Woodlands Discovery Trail** from **Norseman** to **Hyden (3 K7)**. It may surprise many people that the southern Goldfields region has some of the greatest temperate woodlands on earth. The colours of the mallee and gimlet trunks are truly magnificent, as are the salmon gums.

Along this 297km trail are 16 designated stopping points at various places of interest. Each site has informative interpretative signage, which adds to the overall experience. Do the trail in spring and you'll be rewarded with a stunning display of wildflowers, if there has been sufficient winter rain.

Near Norseman, you can take in the scenery from **Lake Cowan Lookout**: the view is especially good near sunset. A good spot to explore one of the most diverse eucalypt woodlands in the world is the **Woodlands rest area (5 H5)**. Take the 900m walk around the base and summit of **Disappointment Rock (5 H4)** to see unusually eroded rock formations and unique woodland vegetation. For a real perspective of the surrounding countryside, stand on a rocky hill and see **Lake Johnston (5 H3)** stretching out toward the horizon. Better still, camp there and have a drink to toast the sunset over this vast and colourful salt lake. To feel a part of the ancient landscape, stop at **The Breakaways (4 K11)** where the rocky outcrops come in an extraordinary array of colours. (This is a bush camping site with a toilet but no power.) For information on Hyden and Wave Rock see boxed text.

The road is mostly good gravel and with care is suitable for all vehicles, including caravans, although a 4WD is recommended. However, check with local shires if rain is about because they will close the trail if it is rain affected. To really make the most of this trail, pick up the *Granite and Woodlands Discovery Trail* booklet at the visitor centres at Hyden or Norseman.

Burra Rock & Cave Hill (Map 5 E4 & F4)

With prospectors flooding into Coolgardie during the gold rush, the township grew rapidly and fuel for the increasing population's power, heating and cooking needs had to come from somewhere. The obvious source of this fuel was timber from the surrounding open woodlands, but once the immediate gimlet and salmon gums had been cleared, train lines had to be laid to access trees further away. Later, base camps were created for men working on these train lines. The **Woodlines**, as they are called, criss-crossed the gimlet forests surrounding Coolgardie. One such Woodline ran between two base camps: **Burra Rock** (1928) and **Cave Hill** (1932). Some of the old sleepers and remnant embankments from this time make up the **4WD track** from Burra Rock to Cave Hill.

Holland Track to Wave Rock

After Bailey and Ford found gold at Fly Flat near Coolgardie in 1892, prospectors from all around arrived in boats at Albany and Perth. Prospectors landing in Albany had to find their way to Perth and York before walking to Coolgardie and, not unsurprisingly, many thought a track from the south directly to Coolgardie would make the trip much quicker. After a few attempts, sandalwood collector and kangaroo shooter, **John Holland** cut a cart track through from Broomehill to Coolgardie in 1893. Holland, and his team of Rudolph and David Krakouer and John Carmody, arrived in Coolgardie the day after Paddy Hannan discovered gold in what is now known as Kalgoorlie. Until the train system was completed three years later, many gold seekers used the 500km track. However, with the advent of the railway in 1896 the track gradually became overrun by bush. In 1992, Broomehill farmer **Graeme Newbey** and **Adrian Malloy** retraced the trail to create the Holland Track we know today. (The track 4WDs use today is the northern half of the original route, as the southern half is now covered by wheat farms.) As 4WD traffic on the track increased, the Toyota LandCruiser Club took on responsibility for upkeeping the track, and today it's well signposted and maintained. (There are no services on this road, nor any towns or roadhouses, so you must be self sufficient for fuel, water and food.)

Hyden (3 K7) is the modern day start (or end – depending which way you are travelling) of the Holland Track. The turnoff is about 60km out of Hyden along the Hyden Norseman Rd. (See Track 15 in Hema's *Western Australia 4WD Top 50 Atlas & Guide* for detailed trip notes.) Hyden is also the home of **Wave Rock (3 K7)**, a granite outcrop with a wave-like formation that is one of WA's most recognisable natural attractions. It is a short walk to Wave Rock from the caravan park. There is a very enthusiastic tourist centre, a small **wildlife park** and even a **Pioneer Town** with a 1920s theme. Above the 15m high wave-like formation itself, check out the **water reservoir**. From Wave Rock there is a short walk to **Hippos Yawn**: an impressive cave formation. It is worth spending some time exploring other less visited rock outcrops that have different features. At **Mulka's Cave** you can see the handprints of the Aboriginal outlaw on the roof.

Near the northern end of the track, is **Victoria Rock Nature Reserve (4 F13)** where the huge granite outcrop of Victoria Rock dominates the landscape. This fascinating rock has some unusual sculptured, eroded shapes, gnamma holes and plenty of places to explore. The reserve is also home to a variety of native animals, including emus, echidnas, ornate dragons and carpet pythons. **Campsites** are located among the trees at the base of the rock. (Ph DEC Goldfields Regional Office in Kalgoorlie 08 9080 5555)

Left to Right: Wave Rock, Crossing a flooded section of Holland Track which is sometimes shut due to rain, Rock formations near Wave Rock PELUSEY PHOTOGRAPHY

COLIN KERR

Cave Hill is the most impressive landmark in this area.

Today as you drive through one of the biggest areas of **temperate woodland forest** in the world, it is hard to believe that for decades 350 000 tonnes of timber were removed every year to fuel the gold industry. **Burra Rock (5 E4)** is one of a number of large granite outcrops found in this region. Early settlers used natural runoff from Burra Rock, and Victoria Rock, by building reservoirs to trap that scarce commodity. These days Burra Rock is protected in a nature reserve which is popular for picnicking and **camping**. The **Woodline Dam** is a popular spot for a swim, and the view from the top of the Rock is well worth the climb.

Cave Hill (5 F4), the most impressive landmark is this area, features a unique cave system and wave-shaped formations. These spectacular geological oddities are the result of erosion – the cave is just further advanced in the erosion process than the wave. Bushland surrounding these rocks is rich in **wildflowers** from August to October, particularly orchids and grevilleas. There is a **camping** area and if you're in the mood you can try your luck looking for yabbies in the dams.

You can head back to the Great Eastern Highway along part of the Holland Track, past Victoria Rock (see boxed text).

Goldfields Woodlands National Park (Map 4 F11)

Along the Great Eastern Highway, the **Goldfields Woodlands National Park** is part of a network of natural bushland that is the world's largest woodland forest. All up the various reserves cover 152 500ha of bushland. The woodlands include a wide variety of eucalyptus trees, including salmon gum, gimlet, ribbon-barked gum, mallee, red morrel, redwood and woodline mallee. In addition to these trees, there are wattles, banksias, bottlebrushes, hakeas, melaleucas, sheoaks, sandalwoods and grasstrees. It is no surprise the woodland is also home to a variety of wildlife, including 17 native mammal species, four frog species, 52 reptile species and more than 100 bird species.

Camping is permitted at **Boondi Rock** where there are toilets. (Ph DEC Goldfields Regional Office in Kalgoorlie 08 9080 5555)

Jaurdi Conservation Park (Map 4 D10)

The **Jaurdi Conservation Park** is another part of the conservation reserve network that includes the Goldfields Woodlands National Park. In the past, Jaurdi was a sheep station but it suffered from overstocking and subsequent land degradation. In 1989, the DEC purchased the land and today the vegetation is recovering. Now the station has become a base for scientists and nature enthusiasts, particularly birdwatchers.

Jaurdi Field Station's main building has bunk accommodation and you can camp around the homestead complex. (Camping fees apply; Ph DEC Goldfields Regional Office, Kalgoorlie 08 9080 5555)

Southern Cross (Map 4 F8)

In 1888, prospectors found gold in what is today called **Southern Cross**, and two years later the town was gazetted. It is named for the prominent star constellation that is so visible in the outback skies. The streets are named after individual stars. Today the area around Southern Cross has large wheat farms, and its location 368km east of Perth makes it the last town on the edge of the Wheatbelt. It is also the first town of the Goldfields.

The **Old Cemetery**, located at the eastern end of Southern Cross, has been redeveloped by the Southern Cross Historical Society as a pioneer memorial. A wander around the cemetery shows typhoid was a major killer of the prospectors and pioneers buried there. For another taste of history, visit the **Yilgarn History Museum** in the old Registrar's Office and Court House. It was at this office that **Paddy Hannan** took out his Miner's Right and it's also where **Arthur Bayley** came to register the claim. The museum explains the history of mining in the area. (Open 9am-noon & 1.30pm-4pm Mon-Sat, 1.30pm-4pm Sun)

Information

The **Shire of Yilgarn** office in Antares St Southern Cross can provide visitors with tourist information. (Open 8.30am-4.30pm Mon-Fri; Ph 08 9049 1001, www.yilgarn.wa.gov.au)

Where to Stay

- *Club Hotel* (Ph 08 9049 1202)
- *Palace Hotel* (Ph 08 9049 1555)
- *Railway Tavern* (Ph 08 9049 1030)
- *Southern Cross Caravan Park* (Ph 08 9149 1212, www.southerncrosscaravanpark.com.au)
- *Southern Cross Motel* (Ph 08 9049 1144)

Golden Pipeline Heritage Trail

When gold was discovered around Kalgoorlie and Coolgardie in the 1890s, it began bringing wealth and fortune to Western Australia. However, early progress was held back by a lack of water in this arid land. An engineer, **C.Y. O'Connor**, had the big picture in mind and designed and oversaw the construction of the pipeline from Perth to Kalgoorlie. An engineering project on such a grand scale had never been attempted, and the sceptics were numerous and unrelenting, especially in the media and government. Eventually all this pressure took a terrible toll on O'Connor, and he committed suicide in Fremantle before the water actually reached Kalgoorlie in 1903.

Today, the **Golden Pipeline Heritage Trail** basically follows what is arguably WA's greatest engineering achievement: the Mundaring to Kalgoorlie water pipeline. Although the trail does follow much of the Great Eastern Highway, it branches off at several points to reveal little known and fascinating aspects of the pipeline. There are 26 informative **interpretive sites** to stop at along the route. For water to flow it had to overcome the 400m climb in altitude to Kalgoorlie, along with pipe friction. O'Connor overcame this engineering obstacle by building an evenly spaced

The thorny devil is not uncommon in the Goldfields Woodlands National Park.

PELUSEY PHOTOGRAPHY

eight **pump system** to get the water to Kalgoorlie. The trail stops at these pump stations and following it turns the trip from Kalgoorlie to Perth into an interesting drive. In fact it is not realistic to do this trail in one day – to really absorb the history, take a few days and stay at some of the important linking towns or interesting campsites. To get the most out of the journey, grab the *Golden Pipeline Heritage Trail Guide* from the Western Australian Visitors Centre (Ph 1300 361 351). You can also visit www.goldenpipeline.com.au for more information.

Kalgoorlie to Southern Cross

Starting your journey in **Kalgoorlie (5 C5)**, make sure you visit **Mount Charlotte** and toast C.Y. O'Connor's triumph at the **final reservoir**. Remember that before the pipeline, many prospectors died of thirst while making their way to the goldfields.

Back road near Merredin

PELUSEY PHOTOGRAPHY

PELUSEY PHOTOGRAPHY

Golden Pipeline Trail signage

About 50km east of **Southern Cross (4 F8)**, visit **Karalee Dam (4 F10)** to see how settlers ingenuously built a rock catchment and aqueduct to supply precious water. There is a **camping** area with toilets at the dam. Just 11km east of Southern Cross, stop at the site of the **Number Six Pumping Station**.

Merredin (Map 3 G5)

Water has also played an important role in the history of **Merredin** and the water catchment scheme on **Merredin Peak** remains a point of interest today. You can walk to the top on the **Merredin Peak Heritage Trail** (60min). Gain an insight into another important factor in the area's history, the railway line, with a visit to the **Merredin Railway Museum**. Highlights include a re-creation of the old station, working windmill and preserved 1897 steam engine. The biggest town in the eastern Wheatbelt, Merredin was important during WWII and also has lots of military heritage. The **Merredin Military Museum** has memorabilia from both WWI and WWII (Ph 08 9041 1204). Ask at the information centre for brochures on the **York to Goldfields Heritage Trail** as well as the **Pioneers' Pathway**.

Information

The **Central Wheatbelt Visitor Centre** is located in Barrack St. (Ph 08 9041 1668, 1300 736 283, www.wheatbelttourism.com)

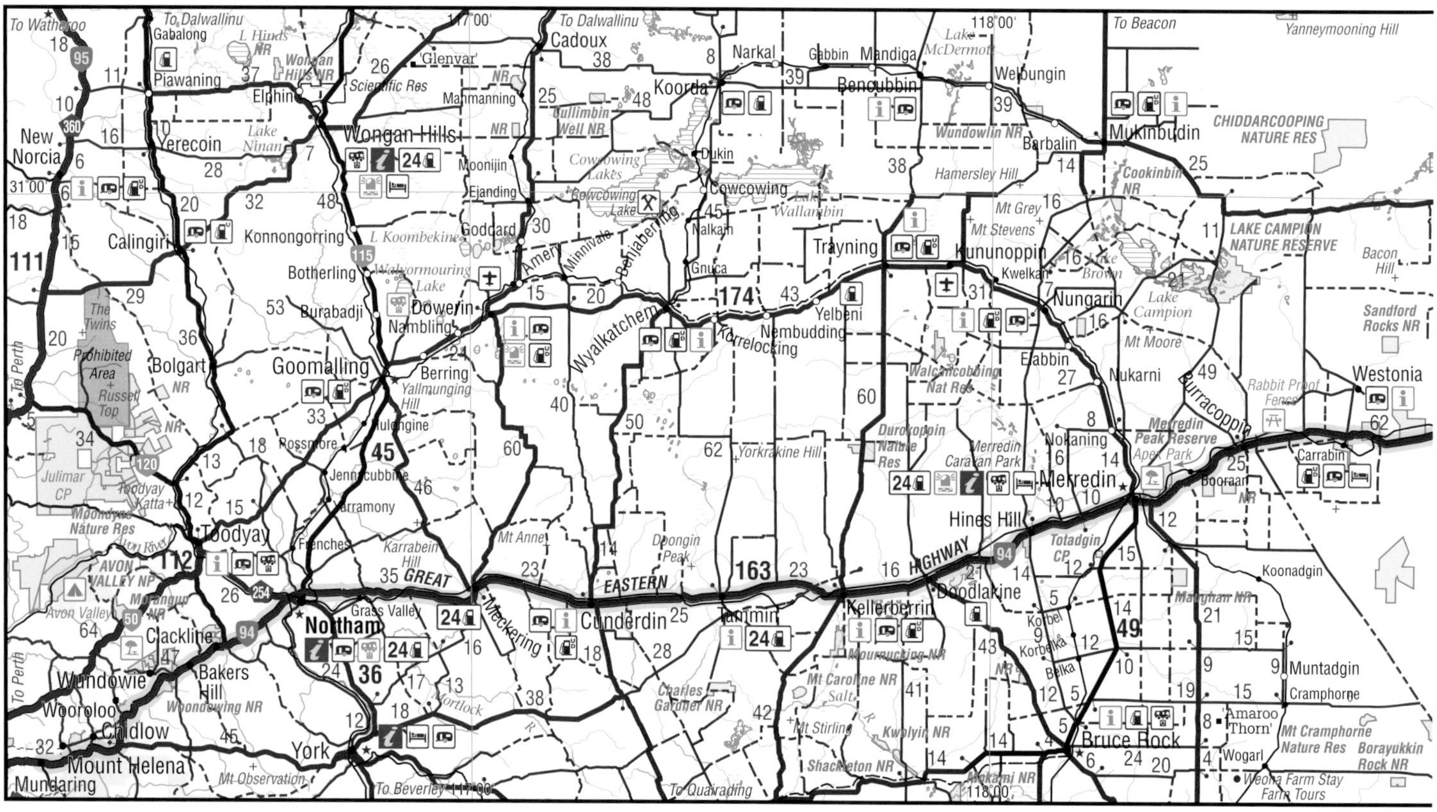

Where to Stay

- *Merredin B&B (Ph 08* 9041 4358*)*
- *Merredin Caravan Park* – also has self-contained units (Ph 08 9041 1535)
- *Merredin Motel* (Ph 08 9041 1886)
- *Merredin Plaza All Suites* (Ph 08 9041 1755)
- *Oasis Hotel/Motel* (Ph 08 9041 1133)
- *Olympic Motel* (Ph 08 9041 1588)

Merredin to Northam

Kellerberrin Hill (3 G4) offers fine views of the surrounding countryside. Drive to **Baandee Lakes Lookout** for interpretive signage and lake views. Visit, the **Tammin Hydrology Model**, an informative display that shows how salt seriously damages farmland and the natural environment. Another highlight along the trail is **pump station number three** at **Cunderdin (3 G2)**. The pump station is quite an impressive building and has been restored and turned into a **museum**. In 1968 **Meckering (3 G2)** was destroyed by a 6.8 strength earthquake. A huge fault line is located 4km west of town.

In **Northam (3 G1)** you can watch the introduced **white swans** while you enjoy a picnic on the banks of the Avon River. Northam boasts 185 **heritage registered buildings**: the most in WA outside Fremantle. The young, and young-at-heart, will enjoy a stop at the area's alpaca and emu farms. If you have a little more time, then organise an early morning **hot-air balloon flight** followed by a champagne breakfast (flights operate from April to late November only).

CY O'Connor's water pipeline

PELUSEY PHOTOGRAPHY

Mundaring (Map 2 H5)

Mundaring Weir, at the Perth end of the trail, has enough to see and do that it would take a good day to cover all the interesting stuff. Learn about CY O'Connor's amazing life by visiting the **Number One Pump Station Museum** at the base of Mundaring Weir. At the same time, take in the wonderful catchment views and go bushwalking in scenic jarrah bushland.

You can also spend a pleasant afternoon in the beer garden of the historic **Mundaring Weir Hotel**. The **Kookaburra Outdoor Cinema** (open between November and April) offers an outdoor cinema experience.

Just 10km from Mundaring is **John Forrest National Park** where you can enjoy waterfalls in winter or wildflowers in spring. There are also numerous trails for walking and tracks for mountain biking.

The **Perth Hills National Parks Centre**, in **Mundaring National Park**, gives a great overview of the Darling Ranges environment. The Centre provides a wide range of activities all year, including guided bush walks, star-gazing, Aboriginal cultural activities and night-time wildlife spotting. ■

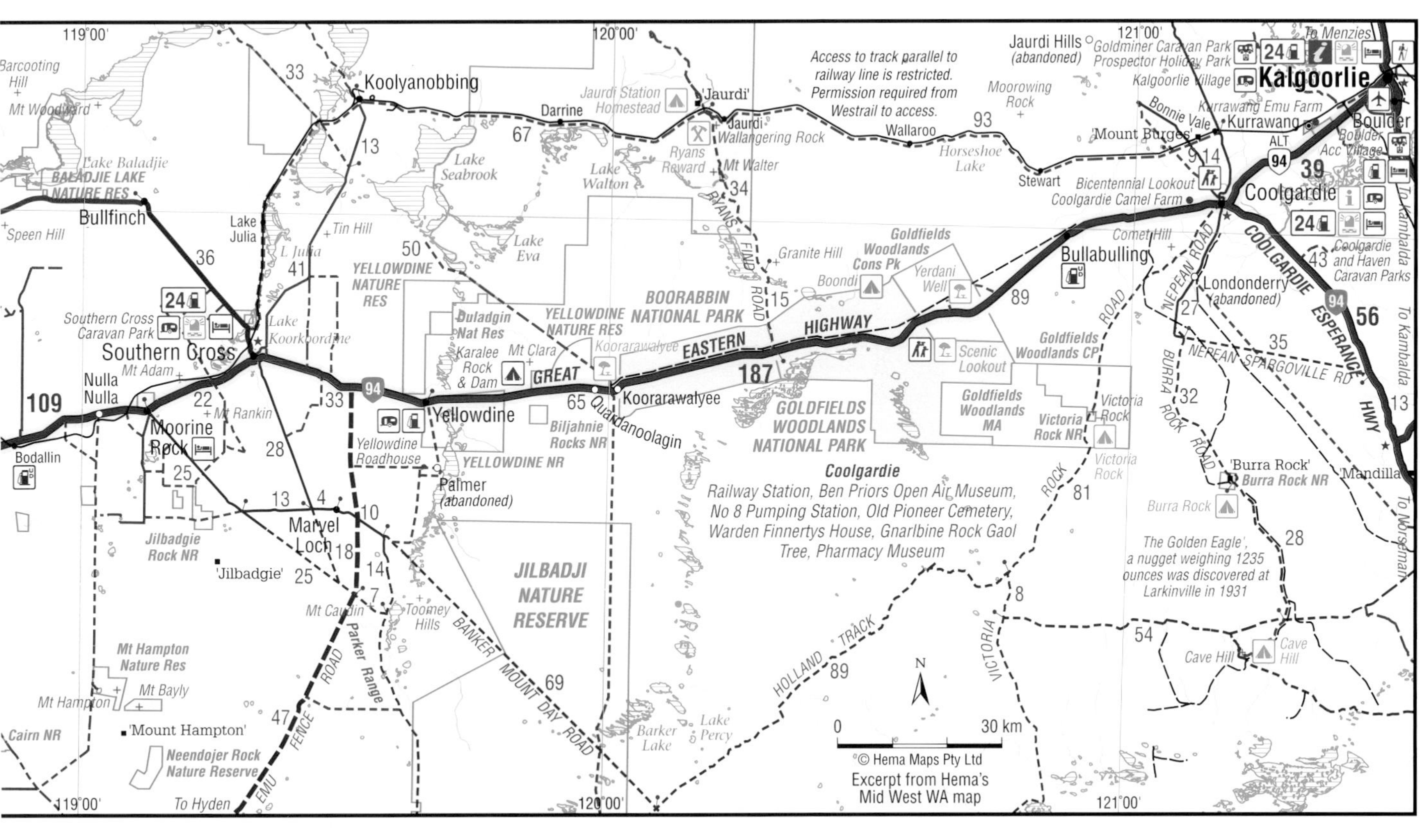

WARLUWAY
WESTERN AUSTRALIA
THE LAND. THE CULTURE. THE JOURNEY.

Experience Western Australia's dramatic Pilbara Region with the Warlu Way Drive Trail

The Warlu Way reveals the mysteries of the warlu and other Aboriginal legends by taking you on a 2500 kilometre self-drive journey through Western Australia's spectacular Gascoyne, Pilbara and Kimberley regions – areas resplendent with sapphire seas, soaring gorges, ancient Aboriginal art, rugged ranges and inland oases.

Open your eyes to the secrets of this country and its historical, cultural and natural wonders.

AUSTRALIA'S northwest

This project is proudly supported by

An Australian Government Initiative
AusIndustry

www.warluway.com.au

warluway@australiasnorthwest.com

Perth to Pilbara Maps

The following maps are from Hema's Western Australia Road & 4WD Atlas

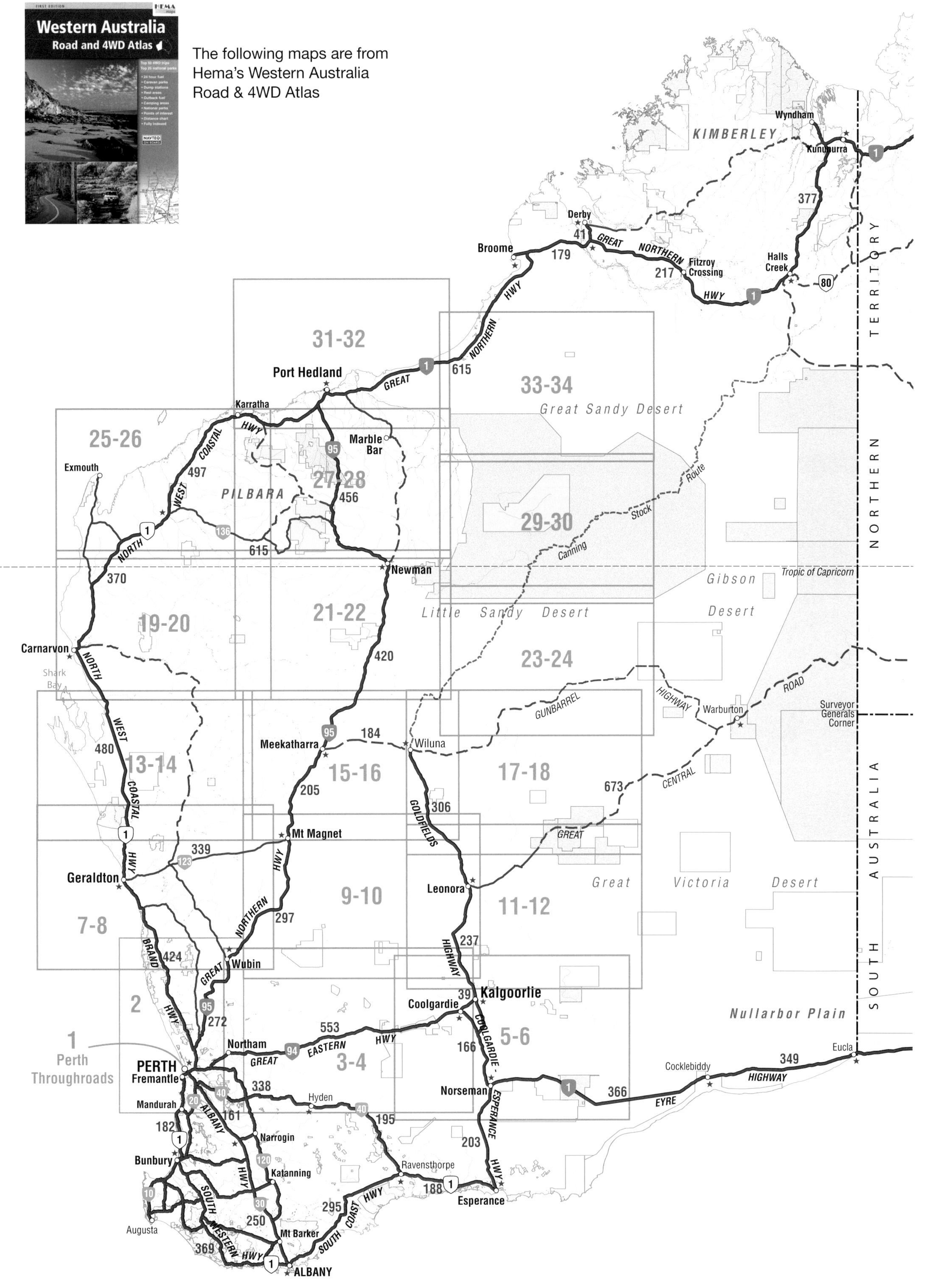

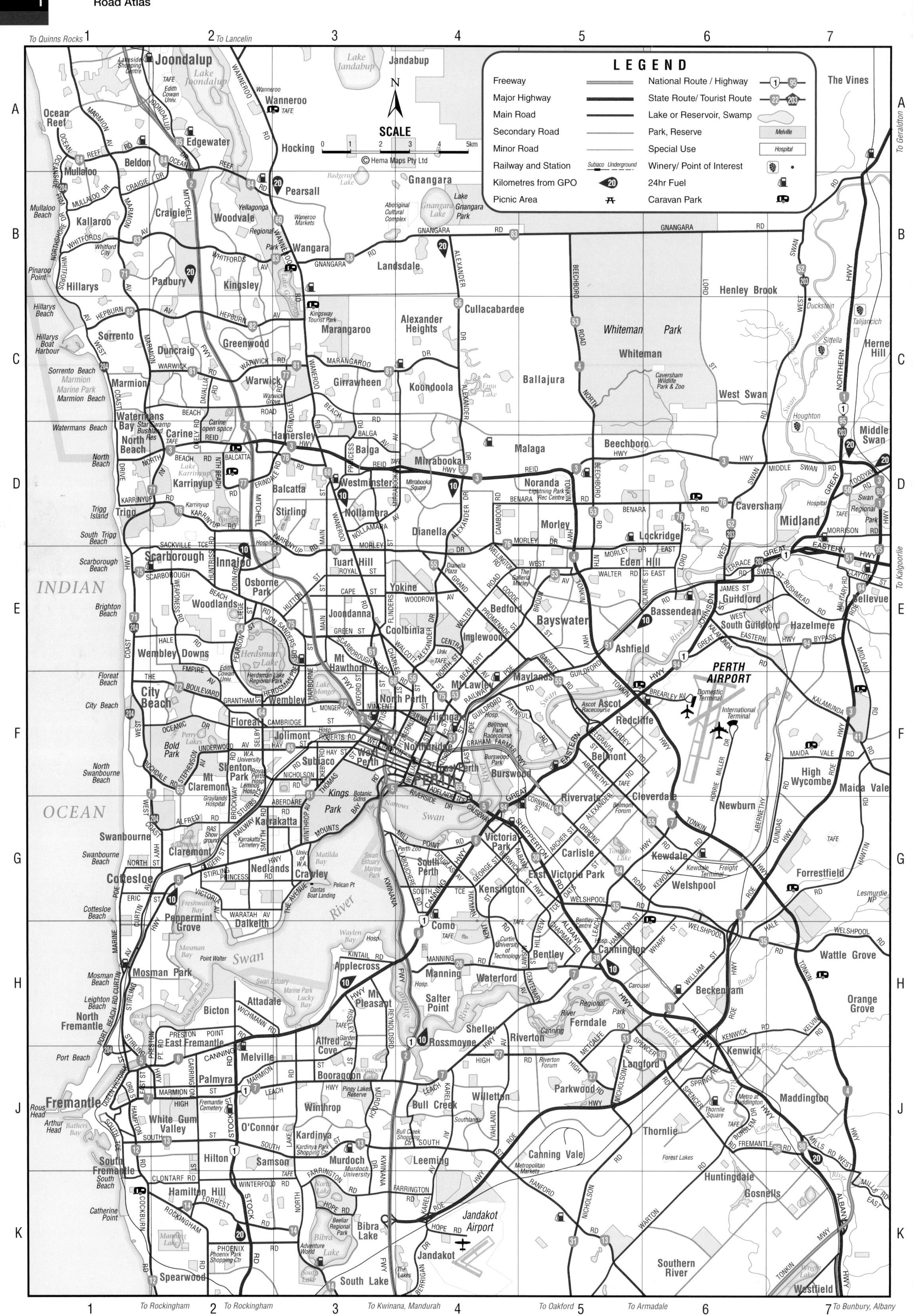
LEGEND
Freeway
Major Highway
Main Road
Secondary Road
Minor Road
Railway and Station
Kilometres from GPO
Picnic Area
National Route / Highway
State Route/ Tourist Route
Lake or Reservoir, Swamp
Park, Reserve
Special Use
Winery/ Point of Interest
24hr Fuel
Caravan Park
SCALE
0 1 2 3 4 5km
© Hema Maps Pty Ltd
To Quinns Rocks
To Lancelin
To Geraldton
To Kalgoorlie
To Rockingham
To Kwinana, Mandurah
To Oakford
To Armadale
To Bunbury, Albany
INDIAN
OCEAN
Joondalup
Wanneroo
Jandabup
Hocking
Ocean Reef
Edgewater
Beldon
Mullaloo
Craigie
Woodvale
Pearsall
Gnangara
Kallaroo
Wangara
Landsdale
Hillarys
Padbury
Kingsley
Cullacabardee
Henley Brook
The Vines
Sorrento
Duncraig
Greenwood
Marangaroo
Alexander Heights
Whiteman Park
Whiteman
Marmion
Warwick
Girrawheen
Koondoola
Ballajura
West Swan
Herne Hill
Waterman Bay
North Beach
Carine
Hamersley
Balga
Mirrabooka
Malaga
Beechboro
Middle Swan
Karrinyup
Balcatta
Westminster
Nollamara
Noranda
Caversham
Midland
Trigg
Stirling
Dianella
Morley
Lockridge
Scarborough
Innaloo
Osborne Park
Tuart Hill
Yokine
Eden Hill
Guildford
Bellevue
Woodlands
Joondanna
Bedford
Bayswater
Bassendean
South Guildford
Hazelmere
Wembley Downs
Coolbinia
Inglewood
Ashfield
Mt Hawthorn
Maylands
PERTH AIRPORT
City Beach
Wembley
North Perth
Mt Lawley
Ascot
Redcliffe
Floreat
Highgate
Jolimont
Northbridge
Bold Park
Subiaco
West Perth
East Perth
Belmont
Shenton Park
PERTH
Burswood
High Wycombe
Maida Vale
Mt Claremont
Kings Park
Rivervale
Cloverdale
Newburn
Swanbourne
Karrakatta
Victoria Park
Claremont
Nedlands
South Perth
Carlisle
Kewdale
Forrestfield
Crawley
East Victoria Park
Cottesloe
Kensington
Welshpool
Peppermint Grove
Dalkeith
Como
Bentley
Cannington
Wattle Grove
Applecross
Manning
Waterford
Mosman Park
Mt Pleasant
Beckenham
Attadale
Salter Point
Orange Grove
Bicton
North Fremantle
Ferndale
Shelley
Riverton
East Fremantle
Rossmoyne
Kenwick
Melville
Alfred Cove
Langford
Palmyra
Booragoon
Fremantle
Parkwood
Maddington
Winthrop
Willetton
Bull Creek
White Gum Valley
O'Connor
Thornlie
Kardinya
Canning Vale
Hilton
Samson
Murdoch
Leeming
South Fremantle
Huntingdale
Gosnells
Hamilton Hill
Jandakot Airport
Bibra Lake
Jandakot
Southern River
Spearwood
South Lake
Westfield

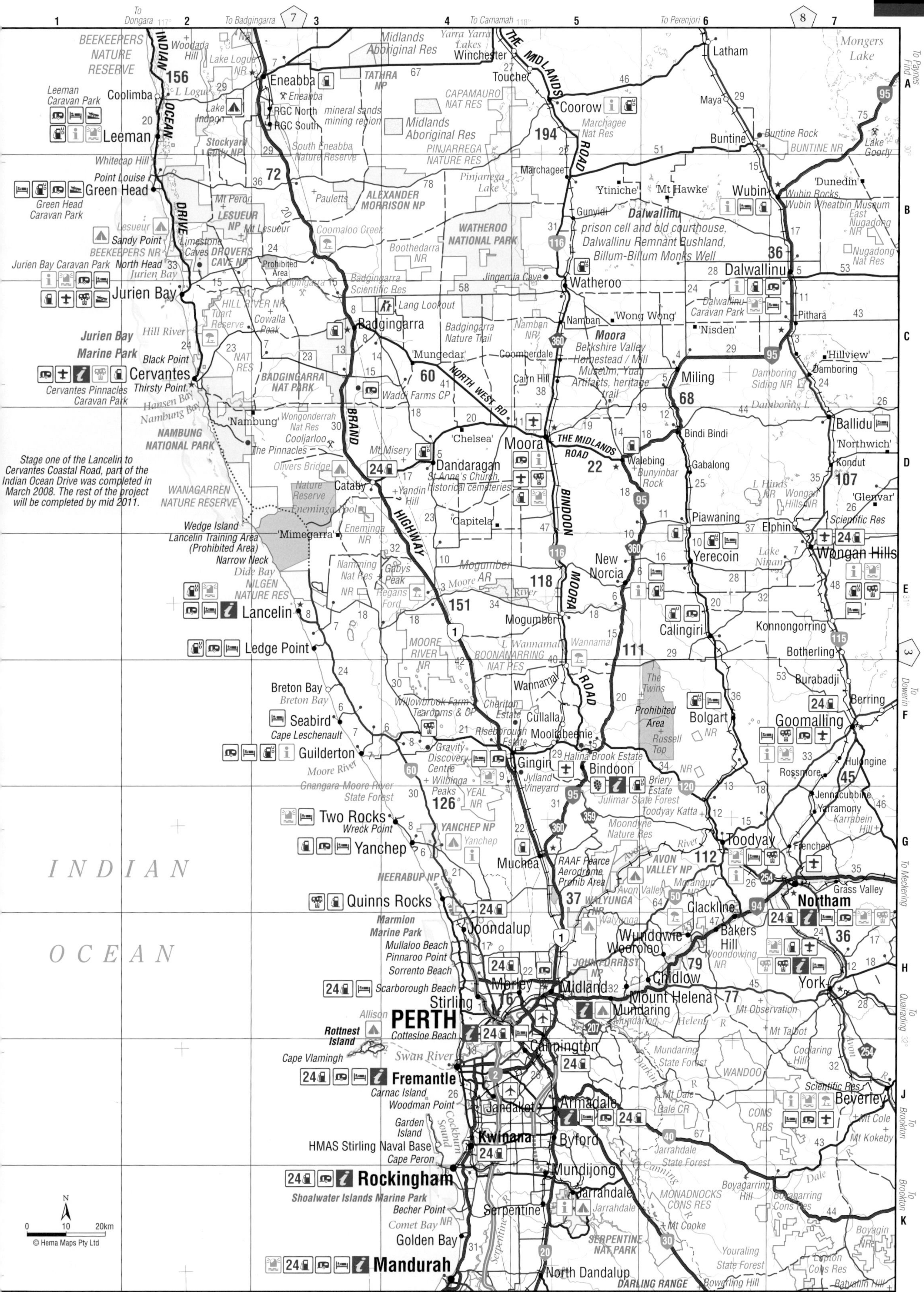
INDIAN OCEAN
PERTH
Fremantle
Rockingham
Mandurah
Joondalup
Midland
Armadale
Kwinana
Northam
York
Toodyay
Beverley
Gingin
Moora
Dalwallinu
Jurien Bay
Cervantes
Lancelin
Leeman
Green Head
Eneabba
Coorow
Wubin
Badgingarra
Dandaragan
New Norcia
Calingiri
Wongan Hills
Goomalling
Bindoon
Yanchep
Two Rocks
Guilderton
Seabird
Ledge Point
Mundaring
Byford
Mundijong
Serpentine
Jarrahdale
North Dandalup
Golden Bay
Stage one of the Lancelin to Cervantes Coastal Road, part of the Indian Ocean Drive was completed in March 2008. The rest of the project will be completed by mid 2011.
Dalwallinu prison cell and old courthouse, Dalwallinu Remnant Bushland, Billum-Billum Monks Well
Moora Berkshire Valley Homestead / Mill Museum, Yued Artifacts, heritage trail
BRAND HIGHWAY
THE MIDLANDS ROAD
BINDOON MOORA ROAD
INDIAN OCEAN DRIVE
NAMBUNG NATIONAL PARK
LESUEUR NP
WATHEROO NATIONAL PARK
BADGINGARRA NAT PARK
YANCHEP NP
NEERABUP NP
AVON VALLEY NP
WALYUNGA NP
JOHN FORREST NP
SERPENTINE NAT PARK
Rottnest Island
Garden Island
Marmion Marine Park
Shoalwater Islands Marine Park
Jurien Bay Marine Park
© Hema Maps Pty Ltd
0 10 20km

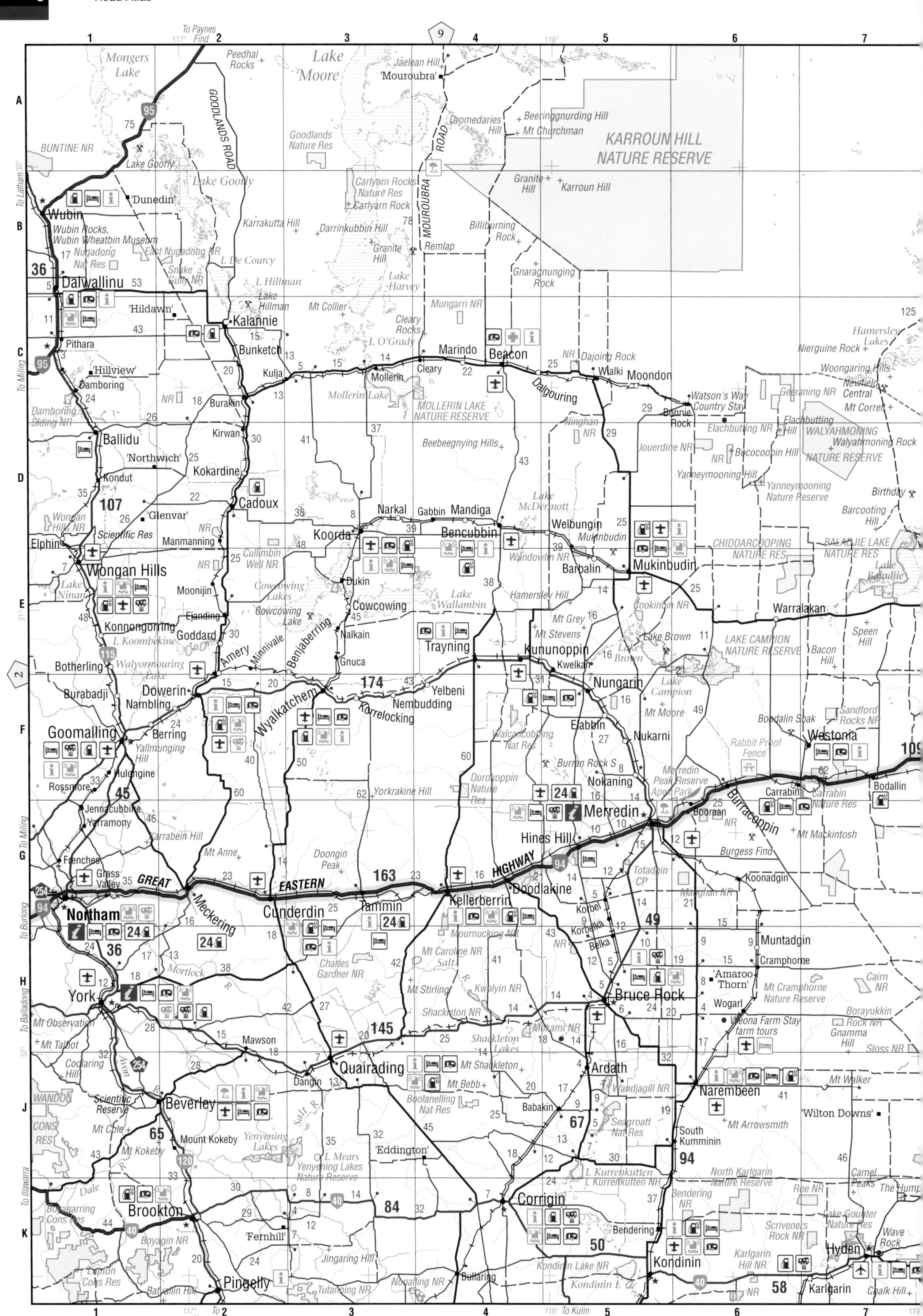
Mongers Lake
Lake Moore
Peedhal Rocks
GOODLANDS ROAD
Jaelean Hill
'Mouroubra'
Goodlands Nature Res
Dromedaries Hill
Beeringgnurding Hill
Mt Churchman
KARROUN HILL NATURE RESERVE
BUNTINE NR
Lake Goorly
Carlyarn Rocks Nature Res
Carlyarn Rock
MOUROUBRA ROAD
Granite Hill
Karroun Hill
Wubin
'Dunedin'
Wubin Rocks, Wubin Wheatbin Museum
Karrakutta Hill
Darrinkubbin Hill
Billiburning Rock
Nugadong Nat Res
East Nugadong NR
L De Courcy
Remlap
Gnaragnunging Rock
Dalwallinu
Snake Gully NR
L Hillman
Lake Harvey
Mungarri NR
'Hildawn'
Lake Hillman
Mt Collier
Cleary Rocks
Kalannie
Pithara
Bunketch
L O'Grady
Marindo
Beacon
Dajoing Rock
Hamersley Lakes
Nierguine Rock
'Hillview'
Damboring
Kulja
Mollerin
Cleary
Walki
Moondon
Woongaring Hills
Newfield
Central
Dalgouring
Mollerin Lake
MOLLERIN LAKE NATURE RESERVE
Watson's Way Country Stay
Geeraning NR
Mt Correll
Burakin
Bonnie Rock
Damboring Siding NR
Ninghan NR
Elachbutting NR
Elachbutting Hill
WALYAHMONING NATURE RESERVE
Walyahmoning Rock
Ballidu
Kirwan
Beebeegnying Hills
Jouerdine NR
Bococoopin Hill
'Northwich'
Kokardine
Yanneymooning Hill
Yanneymooning Nature Reserve
Kondut
Cadoux
Lake McDermott
Birthday
Barcooting Hill
Wongan Hills NR
'Glenvar'
Narkal
Gabbin
Mandiga
Welbungin
Scientific Res
Koorda
Bencubbin
Mukinbudin
CHIDDARCOOPING NATURE RES
BALADJIE LAKE NATURE RES
Elphin
Manmanning
Cullimbin Well NR
Windowlin NR
Barbalin
Lake Baladjie
Wongan Hills
Dukin
Lake Ninan
Moonijin
Cowcowing Lakes
Lake Wallambin
Cookinbin NR
Warralakan
Cowcowing
Hamersley Hill
Ejanding
Cowcowing Lake
Mt Grey
Konnongorring
Goddard
Nalkain
Mt Stevens
Lake Brown
LAKE CAMPION NATURE RESERVE
Speen Hill
L Koombekine
Benjaberring
Trayning
Kununoppin
Kwelkan
Bacon Hill
Botherling
Walyormouring Lake
Amery
Minnivale
Gnuca
Burabadji
Dowerin
Nambling
Wyalkatchem
Yelbeni
Nembudding
Korrelocking
Nungarin
Lake Campion
Mt Moore
Sandford Rocks NR
Goomalling
Berring
Yallmunging Hill
Walcancobbing Nat Res
Elabbin
Nukarni
Boodalin Soak
Westonia
Rabbit Proof Fence
Hulongine
Rossmore
Burran Rock S
Nokaning
Merredin Peak Reserve
Apex Park
Carrabin
Carrabin Nature Res
Bodallin
Jennacubbine
Yarramony
Yorkrakine Hill
Durokoppin Nature Res
Merredin
Booraan
Burracoppin
Mt Mackintosh
Karrabein Hill
Mt Anne
Doongin Peak
Hines Hill
Burgess Find
Frenchess
Grass Valley
GREAT
EASTERN
HIGHWAY
Totadgin CP
Koonadgin
Northam
Meckering
Cunderdin
Tammin
Kellerberrin
Doodlakine
Mangian NR
Korbel
Korbelka
Belka
Mournucking NR
Muntadgin
Cramphorne
Mt Caroline NR
Salt
Charles Gardner NR
'Amaroo Thorn'
Cairn NR
Mortlock
Mt Stirling
Kwolyin NR
Mt Cramphorne Nature Reserve
York
Bruce Rock
Wogarl
Borayukkin Rock NR
Shackleton NR
Mt Observation
Moramj NR
Weona Farm Stay farm tours
Gnamma Hill
Mt Talbot
Mawson
Shackleton Lakes
Sloss NR
Codlaring Hill
Avon
Quairading
Mt Shackleton
Ardath
Dangin
Mt Bebb
Wandjagill NR
Narembeen
Mt Walker
WANDOO CONS RES
Scientific Reserve
Beverley
Boolanelling Nat Res
Babakin
Salt R
Mt Arrowsmith
'Wilton Downs'
Seagroatt Nat Res
Mt Cole
Mount Kokeby
Yenyening Lakes
South Kumminin
Mt Kokeby
L Mears
Yenyening Lakes Nature Reserve
'Eddington'
L Kurrenkutten
L Kurrenkutten NR
North Karlgarin Nature Reserve
Camel Peaks
The Humps
Roe NR
Dale
Corrigin
Bendering NR
Lake Gounter Nature Res
Boyagarring Cons Res
Brookton
'Fernhill'
Bendering
Scriveners Rock NR
Wave Rock
Boyagin NR
Kondinin
Hyden
Jingaring Hill
Kondinin Lake NR
Karlgarin Hill NR
Dryandra Cons Res
Bullaring
Kondinin L
Batyalin Hill
Pingelly
Tutanning NR
Noaaling NR
Karlgarin
Chalk Hill
To Paynes Find
To Latham
To Miling
To Burlong
To Balladong
To Illawarra
To Narrogin
To Kulin

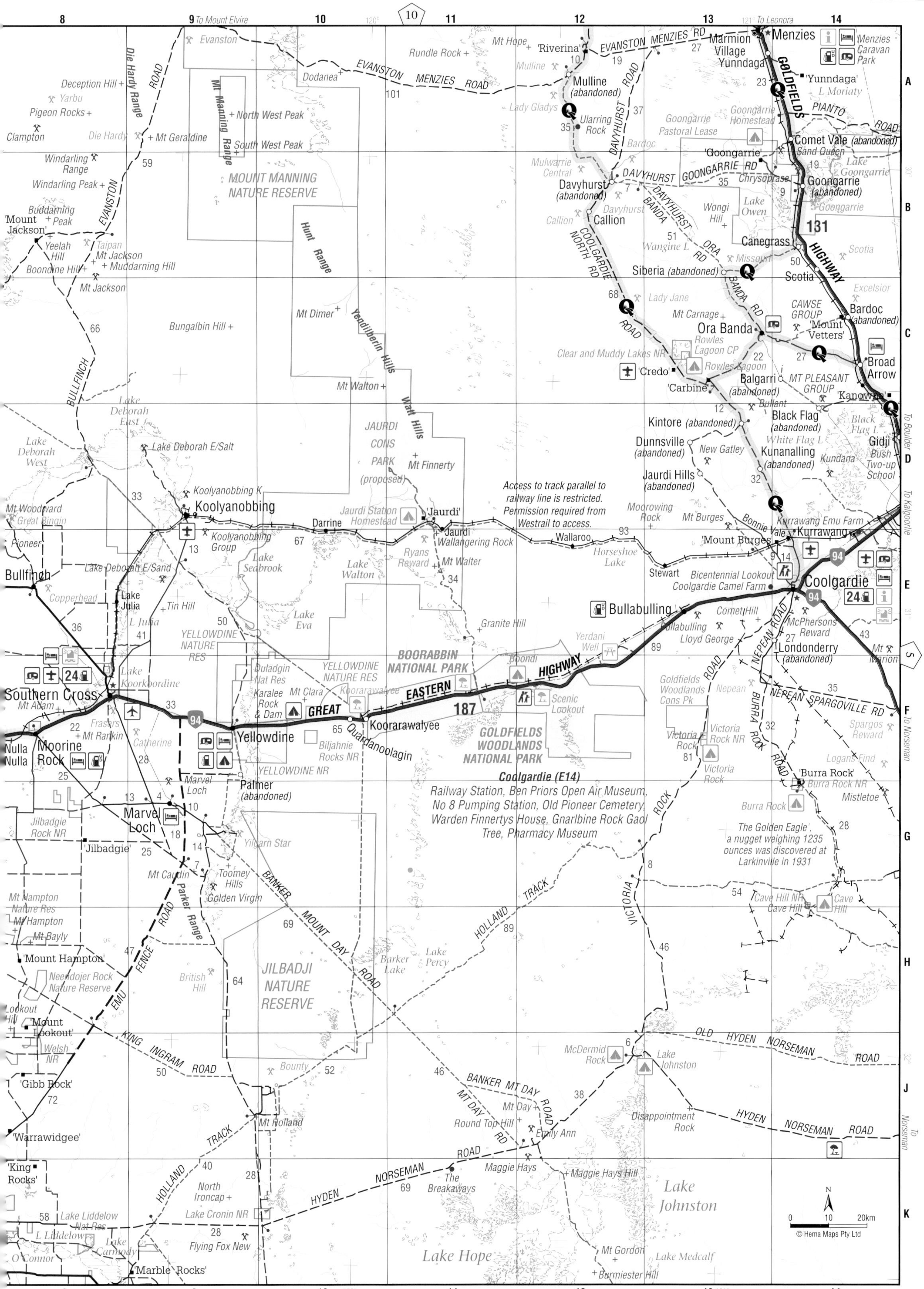

8 9 To Mount Elvire 10 120° 10 11 12 13 121° To Leonora 14

Evanston
Mt Hope
'Riverina'
EVANSTON MENZIES RD
Marmion Village
Menzies
Menzies Caravan Park
Rundle Rock
Mulline
Yunndaga
Die Hardy Range
ROAD
Dodanea
EVANSTON MENZIES ROAD
101
Mulline (abandoned)
DAVYHURST ROAD
GOLDFIELDS
'Yunndaga'
L Moriaty
Deception Hill
Yarbu
Mt Manning Range
Lady Gladys
PIANTO ROAD
Pigeon Rocks
North West Peak
Ularring Rock
Goongarrie Pastoral Lease
Goongarrie Homestead
Clampton
Die Hardy
Mt Geraldine
South West Peak
Bardoc
Comet Vale (abandoned)
Sand Queen
Windarling Range
59
MOUNT MANNING NATURE RESERVE
Mulwarrie Central
'Goongarrie'
Lake Goongarrie
Windarling Peak
EVANSTON
Davyhurst (abandoned)
DAVYHURST GOONGARRIE RD
Chrysoprase
Goongarrie (abandoned)
Buddarning Peak
'Mount Jackson'
Callion
Davyhurst
DAVYHURST BANDA
Wongi Hill
Lake Owen
Goongarrie
Yeelah Hill
Taipan
Mt Jackson
Hunt Range
COOLGARDIE NORTH RD
131
Canegrass
HIGHWAY
Muddarning Hill
Boondine Hill
Wangine L
ORA RD
Missouri
Scotia
Mt Jackson
Siberia (abandoned)
Scotia
Excelsior
BANDA RD
CAWSE GROUP
Bardoc (abandoned)
66
Bungalbin Hill
Mt Dimer
Yendilberin Hills
Lady Jane
Mt Carnage
Ora Banda
'Mount Vetters'
ROAD
Rowles Lagoon CP
BULLFINCH
Clear and Muddy Lakes NR
Rowles Lagoon
Broad Arrow
'Credo'
Balgarri (abandoned)
MT PLEASANT GROUP
Mt Walton
'Carbine'
'Kanowna'
Lake Deborah East
Watt Hills
Bullant
JAURDI CONS PARK (proposed)
Black Flag (abandoned)
Black Flag L
Kintore (abandoned)
Lake Deborah West
Lake Deborah E/Salt
White Flag L
Gidji
To Boulder
Dunnsville (abandoned)
New Gatley
Kunanalling (abandoned)
Kundana
Mt Finnerty
Bush Two-up School
Jaurdi Hills (abandoned)

Access to track parallel to railway line is restricted. Permission required from Westrail to access.

Koolyanobbing K
Koolyanobbing
Mt Woodward
Great Bingin
Jaurdi Station Homestead
'Jaurdi'
Moorowing Rock
Mt Burges
Bonnie Vale
Kurrawang Emu Farm
Kurrawang
To Kalgoorlie
Darrine
93
'Mount Burges'
Wallaroo
Koolyanobbing Group
Jaurdi Wallangering Rock
Pioneer
13
67
Horseshoe Lake
Lake Seabrook
Ryans Reward
Mt Walter
94
Bullfinch
Lake Deborah E/Sand
Lake Walton
Stewart
Bicentennial Lookout
Coolgardie Camel Farm
Coolgardie
34
Copperhead
Lake Julia
Tin Hill
Bullabulling
Comet Hill
Lake Eva
Granite Hill
NEPEAN ROAD
McPhersons Reward
36
L Julia
50
Bullabulling
Lloyd George
43
YELLOWDINE NATURE RES
Yerdani Well
Londonderry (abandoned)
41
89
Mt Marion
BOORABBIN NATIONAL PARK
Boondi
Duladgin Nat Res
YELLOWDINE NATURE RES
HIGHWAY
Goldfields Woodlands Cons Pk
Lake Koorkoordine
Koorarawalyee
EASTERN
NEPEAN SPARGOVILLE RD
Southern Cross
Karalee Rock & Dam
Mt Clara
Scenic Lookout
Nepean
BURRA ROCK
Mt Adam
33
GREAT
187
35
Spargos Reward
Frasers
Koorarawalyee
32
To Norseman
Nulla Nulla
22
Mt Rankin
Yellowdine
65
Quandanoolagin
GOLDFIELDS WOODLANDS NATIONAL PARK
Victoria Rock
Victoria Rock NR
Moorine Rock
Catherine
Biljahnie Rocks NR
ROAD
Logans Find
28
81
Victoria Rock
'Burra Rock'
25
YELLOWDINE NR
Burra Rock NR
Marvel Loch
Palmer (abandoned)

Coolgardie (E14)
Railway Station, Ben Priors Open Air Museum, No 8 Pumping Station, Old Pioneer Cemetery, Warden Finnertys House, Gnarlbine Rock Gaol Tree, Pharmacy Museum

Mistletoe
13
4
10
ROCK
Burra Rock
Marvel Loch
Jilbadgie Rock NR
18
Yilgarn Star
'Jilbadgie'
25
14

The Golden Eagle', a nugget weighing 1235 ounces was discovered at Larkinville in 1931

28
Mt Caudin
7
Toomey Hills
8
Golden Virgin
BANKER
Mt Hampton Nature Res
ROAD
TRACK
VICTORIA
54
Cave Hill NR
Cave Hill
Cave Hill
Mt Hampton
Parker Range
69
MOUNT DAY
HOLLAND
89
Mt Bayly
47
'Mount Hampton'
Barker Lake
Lake Percy
46
Needdojer Rock Nature Reserve
FENCE
British Hill
64
JILBADJI NATURE RESERVE
ROAD
Lookout Hill
'Mount Lookout'
EMU
Welsh NR
KING INGRAM ROAD
OLD HYDEN NORSEMAN ROAD
McDermid Rock
6
Lake Johnston
50
Bounty
52
46
'Gibb Rock'
BANKER MT DAY ROAD
38
72
MT DAY RD
Mt Day
Round Top Hill
Emily Ann
Disappointment Rock
HYDEN NORSEMAN ROAD
To Norseman
Mt Holland
'Warrawidgee'
TRACK
ROAD
Maggie Hays
'King Rocks'
HOLLAND
40
28
HYDEN NORSEMAN
The Breakaways
Maggie Hays Hill
69
North Ironcap
Lake Johnston
58
Lake Liddelow
Lake Cronin NR
L Liddelow Nat Res
28
0 10 20km
© Hema Maps Pty Ltd
Lake Carmody
Flying Fox New
O'Connor
Lake Hope
Mt Gordon
Lake Medcalf
'Marble Rocks'
Burmiester Hill

A B C D E F G H J K

8 9 10 120° 11 12 13 121° 14

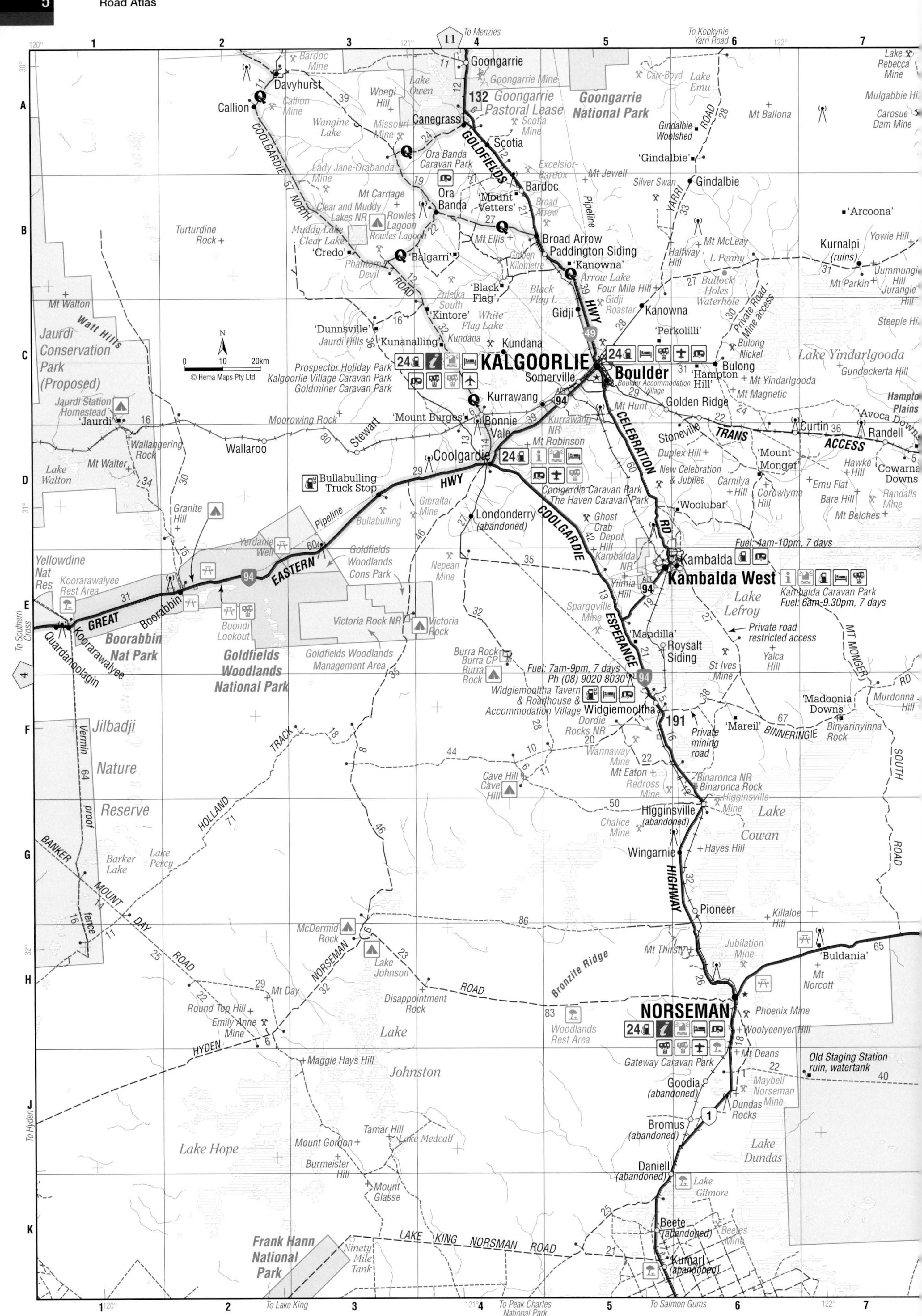
To Menzies
To Kookynie Yarri Road
KALGOORLIE
Boulder
Somerville
Coolgardie
Kambalda
Kambalda West
NORSEMAN
Widgiemooltha
Goongarrie
Goongarrie Pastoral Lease
Goongarrie National Park
Davyhurst
Callion
Canegrass
Scotia
Bardoc
Ora Banda
Ora Banda Caravan Park
Broad Arrow
Paddington Siding
'Kanowna'
Kanowna
Four Mile Hill
Gidji
Kundana
Kurrawang
Bonnie Vale
'Mount Burges'
Stewart
Wallaroo
Moorowing Rock
Turturdine Rock
Mt Walton
Watt Hills
Jaurdi Conservation Park (Proposed)
Jaurdi Station Homestead
'Jaurdi'
Wallangering Rock
Mt Walter
Lake Walton
Granite Hill
Yellowdine Nat Res
Koorarawalyee Rest Area
Boorabbin
Boorabbin Nat Park
Boondi Lookout
Goldfields Woodlands National Park
Goldfields Woodlands Cons Park
Goldfields Woodlands Management Area
Victoria Rock NR
Victoria Rock
Yerdanie Well
Bullabulling
Bullabulling Truck Stop
Gibraltar Mine
Londonderry (abandoned)
Nepean Mine
Burra Rock
Burra CP
Prospector Holiday Park
Kalgoorlie Village Caravan Park
Goldminer Caravan Park
Coolgardie Caravan Park
The Haven Caravan Park
Boulder Accommodation Village
Mt Robinson
Ghost Crab
Depot Hill
Kambalda NR
Yilmia Hill
Spargoville Mine
Fuel: 4am-10pm, 7 days
Kambalda Caravan Park
Fuel: 6am-9.30pm, 7 days
Lake Lefroy
'Mandilla'
Roysalt Siding
St Ives Mine
Private road restricted access
Yalca Hill
Fuel: 7am-9pm, 7 days
Ph (08) 9020 8030
Widgiemooltha Tavern & Roadhouse & Accommodation Village
Dordie Rocks NR
Wannaway Mine
Mt Eaton
Redross Mine
Private mining road
Binaronca NR
Binaronca Rock
Higginsville (abandoned)
Higginsville Mine
Chalice Mine
Wingarnie
Hayes Hill
Lake Cowan
Pioneer
Killaloe Hill
Mt Thirsty
Jubilation Mine
'Buldania'
Mt Norcott
Phoenix Mine
Woolyeenyer Hill
Mt Deans
Gateway Caravan Park
Goodia (abandoned)
Maybell Norseman Mine
Dundas Rocks
Bromus (abandoned)
Lake Dundas
Daniell (abandoned)
Lake Gilmore
Beete (abandoned)
Beetes Mine
Kumarl (abandoned)
Old Staging Station ruin, watertank
Woodlands Rest Area
Bronzite Ridge
Cave Hill
Lake Johnson
Disappointment Rock
McDermid Rock
Lake Johnston
Maggie Hays Hill
Round Top Hill
Emily Anne Mine
Mt Day
Lake Hope
Mount Gordon
Burmeister Hill
Tamar Hill
Lake Medcalf
Mount Glasse
Frank Hann National Park
Ninety Mile Tank
Jilbadji Nature Reserve
Barker Lake
Lake Percy
Vermin proof fence
GREAT EASTERN HWY
GOLDFIELDS HWY
COOLGARDIE NORTH ROAD
COOLGARDIE ESPERANCE HIGHWAY
CELEBRATION RD
TRANS ACCESS
MT MONGER RD
BINNERINGIE
SOUTH ROAD
HOLLAND TRACK
BANKER MOUNT DAY ROAD
NORSEMAN ROAD
HYDEN
LAKE KING NORSMAN ROAD
YARRI ROAD
Private Road - Mine access
Pipeline
Gindalbie
Gindalbie Woolshed
Silver Swan
Mt Jewell
Mt McLeay
Halfway Hill
L Penny
Bullock Holes Waterhole
'Perkolilli'
Bulong
Bulong Nickel
Hampton Hill
Mt Yindarlgooda
Mt Magnetic
Golden Ridge
Mt Hunt
Stoneville
Duplex Hill
New Celebration & Jubilee
'Mount Monger'
Carnilya Hill
Corowlyme Hill
'Woolubar'
Curtin
Randell
Hawke Hill
Emu Flat
Bare Hill
Mt Belches
Cowarna Downs
Randalls Mine
Lake Yindarlgooda
Gundockerta Hill
Kurnalpi (ruins)
Mt Parkin
Yowie Hill
Jummungie Hill
Steeple Hill
'Arcoona'
Mt Ballona
Lake Emu
Carr-Boyd
Lake Rebecca Mine
Mulgabbie Hill
Carosue Dam Mine
'Madoonia Downs'
Murdonna Hill
'Mareil'
Binyarinyinna Rock
Lake Owen
Wongi Hill
Wangine Lake
Missouri Mine
Lady Jane-Orabanda Mine
Mt Carnage
Clear and Muddy Lakes NR
Rowles Lagoon
Muddy Lake
Clear Lake
'Credo'
'Balgarri'
Phantom Devil
'Black Flag'
Black Flag L
Zuleika South
'Kintore'
White Flag Lake
'Dunnsville'
Jaurdi Hills
'Kunanalling'
Kundana
Mount Vetters
Mt Ellis
Golden Kilometre
Excelsior-Bardox
Broad Arrow
Bardoc Mine
Callion Mine
Goongarrie Mine
Scotia Mine
Arrow Lake
Gidji Roaster
To Southern Cross
Quardanoolagin
Koorarawalyee
To Hyden
To Lake King
To Peak Charles National Park
To Salmon Gums
© Hema Maps Pty Ltd
0 10 20km

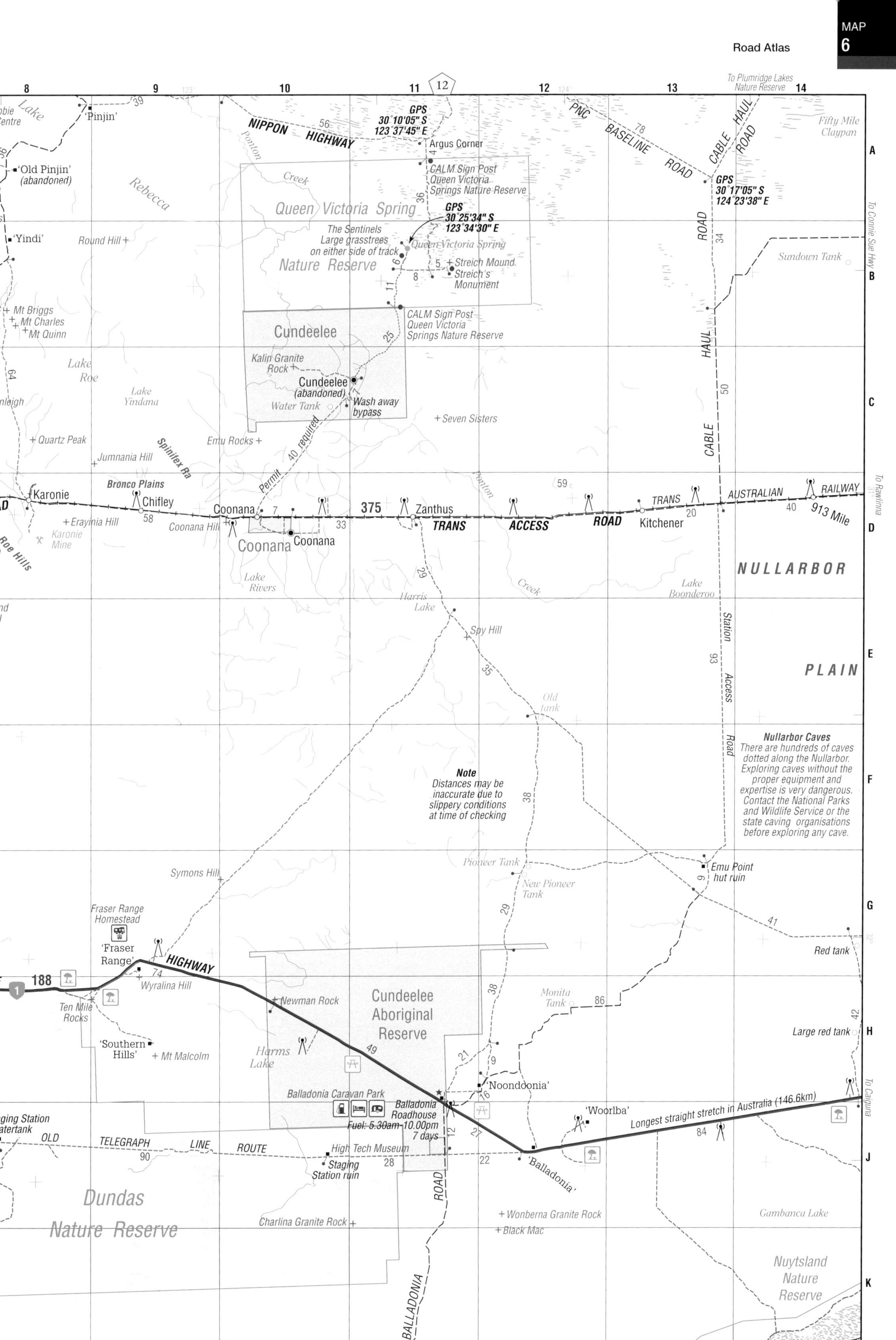
NIPPON HIGHWAY
GPS 30°10'05" S 123°37'45" E
Argus Corner
CALM Sign Post Queen Victoria Springs Nature Reserve
Queen Victoria Spring Nature Reserve
GPS 30°25'34" S 123°34'30" E
The Sentinels Large grasstrees on either side of track
Queen Victoria Spring
Streich Mound
Streich's Monument
CALM Sign Post Queen Victoria Springs Nature Reserve
Cundeelee
Kalin Granite Rock
Cundeelee (abandoned)
Water Tank
Wash away bypass
Seven Sisters
Permit 40 required
Emu Rocks
PNC BASELINE ROAD
CABLE HAUL ROAD
GPS 30°17'05" S 124°23'38" E
Fifty Mile Claypan
To Plumridge Lakes Nature Reserve
To Connie Sue Hwy
Sundown Tank
Mulgabbie Mining Centre
Lake Rebecca
'Pinjin'
'Old Pinjin' (abandoned)
Hunt Pinnacles
'Yindi'
Yangan Hill
Round Hill
Mt Eric
Mt Briggs
Mt Charles
Mt Quinn
Mt Hunt
Mt Turner
Mt Charnleigh
Lake Roe
Lake Yindana
Quartz Peak
Jumnania Hill
Spinifex Ra
Bronco Plains
Karonie
Chifley
Coonana
Coonana Hill
Erayinia Hill
Karonie Mine
Low Trap Hills
Roe Hills
Round Hill
ROAD
375
Zanthus
TRANS ACCESS ROAD
Kitchener
TRANS AUSTRALIAN RAILWAY
913 Mile
To Rawlinna
NULLARBOR PLAIN
Lake Rivers
Harris Lake
Spy Hill
Lake Boonderoo
Station Access Road
Old tank
Nullarbor Caves
There are hundreds of caves dotted along the Nullarbor. Exploring caves without the proper equipment and expertise is very dangerous. Contact the National Parks and Wildlife Service or the state caving organisations before exploring any cave.
Note
Distances may be inaccurate due to slippery conditions at time of checking
Pioneer Tank
New Pioneer Tank
Emu Point hut ruin
Symons Hill
Fraser Range Homestead
'Fraser Range'
EYRE HIGHWAY
188
Wyralina Hill
Ten Mile Rocks
'Southern Hills'
Mt Malcolm
Newman Rock
Cundeelee Aboriginal Reserve
Harms Lake
Red tank
Large red tank
Monita Tank
'Noondoonia'
Balladonia Caravan Park
Balladonia Roadhouse
Fuel: 5.30am-10.00pm 7 days
'Woorlba'
Longest straight stretch in Australia (146.6km)
To Caiguna
Old Staging Station ruin, watertank
OLD TELEGRAPH LINE ROUTE
High Tech Museum
Staging Station ruin
'Balladonia'
Dundas Nature Reserve
Charlina Granite Rock
Wonberna Granite Rock
Black Mac
Gambanca Lake
Nuytsland Nature Reserve
BALLADONIA ROAD
To Parmango Road
118
12

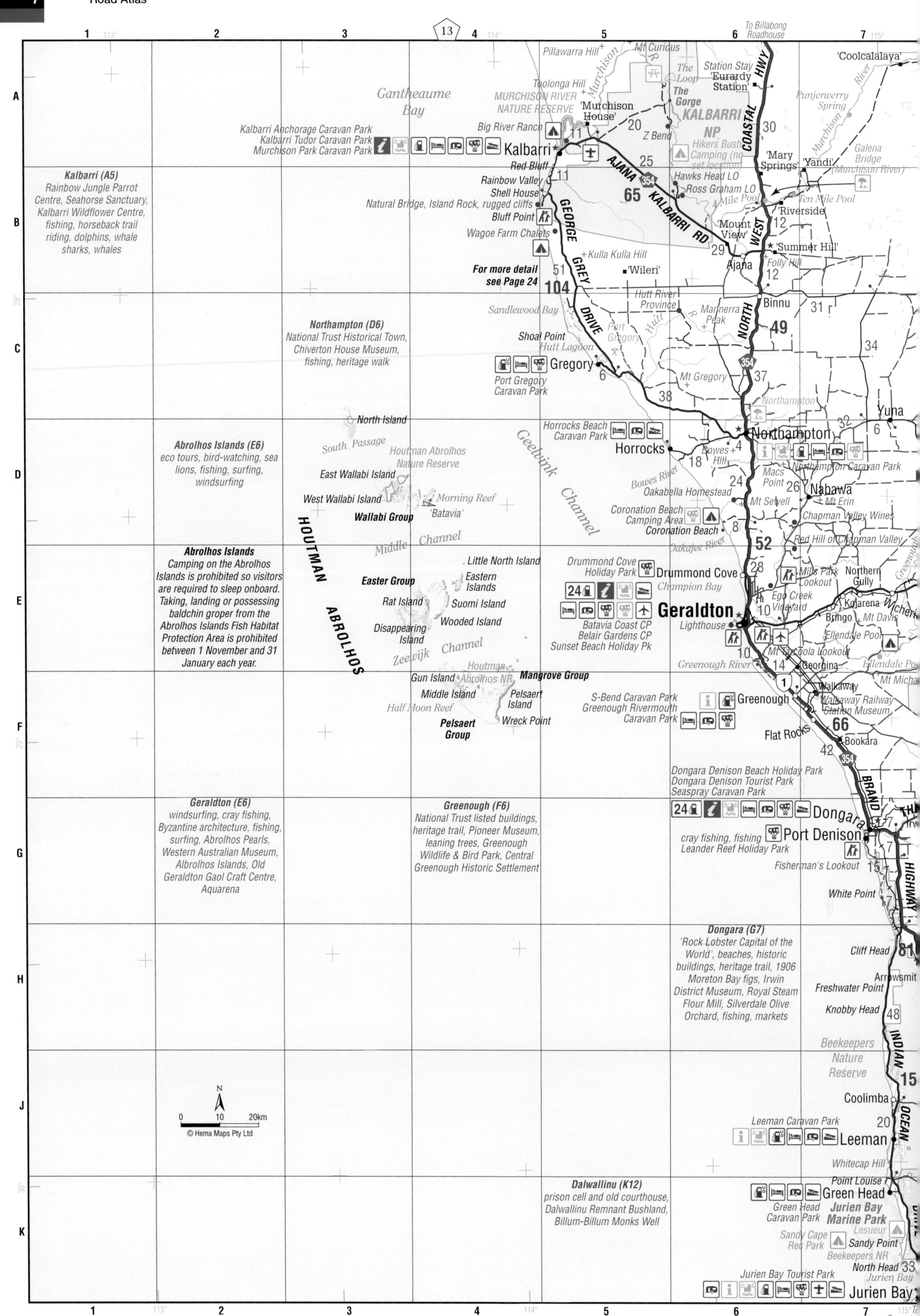
Kalbarri (A5)
Rainbow Jungle Parrot Centre, Seahorse Sanctuary, Kalbarri Wildflower Centre, fishing, horseback trail riding, dolphins, whale sharks, whales
Northampton (D6)
National Trust Historical Town, Chiverton House Museum, fishing, heritage walk
Abrolhos Islands (E6)
eco tours, bird-watching, sea lions, fishing, surfing, windsurfing
Abrolhos Islands
Camping on the Abrolhos Islands is prohibited so visitors are required to sleep onboard. Taking, landing or possessing baldchin groper from the Abrolhos Islands Fish Habitat Protection Area is prohibited between 1 November and 31 January each year.
Geraldton (E6)
windsurfing, cray fishing, Byzantine architecture, fishing, surfing, Abrolhos Pearls, Western Australian Museum, Albrolhos Islands, Old Geraldton Gaol Craft Centre, Aquarena
Greenough (F6)
National Trust listed buildings, heritage trail, Pioneer Museum, leaning trees, Greenough Wildlife & Bird Park, Central Greenough Historic Settlement
Dongara (G7)
'Rock Lobster Capital of the World', beaches, historic buildings, heritage trail, 1906 Moreton Bay figs, Irwin District Museum, Royal Steam Flour Mill, Silverdale Olive Orchard, fishing, markets
Dalwallinu (K12)
prison cell and old courthouse, Dalwallinu Remnant Bushland, Billum-Billum Monks Well
For more detail see Page 24
To Billabong Roadhouse
Gantheaume Bay
Kalbarri Anchorage Caravan Park
Kalbarri Tudor Caravan Park
Murchison Park Caravan Park
Kalbarri
MURCHISON RIVER NATURE RESERVE
KALBARRI NP
Pillawarra Hill
Mt Curious
Toolonga Hill
'Murchison House'
Big River Ranch
Red Bluff
Rainbow Valley
Shell House
Natural Bridge, Island Rock, rugged cliffs
Bluff Point
Wagoe Farm Chalets
The Loop
The Gorge
Z Bend
Hikers Bush Camping (no set location)
Hawks Head LO
Ross Graham LO
Station Stay 'Eurardy Station'
'Coolcalalaya'
Punjerwerry Spring
'Mary Springs'
'Yandi'
Galena Bridge (Murchison River)
Ten Mile Pool
4 Mile Pool
'Riverside'
'Mount View'
'Summer Hill'
Ajana
Folly Hill
AJANA KALBARRI RD
GEORGE GREY DRIVE
NORTH WEST COASTAL HWY
Kulla Kulla Hill
'Wileri'
Binnu
Sandlewood Bay
Hutt River Province
Mannerra Peak
Port Gregory
Shoal Point
Hutt Lagoon
Gregory
Port Gregory Caravan Park
Mt Gregory
Northampton
Yuna
Horrocks Beach Caravan Park
Horrocks
Bowes Hill
Bowes River
Northampton Caravan Park
Macs Point
Nabawa
Mt Erin
Oakabella Homestead
Mt Sewell
Chapman Valley Wines
Coronation Beach Camping Area
Coronation Beach
Red Hill of Chapman Valley
Oakajee River
Drummond Cove Holiday Park
Drummond Cove
Champion Bay
Mills Park Lookout
Northern Gully
Ego Creek Vineyard
Kojarena
Bringo
Mt Davis
Geraldton
Lighthouse
Batavia Coast CP
Belair Gardens CP
Sunset Beach Holiday Pk
Ellendale Pool
Mt Tarcoola Lookout
Georgina
Greenough River
Walkaway
Walkaway Railway Station Museum
Greenough
S-Bend Caravan Park
Greenough Rivermouth Caravan Park
Flat Rocks
Bookara
Geelvink Channel
North Island
South Passage
Houtman Abrolhos Nature Reserve
East Wallabi Island
West Wallabi Island
Morning Reef
'Batavia'
Wallabi Group
HOUTMAN ABROLHOS
Middle Channel
Little North Island
Easter Group
Eastern Islands
Rat Island
Suomi Island
Wooded Island
Disappearing Island
Zeewijk Channel
Houtman Abrolhos NR
Mangrove Group
Gun Island
Middle Island
Pelsaert Island
Half Moon Reef
Wreck Point
Pelsaert Group
Dongara Denison Beach Holiday Park
Dongara Denison Tourist Park
Seaspray Caravan Park
Dongara
Port Denison
cray fishing, fishing
Leander Reef Holiday Park
Fisherman's Lookout
White Point
BRAND HIGHWAY
Cliff Head
Arrowsmith
Freshwater Point
Knobby Head
Beekeepers Nature Reserve
INDIAN OCEAN
Coolimba
Leeman Caravan Park
Leeman
Whitecap Hill
Point Louise
Green Head
Green Head Caravan Park
Jurien Bay Marine Park
Lesueur
Sandy Cape Rec Park
Sandy Point
Beekeepers NR
North Head
Jurien Bay
Jurien Bay Tourist Park
To Cervantes
0 10 20km
N
© Hema Maps Pty Ltd

Mullewa (D9)
heart of the Wildflower Way, old Mullewa -De Grey Stock Route, Tallering Gorge and Peak, old church, Kembla Wildlife Sanctuary
Yalgoo (D12)
Courthouse Museum, railway station, cemetery, old mine sites
Charles Darwin Reserve
ph (03) 6223 2670
To Murchison
To Mount Magnet
To Paynes Find
To Badgingarra
To Moora
To Ballidu
To Kalannie
Mullewa
Yalgoo
Mingenew
Morawa
Perenjori
Three Springs
Carnamah
Coorow
Eneabba
Dalwallinu
Wubin
Watheroo
Latham
Noongal (abandoned)
Gullewa (abandoned)
GERALDTON MOUNT MAGNET ROAD
MULLEWA WUBIN ROAD
MORAWA YALGOO ROAD
MINGENEW MORAWA RD
MIDLANDS ROAD
THE MIDLANDS ROAD
GREAT NORTHERN HIGHWAY
PAYNES FIND YALGOO ROAD
YALGOO NORTH ROAD
CARNARVON MULLEWA RD
MINGENEW MULLEWA RD
WANARRA EAST RD
MT GIBSON RD
GOODLANDS ROAD
WARRIEDAR ROAD
BURNABINMAH NALBARRA RD
MOUNT FARMER ROAD
BERINGARRA PINDAR ROAD
Dividing Range
Lake Moore
Mongers Lake
LESUEUR NP
ALEXANDER MORRISON NP
WATHEROO NATIONAL PARK
DROVERS CAVE NP
TATHRA NP
Midlands Aboriginal Res
Wandana Nature Reserve
Tallering Nature Res
Barrabarra Nature Reserve
Coalseam Conservation Park
Ninghan Station Camping Area
Western Flora Caravan Park
Mingenew Springs Caravan Park
Perenjori Caravan Park
Carnamah Caravan Park
Dalwallinu Caravan Park
Mullewa Caravan Park
Yalgoo Caravan Park
Lake Indoon Camping Area
MacPherson Homestead (1869)
Wubin Rocks, Wubin Wheatbin Museum
museum, heritage trail, Vermin Proof Fence
mineral sands mining region
murals, historic buildings
Historical Site, Wildflowers
Nullewa Lake bird-watching
Dalgaranga Meteorite Crater
John Forrest Lookout
Ballinyoo Bridge (1932)
Joker's Tunnel
Narring Ranges
Gnows Nest Range
Edamurta Ra
Warrakatta Farm Stay
Wandina Station Stay
Tardie Station Stay
Evaside Crossing
Pintharuka Dam
Holy Cross Church
Koolanooka
Bowgada North
Bowgada
Mount Gibson
Ninghan
Thundelarra
Warriedar
Karara
Wurarga
Pindar
Tardun
Canna
Gutha
Wilroy
Sullivan
Tenindewa
Curara
Beatty
Wandanooka
Arrino
Pitfield
Yandanooka
Prowaka
Winchester
Touche
Marchagee
Gunyidi
Buntine
Maya
Caron
Bunjil
Westmine
The Casuarinas
Hildawn

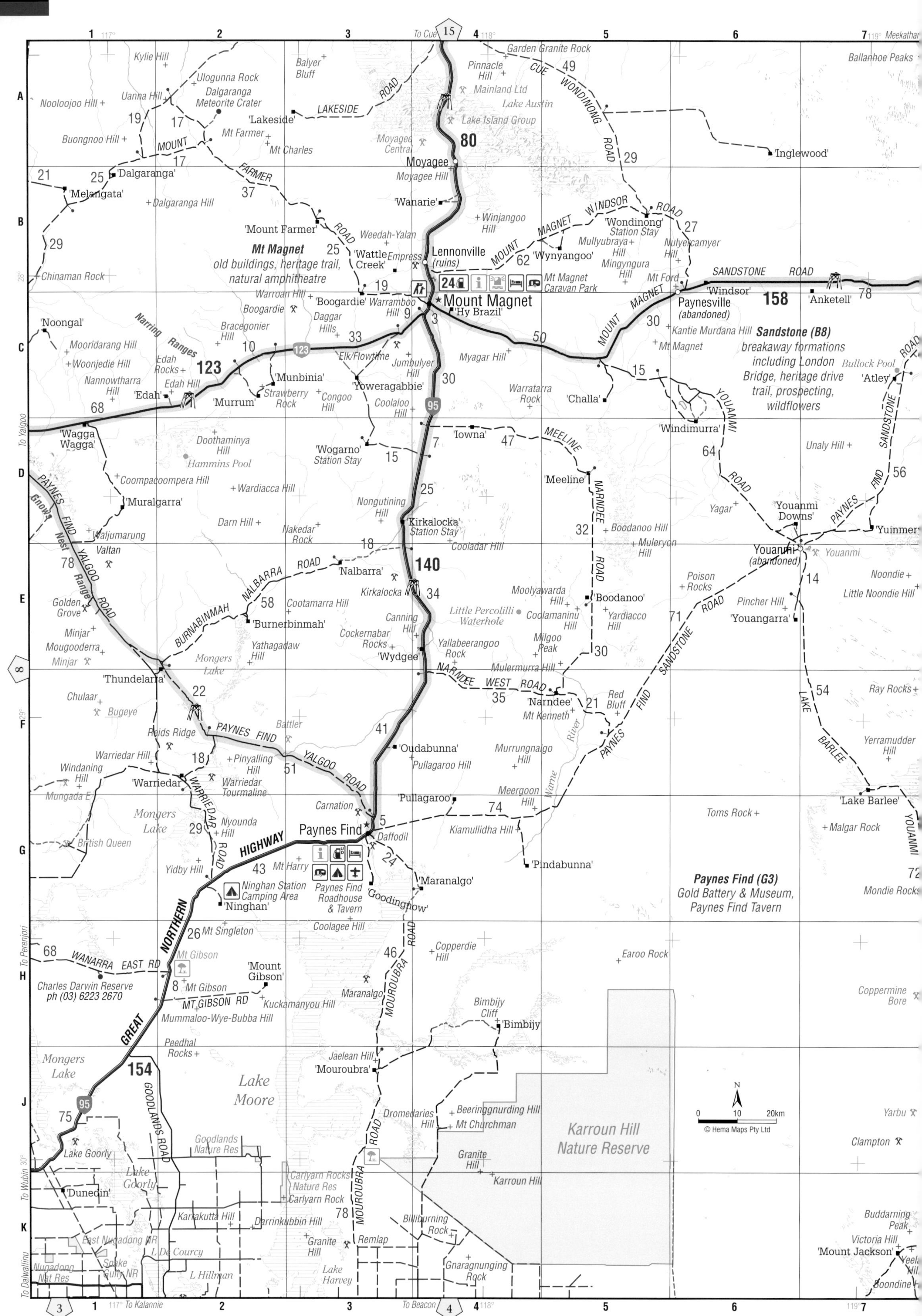
To Cue
15
Meekathara
Garden Granite Rock
Kylie Hill
Balyer Bluff
Pinnacle Hill
Mainland Ltd
Ballanhoe Peaks
Ulogunna Rock
Dalgaranga Meteorite Crater
Nooloojoo Hill
Uanna Hill
LAKESIDE
ROAD
'Lakeside'
Lake Austin
Lake Island Group
CUE WONDINONG ROAD
'Inglewood'
Buongnoo Hill
Mt Farmer
Mt Charles
MOUNT FARMER ROAD
Moyagee Central
80
Moyagee
Moyagee Hill
'Dalgaranga'
'Melangata'
Dalgaranga Hill
'Wanarie'
'Wondinong' Station Stay
WINDSOR ROAD
Winjangoo Hill
'Mount Farmer'
Weedah-Yalan
Mt Magnet
old buildings, heritage trail, natural amphitheatre
'Wattle Creek'
Empress
Lennonville (ruins)
MOUNT MAGNET ROAD
'Wynyangoo'
Mullyubraya Hill
Mingyngura Hill
Nulyercamyer Hill
Chinaman Rock
Warroan Hill
'Boogardie'
Warramboo Hill
Mt Magnet Caravan Park
Mount Magnet
'Hy Brazil'
Mt Ford
SANDSTONE ROAD
'Windsor'
Paynesville (abandoned)
158
'Anketell'
'Noongal'
Boogardie
Daggar Hills
Bracegonier Hill
Narring Ranges
Mooridarang Hill
Woonjedie Hill
Edah Rocks
123
Elk/Flowtime
Jumbulyer Hill
Myagar Hill
Kantie Murdana Hill
Mt Magnet
Sandstone (B8)
breakaway formations including London Bridge, heritage drive trail, prospecting, wildflowers
Bullock Pool
'Atley'
Nannowtharra Hill
'Edah'
Edah Hill
'Munbinia'
Strawberry Rock
'Murrum'
Congoo Hill
'Yoweragabbie'
Coolaloo Hill
Warratarra Rock
'Challa'
YOUANMI
'Windimurra'
'Wagga Wagga'
To Yalgoo
Doothaminya Hill
Hammins Pool
'Wogarno' Station Stay
'Iowna'
MEELINE
Unaly Hill
SANDSTONE
Coompacoompera Hill
Wardiacca Hill
'Meeline'
ROAD
'Muralgarra'
Nonguting Hill
'Kirkalocka' Station Stay
NARNDEE ROAD
Yagar
'Youanmi Downs'
PAYNES FIND
'Yuinmery'
Darn Hill
Nakedar Rock
Cooladar Hill
Boodanoo Hill
Muleryon Hill
Youanmi (abandoned)
Youanmi
PAYNES FIND YALGOO ROAD
Gnows Nest Range
Waljumarung
Valtan
NALBARRA ROAD
'Nalbarra'
140
Poison Rocks
Noondie
Little Noondie Hill
Kirkalocka
Moolyawarda Hill
'Boodanoo'
Golden Grove
BURNERBINMAH
Cootamarra Hill
'Burnerbinmah'
Canning Hill
Little Percolilli Waterhole
Coolamaninu Hill
Yardiacco Hill
Pincher Hill
'Youangarra'
Minjar
Mougooderra
Cockernabar Rocks
Yathagadaw Hill
Yallabeerangoo Rock
Milgoo Peak
'Wydgee'
Mongers Lake
Mulermurra Hill
'Thundelarra'
NARNDEE WEST ROAD
Red Bluff
Chulaar
Bugeye
'Narndee'
Mt Kenneth
Ray Rocks
Reids Ridge
Battler
River
LAKE BARLEE
Yerramudder Hill
Warriedar Hill
Pinyalling Hill
'Oudabunna'
Pullagaroo Hill
Murrungnalgo Hill
Windaning Hill
Mungada E
'Warriedar'
Warriedar Tourmaline
WARRIEDAR ROAD
Carnation
'Pullagaroo'
Meergoon Hill
Warne
'Lake Barlee'
Mongers Lake
Nyounda Hill
Paynes Find
Daffodil
Kiamullidha Hill
Toms Rock
Malgar Rock
British Queen
HIGHWAY
Mt Harry
'Pindabunna'
Yidby Hill
Ninghan Station Camping Area
'Maranalgo'
Paynes Find Roadhouse & Tavern
'Ninghan'
'Goodingnow'
Paynes Find (G3)
Gold Battery & Museum, Paynes Find Tavern
Mondie Rocks
Mt Singleton
Coolagee Hill
GREAT NORTHERN
To Perenjori
WANARRA EAST RD
Mt Gibson
Copperdie Hill
Earoo Rock
Charles Darwin Reserve ph (03) 6223 2670
'Mount Gibson'
Mt Gibson
MT GIBSON RD
Kuckamanyou Hill
Maranalgo
MOUROUBRA ROAD
Coppermine Bore
Mummaloo-Wye-Bubba Hill
Bimbijy Cliff
'Bimbijy'
Peedhal Rocks
Jaelean Hill
Mongers Lake
154
'Mouroubra'
Lake Moore
GOODLANDS ROAD
Dromedaries Hill
Beeringgnurding Hill
Mt Churchman
Karroun Hill Nature Reserve
Yarbu
© Hema Maps Pty Ltd
Lake Goorly
Goodlands Nature Res
Granite Hill
Karroun Hill
Clampton
Lake Goorly
Carlyarn Rocks Nature Res
Carlyarn Rock
To Wubin
'Dunedin'
Karrakutta Hill
Darrinkubbin Hill
Billiburning Rock
Buddarning Peak
East Nugadong NR
Granite Hill
Remlap
Victoria Hill
'Mount Jackson'
L De Courcy
Nugadong Nat Res
Snake Gully NR
L Hillman
Lake Harvey
Gnaragnunging Rock
Boondine
To Dalwallinu
To Kalannie
To Beacon

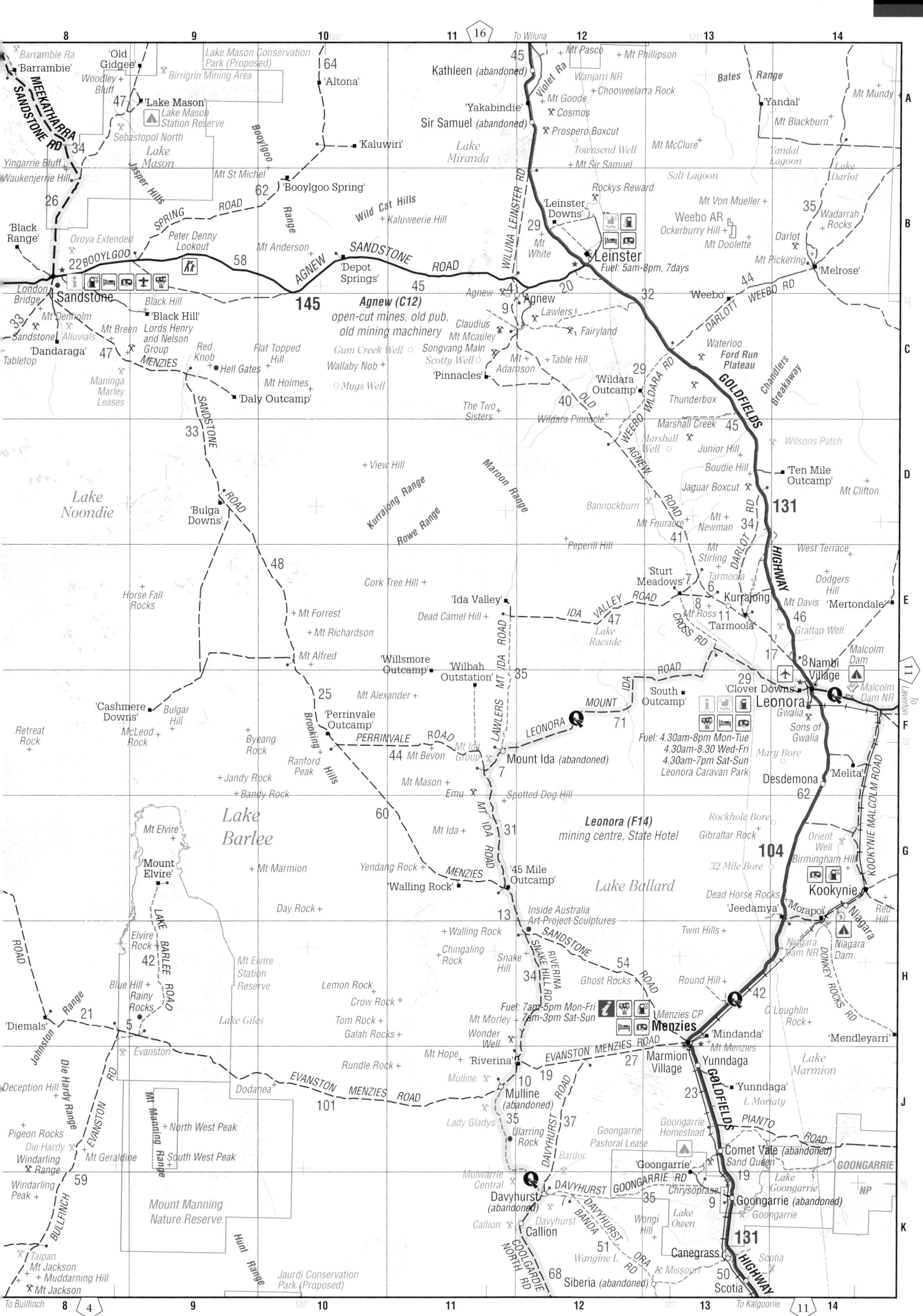
Sandstone
Leinster
Fuel: 5am-8pm, 7days
Agnew (C12)
open-cut mines, old pub,
old mining machinery
Leonora
Fuel: 4.30am-8pm Mon-Tue
4.30am-8.30 Wed-Fri
4.30am-7pm Sat-Sun
Leonora Caravan Park
Leonora (F14)
mining centre, State Hotel
Kookynie
Menzies
Fuel: 7am-5pm Mon-Fri
7am-3pm Sat-Sun
Menzies CP
Lake Barlee
Lake Ballard
Lake Noondie
Lake Mason
Mount Manning Nature Reserve
Inside Australia Art Project Sculptures
GOLDFIELDS HIGHWAY
SANDSTONE AGNEW ROAD
MEEKATHARRA SANDSTONE RD
WILUNA LEINSTER RD
EVANSTON MENZIES ROAD
To Wiluna
To Laverton
To Bullfinch
To Kalgoorlie

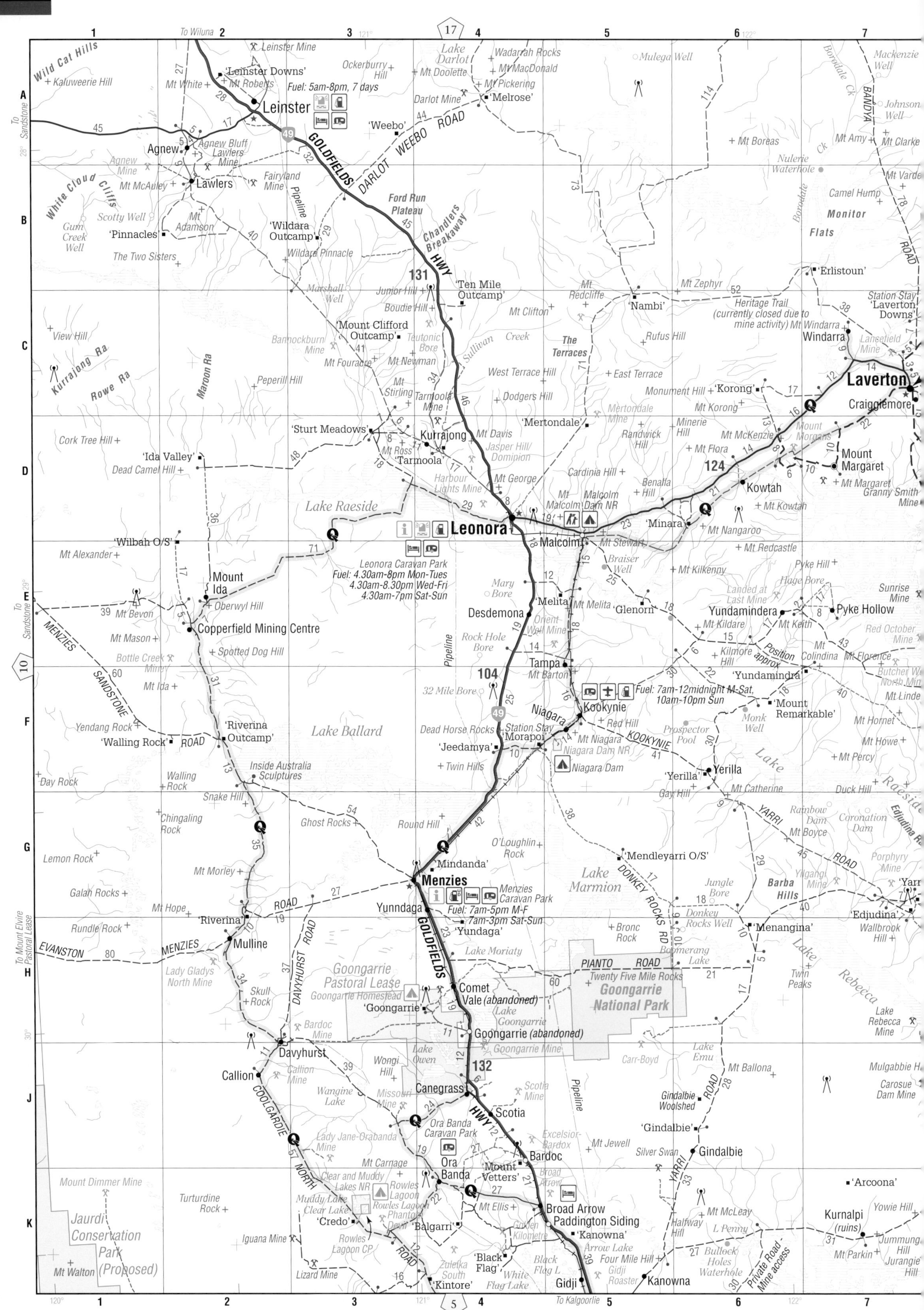
To Wiluna
17
To Sandstone
To Mount Elvire Pastoral Lease
10
To Kalgoorlie
5
Wild Cat Hills
Kaluweerie Hill
Leinster Mine
'Leinster Downs'
Mt White
Mt Roberts
Leinster
Fuel: 5am-8pm, 7 days
Ockerburry Hill
Lake Darlot
Mt Doolette
Wadarrah Rocks
Mt MacDonald
Mt Pickering
Darlot Mine
'Melrose'
Mulega Well
Mackenzie Well
Johnson Well
BANDYA
Borodale Ck
'Weebo'
DARLOT WEEBO ROAD
GOLDFIELDS
Agnew
Agnew Bluff
Lawlers Mine
Agnew Mine
Mt McAuley
Lawlers
Fairyland Mine
Pipeline
White Cloud Cliffs
Scotty Well
Mt Adamson
Gum Creek Well
'Pinnacles'
'Wildara Outcamp'
Wildara Pinnacle
The Two Sisters
Ford Run Plateau
Chandlers Breakaway
HWY
Mt Boreas
Mt Amy
Mt Clarke
Nulerie Waterhole
Mt Varde
Camel Hump
Monitor Flats
ROAD
'Erlistoun'
Marshall Well
Junior Hill
Boudie Hill
'Ten Mile Outcamp'
Mt Redcliffe
'Nambi'
Mt Zephyr
Heritage Trail (currently closed due to mine activity)
Mt Windarra
Station Stay 'Laverton Downs'
Windarra
Lancefield Mine
View Hill
Kurrajong Ra
Rowe Ra
Maroon Ra
Bannockburn Mine
'Mount Clifford Outcamp'
Teutonic Bore
Mt Fouracre
Mt Newman
Sullivan Creek
Mt Clifton
The Terraces
Rufus Hill
West Terrace Hill
East Terrace
Peterill Hill
Mt Stirling
Tarmoola Mine
Dodgers Hill
Monument Hill
'Korong'
Laverton
Mt Korong
Craiggiemore
Cork Tree Hill
'Sturt Meadows'
Kurrajong
Mt Davis
Mt Ross
'Tarmoola'
Jasper Hill/ Dominion
'Mertondale'
Mertondale Mine
Randwick Hill
Minerie Hill
Mt McKenzie
Mount Morgans
Mount Margaret
'Ida Valley'
Dead Camel Hill
Mt Flora
Harbour Lights Mine
Mt George
Cardinia Hill
Benalla Hill
Kowtah
Mt Margaret
Granny Smith Mine
Mt Malcolm
Malcolm Dam NR
Lake Raeside
Leonora
Malcolm
Mt Stewart
'Minara'
Mt Kowtah
Mt Nangaroo
'Wilbah O/S'
Mt Alexander
Leonora Caravan Park
Fuel: 4.30am-8pm Mon-Tues
4.30am-8.30pm Wed-Fri
4.30am-7pm Sat-Sun
Braiser Well
Mt Redcastle
Mt Kilkenny
Pyke Hill
Mount Ida
Oberwyl Hill
Mt Bevon
Mary Bore
'Melita'
Mt Melita
Glenorn
Hage Bore
Landed at Last Mine
Sunrise Mine
Desdemona
Yundamindera
Pyke Hollow
MENZIES
Copperfield Mining Centre
Orient Well Mine
Mt Kildare
Mt Keith
Red October Mine
Mt Mason
Rock Hole Bore
Spotted Dog Hill
Bottle Creek Mine
Tampa
Kilmore Hill
Position approx
Mt Colindina
Mt Florence
Mt Barton
'Yundamindra'
Butcher Well North Mine
SANDSTONE
Mt Ida
32 Mile Bore
Fuel: 7am-12midnight M-Sat, 10am-10pm Sun
Mt Linde
Kookynie
'Mount Remarkable'
Monk Well
Niagara
Red Hill
Prospector Pool
Mt Hornet
Yendang Rock
Riverina Outcamp
Lake Ballard
Dead Horse Rocks
Station Stay Morapoi
Mt Niagara
KOOKYNIE
'Walling Rock'
ROAD
'Jeedamya'
Niagara Dam NR
Mt Howe
Mt Percy
Niagara Dam
Twin Hills
'Yerilla'
Yerilla
Lake Raeside
Day Rock
Walling Rock
Inside Australia Sculptures
Gay Hill
Mt Catherine
Duck Hill
Snake Hill
Chingaling Rock
Ghost Rocks
Round Hill
YARRI
Rainbow Dam
Coronation Dam
Edjudina Ra
Mt Boyce
O'Loughlin Rock
Lemon Rock
'Mindanda'
'Mendleyarri O/S'
ROAD
Porphyry Mine
Mt Morley
Menzies
Lake Marmion
DONKEY ROCKS RD
Jungle Bore
Yilgangi Mine
Barba Hills
Galah Rocks
Menzies Caravan Park
Fuel: 7am-5pm M-F
7am-3pm Sat-Sun
'Yundaga'
Yunndaga
Mt Hope
ROAD
'Riverina'
Donkey Rocks Well
'Edjudina'
Wallbrook Hill
Rundle Rock
Bronc Rock
'Menangina'
EVANSTON
MENZIES
Mulline
Lake Moriaty
Boomerang Lake
Lake Rebecca
Lady Gladys North Mine
DAVYHURST ROAD
Goongarrie Pastoral Lease
PIANTO ROAD
Twenty Five Mile Rocks
Goongarrie National Park
Twin Peaks
Goongarrie Homestead
Comet Vale (abandoned)
Skull Rock
'Goongarrie'
Lake Goongarrie
Lake Rebecca Mine
Bardoc Mine
Goongarrie (abandoned)
Goongarrie Mine
Davyhurst
Lake Owen
Carr-Boyd
Lake Emu
Mt Ballona
Mulgabbie H.
Callion
Callion Mine
Wongi Hill
Canegrass
Scotia Mine
Gindalbie Woolshed
Carosue Dam Mine
Wangine Lake
Missouri Mine
Scotia
COOLGARDIE
Ora Banda Caravan Park
'Gindalbie'
Lady Jane-Orabanda Mine
Excelsior-Bardox
Mt Jewell
Silver Swan
Gindalbie
Mt Carnage
Ora Banda
Bardoc
Clear and Muddy Lakes NR
Mount Dimmer Mine
'Mount Vetters'
Broad Arrow
'Arcoona'
Turturdine Rock
Rowles Lagoon
Muddy Lake
Clear Lake
Rowles Lagoon
Phantom Dam
Mt Ellis
Broad Arrow
Paddington Siding
Mt McLeay
Yowie Hill
Jaurdi Conservation Park (Proposed)
'Credo'
'Balgarri'
Golden Kilometre
'Kanowna'
Halfway Hill
L Penny
Kurnalpi (ruins)
Iguana Mine
Rowles Lagoon CP
Arrow Lake
Four Mile Hill
Bullock Holes Waterhole
Jummung Hill
Mt Parkin
Jurangie Hill
'Black Flag'
Black Flag L
Gidji Roaster
Private Road - Mine access
Mt Walton
Lizard Mine
Zuleika South
White Flag Lake
Gidji
Kanowna
'Kintore'
NORTH ROAD
Fuel: 7am-3pm Sat-Sun

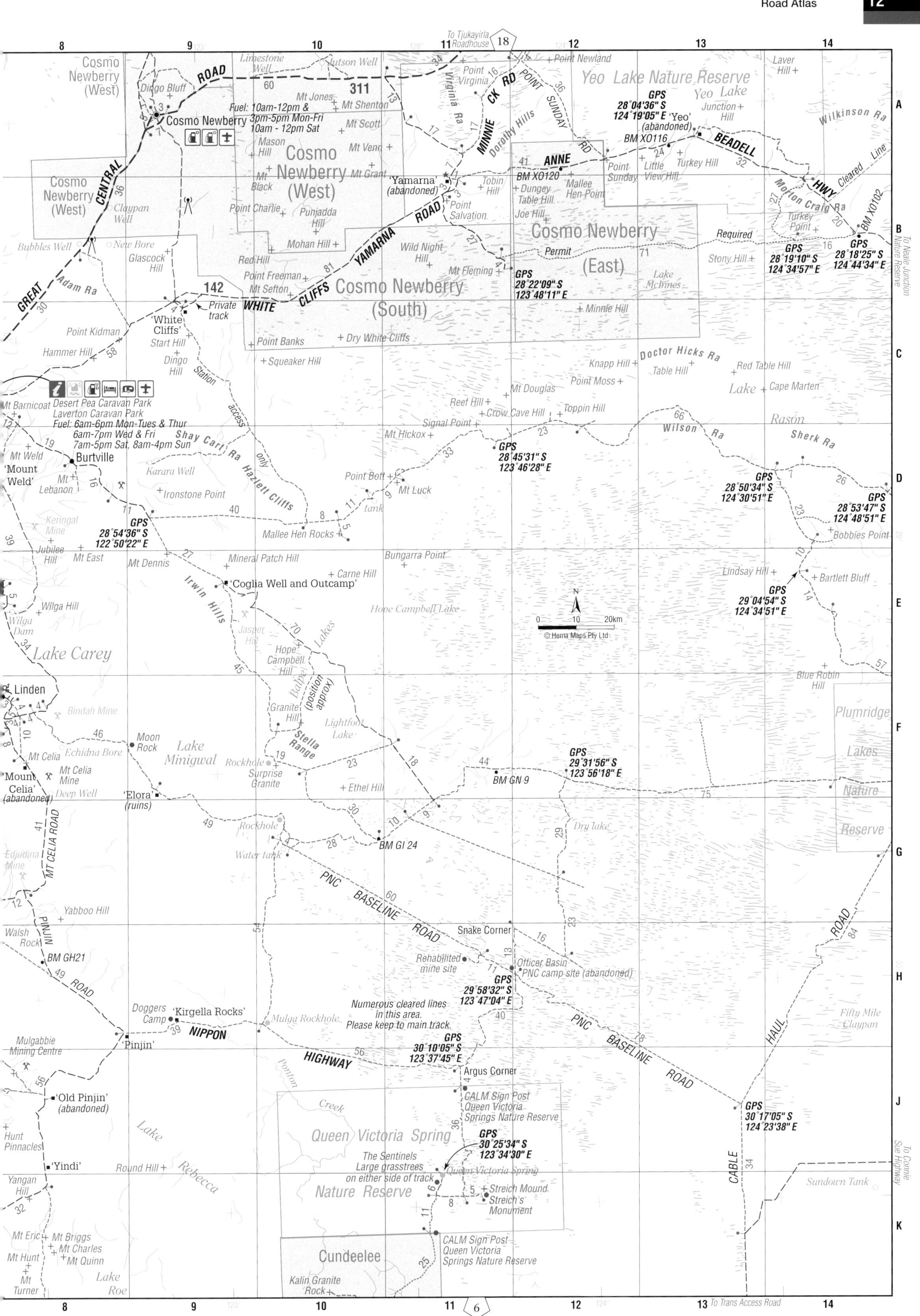
Cosmo Newberry (West)
Cosmo Newberry
Fuel: 10am-12pm & 3pm-5pm Mon-Fri 10am - 12pm Sat
GREAT CENTRAL ROAD
Yeo Lake Nature Reserve
Cosmo Newberry (East)
Cosmo Newberry (South)
Permit Required
WHITE CLIFFS YAMARNA ROAD
ANNE BEADELL HWY
MINNIE CK RD
POINT SUNDAY RD
'Yamarna' (abandoned)
'Yeo' (abandoned)
GPS 28°04'36" S 124°19'05" E
GPS 28°22'09" S 123°48'11" E
GPS 28°19'10" S 124°34'57" E
GPS 28°18'25" S 124°44'34" E
Desert Pea Caravan Park
Laverton Caravan Park
Fuel: 6am-6pm Mon-Tues & Thur 6am-7pm Wed & Fri 7am-5pm Sat, 8am-4pm Sun
Burtville
GPS 28°45'31" S 123°46'28" E
GPS 28°50'34" S 124°30'51" E
GPS 28°53'47" S 124°48'51" E
GPS 28°54'36" S 122°50'22" E
'Coglia Well and Outcamp'
Lake Rason
Hope Campbell Lake
GPS 29°04'54" S 124°34'51" E
Lake Carey
Linden
Lake Minigwal
Plumridge Lakes Nature Reserve
GPS 29°31'56" S 123°56'18" E
MT CELIA ROAD
PNC BASELINE ROAD
Snake Corner
Officer Basin PNC camp site (abandoned)
GPS 29°58'32" S 123°47'04" E
Numerous cleared lines in this area. Please keep to main track.
'Kirgella Rocks'
NIPPON HIGHWAY
PINJIN ROAD
'Pinjin'
GPS 30°10'05" S 123°37'45" E
Argus Corner
CALM Sign Post Queen Victoria Springs Nature Reserve
Queen Victoria Spring Nature Reserve
GPS 30°25'34" S 123°34'30" E
The Sentinels Large grasstrees on either side of track
Streich Mound
Streich's Monument
GPS 30°17'05" S 124°23'38" E
CABLE HAUL ROAD
Cundeelee
Lake Rebecca
Lake Roe
To Tjukayirla Roadhouse
To Neale Junction Nature Reserve
To Connie Sue Highway
To Trans Access Road
© Hema Maps Pty Ltd

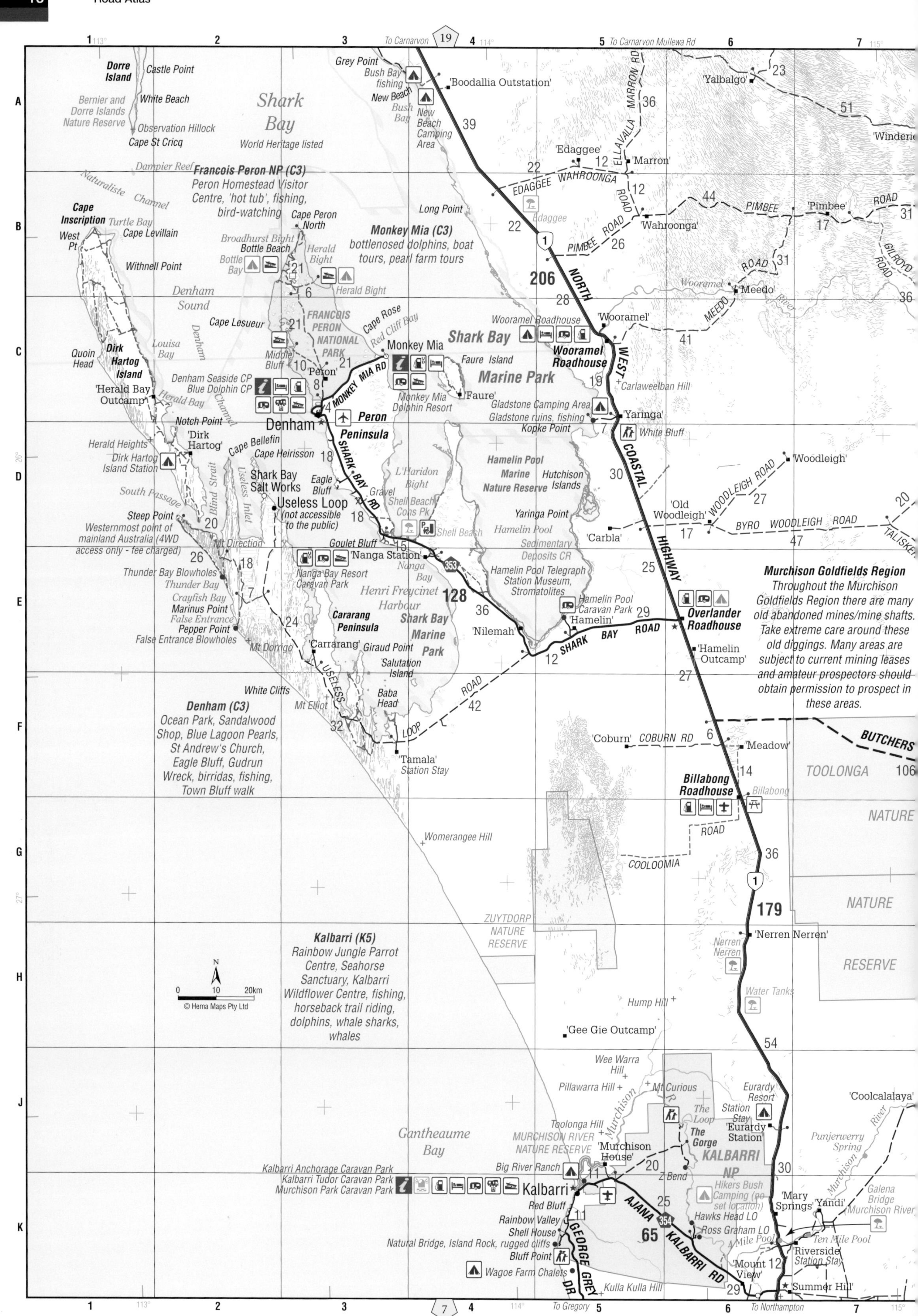

To Carnarvon
To Carnarvon Mullewa Rd
Dorre Island
Castle Point
White Beach
Bernier and Dorre Islands Nature Reserve
Observation Hillock
Cape St Cricq
Shark Bay
World Heritage listed
Grey Point
Bush Bay fishing
New Beach
Bush Bay
New Beach Camping Area
'Boodallia Outstation'
'Yalbalgo'
'Winderie'
'Edaggee'
'Marron'
ELLAVALLA MARRON RD
EDAGGEE WAHROONGA ROAD
'Wahroonga'
PIMBEE ROAD
'Pimbee'
GILROYD ROAD
Dampier Reef
Naturaliste Channel
Francois Peron NP (C3)
Peron Homestead Visitor Centre, 'hot tub', fishing, bird-watching
Cape Inscription
Turtle Bay
Cape Levillain
West Pt
Withnell Point
Cape Peron North
Long Point
Edaggee
Broadhurst Bight
Bottle Beach
Bottle Bay
Herald Bight
Monkey Mia (C3)
bottlenosed dolphins, boat tours, pearl farm tours
NORTH WEST COASTAL HIGHWAY
Wooramel
'Meedo'
MEEDO ROAD
Wooramel River
Denham Sound
Cape Lesueur
Louisa Bay
Denham
FRANCOIS PERON NATIONAL PARK
Cape Rose
Red Cliff Bay
Monkey Mia
Shark Bay Marine Park
Wooramel Roadhouse
'Wooramel'
Quoin Head
Dirk Hartog Island
'Herald Bay Outcamp'
Herald Bay
Denham Seaside CP
Blue Dolphin CP
Middle Bluff
'Peron'
MONKEY MIA RD
Faure Island
'Faure'
Monkey Mia Dolphin Resort
Carlaweelban Hill
Gladstone Camping Area
Gladstone ruins, fishing
Kopke Point
'Yaringa'
White Bluff
Notch Point
Denham
Peron Peninsula
'Dirk Hartog'
Herald Heights
Dirk Hartog Island Station
Cape Bellefin
Cape Heirisson
SHARK BAY RD
Hamelin Pool Marine Nature Reserve
Hutchison Islands
'Woodleigh'
WOODLEIGH ROAD
'Old Woodleigh'
BYRO WOODLEIGH ROAD
TALISKER
Shark Bay Salt Works
Eagle Bluff
L'Haridon Bight
Shell Beach
Cons Pk
Gravel
South Passage
Blind Strait
Useless Inlet
Useless Loop
(not accessible to the public)
Steep Point
Westernmost point of mainland Australia (4WD access only - fee charged)
Yaringa Point
Hamelin Pool
Sedimentary Deposits CR
'Carbla'
Mt Direction
Goulet Bluff
'Nanga Station'
Nanga Bay
Nanga Bay Resort Caravan Park
Hamelin Pool Telegraph Station Museum, Stromatolites
Thunder Bay Blowholes
Thunder Bay
Crayfish Bay
Marinus Point
False Entrance
Pepper Point
False Entrance Blowholes
Henri Freycinet Harbour
Shark Bay Marine Park
Cararang Peninsula
Hamelin Pool Caravan Park
'Hamelin'
Overlander Roadhouse
Murchison Goldfields Region
Throughout the Murchison Goldfields Region there are many old abandoned mines/mine shafts. Take extreme care around these old diggings. Many areas are subject to current mining leases and amateur prospectors should obtain permission to prospect in these areas.
Mt Dorngo
'Carrarang'
Giraud Point
'Nilemah'
SHARK BAY ROAD
'Hamelin Outcamp'
Salutation Island
White Cliffs
Mt Elliot
USELESS LOOP ROAD
Baba Head
Denham (C3)
Ocean Park, Sandalwood Shop, Blue Lagoon Pearls, St Andrew's Church, Eagle Bluff, Gudrun Wreck, birridas, fishing, Town Bluff walk
'Tamala' Station Stay
'Coburn'
COBURN RD
'Meadow'
BUTCHERS
TOOLONGA NATURE RESERVE
Billabong Roadhouse
Billabong
COOLOOMIA ROAD
Womerangee Hill
ZUYTDORP NATURE RESERVE
'Nerren Nerren'
Nerren Nerren
Kalbarri (K5)
Rainbow Jungle Parrot Centre, Seahorse Sanctuary, Kalbarri Wildflower Centre, fishing, horseback trail riding, dolphins, whale sharks, whales
© Hema Maps Pty Ltd
Hump Hill
Water Tanks
'Gee Gie Outcamp'
Wee Warra Hill
Pillawarra Hill
Mt Curious
Murchison R
The Loop
Eurardy Resort
Station Stay
'Eurardy Station'
'Coolcalalaya'
Punjerwerry Spring
Murchison River
Toolonga Hill
MURCHISON RIVER NATURE RESERVE
The Gorge
KALBARRI NP
Gantheaume Bay
'Murchison House'
Z Bend
Hikers Bush Camping (no set location)
Big River Ranch
Kalbarri Anchorage Caravan Park
Kalbarri Tudor Caravan Park
Murchison Park Caravan Park
Kalbarri
Red Bluff
Rainbow Valley
Shell House
Natural Bridge, Island Rock, rugged cliffs
Bluff Point
Wagoe Farm Chalets
AJANA KALBARRI RD
GEORGE GREY DR
Hawks Head LO
Ross Graham LO
4 Mile Pool
'Mary Springs'
'Yandi'
Galena Bridge Murchison River
Ten Mile Pool
'Riverside' Station Stay
'Mount View'
'Summer Hill'
Kulla Kulla Hill
To Gregory
To Northampton

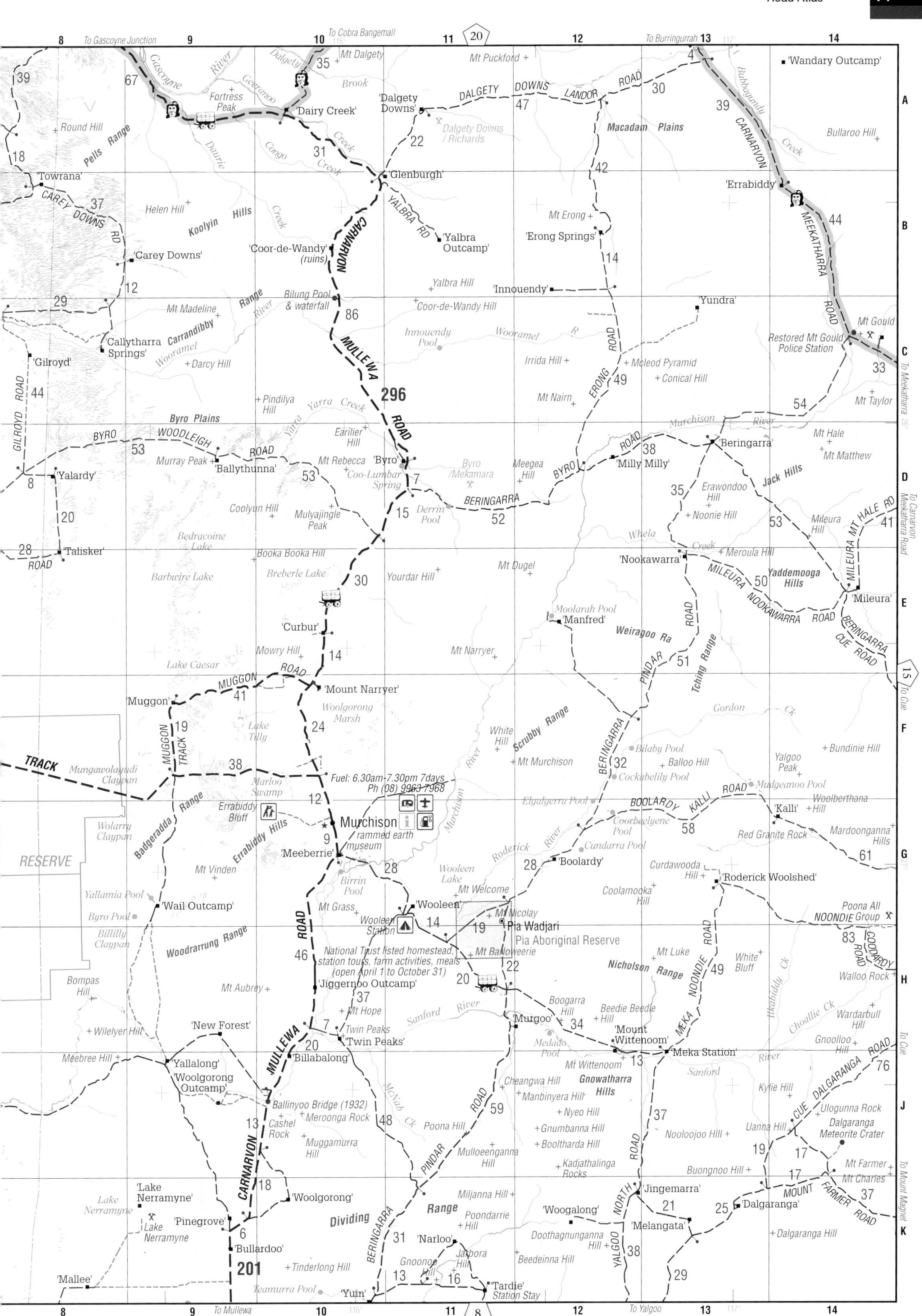
To Gascoyne Junction
To Cobra Bangemall
To Burringurrah
'Wandary Outcamp'
Mt Dalgety
'Dairy Creek'
'Dalgety Downs'
DALGETY DOWNS LANDOR ROAD
Macadam Plains
Round Hill
Pells Range
Fortress Peak
Dalgety Downs / Richards
Bullaroo Hill
'Towrana'
'Glenburgh'
'Errabiddy'
CAREY DOWNS RD
Helen Hill
Koolyin Hills
YALBRA RD
Mt Erong
'Yalbra Outcamp'
'Erong Springs'
MEEKATHARRA
'Carey Downs'
'Coor-de-Wandy' (ruins)
CARNARVON
Yalbra Hill
'Innouendy'
'Yundra'
Mt Madeline
Bilung Pool & waterfall
Coor-de-Wandy Hill
Mt Gould
Restored Mt Gould Police Station
'Callytharra Springs'
Carrandibby Range
Innouendy Pool
Wooramel
'Gilroyd'
Darcy Hill
Irrida Hill
Mcleod Pyramid
Conical Hill
To Meekatharra
GILROYD ROAD
MULLEWA
296
ROAD
Pindilya Hill
Yarra Yarra Creek
Mt Nairn
ERONG ROAD
Mt Taylor
Byro Plains
Murchison River
Mt Hale
BYRO WOODLEIGH ROAD
Earilier Hill
'Beringarra'
Mt Matthew
Murray Peak
'Ballythunna'
Mt Rebecca
'Byro'
Byro /Mekamara
Meegea Hill
BYRO ROAD
'Milly Milly'
'Yalardy'
Coo-Lumbar Spring
Erawondoo Hill
Jack Hills
BERINGARRA
Derrin Pool
Noonie Hill
Mileura Hill
Coolyun Hill
Mulyajingle Peak
Whela Creek
MILEURA MT HALE RD
To Carnarvon Meekatharra Road
Bedracoine Lake
'Talisker'
Booka Booka Hill
Meroula Hill
ROAD
'Nookawarra'
Mt Dugel
Yaddemooga Hills
Barbwire Lake
Breberle Lake
Yourdar Hill
MILEURA NOOKAWARRA ROAD
'Mileura'
Moolarah Pool
'Manfred'
'Curbur'
Weiragoo Ra
BERINGARRA CUE ROAD
Mowry Hill
Mt Narryer
Tching Range
Lake Caesar
MUGGON ROAD
PINDAR
'Mount Narryer'
To Cue
'Muggon'
Woolgorong Marsh
Gordon Ck
Lake Tilly
White Hill
Scrubby Range
MUGGON TRACK
TRACK
Mungawolagudi Claypan
Bilaby Pool
Bundinie Hill
Mt Murchison
Balloo Hill
Yalgoo Peak
Cockabelily Pool
Marloo Swamp
Fuel: 6.30am-7.30pm 7days Ph (08) 9963 7968
Mudgeanoo Pool
Elgalgerra Pool
BOOLARDY KALLI ROAD
Woolberthana Hill
Errabiddy Bluff
Badgeradda Range
'Kalli'
Wolarry Claypan
Errabiddy Hills
Murchison rammed earth museum
Coorbeelyene Pool
Mardoonganna Hills
Red Granite Rock
RESERVE
'Meeberrie'
Roderick River
Cundarra Pool
'Boolardy'
Mt Vinden
Curdawooda Hill
'Roderick Woolshed'
Wooleen Lake
Birrin Pool
Mt Welcome
Coolamooka Hill
Yallamia Pool
'Wooleen'
'Wail Outcamp'
Mt Grass
Poona All Group
NOONDIE
Mt Nicolay
Byro Pool
Wooleen Station
Pia Wadjari
Pia Aboriginal Reserve
Billilly Claypan
Woodrarrung Range
National Trust listed homestead, station tours, farm activities, meals (open April 1 to October 31)
Mt Balloweerie
Mt Luke
White Bluff
GOODARDY ROAD
Nicholson Range
NOONDIE ROAD
Walloo Rock
Bompas Hill
'Jiggernoo Outcamp'
Mt Aubrey
Mt Hope
Boogarra Hill
Beedie Beedie Hill
Chollie Ck
Wardarbull Hill
Sanford River
Ilkabiddy Ck
Twin Peaks
'Murgoo'
Wilelyer Hill
'New Forest'
'Twin Peaks'
'Mount Wittenoom'
Gnoolloo Hill
Medado Pool
MEKA
Meebree Hill
'Billabalong'
'Meka Station'
'Yallalong'
Mt Wittenoom
'Woolgorong Outcamp'
Gnowatharra Hills
Cheangwa Hill
Kylie Hill
Manbinyera Hill
CUE DALGARANGA ROAD
Ballinyoo Bridge (1932)
Meroonga Rock
Ulogunna Rock
Cashel Rock
McNab Ck
Nyeo Hill
Poona Hill
Dalgaranga Meteorite Crater
Gnumbanna Hill
Nooloojoo Hill
Uanna Hill
Muggamurra Hill
Boolthardha Hill
Mulloeenganna Hill
Kadjathalinga Rocks
Buongnoo Hill
Mt Farmer
To Mount Magnet
Mt Charles
'Lake Nerramyne'
'Woolgorong'
'Jingemarra'
MOUNT FARMER ROAD
Lake Nerramyne
Miljanna Hill
NORTH ROAD
'Dalgaranga'
Range
Dividing
Poondarrie Hill
'Woogalong'
'Melangata'
'Pinegrove'
Dalgaranga Hill
'Narloo'
Doothagnunganna Hill
'Bullardoo'
Jatbora Hill
Beedeinna Hill
YALGOO
201
Tinderlong Hill
Gnoono Hill
'Mallee'
'Tardie' Station Stay
Teamurra Pool
'Yuin'
To Mullewa
To Yalgoo

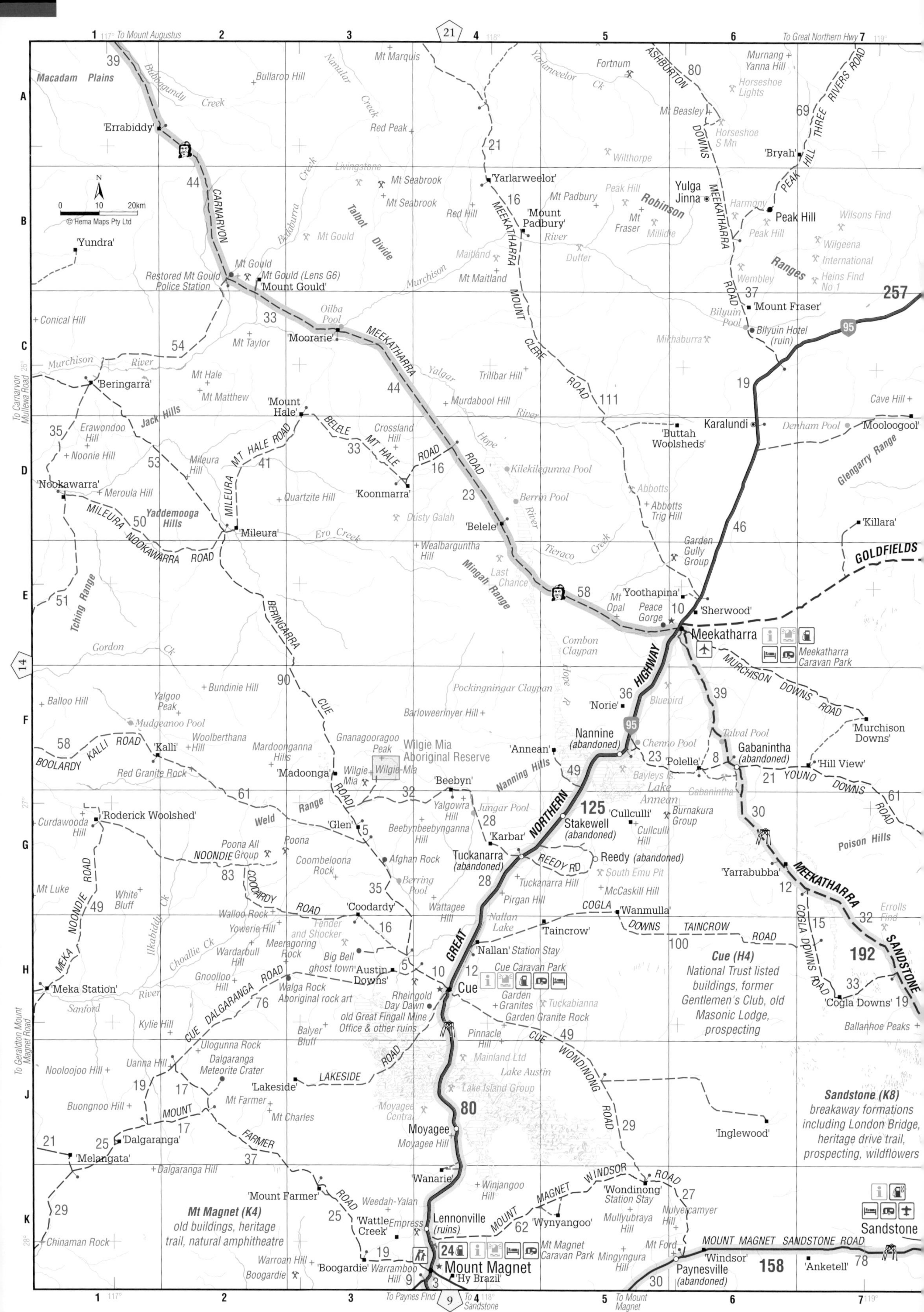
To Mount Augustus
To Great Northern Hwy
Macadam Plains
'Errabiddy'
Bullaroo Hill
Mt Marquis
Fortnum
Murnang
Yanna Hill
Horseshoe Lights
Mt Beasley
Horseshoe S Mn
Wilthorpe
'Bryah'
THREE RIVERS ROAD
PEAK HILL
ASHBURTON DOWNS MEEKATHARRA ROAD
Red Peak
Livingstone
Mt Seabrook
Talbot Divide
Red Hill
'Yarlarweelor'
MEEKATHARRA MOUNT CLERE ROAD
Mt Padbury
'Mount Padbury'
Peak Hill
Robinson Ranges
Yulga Jinna
Mt Fraser
Millidie
Harmony
Peak Hill
Wilsons Find
Wilgeena
International
Heins Find No 1
Wembley
'Yundra'
CARNARVON
© Hema Maps Pty Ltd
Mt Gould
Restored Mt Gould Police Station
Mt Gould (Lens G6)
'Mount Gould'
Maitland
Mt Maitland
Duffer
'Mount Fraser'
Bilyuin Pool
Bilyuin Hotel (ruin)
Mikhaburra
Conical Hill
Oilba Pool
'Moorarie'
MEEKATHARRA
Mt Taylor
Murchison River
'Beringarra'
Mt Hale
Mt Matthew
Trillbar Hill
Murdabool Hill
'Mount Hale'
BELELE MT HALE ROAD
Crossland Hill
Karalundi
Denham Pool
'Mooloogool'
Cave Hill
'Buttah Woolsheds'
Glengarry Range
Erawondoo Hill
Noonie Hill
Jack Hills
Mileura Hill
MT HALE ROAD
Kilekilegunna Pool
'Nookawarra'
Meroula Hill
Quartzite Hill
'Koonmarra'
Berrin Pool
Abbotts
Abbotts Trig Hill
MILEURA NOOKAWARRA ROAD
Yaddemooga Hills
'Mileura'
Ero Creek
Dusty Galah
'Belele'
'Killara'
Wealbarguntha Hill
Tieraco Creek
Garden Gully Group
GOLDFIELDS
Tching Range
BERINGARRA CUE ROAD
Mingah Range
Last Chance
Mt Opal
'Yoothapina'
Peace Gorge
'Sherwood'
Meekatharra
Meekatharra Caravan Park
Gordon Ck
Combon Claypan
MURCHISON DOWNS ROAD
Bundinie Hill
Pockingningar Claypan
Balloo Hill
Yalgoo Peak
Barloweerinyer Hill
'Norie'
Bluebird
Mudgeamoo Pool
Woolberthana Hill
Mardoonganna Hills
Gnanagooragoo Peak
Wilgie Mia Aboriginal Reserve
'Annean'
Nannine (abandoned)
Chemo Pool
Talval Pool
Gabanintha (abandoned)
'Murchison Downs'
'Hill View'
BOOLARDY KALLI ROAD
'Kalli'
Red Granite Rock
'Madoonga'
Wilgie Mia
'Beebyn'
Nanning Hills
'Polelle'
Bayleys Is.
Lake Annean
YOUNO DOWNS ROAD
'Roderick Woolshed'
Curdawooda Hill
Weld Range
Yalgowra Hill
Jungar Pool
NORTHERN
'Cullculli'
Burnakura Group
Stakewell (abandoned)
Cullculli Hill
'Glen'
Beebynbeebynganna Hill
'Karbar'
Poison Hills
Poona All Group
Poona
NOONDIE
Coombeloona Rock
Afghan Rock
Tuckanarra (abandoned)
REEDY RD
Reedy (abandoned)
South Emu Pit
'Yarrabubba'
MEEKATHARRA SANDSTONE
Mt Luke
White Bluff
NOONDIE ROAD
COODARDY ROAD
Berring Pool
Tuckanarra Hill
McCaskill Hill
Pirgan Hill
Walloo Rock
'Coodardy'
Wattagee Hill
COGLA DOWNS TAINCROW ROAD
'Wanmulla'
Errolls Find
Yowerie Hill
Fender and Shocker
Meeragoring Rock
Nallan Lake
'Taincrow'
Cue (H4)
National Trust listed buildings, former Gentlemen's Club, old Masonic Lodge, prospecting
Wardarbull Hill
Big Bell ghost town
'Austin Downs'
GREAT
'Nallan' Station Stay
Cue Caravan Park
COGLA DOWNS ROAD
MEKA
Ilkabiddy Ck
Chodlie Ck
Gnoolloo Hill
CUE DALGARANGA ROAD
Walga Rock Aboriginal rock art
Rheingold Day Dawn
Cue
Garden Granites
Tuckabianna
'Cogla Downs'
'Meka Station'
Sanford River
Kylie Hill
old Great Fingall Mine Office & other ruins
Garden Granite Rock
Balyer Bluff
Pinnacle Hill
CUE WONDINONG ROAD
Ballanhoe Peaks
To Geraldton Mount Magnet Road
Ulogunna Rock
Dalgaranga Meteorite Crater
Mainland Ltd
Lake Austin
Nooloojoo Hill
Uanna Hill
LAKESIDE ROAD
'Lakeside'
Lake Island Group
Sandstone (K8)
breakaway formations including London Bridge, heritage drive trail, prospecting, wildflowers
Mt Farmer
Mt Charles
Buongnoo Hill
MOUNT FARMER
Moyagee Central
Moyagee
Moyagee Hill
'Inglewood'
'Dalgaranga'
'Melangata'
Dalgaranga Hill
'Wanarie'
WINDSOR ROAD
Winjangoo Hill
'Mount Farmer'
Weedah-Yalan
'Wondinong' Station Stay
Mullyubraya Hill
Nulyercamyer Hill
MOUNT MAGNET
Mt Magnet (K4)
old buildings, heritage trail, natural amphitheatre
'Wattle Creek'
Empress
Lennonville (ruins)
'Wynyangoo'
Sandstone
Chinaman Rock
Warroan Hill
Mt Magnet Caravan Park
Mingyngura Hill
Mt Ford
MOUNT MAGNET SANDSTONE ROAD
'Windsor'
Paynesville (abandoned)
'Anketell'
Boogardie
'Boogardie'
Warramboo Hill
Mount Magnet
'Hy Brazil'
To Paynes Find
To Sandstone
To Mount Magnet
To Carnarvon Mullewa Road

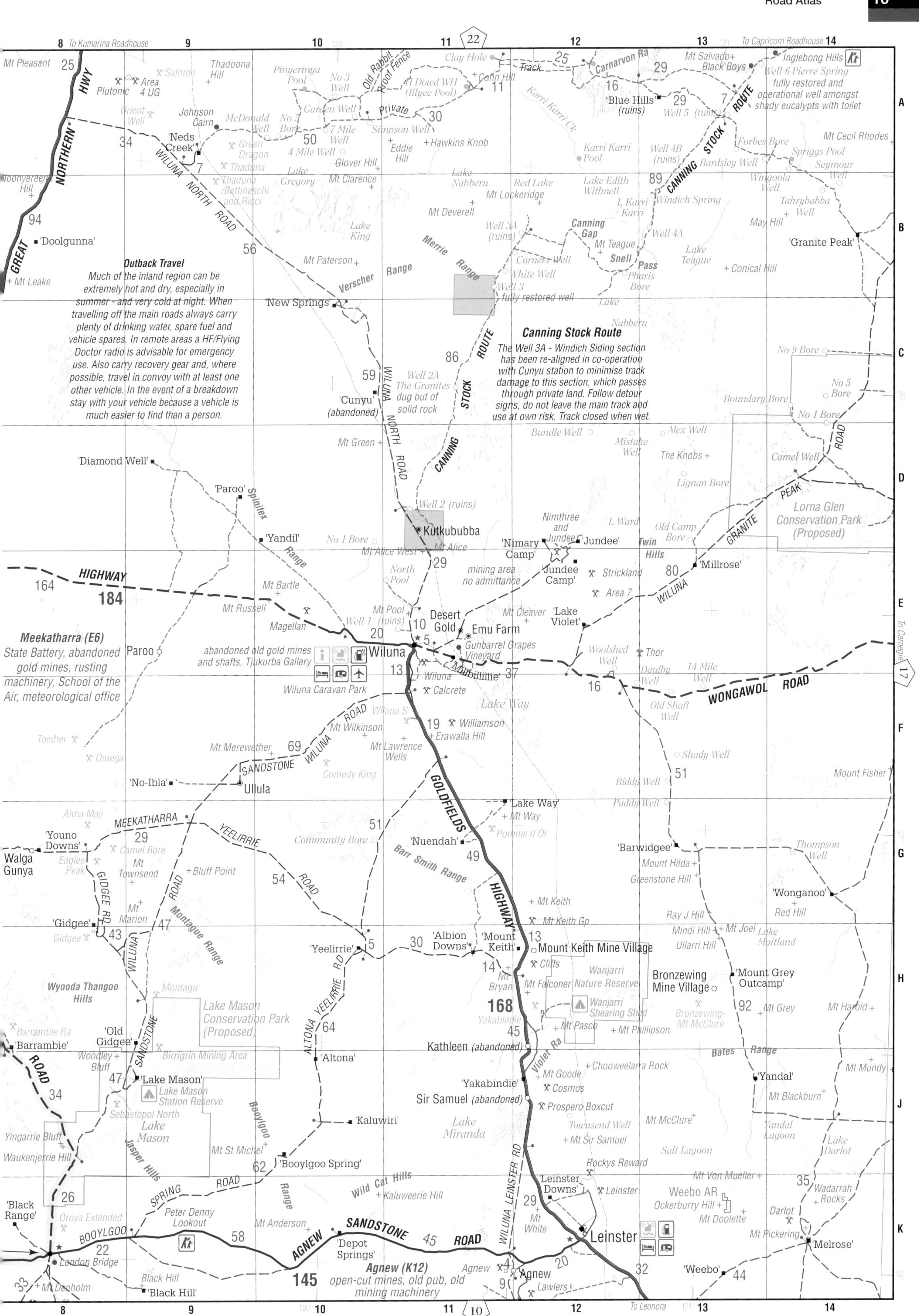
To Kumarina Roadhouse
To Capricorn Roadhouse
To Carnegie
To Leonora
22
17
10
Outback Travel
Much of the inland region can be extremely hot and dry, especially in summer - and very cold at night. When travelling off the main roads always carry plenty of drinking water, spare fuel and vehicle spares. In remote areas a HF/Flying Doctor radio is advisable for emergency use. Also carry recovery gear and, where possible, travel in convoy with at least one other vehicle. In the event of a breakdown stay with your vehicle because a vehicle is much easier to find than a person.
Canning Stock Route
The Well 3A - Windich Siding section has been re-aligned in co-operation with Cunyu station to minimise track damage to this section, which passes through private land. Follow detour signs, do not leave the main track and use at own risk. Track closed when wet.
Meekatharra (E6)
State Battery, abandoned gold mines, rusting machinery, School of the Air, meteorological office
Agnew (K12)
open-cut mines, old pub, old mining machinery
abandoned old gold mines and shafts, Tjukurba Gallery
Wiluna Caravan Park
Well 6 Pierre Spring fully restored and operational well amongst shady eucalypts with toilet
Well 3 fully restored well
mining area no admittance
GREAT NORTHERN HWY
WILUNA NORTH ROAD
CANNING STOCK ROUTE
GOLDFIELDS HIGHWAY
HIGHWAY 184
WONGAWOL ROAD
AGNEW SANDSTONE ROAD
GRANITE PEAK WILUNA ROAD
Wiluna
Leinster
Kutkububba
Desert Gold
Emu Farm
Gunbarrel Grapes Vineyard
Mount Keith Mine Village
Bronzewing Mine Village
Ullula
Paroo
Walga Gunya
Lorna Glen Conservation Park (Proposed)
Lake Mason Conservation Park (Proposed)
Wanjarri Nature Reserve
Lake Way
Lake Miranda
Kathleen (abandoned)
Sir Samuel (abandoned)
'Cunyu' (abandoned)
'Lake Violet'
'Millrose'
'Granite Peak'
'Doolgunna'
'New Springs'
'Yeelirrie'
'Albion Downs'
'Mount Keith'
'Yakabindie'
'Leinster Downs'
'Barwidgee'
'Wonganoo'
'Mount Grey Outcamp'
'Yandal'
'Weebo'
'Melrose'
'Depot Springs'
'Black Hill'
'Booylgoo Spring'
'Kaluwiri'
'Altona'
'Lake Mason'
'Old Gidgee'
'Gidgee'
'Youno Downs'
'Barrambie'
'Black Range'
'No-Ibla'
'Yandil'
'Paroo'
'Diamond Well'
'Nuendah'
'Lake Way'
'Jundee'
'Nimary Camp'
'Jundee Camp'
'Blue Hills' (ruins)
'Neds Creek'
Inglebong Hills
Weebo AR
London Bridge

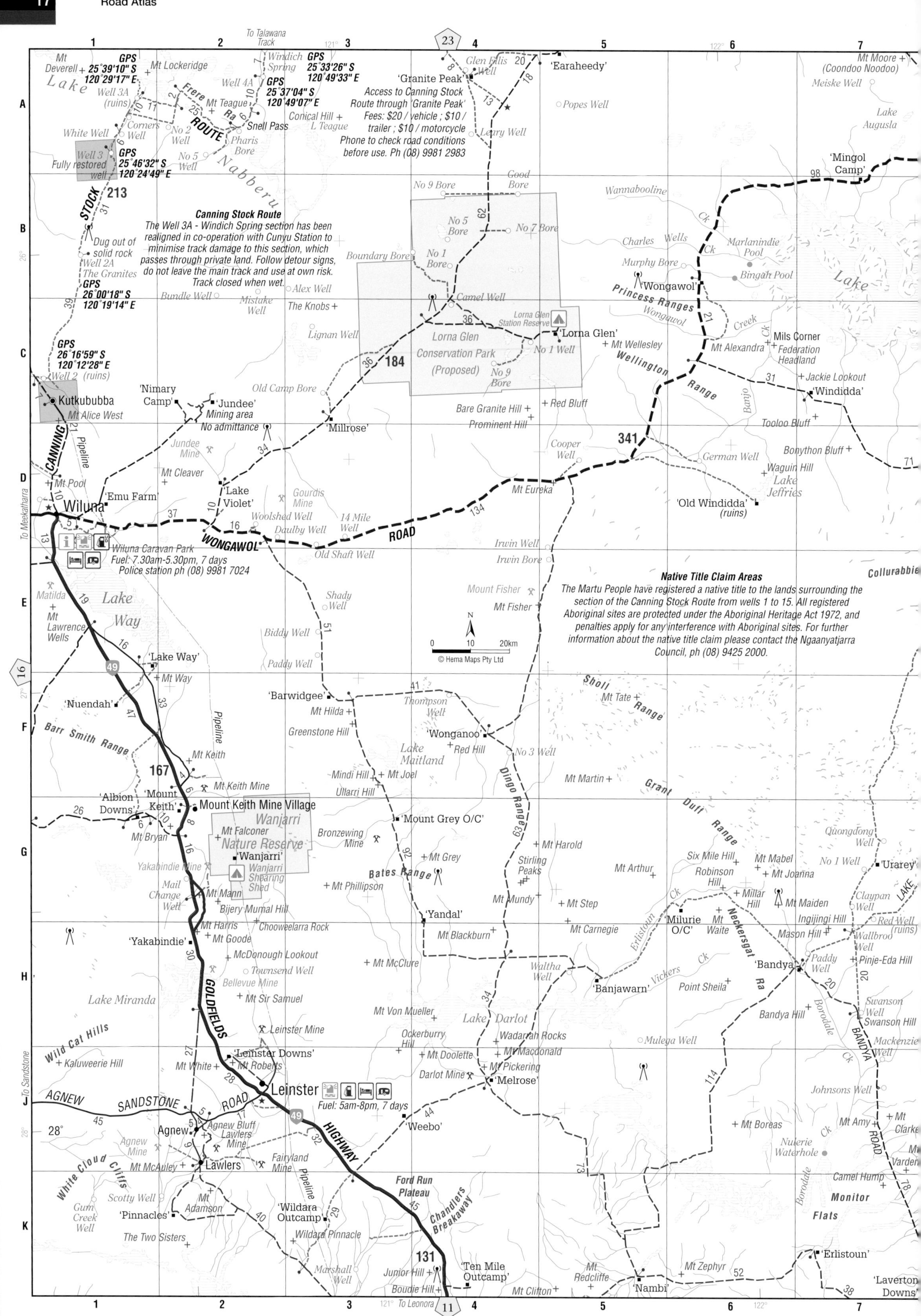

Canning Stock Route
The Well 3A - Windich Spring section has been realigned in co-operation with Cunyu Station to minimise track damage to this section, which passes through private land. Follow detour signs, do not leave the main track and use at own risk. Track closed when wet.
Access to Canning Stock Route through 'Granite Peak' Fees: $20 / vehicle ; $10 / trailer ; $10 / motorcycle Phone to check road conditions before use. Ph (08) 9981 2983
Native Title Claim Areas
The Martu People have registered a native title to the lands surrounding the section of the Canning Stock Route from wells 1 to 15. All registered Aboriginal sites are protected under the Aboriginal Heritage Act 1972, and penalties apply for any interference with Aboriginal sites. For further information about the native title claim please contact the Ngaanyatjarra Council, ph (08) 9425 2000.
Wiluna Caravan Park
Fuel: 7.30am-5.30pm, 7 days
Police station ph (08) 9981 7024
Leinster
Fuel: 5am-8pm, 7 days
© Hema Maps Pty Ltd
0 10 20km
GPS 25°39'10" S 120°29'17" E
GPS 25°33'26" S 120°49'33" E
GPS 25°37'04" S 120°49'07" E
GPS 25°46'32" S 120°24'49" E
GPS 26°00'18" S 120°19'14" E
GPS 26°16'59" S 120°12'28" E
To Talawana Track
To Meekatharra
To Sandstone
To Leonora
Mt Deverell
Mt Lockeridge
Lake Nabberu
Well 3A (ruins)
Windich Spring
Well 4A
Mt Teague
Frere Ra
Snell Pass
Conical Hill
L Teague
White Well
Corners Well
No 2 Well
Pharis Bore
No 5 Well
Well 3 Fully restored well
Dug out of solid rock
Well 2A
The Granites
Bundle Well
Mistake Well
Alex Well
The Knobs
Lignan Well
Well 2 (ruins)
Kutkububba
Mt Alice West
'Nimary Camp'
'Jundee' Mining area No admittance
Old Camp Bore
'Millrose'
Jundee Mine
Mt Cleaver
'Lake Violet'
Gourdis Mine
Mt Pool
Wiluna
'Emu Farm'
Woolshed Well
Daulby Well
14 Mile Well
Old Shaft Well
WONGAWOL ROAD
CANNING STOCK ROUTE
Pipeline
'Granite Peak'
Glen Ellis Well
Leary Well
'Earaheedy'
Popes Well
No 9 Bore
Good Bore
No 5 Bore
No 7 Bore
Boundary Bore
No 1 Bore
Camel Well
Lorna Glen Station Reserve
'Lorna Glen'
No 1 Well
Lorna Glen Conservation Park (Proposed)
No 9 Bore
Bare Granite Hill
Prominent Hill
Red Bluff
Cooper Well
Mt Eureka
Irwin Well
Irwin Bore
Mount Fisher
Mt Fisher
Mt Moore (Coondoo Noodoo)
Meiske Well
Lake Augusta
'Mingol Camp'
Wannabooline
Charles Wells
Marlanindie Pool
Murphy Bore
Bingah Pool
'Wongawol'
Princess Ranges
Wongawol Creek
Lake
Mt Wellesley
Mt Alexandra
Mils Corner
Federation Headland
Wellington Range
Jackie Lookout
'Windidda'
Banjo Ck
Tooloo Bluff
Bonython Bluff
German Well
Waguin Hill
Lake Jeffries
'Old Windidda' (ruins)
Collurabbie
Matilda
Mt Lawrence Wells
Lake Way
'Lake Way'
Mt Way
'Nuendah'
Barr Smith Range
Mt Keith
Mt Keith Mine
'Albion Downs'
'Mount Keith'
Mount Keith Mine Village
Wanjarri Nature Reserve
Mt Falconer
'Wanjarri'
Wanjarri Shearing Shed
Mt Bryan
Yakabindie Mine
Mail Change Well
Mt Mann
Bijery Mumal Hill
Mt Harris
Chooweelarra Rock
'Yakabindie'
Mt Goode
McDonough Lookout
Townsend Well
Bellevue Mine
Mt Sir Samuel
Lake Miranda
GOLDFIELDS HIGHWAY
Leinster Mine
Wild Cat Hills
Kaluweerie Hill
'Leinster Downs'
Mt Roberts
Mt White
AGNEW SANDSTONE ROAD
Agnew
Agnew Bluff
Lawlers Mine
Agnew Mine
Mt McAuley
Lawlers
Fairyland Mine
White Cloud Cliffs
Scotty Well
Gum Creek Well
'Pinnacles'
Mt Adamson
The Two Sisters
Shady Well
Biddy Well
Paddy Well
'Barwidgee'
Mt Hilda
Greenstone Hill
Thompson Well
'Wonganoo'
Red Hill
Lake Maitland
Mindi Hill
Mt Joel
Ullarri Hill
'Mount Grey O/C'
Bronzewing Mine
Bates Range
Mt Grey
Mt Phillipson
'Yandal'
Mt Blackburn
Mt McClure
Mt Von Mueller
Ockerburry Hill
Lake Darlot
Wadarrah Rocks
Mt Macdonald
Mt Doolette
Mt Pickering
Darlot Mine
'Melrose'
'Weebo'
'Wildara Outcamp'
Wildara Pinnacle
Ford Run Plateau
Chandlers Breakaway
Marshall Well
Junior Hill
Boudie Hill
'Ten Mile Outcamp'
Mt Clifton
Sholl Range
Mt Tate
No 3 Well
Dingo Range
Mt Martin
Grant Duff Range
Mt Harold
Stirling Peaks
Mt Mundy
Mt Step
Mt Arthur
Mt Carnegie
Waltha Well
'Banjawarn'
Erlistoun Ck
Vickers Ck
Mulega Well
Mt Redcliffe
'Nambi'
Mt Zephyr
Quongdong Well
'Urarey'
No 1 Well
Six Mile Hill
Robinson Hill
Mt Mabel
Mt Joanna
Millar Hill
Mt Maiden
Claypan Well
Milurie O/C'
Mt Waite
Neckersgat Ra
Ingijingi Hill
Mason Hill
Red Well (ruins)
Wallbrod Well
'Bandya'
Paddy Well
Pinje-Eda Hill
Point Sheila
Bandya Hill
Swanson Well
Swanson Hill
Mackenzie Well
Borodale Ck
BANDYA ROAD
Johnsons Well
Mt Boreas
Mt Amy
Mt Clarke
Nuerie Waterhole
Camel Hump
Monitor Flats
'Erlistoun'
'Laverton Downs'
LAKE

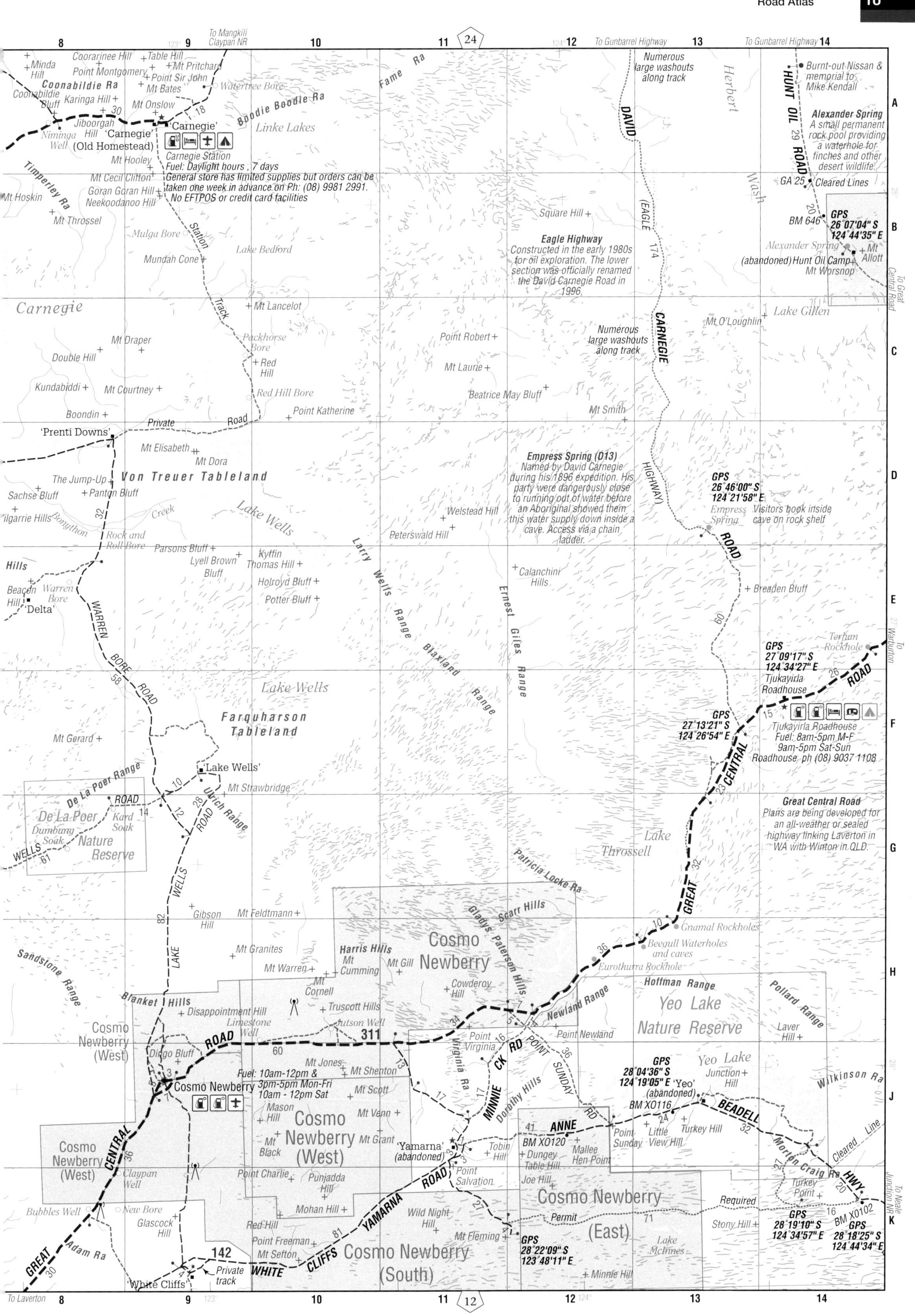
To Mangkili Claypan NR
To Gunbarrel Highway
To Gunbarrel Highway
24
8
9
10
11
12
13
14
A
B
C
D
E
F
G
H
J
K
Minda Hill
Coorarinee Hill
Table Hill
Mt Pritchard
Point Montgomery
Point Sir John
Mt Bates
Coonabildie Ra
Coonabildie Bluff
Karinga Hill
Watertree Bore
Mt Onslow
Jiboorgah Hill
Niminga Well
'Carnegie'
'Carnegie' (Old Homestead)
Boodie Boodie Ra
Linke Lakes
Fame Ra
Carnegie Station
Fuel: Daylight hours , 7 days
General store has limited supplies but orders can be taken one week in advance on Ph: (08) 9981 2991.
No EFTPOS or credit card facilities
Mt Hooley
Mt Cecil Clifton
Goran Goran Hill
Neekoodanoo Hill
Timperley Ra
Mt Hoskin
Mt Throssel
Mulga Bore
Station
Lake Bedford
Mundah Cone
Track
Carnegie
Mt Lancelot
Packhorse Bore
Red Hill
Red Hill Bore
Mt Draper
Double Hill
Kundabiddi
Mt Courtney
Boondin
Point Katherine
Private
Road
'Prenti Downs'
Mt Elisabeth
Mt Dora
The Jump-Up
Von Treuer Tableland
Sachse Bluff
Panton Bluff
Bonython
Creek
Lake Wells
Rock and Roll Bore
Parsons Bluff
Lyell Brown Bluff
Kyffin Thomas Hill
Holroyd Bluff
Potter Bluff
Hills
Beacon Hill
Warren Bore
'Delta'
WARREN BORE ROAD
Larry Wells Range
Blaxland Range
Lake Wells
Farquharson Tableland
Mt Gerard
'Lake Wells'
Mt Strawbridge
De La Poer Range
ROAD
De La Poer Nature Reserve
Kard Soak
Dumbung Soak
WELLS
Ulrich Range
ROAD
WELLS
LAKE
Gibson Hill
Mt Feldtmann
Sandstone Range
Mt Granites
Mt Warren
Blanket Hills
Disappointment Hill
Limestone Well
Cosmo Newberry (West)
Dingo Bluff
ROAD
311
Cosmo Newberry
Fuel: 10am-12pm & 3pm-5pm Mon-Fri 10am - 12pm Sat
Mt Jones
Mt Shenton
Mt Scott
Mason Hill
Cosmo Newberry (West)
Mt Venn
Mt Black
Mt Grant
Claypan Well
Point Charlie
Punjadda Hill
Mohan Hill
Bubbles Well
New Bore
Glasscock Hill
Red Hill
Point Freeman
Mt Sefton
Adam Ra
GREAT
CENTRAL
142
Private track
'White Cliffs'
WHITE CLIFFS
YAMARNA ROAD
Cosmo Newberry (South)
Wild Night Hill
Mt Fleming
Harris Hills
Mt Cumming
Mt Gill
Cosmo Newberry
Mt Cornell
Truscott Hills
Jutson Well
Cowderoy Hill
Gladys Paterson Hills
Scarr Hills
Point Virginia
Virginia Ra
MINNIE CK RD
Dorothy Hills
'Yamarna' (abandoned)
Point Salvation
Tobin Hill
GPS 28°22'09" S 123°48'11" E
Numerous large washouts along track
DAVID CARNEGIE (EAGLE HIGHWAY) ROAD
Herbert Wash
HUNT OIL ROAD
Burnt-out Nissan & memorial to Mike Kendall
Alexander Spring
A small permanent rock pool providing a waterhole for finches and other desert wildlife.
GA 25
Cleared Lines
BM 646
GPS 26°07'04" S 124°44'35" E
Alexander Spring
Mt Allott
(abandoned) Hunt Oil Camp
Mt Worsnop
To Great Central Road
Square Hill
Eagle Highway
Constructed in the early 1980s for oil exploration. The lower section was officially renamed the David Carnegie Road in 1996.
Lake Gillen
Mt O'Loughlin
Numerous large washouts along track
Point Robert
Mt Laurie
Beatrice May Bluff
Mt Smith
Empress Spring (D13)
Named by David Carnegie during his 1896 expedition. His party were dangerously close to running out of water before an Aboriginal showed them this water supply down inside a cave. Access via a chain ladder.
GPS 26°46'00" S 124°21'58" E
Empress Spring
Visitors book inside cave on rock shelf
Welstead Hill
Peterswald Hill
Calanchini Hills
Ernest Giles Range
Breaden Bluff
Terhan Rockhole
To Warburton
GPS 27°09'17" S 124°34'27" E
Tjukayirla Roadhouse
GPS 27°13'21" S 124°26'54" E
Tjukayirla Roadhouse
Fuel: 8am-5pm M-F 9am-5pm Sat-Sun
Roadhouse ph (08) 9037 1108
Great Central Road
Plans are being developed for an all-weather or sealed highway linking Laverton in WA with Winton in QLD.
Lake Throssell
Patricia Locke Ra
Gnamal Rockholes
Beegull Waterholes and caves
Eurothurra Rockhole
Newland Range
Point Newland
POINT SUNDAY RD
Hoffman Range
Yeo Lake Nature Reserve
Pollard Range
Laver Hill
Yeo Lake
Junction Hill
GPS 28°04'36" S 124°19'05" E
'Yeo' (abandoned)
BM XO116
BEADELL
Wilkinson Ra
ANNE
BM XO120
Dungey Table Hill
Mallee Hen Point
Point Sunday
Little View Hill
Turkey Hill
Morton Craig Ra
Cleared Line
HWY
Joe Hill
Cosmo Newberry (East)
Permit
Required
Turkey Point
Stony Hill
Lake McInnes
Minnie Hill
GPS 28°19'10" S 124°34'57" E
BM XO102
GPS 28°18'25" S 124°44'34" E
To Neale Junction NR
To Laverton
12

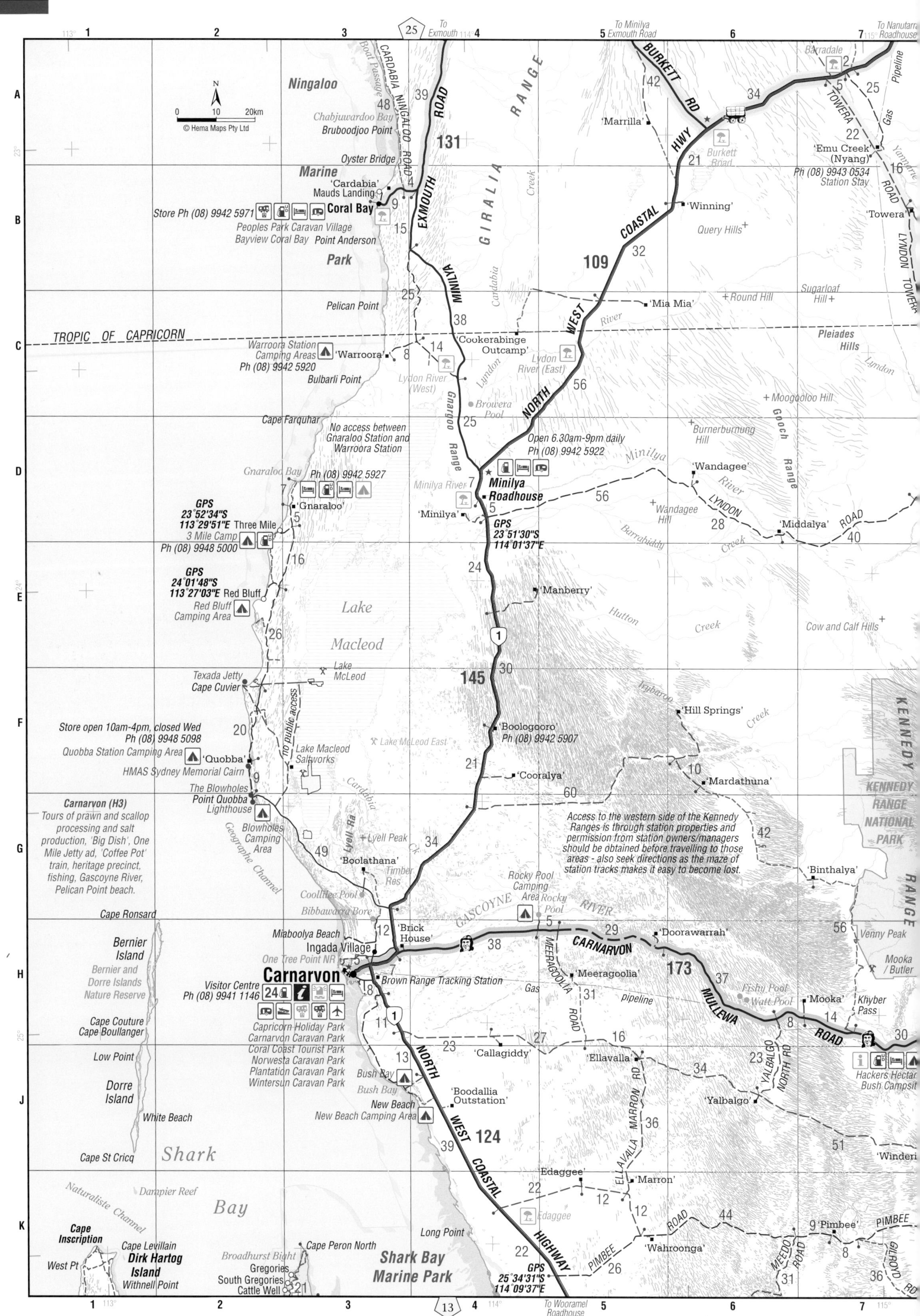

To Exmouth
To Minilya Exmouth Road
To Nanutarra Roadhouse
Ningaloo
Marine
Park
© Hema Maps Pty Ltd
Chabjuwardoo Bay
Bruboodjoo Point
Oyster Bridge
'Cardabia'
Mauds Landing
Coral Bay
Store Ph (08) 9942 5971
Peoples Park Caravan Village
Bayview Coral Bay
Point Anderson
Boat Passage
CARDABIA NINGALOO ROAD
EXMOUTH ROAD
MINILYA
131
GIRALIA RANGE
BURKETT RD
'Marrilla'
Burkett Road
'Winning'
Query Hills
COASTAL HWY
NORTH WEST
109
Baradale
TOWERA
'Emu Creek' (Nyang)
Ph (08) 9943 0534 Station Stay
'Towera'
LYNDON TOWERA
Pipeline
Gas
Pelican Point
TROPIC OF CAPRICORN
'Mia Mia'
Round Hill
Sugarloaf Hill
Pleiades Hills
Cookerabinge Outcamp'
Warroora Station Camping Areas
Ph (08) 9942 5920
'Warroora'
Bulbarli Point
Lydon River (West)
Lydon River (East)
Browera Pool
Gnargoo Range
Moogooloo Hill
Burnerbunung Hill
Gooch Range
Cape Farquhar
No access between Gnaraloo Station and Warroora Station
Open 6.30am-9pm daily
Ph (08) 9942 5922
Minilya River
'Wandagee'
Gnaraloo Bay
Ph (08) 9942 5927
'Gnaraloo'
Minilya Roadhouse
'Minilya'
Wandagee Hill
LYNDON ROAD
'Middalya'
GPS 23°52'34"S 113°29'51"E
Three Mile
3 Mile Camp
Ph (08) 9948 5000
GPS 23°51'30"S 114°01'37"E
Barrabiddy Creek
GPS 24°01'48"S 113°27'03"E
Red Bluff
Red Bluff Camping Area
'Manberry'
Hutton Creek
Cow and Calf Hills
Lake Macleod
Lake McLeod
Texada Jetty
Cape Cuvier
145
'Hill Springs'
Store open 10am-4pm, closed Wed
Ph (08) 9948 5098
Quobba Station Camping Area
'Quobba'
no public access
Lake Macleod Saltworks
Lake McLeod East
'Boologooro'
Ph (08) 9942 5907
HMAS Sydney Memorial Cairn
The Blowholes
Point Quobba Lighthouse
'Cooralya'
'Mardathuna'
KENNEDY RANGE NATIONAL PARK
KENNEDY RANGE
Carnarvon (H3)
Tours of prawn and scallop processing and salt production, 'Big Dish', One Mile Jetty ad, 'Coffee Pot' train, heritage precinct, fishing, Gascoyne River, Pelican Point beach.
Blowholes Camping Area
Geographe Channel
Lyell Ra
Lyell Peak
'Boolathana'
Timber Res
Access to the western side of the Kennedy Ranges is through station properties and permission from station owners/managers should be obtained before travelling to those areas - also seek directions as the maze of station tracks makes it easy to become lost.
'Binthalya'
Coolliffee Pool
Bibbawarra Bore
Rocky Pool Camping Area
Rocky Pool
GASCOYNE RIVER
Cape Ronsard
Miaboolya Beach
Ingada Village
'Brick House'
'Doorawarrah'
CARNARVON
173
Venny Peak
Mooka / Butler
Bernier Island
Bernier and Dorre Islands Nature Reserve
One Tree Point NR
Carnarvon
Visitor Centre
Ph (08) 9941 1146
Brown Range Tracking Station
MEERAGOOLIA ROAD
'Meeragoolia'
Gas pipeline
MULLEWA ROAD
Fishy Pool
Watt Pool
'Mooka'
Khyber Pass
Cape Couture
Cape Boullanger
Capricorn Holiday Park
Carnarvon Caravan Park
Coral Coast Tourist Park
Norwesta Caravan Park
Plantation Caravan Park
Wintersun Caravan Park
'Callagiddy'
'Ellavalla'
Low Point
Bush Bay
NORTH WEST COASTAL HIGHWAY
YALBALGO NORTH RD
Hackers Hectar Bush Campsit
Dorre Island
'Boodallia Outstation'
New Beach
New Beach Camping Area
'Yalbalgo'
White Beach
124
MARRON RD
ELLAVALLA
'Winderi
Cape St Cricq
Shark Bay
Edaggee'
'Marron'
Naturaliste Channel
Dampier Reef
Edaggee
PIMBEE ROAD
'Pimbee'
Cape Inscription
Cape Levillain
Dirk Hartog Island
West Pt
Broadhurst Bight
Cape Peron North
Gregories
South Gregories
Cattle Well
Shark Bay Marine Park
Long Point
'Wahroonga'
MEEDO ROAD
GILROYD RD
GPS 25°34'31"S 114°09'37"E
Withnell Point
To Wooramel Roadhouse

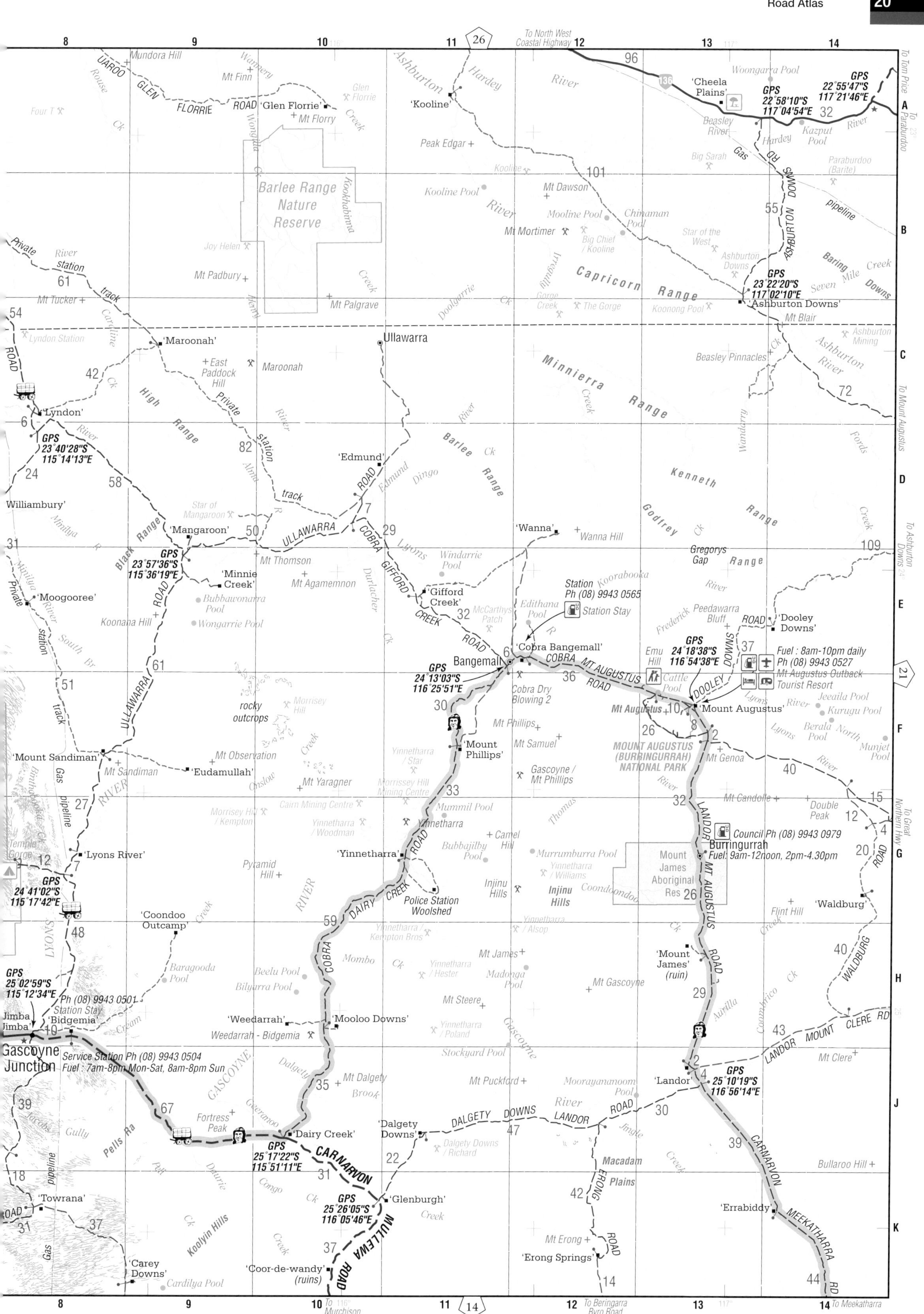
To North West Coastal Highway
To Tom Price
To Paraburdoo
To Mount Augustus
To Ashburton Downs
To Great Northern Hwy
To Meekatharra
To Beringarra Byro Road
To Murchison
Mundora Hill
UAROO GLEN FLORRIE ROAD
Mt Finn
'Glen Florrie'
Mt Florry
Glen Florrie
Ashburton River
Hardey
'Kooline'
Peak Edgar
'Cheela Plains'
Woongarra Pool
GPS 22°58'10"S 117°04'54"E
GPS 22°55'47"S 117°21'46"E
Beasley River
Kazput Pool
Paraburdoo (Barite)
Big Sarah
Gas pipeline
ASHBURTON DOWNS RD
Barlee Range Nature Reserve
Kooline Pool
Kooline
Mt Dawson
Mooline Pool
Chinaman Pool
Mt Mortimer
Big Chief / Kooline
Star of the West
Ashburton Downs
Baring Mile Creek
Seven Mile Downs
Joy Helen
Private station track
River station
Mt Padbury
Mt Palgrave
Mt Tucker
Capricorn Range
Gorge Creek
The Gorge
Koonong Pool
GPS 23°22'20"S 117°02'10"E
'Ashburton Downs'
Mt Blair
Lyndon Station
'Maroonah'
Ullawarra
Ashburton Mining
East Paddock Hill
Maroonah
Minnierra Range
Beasley Pinnacles
Ashburton River
'Lyndon'
High Range
Private station track
GPS 23°40'28"S 115°14'13"E
Williambury'
'Edmund'
Barlee Range
Kenneth Range
Godfrey Range
Dingo
Star of Mangaroon
'Mangaroon'
ULLAWARRA
COBRA GIFFORD CREEK ROAD
'Wanna'
Wanna Hill
Gregorys Gap
Range
GPS 23°57'36"S 115°36'19"E
Black Range
Mt Thomson
'Minnie Creek'
Mt Agamemnon
Windarrie Pool
Station Ph (08) 9943 0565
Station Stay
Koorabooka
'Moogooree'
Bubbawonarra Pool
Wongarrie Pool
Koonana Hill
'Gifford Creek'
McCarthys Patch
Editbana Pool
Peedawarra Bluff
'Dooley Downs'
DOOLEY DOWNS ROAD
Frederick River
Emu Hill
GPS 24°18'38"S 116°54'38"E
Fuel : 8am-10pm daily
Ph (08) 9943 0527
Mt Augustus Outback Tourist Resort
Cattle Pool
'Cobra Bangemall'
Bangemall
COBRA MT AUGUSTUS ROAD
GPS 24°13'03"S 116°25'51"E
Cobra Dry Blowing 2
Mt Augustus
'Mount Augustus'
Jeeaila Pool
Kurugu Pool
Berala Pool
Munjet Pool
Lyons River
Lyons North River
rocky outcrops
Morrisey Hill
Mt Phillips
Mt Samuel
'Mount Phillips'
MOUNT AUGUSTUS (BURRINGURRAH) NATIONAL PARK
Mt Genoa
'Mount Sandiman'
Mt Sandiman
Mt Observation
'Eudamullah'
Onslow Creek
Ynnetharra / Star
Gascoyne / Mt Phillips
Mt Yaragner
Morrissey Hill Mining Centre
Cairn Mining Centre
Mt Candolle
Double Peak
Gas pipeline
LYONS RIVER
Morrisey Hill / Kempton
Yinnetharra / Woodman
Mummil Pool
Yinnetharra
Camel Hill
LANDOR MT AUGUSTUS ROAD
Council Ph (08) 9943 0979
Burringurrah
Fuel: 9am-12noon, 2pm-4.30pm
'Lyons River'
Temple Gorge
Pyramid Hill
'Yinnetharra'
Bubbajilby Pool
Murrumburra Pool
Yinnetharra / Williams
Mount James Aboriginal Res
GPS 24°41'02"S 115°17'42"E
Injinu Hills
Coondoondoo
Police Station Woolshed
Flint Hill
'Waldburg'
WALDBURG ROAD
'Coondoo Outcamp'
COBRA DAIRY CREEK ROAD
Yinnetharra / Kempton Bros
Yinnetharra / Alsop
Mombo Ck
'Mount James' (ruin)
GPS 25°02'59"S 115°12'34"E
Baragooda Pool
Beelu Pool
Bilyarra Pool
Mt James
Yinnetharra / Hester
Madonga Pool
Mt Gascoyne
Ph (08) 9943 0501
Station Stay
'Bidgemia'
Jimba Jimba'
Mt Steere
Aurilla
'Weedarrah'
'Mooloo Downs'
Weedarrah - Bidgemia
Yinnetharra / Poland
LANDOR MOUNT CLERE RD
Gascoyne Junction
Service Station Ph (08) 9943 0504
Fuel : 7am-8pm Mon-Sat, 8am-8pm Sun
Stockyard Pool
Mt Clere
Gascoyne
Mt Dalgety
Dalgety Brook
Mt Puckford
Moorayanunoom Pool
'Landor'
GPS 25°10'19"S 116°56'14"E
Jacobs Gully
Fortress Peak
Pells Ra
'Dalgety Downs'
DALGETY DOWNS LANDOR ROAD
Jingle Creek
'Dairy Creek'
GPS 25°17'22"S 115°51'11"E
CARNARVON MULLEWA ROAD
Dalgety Downs / Richard
Macadam Plains
ERONG ROAD
Bullaroo Hill
CARNARVON MEEKATHARRA RD
Congo Ck
'Glenburgh'
GPS 25°26'05"S 116°05'46"E
'Towrana'
Koolyin Hills
'Errabiddy'
Mt Erong
'Erong Springs'
'Carey Downs'
Cardilya Pool
'Coor-de-wandy' (ruins)
Gas pipeline

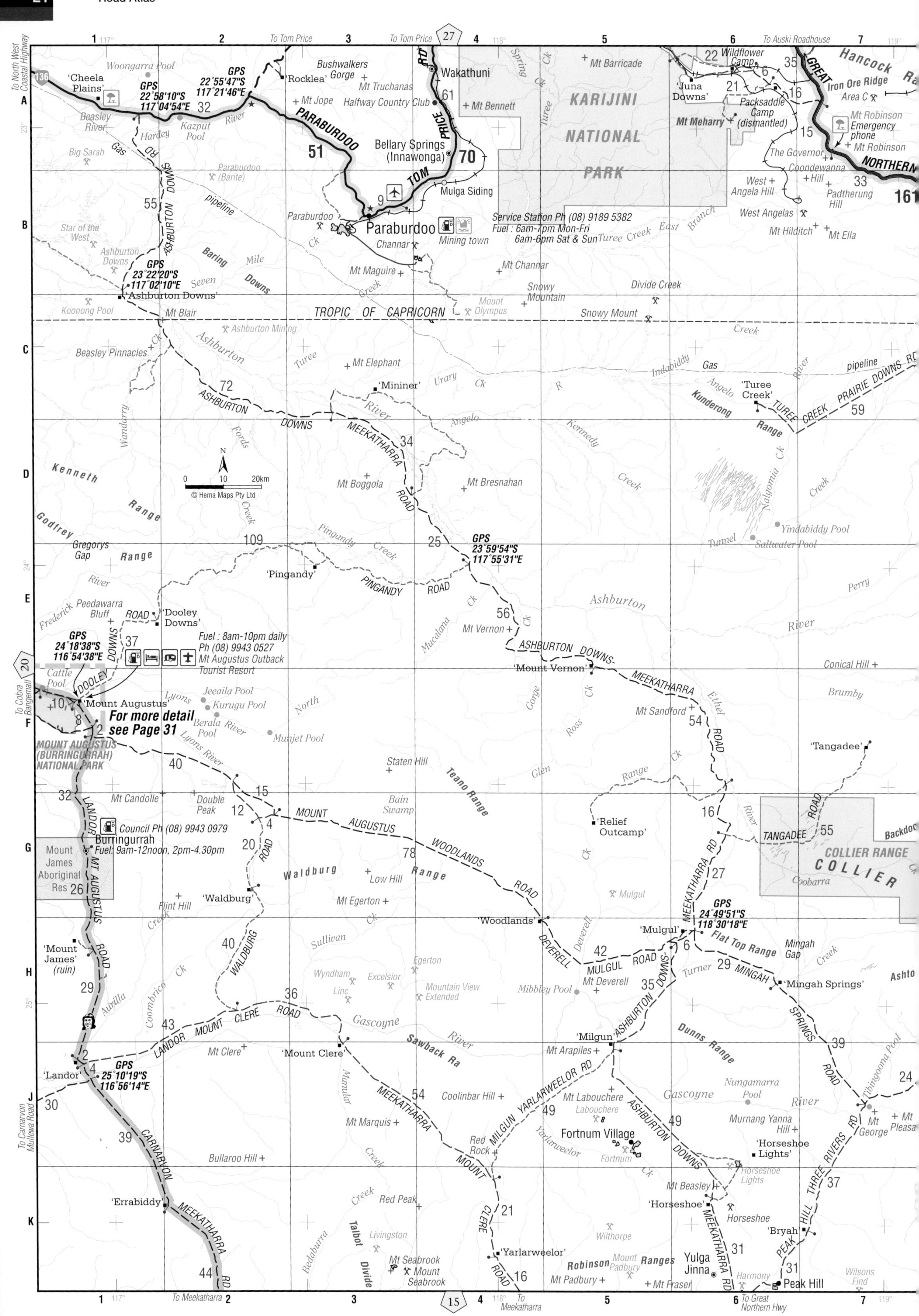
To Tom Price
To Tom Price
To Auski Roadhouse
To North West Coastal Highway
136
Woongarra Pool
'Cheela Plains'
GPS 22°58'10"S 117°04'54"E
GPS 22°55'47"S 117°21'46"E
32
Beasley River
Hardey
Kazput Pool
River
'Rocklea'
Bushwalkers Gorge
Mt Truchanas
Mt Jope
Halfway Country Club
PARABURDOO
51
Wakathuni
61
Mt Bennett
TOM PRICE RD
Bellary Springs (Innawonga)
70
Mulga Siding
9
Paraburdoo
Paraburdoo
Channar
Mining town
Service Station Ph (08) 9189 5382
Fuel : 6am-7pm Mon-Fri
6am-6pm Sat & Sun
Mt Barricade
KARIJINI NATIONAL PARK
Spring Ck
Turee Ck
22 Wildflower Camp
'Juna Downs'
21
6
35
16
Packsaddle Camp (dismantled)
Mt Meharry
15
The Governor
Coondewanna Hill
West Angela Hill
33
Padtherung Hill
West Angelas
Mt Hilditch
Mt Ella
Hancock Ra
GREAT NORTHERN
Iron Ore Ridge Area C
Mt Robinson Emergency phone
Mt Robinson
161
Big Sarah
Gas
Paraburdoo (Barite)
pipeline
ASHBURTON DOWNS RD
55
Star of the West
Ashburton Downs
GPS 23°22'20"S 117°02'10"E
Baring
Mile
Seven
Downs
'Ashburton Downs'
Koonong Pool
Mt Blair
Mt Maguire
Creek
Ck
Mt Channar
Turee Creek
East Branch
Snowy Mountain
Mount Olympus
Divide Creek
Snowy Mount
TROPIC OF CAPRICORN
Ashburton Mining
Beasley Pinnacles
Ashburton
Turee
Mt Elephant
'Mininer'
Urary Ck
Indabiddy
Gas
pipeline
'Turee Creek'
Angelo
Kunderong Range
TUREE CREEK PRAIRIE DOWNS RD
59
72
ASHBURTON DOWNS
River
Angelo
Kennedy
MEEKATHARRA ROAD
34
Wandarry
Fords
Kenneth Range
Mt Boggola
Mt Bresnahan
Creek
Nalgomia Ck
Creek
Godfrey Range
Gregorys Gap
109
Pingandy Creek
25
GPS 23°59'54"S 117°55'31"E
Yindabiddy Pool
Tunnel
Saltwater Pool
'Pingandy'
PINGANDY ROAD
River
Frederick
Peedawarra Bluff
ROAD
'Dooley Downs'
Ashburton
Perry
56
Mt Vernon
Mucalana
GPS 24°18'38"S 116°54'38"E
37
Fuel : 8am-10pm daily
Ph (08) 9943 0527
Mt Augustus Outback Tourist Resort
ASHBURTON DOWNS-
River
Conical Hill
20
Cattle Pool
DOOLEY
'Mount Augustus'
10
8
2
Lyons
Jeeaila Pool
Kurugu Pool
For more detail see Page 31
Berala Pool
River
North
Munjet Pool
'Mount Vernon'
MEEKATHARRA
Gorge
Ck
Ethel
Brumby
Mt Sandford
54
ROAD
Ross
MOUNT AUGUSTUS (BURRINGURRAH) NATIONAL PARK
Lyons River
40
Staten Hill
Teano Range
Glen
Ck
Range
'Tangadee'
32
Mt Candolle
Double Peak
15
12
4
Bain Swamp
MOUNT AUGUSTUS WOODLANDS ROAD
16
River
'Relief Outcamp'
LANDOR
Council Ph (08) 9943 0979
Burringurrah
Fuel: 9am-12noon, 2pm-4.30pm
20
ROAD
78
TANGADEE ROAD
55
Backdoor
COLLIER RANGE
COLLIER
Coobarra
Mount James Aboriginal Res
26
MT AUGUSTUS
Waldburg
Low Hill
Range
ROAD
Ck
MEEKATHARRA RD
27
'Waldburg'
Flint Hill
Mt Egerton
Mulgul
GPS 24°49'51"S 118°30'18"E
Creek
Ck
'Woodlands'
Deverell
'Mulgul'
6
Flat Top Range
Mingah Gap
Creek
'Mount James' (ruin)
40
WALDBURG
Sullivan
Egerton
DEVERELL
42
MULGUL ROAD
29 MINGAH
Turner
Ashto
ROAD
Wyndham
Excelsior
Linc
Mountain View Extended
Mibbley Pool
Mt Deverell
35
'Mingah Springs'
29
Aurilla
Ck
Coombrico
36
LANDOR MOUNT CLERE ROAD
43
Gascoyne
ASHBURTON DOWNS-
Dunns Range
SPRINGS
39
ROAD
Sawback Ra
River
'Milgun'
Mt Clere
'Mount Clere'
Mt Arapiles
2
'Landor'
4
GPS 25°10'19"S 116°56'14"E
Mullar
MEEKATHARRA
54
Coolinbar Hill
MILGUN YARLARWEELOR RD
Mt Labouchere
Labouchere
ASHBURTON
Gascoyne
Nungamarra Pool
River
24
30
49
49
Murnang Yanna Hill
Tibingoona Pool
Mt George
Mt Pleasa
Mt Marquis
Fortnum Village
Yarlarweelor
Fortnum
DOWNS
'Horseshoe Lights'
THREE RIVERS RD
39
CARNARVON
Red Rock
Creek
Bullaroo Hill
Ck
MOUNT
Horseshoe Lights
Mt Beasley
37
'Errabiddy'
Red Peak
Creek
'Horseshoe'
Horseshoe
MEEKATHARRA
CLERE ROAD
21
Livingston
Bedaburra
Talbot Divide
Wilthorpe
'Bryah'
PEAK HILL
Mt Seabrook
Mount Seabrook
'Yarlarweelor'
Robinson Ranges
Mount Padbury
Yulga Jinna
31
31
44
RD
16
Mt Padbury
Mt Fraser
MEEKATHARRA RD
Harmony
Peak Hill
Wilsons Find
To Carnarvon Mullewa Road
To Cobra Bangemall
To Meekatharra
15
To Meekatharra
To Great Northern Hwy
© Hema Maps Pty Ltd

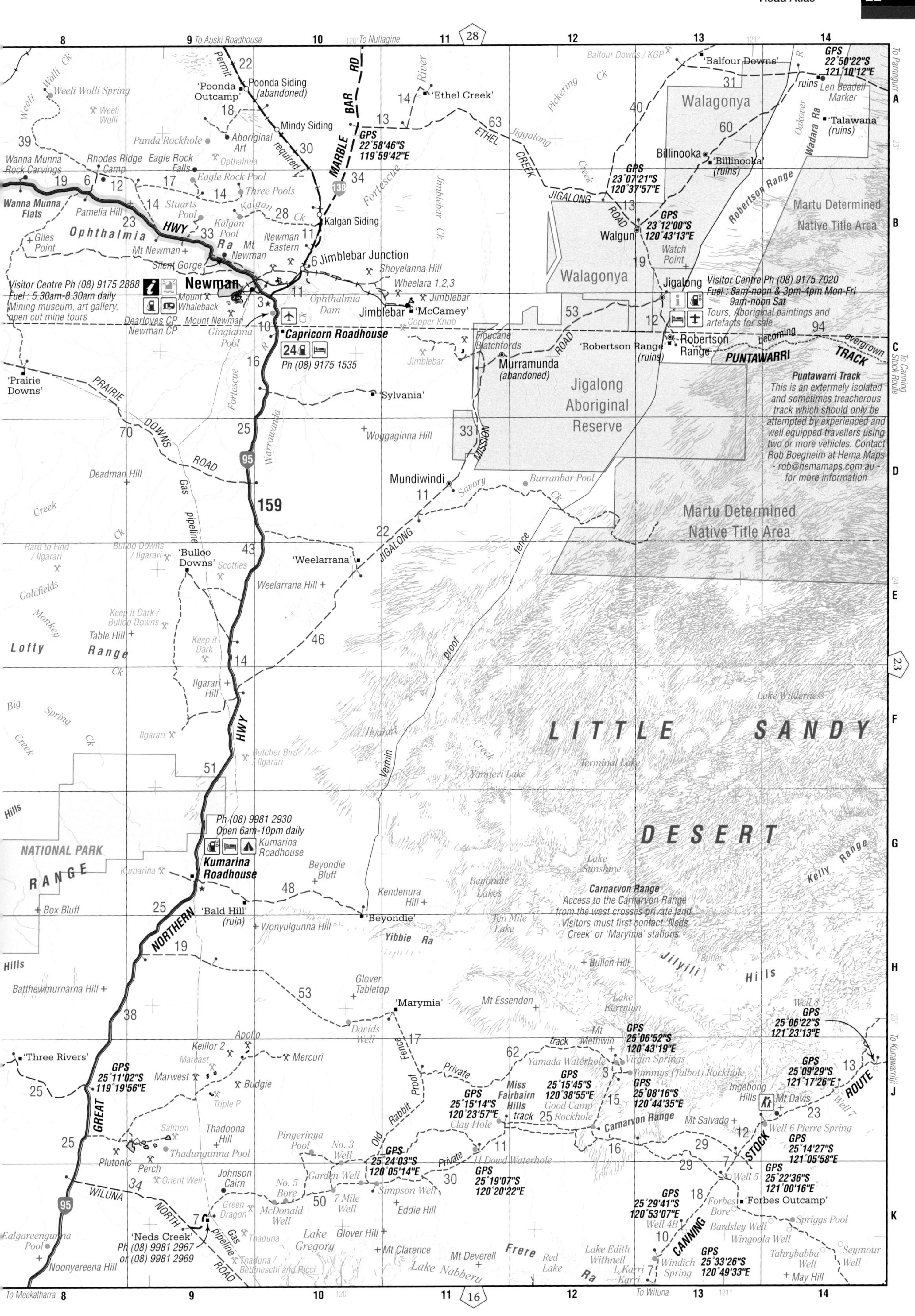
Newman
Visitor Centre Ph (08) 9175 2888
Fuel : 5.30am-8.30am daily
Mining museum, art gallery, open cut mine tours
Capricorn Roadhouse
Ph (08) 9175 1535
Jigalong
Visitor Centre Ph (08) 9175 7020
Fuel : 8am-noon & 3pm-4pm Mon-Fri 9am-noon Sat
Tours, Aboriginal paintings and artefacts for sale
Puntawarri Track
This is an extermely isolated and sometimes treacherous track which should only be attempted by experienced and well equipped travellers using two or more vehicles. Contact Rob Boegheim at Hema Maps - rob@hemamaps.com.au - for more information
Martu Determined Native Title Area
Jigalong Aboriginal Reserve
Walagonya
LITTLE SANDY DESERT
Kumarina Roadhouse
Ph (08) 9981 2930
Open 6am-10pm daily
Carnarvon Range
Access to the Carnarvon Range from the west crosses private land. Visitors must first contact 'Neds Creek' or 'Marymia' stations.
'Neds Creek'
Ph (08) 9981 2967 or (08) 9981 2969
GREAT NORTHERN HWY
CANNING STOCK ROUTE
To Meekatharra
To Wiluna
To Nullagine
To Auski Roadhouse
To Parngurr
To Kunawarritji
To Canning Stock Route

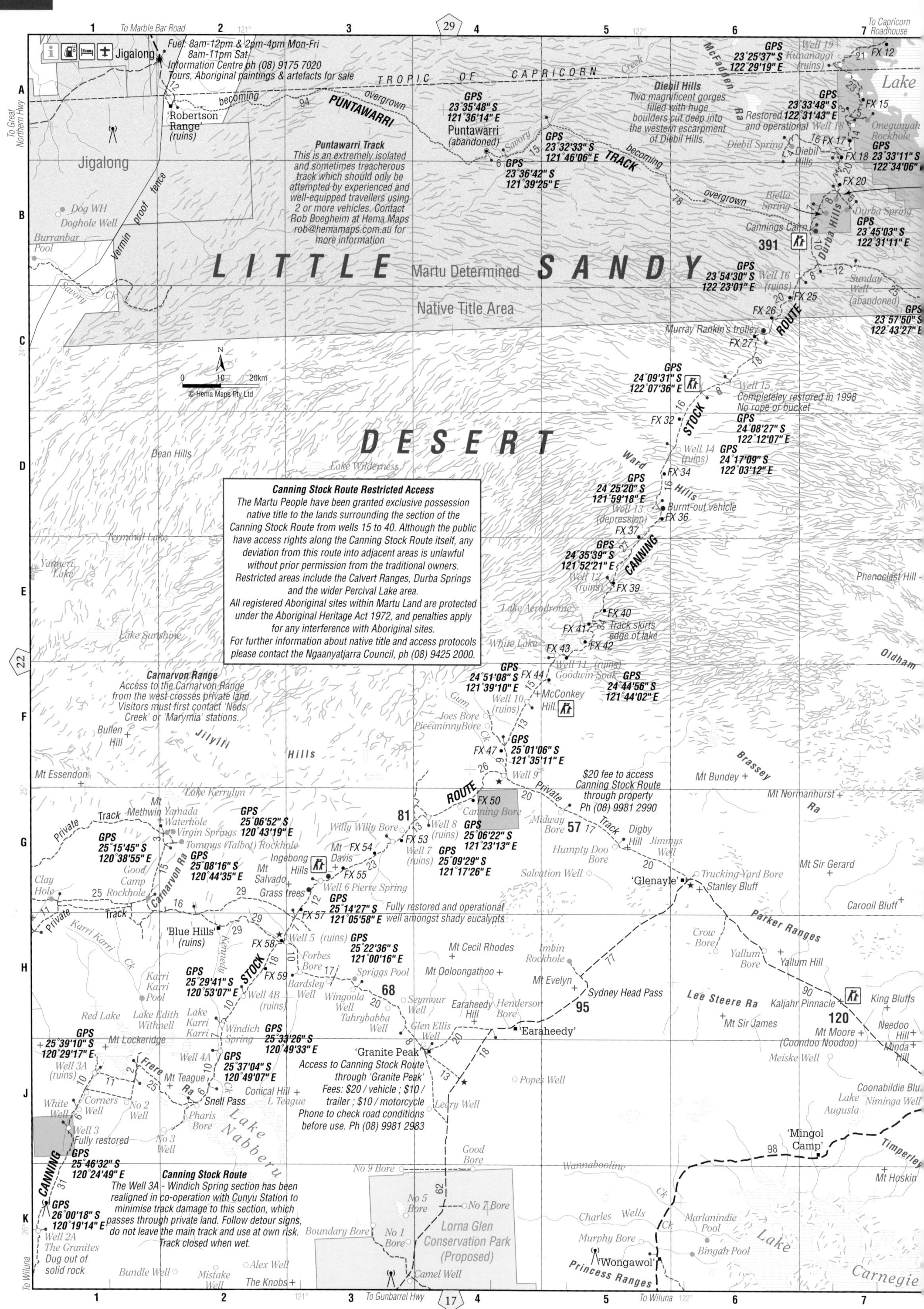
Jigalong
Fuel: 8am-12pm & 2pm-4pm Mon-Fri
8am-11pm Sat
Information Centre ph (08) 9175 7020
Tours, Aboriginal paintings & artefacts for sale
TROPIC OF CAPRICORN
PUNTAWARRI TRACK
Puntawarri Track
This is an extremely isolated and sometimes treacherous track which should only be attempted by experienced and well-equipped travellers using 2 or more vehicles. Contact Rob Boegheim at Hema Maps rob@hemamaps.com.au for more information
Diebil Hills
Two magnificent gorges filled with huge boulders cut deep into the western escarpment of Diebil Hills.
LITTLE SANDY DESERT
Martu Determined Native Title Area
Canning Stock Route Restricted Access
The Martu People have been granted exclusive possession native title to the lands surrounding the section of the Canning Stock Route from wells 15 to 40. Although the public have access rights along the Canning Stock Route itself, any deviation from this route into adjacent areas is unlawful without prior permission from the traditional owners.
Restricted areas include the Calvert Ranges, Durba Springs and the wider Percival Lake area.
All registered Aboriginal sites within Martu Land are protected under the Aboriginal Heritage Act 1972, and penalties apply for any interference with Aboriginal sites.
For further information about native title and access protocols please contact the Ngaanyatjarra Council, ph (08) 9425 2000.
Carnarvon Range
Access to the Carnarvon Range from the west crosses private land. Visitors must first contact 'Neds Creek' or 'Marymia' stations.
CANNING STOCK ROUTE
$20 fee to access Canning Stock Route through property Ph (08) 9981 2990
Fully restored and operational well amongst shady eucalypts
Access to Canning Stock Route through 'Granite Peak'
Fees: $20 / vehicle ; $10 / trailer ; $10 / motorcycle
Phone to check road conditions before use. Ph (08) 9981 2983
Canning Stock Route
The Well 3A - Windich Spring section has been realigned in co-operation with Cunyu Station to minimise track damage to this section, which passes through private land. Follow detour signs, do not leave the main track and use at own risk. Track closed when wet.
Well 15 Completeley restored in 1998 No rope or bucket
Lorna Glen Conservation Park (Proposed)
To Marble Bar Road
To Capricorn Roadhouse
To Great Northern Hwy
To Wiluna
To Gunbarrel Hwy
© Hema Maps Pty Ltd

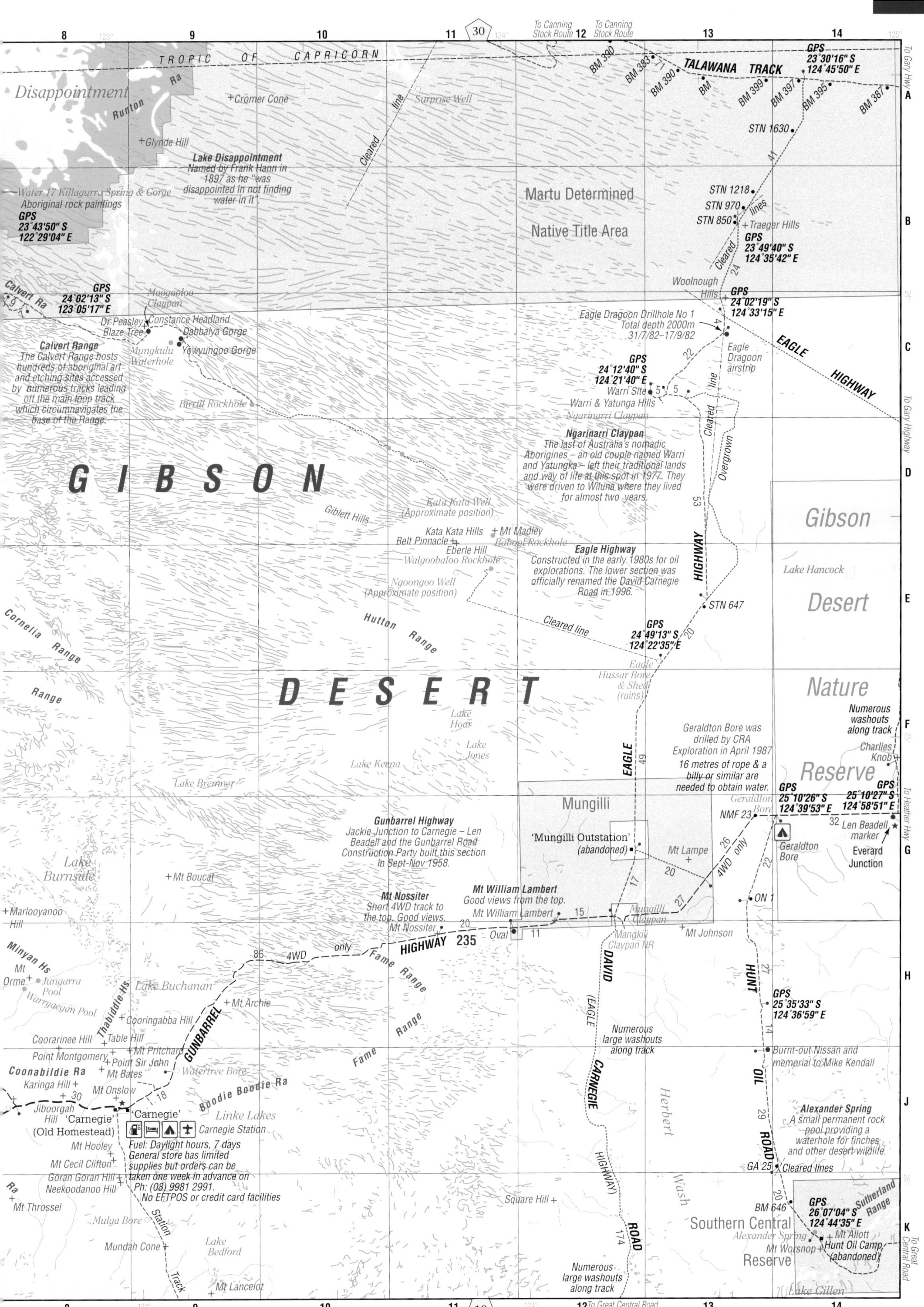
TROPIC OF CAPRICORN
Disappointment
Runton Ra
Cromer Cone
Surprise Well
Glynde Hill
Lake Disappointment
Named by Frank Hann in 1897 as he "was disappointed in not finding water in it".
Water 17 Killagurra Spring & Gorge
Aboriginal rock paintings
GPS 23°43'50" S 122°29'04" E
Martu Determined Native Title Area
TALAWANA TRACK
GPS 23°30'16" S 124°45'50" E
To Canning Stock Route
Calvert Ra
GPS 24°02'13" S 123°05'17" E
Dr Peasley Blaze Tree
Constance Headland
Dabbalya Gorge
Yowyungoo Gorge
Calvert Range
The Calvert Range hosts hundreds of aboriginal art and etching sites accessed by numerous tracks leading off the main loop track which circumnavigates the base of the Range.
Eagle Dragoon Drillhole No 1
Total depth 2000m
31/7/82–17/9/82
GPS 24°02'19" S 124°33'15" E
GPS 23°49'40" S 124°35'42" E
EAGLE HIGHWAY
GPS 24°12'40" S 124°21'40" E
Warri Site
Warri & Yatunga Hills
Ngarinarri Claypan
The last of Australia's nomadic Aborigines – an old couple named Warri and Yatungka – left their traditional lands and way of life at this spot in 1977. They were driven to Wiluna where they lived for almost two years.
GIBSON DESERT
Eagle Highway
Constructed in the early 1980s for oil explorations. The lower section was officially renamed the David Carnegie Road in 1996.
GPS 24°49'13" S 124°22'35" E
Gibson Desert Nature Reserve
Geraldton Bore was drilled by CRA Exploration in April 1987
16 metres of rope & a billy or similar are needed to obtain water.
GPS 25°10'26" S 124°39'53" E
GPS 25°10'27" S 124°58'51" E
Len Beadell marker
Everard Junction
Mungilli
'Mungilli Outstation' (abandoned)
Gunbarrel Highway
Jackie Junction to Carnegie – Len Beadell and the Gunbarrel Road Construction Party built this section in Sept-Nov 1958.
Mt Nossiter
Short 4WD track to the top. Good views.
Mt William Lambert
Good views from the top.
HIGHWAY 235
DAVID CARNEGIE ROAD (EAGLE HIGHWAY)
HUNT OIL ROAD
GPS 25°35'33" S 124°36'59" E
Burnt-out Nissan and memorial to Mike Kendall
Alexander Spring
A small permanent rock pool providing a waterhole for finches and other desert wildlife.
GPS 26°07'04" S 124°44'35" E
Hunt Oil Camp (abandoned)
Southern Central Reserve
'Carnegie' (Old Homestead)
Carnegie Station
Fuel: Daylight hours, 7 days
General store has limited supplies but orders can be taken one week in advance on Ph: (08) 9981 2991.
No EFTPOS or credit card facilities
Numerous large washouts along track
To Great Central Road
To Gary Hwy
To Heather Hwy

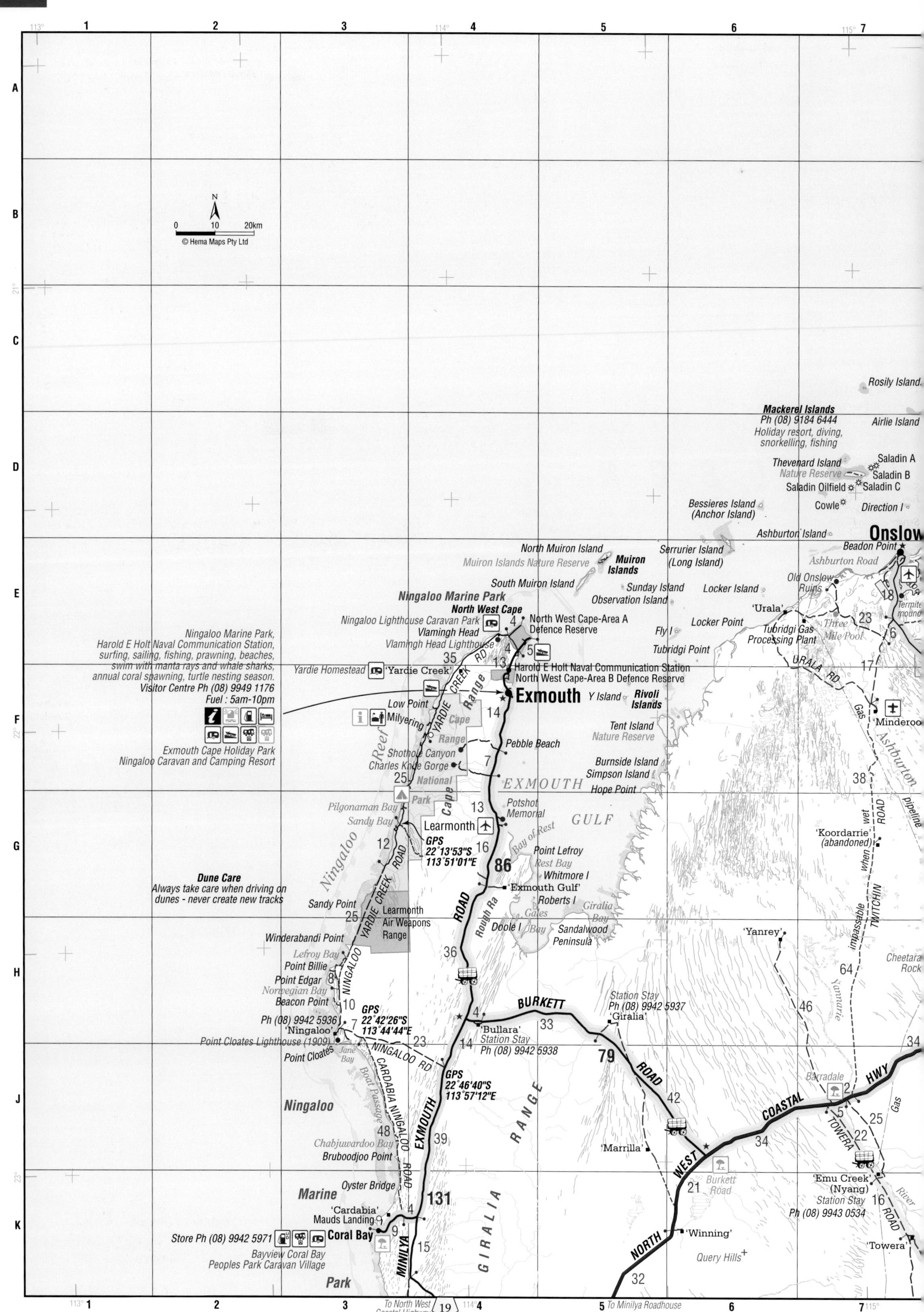
© Hema Maps Pty Ltd
Onslow
Exmouth
Coral Bay
Ningaloo Marine Park
North West Cape
Mackerel Islands
Ph (08) 9184 6444
Holiday resort, diving, snorkelling, fishing
Ningaloo Marine Park, Harold E Holt Naval Communication Station, surfing, sailing, fishing, prawning, beaches, swim with manta rays and whale sharks, annual coral spawning, turtle nesting season.
Visitor Centre Ph (08) 9949 1176
Fuel : 5am-10pm
Exmouth Cape Holiday Park
Ningaloo Caravan and Camping Resort
Dune Care
Always take care when driving on dunes - never create new tracks
Store Ph (08) 9942 5971
Bayview Coral Bay
Peoples Park Caravan Village
Learmonth
GPS 22°13'53"S 113°51'01"E
GPS 22°42'26"S 113°44'44"E
GPS 22°46'40"S 113°57'12"E
Station Stay Ph (08) 9942 5937
'Bullara' Station Stay Ph (08) 9942 5938
'Emu Creek' (Nyang) Station Stay Ph (08) 9943 0534
Cape Range National Park
Exmouth Gulf
Giralia Range
To North West Coastal Highway
To Minilya Roadhouse

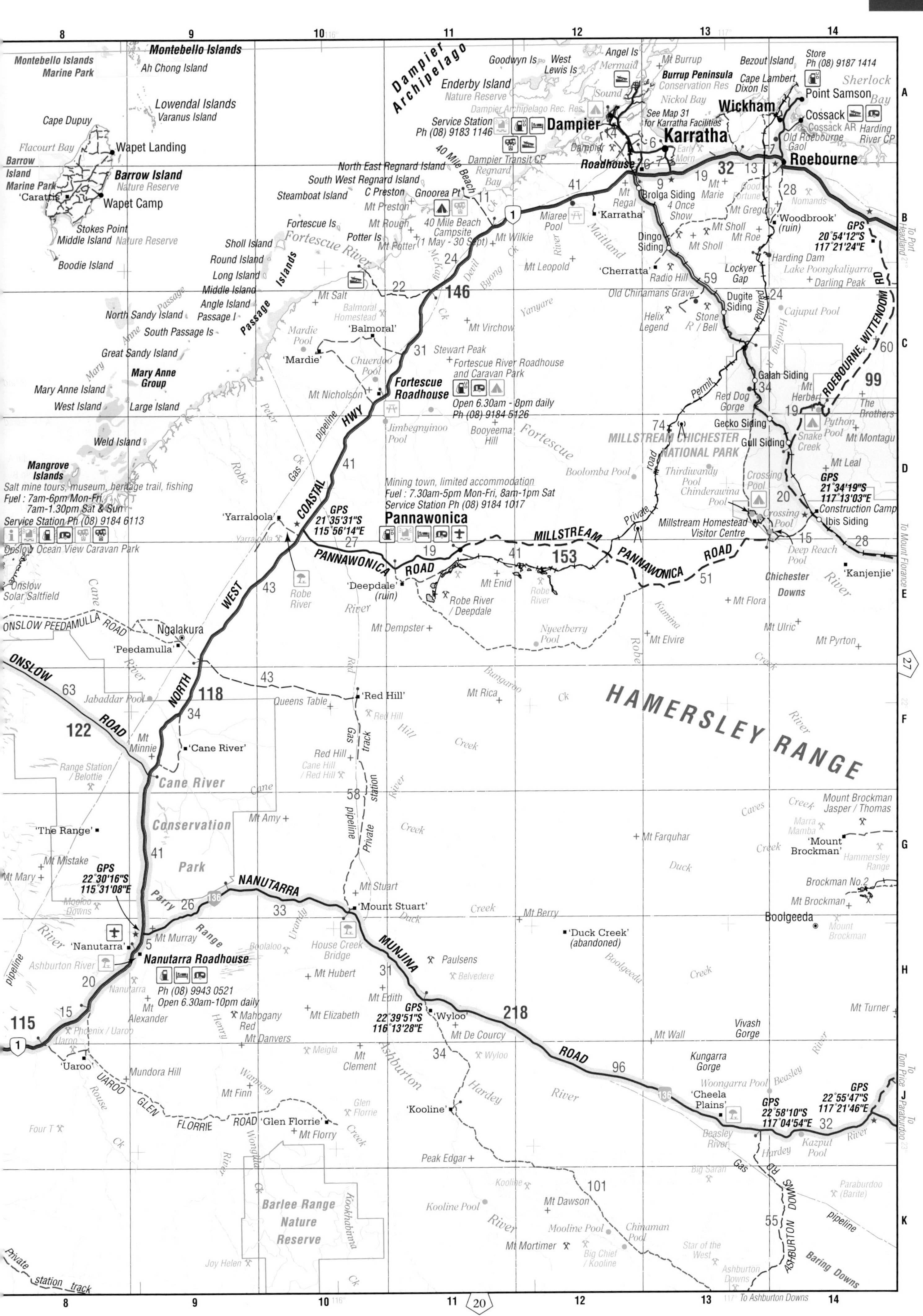
Montebello Islands
Montebello Islands Marine Park
Ah Chong Island
Lowendal Islands
Varanus Island
Cape Dupuy
Wapet Landing
Barrow Island Marine Park
Barrow Island Nature Reserve
Wapet Camp
Stokes Point
Middle Island Nature Reserve
Boodie Island
Dampier Archipelago
Enderby Island Nature Reserve
Service Station Ph (08) 9183 1146
Dampier
Karratha
Wickham
Point Samson
Cossack
Roebourne
Burrup Peninsula Conservation Res
Fortescue Roadhouse
Open 6.30am - 8pm daily Ph (08) 9184 5126
Fortescue River Roadhouse and Caravan Park
Pannawonica
Mining town, limited accommodation
Fuel : 7.30am-5pm Mon-Fri, 8am-1pm Sat
Service Station Ph (08) 9184 1017
MILLSTREAM CHICHESTER NATIONAL PARK
Millstream Homestead Visitor Centre
Salt mine tours, museum, heritage trail, fishing
Fuel : 7am-6pm Mon-Fri, 7am-1.30pm Sat & Sun
Service Station Ph (08) 9184 6113
Onslow Ocean View Caravan Park
ONSLOW ROAD
NORTH WEST COASTAL HWY
PANNAWONICA ROAD
MILLSTREAM PANNAWONICA ROAD
ROEBOURNE WITTENOOM RD
HAMERSLEY RANGE
Cane River Conservation Park
NANUTARRA MUNJINA ROAD
Nanutarra Roadhouse
Ph (08) 9943 0521 Open 6.30am-10pm daily
Barlee Range Nature Reserve
UAROO GLEN FLORRIE ROAD
ASHBURTON DOWNS RD
To Port Hedland
To Mount Florance
To Tom Price
To Paraburdoo
To Ashburton Downs
GPS 22°30'16"S 115°31'08"E
GPS 21°35'31"S 115°56'14"E
GPS 20°54'12"S 117°21'24"E
GPS 21°34'19"S 117°13'03"E
GPS 22°39'51"S 116°13'28"E
GPS 22°58'10"S 117°04'54"E
GPS 22°55'47"S 117°21'46"E

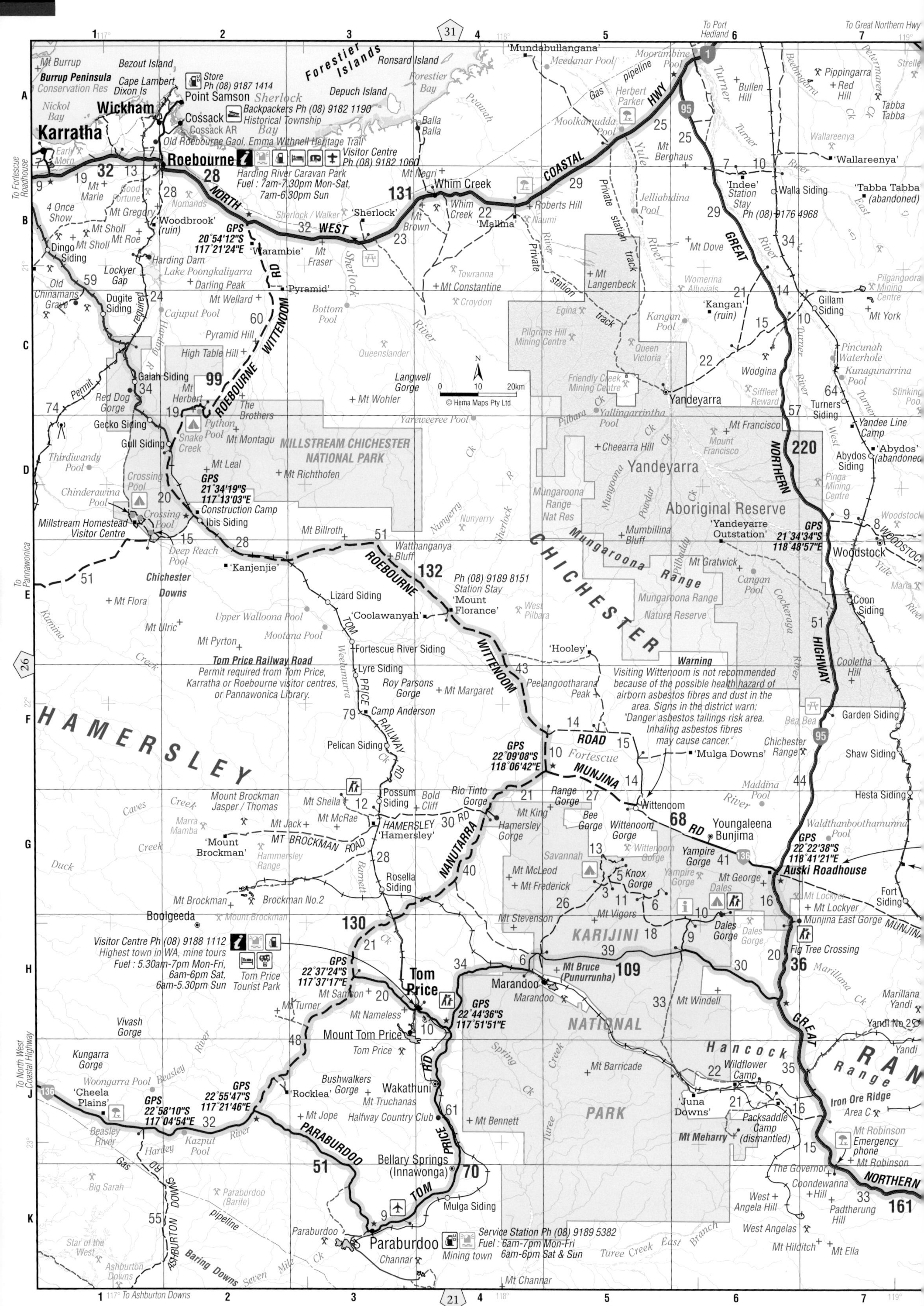
Karratha
Wickham
Point Samson
Cossack
Roebourne
Whim Creek
Yandeyarra
Wittenoom
Tom Price
Paraburdoo
Auski Roadhouse
Woodstock
MILLSTREAM CHICHESTER NATIONAL PARK
HAMERSLEY
CHICHESTER
Yandeyarra Aboriginal Reserve
KARIJINI NATIONAL PARK
Warning
Visiting Wittenoom is not recommended because of the possible health hazard of airborn asbestos fibres and dust in the area. Signs in the district warn: "Danger asbestos tailings risk area. Inhaling asbestos fibres may cause cancer."
Tom Price Railway Road
Permit required from Tom Price, Karratha or Roebourne visitor centres, or Pannawonica Library.
Visitor Centre Ph (08) 9188 1112
Highest town in WA, mine tours
Fuel : 5.30am-7pm Mon-Fri, 6am-6pm Sat, 6am-5.30pm Sun
Service Station Ph (08) 9189 5382
Fuel : 6am-7pm Mon-Fri 6am-6pm Sat & Sun
Harding River Caravan Park
Fuel : 7am-7.30pm Mon-Sat, 7am-6.30pm Sun
Visitor Centre Ph (08) 9182 1060
Store Ph (08) 9187 1414
Backpackers Ph (08) 9182 1190
Historical Township
Old Roebourne Gaol, Emma Withnell Heritage Trail
Ph (08) 9189 8151 Station Stay 'Mount Florance'
Ph (08) 9176 4968
© Hema Maps Pty Ltd

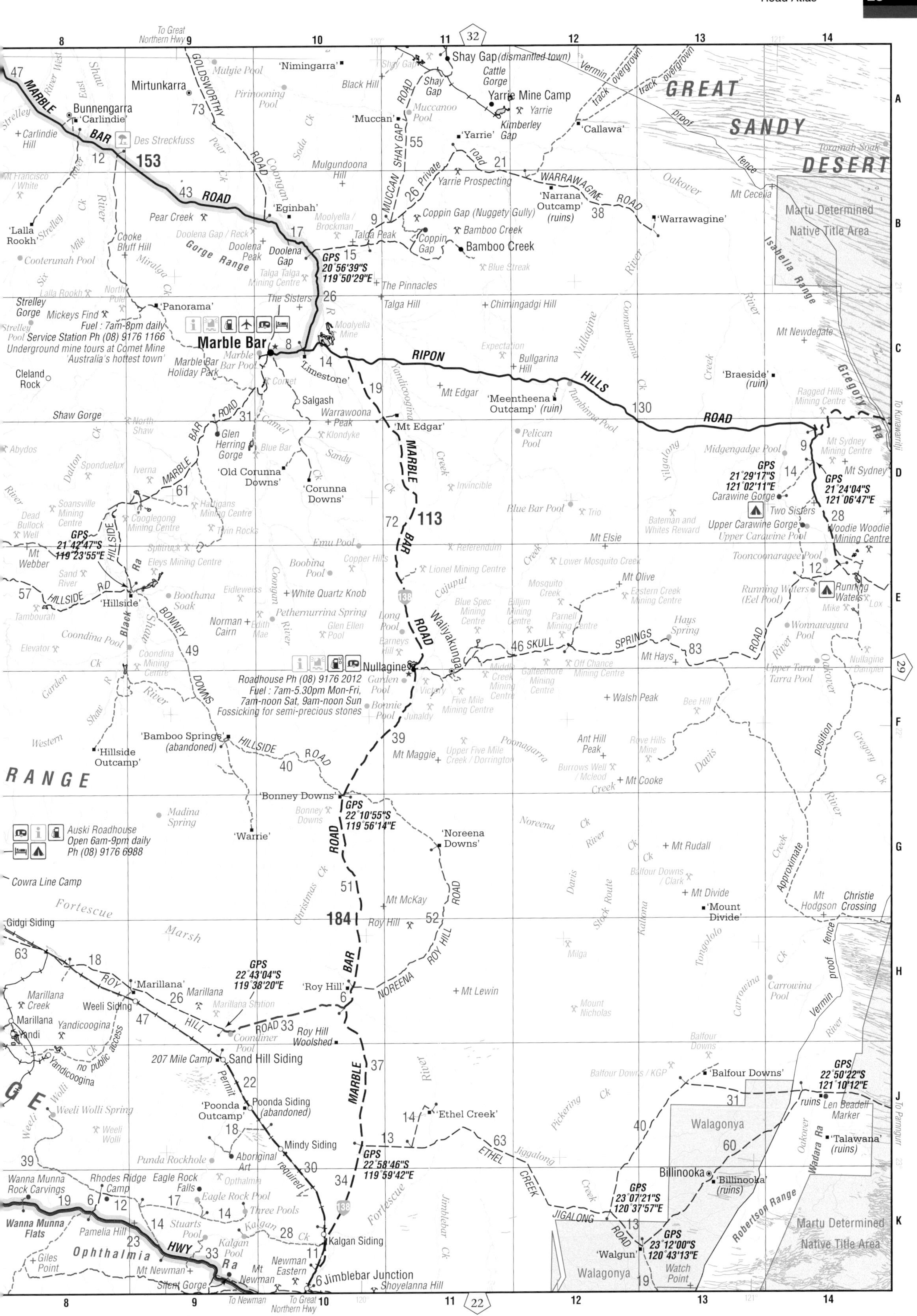
To Great Northern Hwy
GREAT SANDY DESERT
Martu Determined Native Title Area
Shay Gap (dismantled town)
Cattle Gorge
Yarrie Mine Camp
Yarrie
Kimberley Gap
'Callawa'
Vermin track overgrown
proof fence
Toramah Soak
'Nimingarra'
Mulgie Pool
Mirtunkarra
Bunnengarra
'Carlindie'
Carlindie Hill
MARBLE BAR ROAD
153
Des Streckfuss
GOLDSWORTHY ROAD
Pirinooning Pool
Black Hill
'Muccan'
Muccanoo Pool
SHAY GAP ROAD
MUCCAN
'Yarrie'
Mulgundoona Hill
Private road
Yarrie Prospecting
WARRAWAGINE ROAD
'Narrana Outcamp' (ruins)
'Warrawagine'
Oakover River
Mt Cecelia
Isabella Range
'Lalla Rookh'
Pear Creek
'Egginbah'
Moolyella / Brockman
Coppin Gap (Nuggety Gully)
Bamboo Creek
Coppin Gap
Talga Peak
Cooke Bluff Hill
Doolena Gap / Reck
Doolena Peak
Doolena Gap
Gorge Range
GPS 20°56'39"S 119°50'29"E
Cooterunah Pool
Talga Talga Mining Centre
The Pinnacles
Blue Streak
Lalla Rookh
North Pole
Strelley Gorge
Mickeys Find
'Panorama'
The Sisters
Talga Hill
Chimingadgi Hill
Coonambunna Ck
Nullagine River
Mt Newdegate
Fuel: 7am-8pm daily
Service Station Ph (08) 9176 1166
Underground mine tours at Comet Mine
'Australia's hottest town'
Marble Bar
Moolyella Mine
Marble Bar Holiday Park
Marble Bar Pool
Cleland Rock
'Limestone'
RIPON HILLS ROAD
Expectation
Bullgarina Hill
'Braeside' (ruin)
Gregory Ra
Comet
Salgash
Mt Edgar
'Meentheena Outcamp' (ruin)
Ragged Hills Mining Centre
To Kunawarritji
Shaw Gorge
Warrawoona Peak
'Mt Edgar'
Turnbing Pool
130
Glen Herring Gorge
Blue Bar
Klondyke
Pelican Pool
Midgengadge Pool
Mt Sydney Mining Centre
Mt Sydney
Abydos
'Old Corunna Downs'
'Corunna Downs'
Invincible
GPS 21°29'17"S 121°02'11"E
Carawine Gorge
GPS 21°24'04"S 121°06'47"E
Two Sisters
Soansville Mining Centre
Cooglegong Mining Centre
Hatigans Mining Centre
Twin Rocks
113
Blue Bar Pool
Trio
Bateman and Whites Reward
Upper Carawine Gorge
Upper Carawine Pool
Woodie Woodie Mining Centre
Dead Bullock Well
GPS 21°42'47"S 119°23'55"E
Mt Webber
Eleys Mining Centre
Emu Pool
Copper Hills
Referendum
Mt Elsie
Lower Mosquito Creek
Tooncoonaragee Pool
HILLSIDE RD
Boobina Pool
Lionel Mining Centre
Mt Olive
'Hillside'
Boothana Soak
Eidleweiss
White Quartz Knob
Cajuput
Mosquito Creek
Eastern Creek Mining Centre
Running Waters (Eel Pool)
Running Waters
Tambourah
Pethernurrina Spring
Glen Ellen Pool
Long Pool
Blue Spec Mining Centre
Billjim Mining Centre
Parnell Mining Centre
Hays Spring
Wonnawaywa Pool
Coondina Pool
Norman Cairn
Edith Mae
Waliyakunga
SKULL SPRINGS ROAD
Mt Hays
Nullagine Damper
Elevator
Coondina Mining Centre
BONNEY DOWNS
Barneys Hill
Roadhouse Ph (08) 9176 2012
Fuel: 7am-5.30pm Mon-Fri, 7am-noon Sat, 9am-noon Sun
Fossicking for semi-precious stones
Nullagine
Garden Pool
Victory
Five Mile Mining Centre
Middle Creek Mining Centre
Gallemore Mining Centre
Off Chance Mining Centre
Upper Tarra Tarra Pool
Walsh Peak
Bee Hill
Bonnie Pool
Junaldy
'Hillside Outcamp'
'Bamboo Springs' (abandoned)
HILLSIDE ROAD
Mt Maggie
Upper Five Mile Creek / Dorrington
Poonagarra
Ant Hill Peak
Rose Hills Mine
Burrows Well / Mcleod
Mt Cooke
Davis
approximate position
RANGE
'Bonney Downs'
Bonney Downs
GPS 22°10'55"S 119°56'14"E
Madina Spring
'Warrie'
Noreena
'Noreena Downs'
Mt Rudall
Auski Roadhouse
Open 6am-9pm daily
Ph (08) 9176 6988
Cowra Line Camp
Fortescue Marsh
Christmas Ck
Mt McKay
ROY HILL ROAD
Balfour Downs / Clark
Mt Divide
'Mount Divide'
Stock Route
Kalkuna
Tongololo
Mt Hodgson
Christie Crossing
Gidgi Siding
Roy Hill
184
Milga
NOREENA
'Roy Hill'
Mt Lewin
Carrowina Pool
GPS 22°43'04"S 119°38'20"E
ROY HILL ROAD
'Marillana'
Marillana
Marillana Station
Weeli Siding
Marillana Creek
Yandicoogina
Yandi
Coondiner Pool
Roy Hill Woolshed
Mount Nicholas
Balfour Downs
no public access
207 Mile Camp
Sand Hill Siding
Permit required
Balfour Downs / KGP
'Balfour Downs'
GPS 22°50'22"S 121°10'12"E
Len Beadell Marker
ruins
Weeli Wolli Spring
'Poonda Outcamp'
Poonda Siding (abandoned)
'Ethel Creek'
Walagonya
'Talawana' (ruins)
Weeli Wolli
Mindy Siding
ETHEL CREEK
Jiggalong
Punda Rockhole
Aboriginal Art
GPS 22°58'46"S 119°59'42"E
Billinooka
'Billinooka' (ruins)
Wadara Ra
Robertson Range
Wanna Munna Rock Carvings
Rhodes Ridge Camp
Eagle Rock Falls
Opthalmia
Eagle Rock Pool
Three Pools
JIGALONG ROAD
GPS 23°07'21"S 120°37'57"E
GPS 23°12'00"S 120°43'13"E
Wanna Munna Flats
Pamelia Hill
Stuarts Pool
Kalgan
Kalgan Pool
Kalgan Siding
'Walgun'
Watch Point
Giles Point
Ophthalmia Ra
HWY
Mt Newman
Newman Eastern
Jimblebar Junction
Shoyelanna Hill
Silent Gorge
To Newman
To Great Northern Hwy
To Parnngurr
Jimblebar Ck

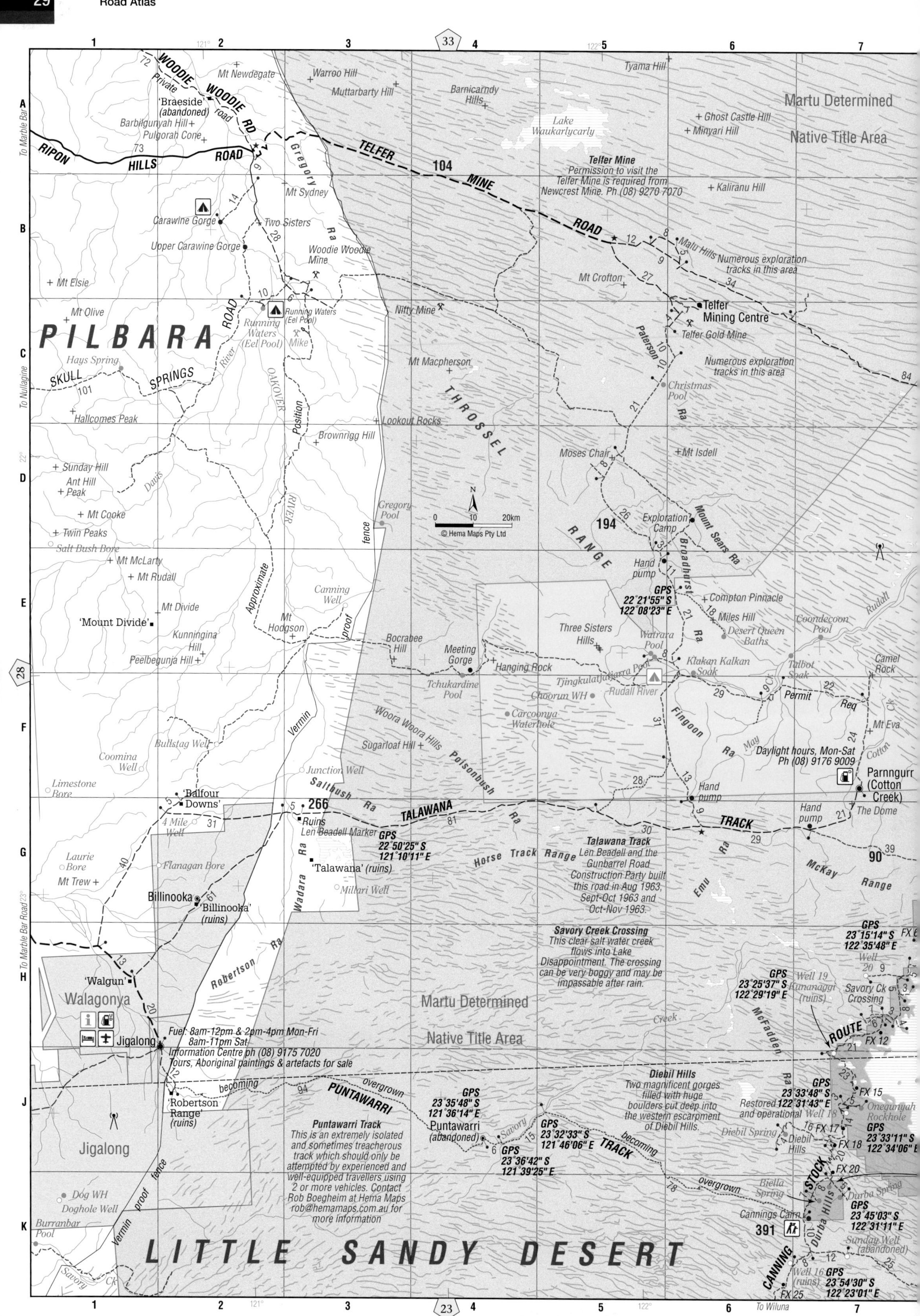
PILBARA
LITTLE SANDY DESERT
Martu Determined Native Title Area
WOODIE WOODIE RD
RIPON HILLS ROAD
TELFER MINE ROAD
SKULL SPRINGS ROAD
TALAWANA TRACK
PUNTAWARRI TRACK
CANNING STOCK ROUTE
THROSSEL RANGE
Telfer Mine
Permission to visit the Telfer Mine is required from Newcrest Mine. Ph (08) 9270 7070
Telfer Mining Centre
Telfer Gold Mine
Numerous exploration tracks in this area
Talawana Track
Len Beadell and the Gunbarrel Road Construction Party built this road in Aug 1963, Sept-Oct 1963 and Oct-Nov 1963.
Savory Creek Crossing
This clear salt water creek flows into Lake Disappointment. The crossing can be very boggy and may be impassable after rain.
Diebil Hills
Two magnificent gorges filled with huge boulders cut deep into the western escarpment of Diebil Hills.
Puntawarri Track
This is an extremely isolated and sometimes treacherous track which should only be attempted by experienced and well-equipped travellers using 2 or more vehicles. Contact Rob Boegheim at Hema Maps rob@hemamaps.com.au for more information
Fuel: 8am-12pm & 2pm-4pm Mon-Fri
8am-11pm Sat
Information Centre ph (08) 9175 7020
Tours, Aboriginal paintings & artefacts for sale
Jigalong
Walagonya
'Walgun'
Billinooka
'Robertson Range' (ruins)
'Talawana' (ruins)
'Balfour Downs'
'Mount Divide'
'Braeside' (abandoned)
Carawine Gorge
Upper Carawine Gorge
Running Waters (Eel Pool)
Woodie Woodie Mine
Nifty Mine
Lake Waukarlycarly
Mt Crofton
Christmas Pool
Moses Chair
Mt Isdell
Exploration Camp
Mount Sears Ra
Hand pump
GPS 22°21'55" S 122°08'23" E
Three Sisters Hills
Watrara Pool
Rudall River
Parnngurr (Cotton Creek)
Daylight hours, Mon-Sat Ph (08) 9176 9009
The Dome
McKay Range
Horse Track Range
Emu Ra
McFadden Ra
Durba Hills
Cannings Cairn
Len Beadell Marker
GPS 22°50'25" S 121°10'11" E
GPS 23°35'48" S 121°36'14" E
Puntawarri (abandoned)
GPS 23°32'33" S 121°46'06" E
GPS 23°36'42" S 121°39'25" E
GPS 23°25'37" S 122°29'19" E
GPS 23°15'14" S 122°35'48" E
GPS 23°33'48" S 122°31'43" E
GPS 23°33'11" S 122°34'06" E
GPS 23°45'03" S 122°31'11" E
GPS 23°54'30" S 122°23'01" E
Restored and operational Well 18
Savory Ck Crossing
Sunday Well (abandoned)
To Marble Bar
To Nullagine
To Marble Bar Road
To Wiluna
© Hema Maps Pty Ltd

Rudall River National Park
Rudall was a government surveyor who lead the search party for the lost members of the 1896 Calvert Expedition. He explored the river's length during the search in 1897. The Rudall River is known by the Aboriginal people as Waturarra (upper reaches) and Karlamilyi (lower reaches).
Gindarjarie Native Well (Approximate position)
FV65
FV66
Mendigigil Rockhole (Approximate position)
GPS 21°22'37" S 123°26'22" E
Bore and windmill
Bremner Peak
Sahara Well (Approximate position)
LAKES
PERCIVAL
Old lake bed
Old track – mostly overgrown
Twin Gum Hill
Cleared lines
Windmill & tank
GPS 21°33'13" S 123°21'42" E
Earsen Claypan
Picture Hill
GPS 21°40'59" S 123°42'19" E
Martu Determined Native Title Area
FV77
Old lake beds
Numerous gravel scrapes next to track
FV78
Overgrown
FV79
FV80
FV81
Numerous small claypans – impassable in wet
Canning Stock Route (CSR)
From 1906-08 Alfred Canning and his team surveyed the Stock Route and built the 51 wells along its 1600km length. Travelling the CSR is Australia's greatest Desert Tracks adventure. Extra care is required on large sandhills, extreme corrugations & patches of very soft sand. Take care of the wells & replace well lids.
Fuel: 8am-5pm Mon-Fri
Available 24 hrs upon request
Hot showers $5
Aboriginal Art Souvenir shop
Ph (08) 9176 9040
Kunawarritji Aboriginal Community
Camping Area
216
Daylight hours Ph (08) 9176 9006
Punmu
Lake Dora
Rudall River (Karlamilyi) National Park
GPS 22°06'23" S 123°45'19" E
WAPET D47
Rocky knoll
FV83
GPS 22°15'33" S 124°54'09" E
GPS 22°19'44" S 124°43'38" E
Well 34 Nibil (ruins)
WAPET ROAD (KIDSON TRACK)
113
FV84
FV85
FV87
FV88
FV90
FV92
FV93
FV94
Rocky outcrops
Wa Wa Bore (aband)
Kunawarritji Community
Wa Wa Bore
Well 33 Gunowaggi
Kunawarritji Airstrip
Mallowa Native Well
Lake Auld
GPS 22°30'15" S 124°08'23" E
Nangabbittajarra Native Well
Well 30 Dunda Jimnda (ruins)
Heavily corrugated
Well 32 (abandoned)
JENKINS TRACK
To Gary Junction
GPS 22°24'22" S 124°35'08" E
Lake Blanche
Scott Bluff
GPS 22°33'17" S 123°52'44" E
Tabletop
Well 29 (ruins)
King Hill
ROUTE 253
Mujingerra Cave
Nurgurga Soak
Well 31 (ruins)
Windmill and tank
GPS 22°31'32" S 124°24'26" E
GPS 22°32'33" S 124°54'35" E
Thring Rock
Lake George
No 11 Bore
Cleared line
Well 28 (ruins)
GPS 22°47'41" S 123°38'39" E
STOCK
GPS 22°38'35" S 123°45'26" E
Well 27 (ruins)
Lake Winifred
Helen Hill
GPS 22°51'03" S 124°00'57" E
Separation Well
Canning Stock Route Restricted Access
The Martu People have been granted exclusive possession native title to the lands surrounding the section of the Canning Stock Route from wells 15 to 40. Although the public have access rights along the Canning Stock Route itself, any deviation from this route into adjacent areas is unlawful without prior permission from the traditional owners. Restricted areas include the Calvert Ranges, Durba Springs and the wider Percival Lake area.
All registered Aboriginal sites within Martu Land are protected under the Aboriginal Heritage Act 1972, and penalties apply for any interference with Aboriginal sites.
For further information about native title and access protocols please contact the Ngaanyatjarra Council, ph (08) 9425 2000.
Canning Camp (1907)
Small hill
Slate Range
Separation Well
Separation Well was first discovered by Wells in 1896 during the Calvert Expedition and re-discovered in 1979 by a group retracing the explorer's footsteps
Harbutt Range
GPS 22°58'58" S 123°23'48" E
CANNING
Well 26 (Tiwa Well)
Restored and operational
GPS 23°04'45" S 123°13'14" E
Well 25 (ruins)
GPS 22°54'58" S 123°30'21" E
GIBSON
Well 23 (ruins)
GPS 23°05'11" S 123°21'12" E
BM 326
Georgia Bore
39
Capricorn Roadhouse
Well 24
FX 3
FX 2
FX 4
Well 22 (ruins)
fuel dump
Curara Soak (Ruins)
Alternate
Well 21 (ruins)
GPS 23°07'14" S 123°02'32" E
GPS 23°06'34" S 123°20'37" E
TALAWANA
Fuel dump (aband)
Winnecke Rock
GPS 23°10'40" S 122°48'34" E
Track splits around edge of claypan
Fuel available April-October and must be pre-arranged through Capricorn Roadhouse (08) 9175 1535 6-8 weeks in advance
Midway Well (aband)
201
DESERT
Windmill & tank
Lake Disappointment
TROPIC OF CAPRICORN
GPS 23°24'03" S 124°08'01" E
TRACK
GPS 23°30'16" S 124°45'50" E
To Windy Corner
Runton Ra
Cromer Cone
Surprise Well
STN 1630
Glynde Hill
GPS 23°43'50" S 122°29'04" E
Water 17
Killagurra Spring & Gorge
Aboriginal rock paintings
Lake Disappointment
Named by Frank Hann in 1897 as he "was disappointed in not finding water in it".
Cleared line
Martu Determined Native Title Area
STN 1218
STN 970
STN 850
Cleared lines
Traeger Hills
GPS 23°49'40" S 124°35'42" E
Woolnough Hills
GPS 24°02'19" S 124°33'15" E
Calvert Ra
34
24

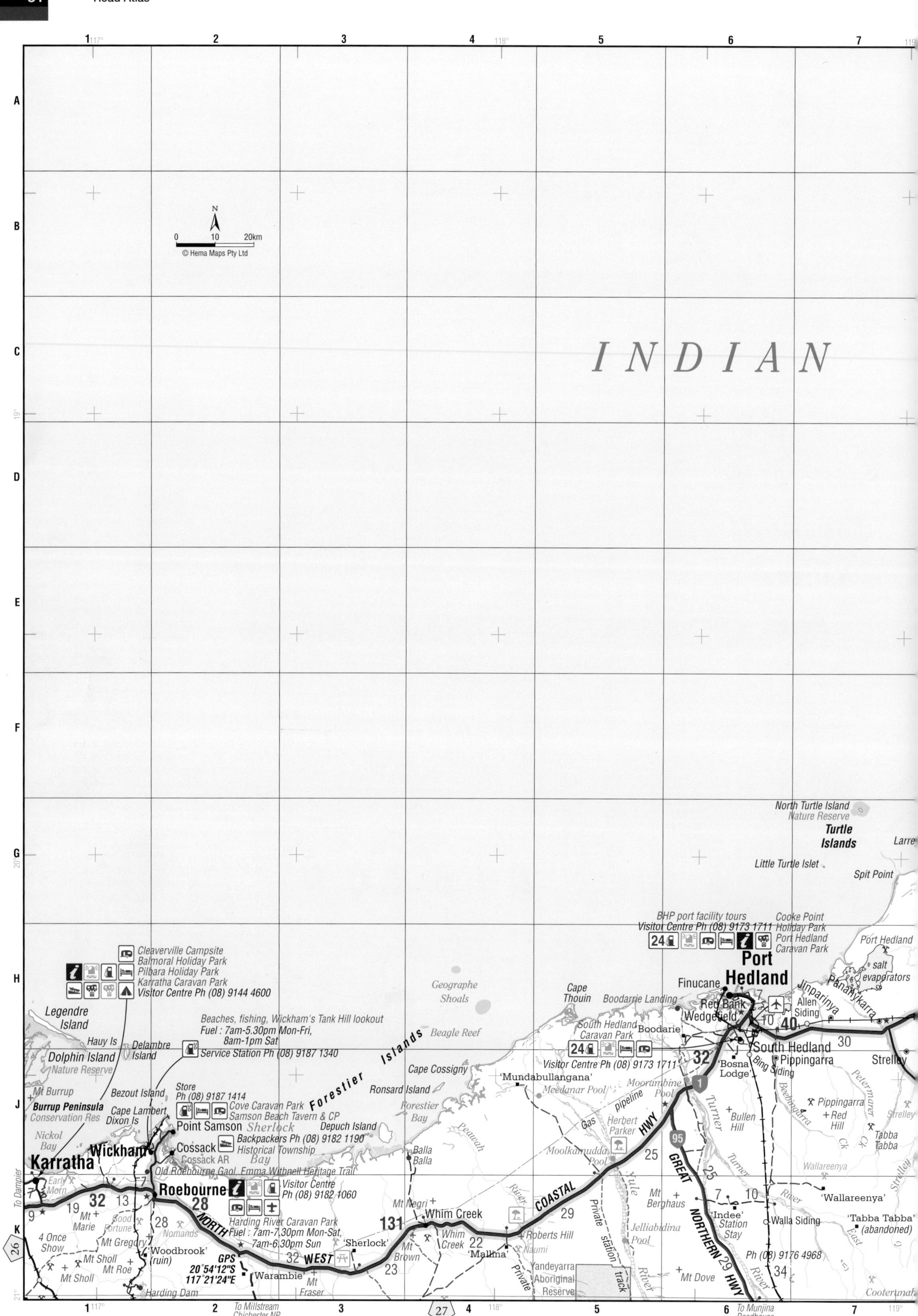
INDIAN
© Hema Maps Pty Ltd
North Turtle Island Nature Reserve
Turtle Islands
Little Turtle Islet
Spit Point
BHP port facility tours
Visitor Centre Ph (08) 9173 1711
Cooke Point Holiday Park
Port Hedland Caravan Park
Port Hedland
Finucane
Cape Thouin
Boodarrie Landing
Red Bank
Wedgefield
South Hedland Caravan Park
Visitor Centre Ph (08) 9173 1711
South Hedland
Pippingarra
Strelley
Cleaverville Campsite
Balmoral Holiday Park
Pilbara Holiday Park
Karratha Caravan Park
Visitor Centre Ph (08) 9144 4600
Legendre Island
Dolphin Island Nature Reserve
Beaches, fishing, Wickham's Tank Hill lookout
Fuel : 7am-5.30pm Mon-Fri, 8am-1pm Sat
Service Station Ph (08) 9187 1340
Forestier Islands
Geographe Shoals
Beagle Reef
Cape Cossigny
Ronsard Island
Depuch Island
Burrup Peninsula Conservation Res
Cape Lambert
Point Samson
Cove Caravan Park
Samson Beach Tavern & CP
Backpackers Ph (08) 9182 1190
Historical Township
Wickham
Cossack
Karratha
Roebourne
Visitor Centre Ph (08) 9182 1060
Harding River Caravan Park
Fuel : 7am-7.30pm Mon-Sat, 7am-6.30pm Sun
GPS 20°54'12"S 117°21'24"E
Whim Creek
'Sherlock'
'Mallina'
'Mundabullangana'
Yandeyarra Aboriginal Reserve
COASTAL HWY
GREAT NORTHERN HWY
NORTH WEST
To Millstream Chichester NP
To Munjina Roadhouse
'Wallareenya'
Walla Siding
'Tabba Tabba' (abandoned)
'Indee' Station Stay
Ph (08) 9176 4968
Mt Dove
Harding Dam

OCEAN
Bedout Island
Nature Reserve
Poissonnier Point
Breaker Inlet
Condini Landing
Cape Keraudren
Cape Keraudren Coastal Reserve
Point Poolingerena
Yegin Pool
Ripon Island
Salt Pool
'De Grey'
Station Stay 'Pardoo'
Ph (08) 9176 4930
GPS
20°03'18"S
119°49'42"E
Pardoo Roadhouse
Pardoo Roadhouse
Open 6am to 10pm daily
Ph (08) 9176 4916
Marloo Pool
Ord Ranges
Hardy Siding
Ryan Siding
Goldsworthy
(dismantled town)
Mount Goldsworthy
Taplin Siding
Rubin Junction
Nimingarra
Sunrise Hill
Shay Gap
(dismantled town)
Cattle Gorge
Yarrie Mine Camp
Yarrie
Kimberley Gap
'Mulyie'
Carleecarleethong Pool
Mulgie Pool
'Nimingarra'
Mirtunkarra
Pirinooning Pool
Black Hill
Shay Gap
Muccanoo Pool
'Muccan'
'Yarrie'
Bunnengarra
'Carlindie'
Des Streckfuss
Carlindie Hill
Mt Francisco / White
Mulgundoona Hill
Yarrie Prospecting
'Lalla Rookh'
Pear Creek
'Egînbah'
Moolyella / Brockman
Coppin Gap (Nuggety Gully)
Bamboo Creek
Bamboo Creek
Coppin Gap
Talga Peak
Cooke Bluff Hill
Doolena Gap / Reck
Doolena Peak
Doolena Gap
Gorge Range
Blue Streak
To Marble Bar
'Narrana Outcamp'
(ruins)
'Warrawagine'
'Callawa'
Shoonta Hill
NORTHERN
HIGHWAY
GREAT
139
101
1
153
138
MARBLE BAR ROAD
SHAY GAP ROAD
MUCCAN SHAY GAP ROAD
GOLDSWORTHY
COONGAN ROAD
BORELINE ROAD
Boreline Road
Ph (08) 9176 1008
for road conditions
WARRAWAGINE ROAD
Private road
WAPET (KIDSON) ROAD
Private Track
OLD TELEGRAPH TRACK
Wapet Road (Kidson Track)
This track carries very little traffic.
Don't travel this track unless you have effective communication equipment.
Allow a minimum of two days to travel its full length to Kunawarritji. Numerous washouts and soft sandy patches.
rocky outcrops
overgrown track
Vermin proof fence
Eighty Mile Beach
Ph (08) 9176 5941
Eighty Mile Beach
Caravan Park
'Wallal Downs'
GPS
19°50'02"S
120°41'32"E
'Mandora'
Locked Gate
Permission required
from Anna Plains Station
GPS
19°46'13"S
121°05'22"E
Sandfire Roadhouse
Sandfire Roadhouse
Fuel available 7am-10pm daily
Ph (08) 9176 5944
Radi Hills
To Broome
GREAT SANDY DESERT
Toramah Soak
Mt Cecelia
Isabella Range
Oakover River
Martu Determined Native Title Area
De Grey River
West River
Shaw River
East Strelley River
Six Mile Ck
Soda Ck
Pardoo Ck
Pear Ck
Coongan River
33
28
8
9
10
11
12
13
14
A
B
C
D
E
F
G
H
J
K

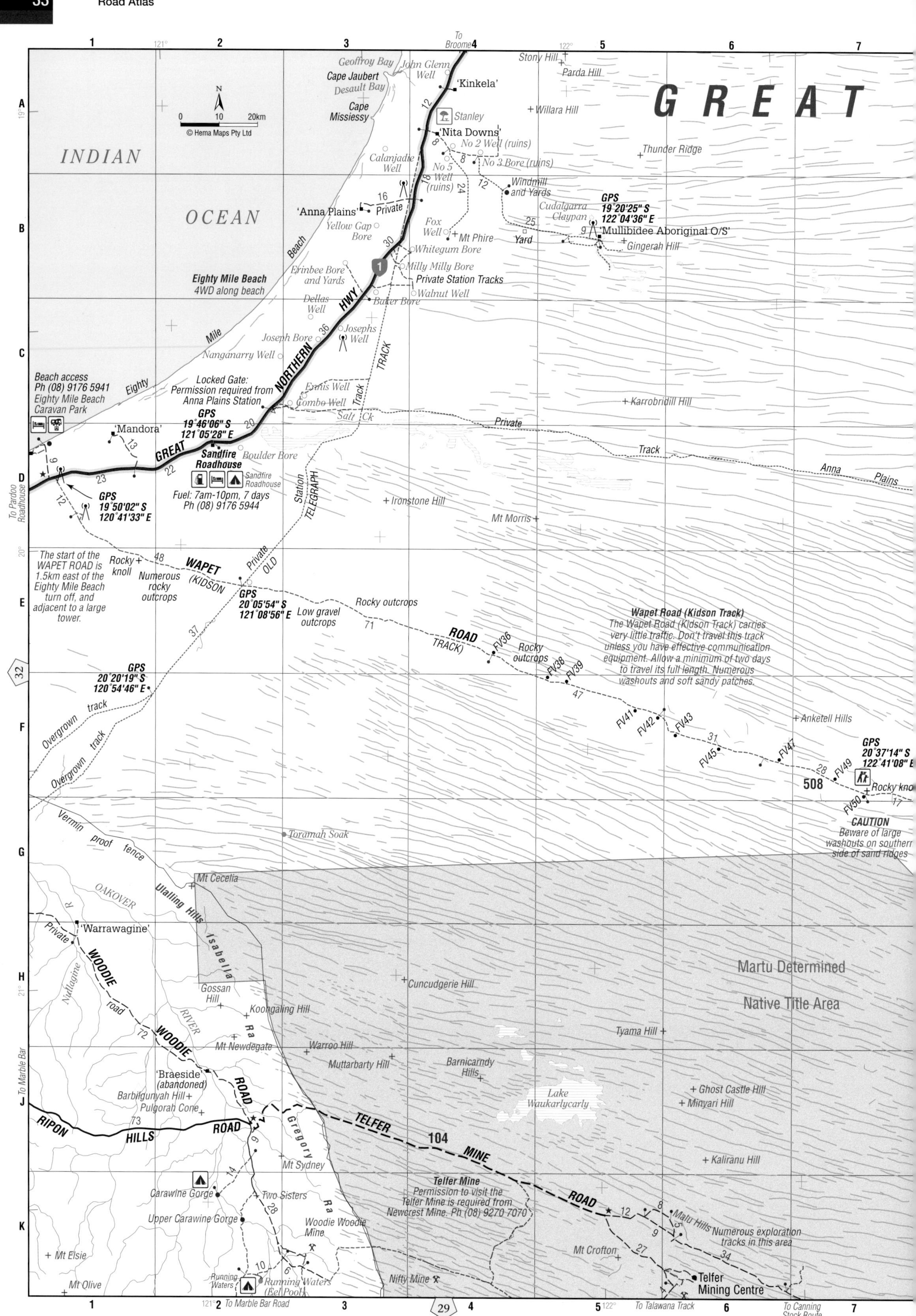
GREAT
INDIAN
OCEAN
© Hema Maps Pty Ltd
Cape Jaubert
Cape Missiessy
'Kinkela'
Stanley
'Nita Downs'
'Anna Plains'
Eighty Mile Beach
4WD along beach
Beach access
Ph (08) 9176 5941
Eighty Mile Beach
Caravan Park
Locked Gate:
Permission required from
Anna Plains Station
GPS
19°46'06" S
121°05'28" E
Sandfire Roadhouse
Fuel: 7am-10pm, 7 days
Ph (08) 9176 5944
GPS
19°50'02" S
120°41'33" E
GPS
19°20'25" S
122°04'36" E
'Mullibidee Aboriginal O/S'
GREAT NORTHERN HWY
Private Station Tracks
The start of the WAPET ROAD is 1.5km east of the Eighty Mile Beach turn off, and adjacent to a large tower.
WAPET (KIDSON ROAD TRACK)
GPS
20°05'54" S
121°08'56" E
GPS
20°20'19" S
120°54'46" E
Wapet Road (Kidson Track)
The Wapet Road (Kidson Track) carries very little traffic. Don't travel this track unless you have effective communication equipment. Allow a minimum of two days to travel its full length. Numerous washouts and soft sandy patches.
GPS
20°37'14" S
122°41'08" E
CAUTION
Beware of large washouts on southern side of sand ridges
Martu Determined
Native Title Area
'Warrawagine'
WOODIE WOODIE ROAD
RIPON HILLS ROAD
TELFER MINE ROAD
Telfer Mine
Permission to visit the Telfer Mine is required from Newcrest Mine. Ph (08) 9270 7070
Numerous exploration tracks in this area
Telfer Mining Centre
Lake Waukarlycarly
To Broome
To Marble Bar Road
To Talawana Track
To Canning Stock Route

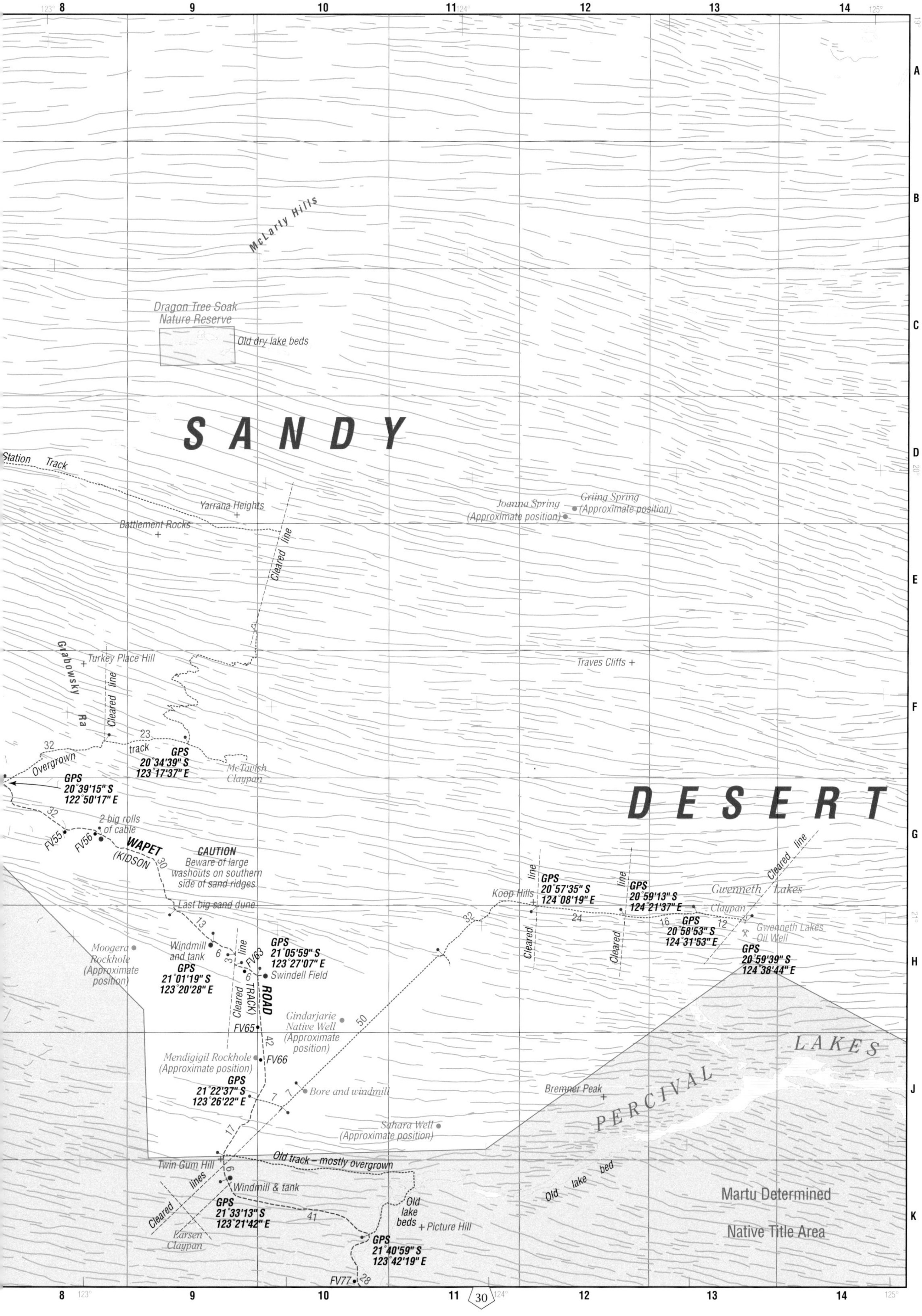

8 9 10 11 12 13 14

McLarty Hills

Dragon Tree Soak Nature Reserve

Old dry lake beds

SANDY

Station Track

Yarrana Heights

Battlement Rocks

Cleared line

Joanna Spring (Approximate position)

Griing Spring (Approximate position)

Grabowsky Ra

Turkey Place Hill

Cleared line

Traves Cliffs

23

track

GPS 20°34'39" S 123°17'37" E

McTavish Claypan

32

Overgrown

GPS 20°39'15" S 122°50'17" E

DESERT

32

2 big rolls of cable

FV55

FV56

WAPET (KIDSON

30

CAUTION Beware of large washouts on southern side of sand ridges

Last big sand dune

13

Moogera Rockhole (Approximate position)

Windmill and tank

6

3

FV63

GPS 21°05'59" S 123°27'07" E

Swindell Field

GPS 21°01'19" S 123°20'28" E

Cleared line

6 TRACK)

ROAD

Gindarjarie Native Well (Approximate position)

50

FV65

42

Mendigigil Rockhole (Approximate position)

FV66

GPS 21°22'37" S 123°26'22" E

7

7

Bore and windmill

Sahara Well (Approximate position)

17

Twin Gum Hill

Old track – mostly overgrown

Cleared lines

9

Windmill & tank

GPS 21°33'13" S 123°21'42" E

41

Old lake beds

Picture Hill

Larsen Claypan

GPS 21°40'59" S 123°42'19" E

FV77

28

Koop Hills

line

GPS 20°57'35" S 124°08'19" E

Cleared

32

24

line

GPS 20°59'13" S 124°21'37" E

Cleared

Gwenneth Lakes

Claypan

16

GPS 20°58'53" S 124°31'53" E

12

Gwenneth Lakes Oil Well

Cleared line

GPS 20°59'39" S 124°38'44" E

Bremner Peak

PERCIVAL LAKES

Old lake bed

Martu Determined Native Title Area

A B C D E F G H J K

8 9 10 11 12 13 14

30

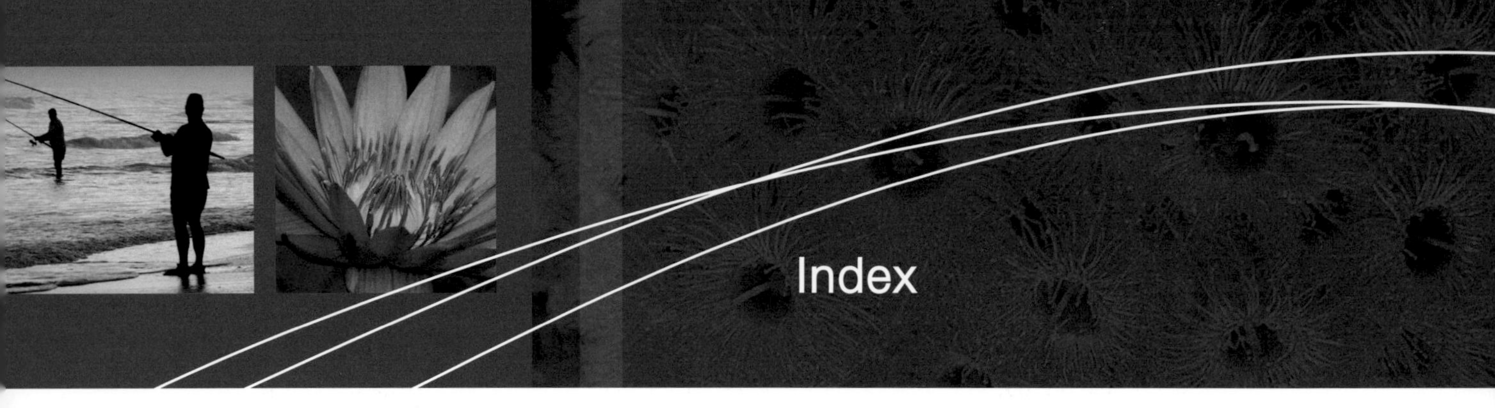

Index

TEXT & ATLAS REFERENCES

- **bold** – major text references
- normal – text references (minor references ignored)
- *blue italics* – map references specified by map number followed by grid, e.g. "6 G6" means map 6, grid G6